Warfare and Shamanism in Amazonia

Warfare and Shamanism in Amazonia is an ethnographic study of the Parakanã, a little-known indigenous people of Amazonia, who inhabit the Xingu-Tocantins interfluvial region in the state of Pará, Brazil. This book analyzes the relationship between warfare and shamanism in Parakanã society from the late nineteenth century until the end of the twentieth century. Based on the author's extensive fieldwork, the book presents first-hand ethnographic data collected among a generation still deeply involved in conflicts. The result is an innovative work with a broad thematic and comparative scope.

Carlos Fausto is Associate Professor of Anthropology at the Museu Nacional, Universidade Federal do Rio de Janeiro. Fausto has been conducting fieldwork among Amazonian indigenous peoples since 1988. His articles have appeared in the *Journal of the Royal Anthropological Institute, Current Anthropology, American Ethnologist, Religion and Society, Science, Mana, L'Homme, Gradhiva*, and *Journal de la Société des Américanistes*. He co-edited *Time and Memory in Indigenous Amazonia* (2007) with Michael Heckenberger. He directed a number of documentary films in collaboration with the Kuikuro people, including the feature film *The Hyper Women*.

CAMBRIDGE LATIN AMERICAN STUDIES

General Editor
Herbert S. Klein
Gouverneur Morris Emeritus Professor of History, Columbia University
Hoover Curator and Research Fellow, Stanford University

96
Warfare and Shamanism in Amazonia

Other Books in the Series

(continued after index)

Warfare and Shamanism in Amazonia

CARLOS FAUSTO

Universidade Federal do Rio de Janeiro

translated by David Rodgers

CAMBRIDGE
UNIVERSITY PRESS

CAMBRIDGE
UNIVERSITY PRESS

32 Avenue of the Americas, New York NY 10013-2473, USA

Cambridge University Press is part of the University of Cambridge.

It furthers the University's mission by disseminating knowledge in the pursuit of
education, learning and research at the highest international levels of excellence.

www.cambridge.org
Information on this title: www.cambridge.org/9781107449428

© Carlos Fausto 2001
English translation © Carlos Fausto 2012

First published in Portuguese by University of São Paulo Press, Brazil
First published in English 2012
First paperback edition 2014

A catalogue record for this publication is available from the British Library

Library of Congress Cataloguing in Publication data
Fausto, Carlos.
Warfare and shamanism in Amazonia / Carlos Fausto.
p.   cm. – (Cambridge Latin American studies ; 96)
Includes bibliographical references and index.
ISBN 978-1-107-02006-1 (hardback)
1. Parakanã Indians – Warfare.   2. Parakanã Indians – Religion.   3. Parakanã Indians –
Rites and ceremonies.   4. Shamanism – Brazil – Pará (State)   5. Pará (Brazil : State) –
Social life and customs.   6. Pará (Brazil : State) – Religious life and customs.   I. Title.
F2520.1.P38F39   2012
299′.8911–dc23   2011040933

ISBN 978-1-107-02006-1 Hardback
ISBN 978-1-107-44942-8 Paperback

to my father and my mother
to Iatora, Arakytá e Pi'awa.
eipo pejawareté
here's your true jaguar

Location of indigenous peoples

Contents

Illustrations

Maps

Figures

Tables

Photos

Foreword to the English Edition

Published originally in Portuguese in 2001, this book was awarded the José Honório Rodrigues Prize for the best book in Social Sciences of that year, a distinction conferred by the Brazilian Association of Graduate Programs in Social Sciences (ANPOCS). Since then it has followed its natural course as an autonomous object. And so have I. Over the years I further elaborated some of the ideas contained in the book and also moved into new areas of research. When I finally decided it was time to stop, rewrite, shorten, and translate the text, choices had to be made. I opted to preserve as much ethnographic data as possible and drop the lengthier comparative and theoretical digressions. I tried to ensure that all my claims were entwined with the data, not only because this is my idea of what anthropology is about, but also because I feel that, twenty years after my first arrival at a Parakanã village, the data I gathered amounts to invaluable oral testimonies given to me by old, and now dead, people. I talked to and interviewed the last Parakanã generation deeply involved in indigenous warfare. I heard their histories, shared some of their feelings, and walked with them in the forest. This book is a part of what they told me, one that I struggled for years to understand both anthropologically and humanly.

Although primarily focused on warfare and shamanism, the book's argument is constructed within the general framework of Parakanã social life and history. Its historical period spans from the end of the nineteenth century until the end of the twentieth century, and its ethnographic period is from 1988 to 1999. I intended this book to be quite innovative, both in theoretical terms and within the context of Amazonian ethnology. My aim was to integrate a historical approach with a structural one. Being formed in a structuralist school and informed by a family academic background in history, I rapidly plunged myself into the intellectual climate of the 1980s and 1990s. My ethnography of the Parakanã clearly spells these issues out through its own mode of presentation, especially in the way historical data is enmeshed with long-term sociocultural forms. Through a detailed analysis of particular events sensible both to the hazards of experience and the resilience of culture, I intended to intervene in what we all saw at the time as an overly simplified dichotomy between structure and social action – a topic to which I came back in subsequent publications (Fausto 2002a; 2002b, Fausto 2007b; Fausto & Heckenberger 2007).

I also wanted to intervene in two issues important for Amazonian anthropology at the time. The first was the opposition between materialistic and symbolic approaches to culture, the former mainly represented by ecofunctionalism, and the latter by both French structuralism and American culturalism. The second issue was the different emphasis given to the inside and outside by ethnographers describing Amerindian social life. This dichotomy was closely interconnected with a number of others, such as consanguinity versus affinity, production versus exchange, sharing versus reciprocity, conviviality versus predation, and so on. In the book, I intended to surpass these oppositions through a model of how external and internal relations were articulated in shamanism and warfare. In rethinking these dualisms, I proposed a general model for understanding both Amazonian warfare and shamanism, based on the idea of a conversion of predation into familiarization – a central point of this work to which I also returned later at various times (Fausto 2004, 2007a, 2008, in press).

I treated Parakanã and other Amazonian warfare rituals as the apex of this conversion of a predatory relationship into a productive one, as the most public and collective moment for the production of persons and peoples. In the book, the analysis of rituals served the ends of the model, but it also contained data that has recently assisted me in thinking about ritual in its own right, particularly through the investigation of its form and pragmatics among the Kuikuro of the Upper Xingu, where I have now been working for more than ten years (Fausto 2011a, Fausto, Franchetto and Montagnani 2011, Fausto and Penoni in press).

The book did not focus on the transformations in course during those voracious years of the end of the twentieth century. In the space of a decade, the Parakanã and I watched 500 years of Brazilian history reenacted in front of our hearts and minds, as the region passed from isolation to lumbering and gold mining, from cattle ranches to colonization, from migration to urban expansion. I left before the advent of the brave new world of technology, a world in which I would deeply immerse myself in another setting (Fausto 2011b).

A final note on the English version: I restricted the bibliography to the texts I had actually handled during the writing of the original book. Some of the theses to which I refer here were later published in a modified form, but I have kept the earlier reference.

Last, but not least, let me acknowledge two friends without whom this book would never have come to life. I would have become lost in translation had it not been for David Rodgers, a fellow anthropologist who, as a translator, has both a fine sense of what a style means for an author, and a deep understanding of the dilemmas involved in the translation of concepts that are already translations of others' concepts. I would also have become lost (in different ways) had it not been for Herb Klein, who since I met him many years ago in his self-inflicted exile in Washington DC, has given me more advice than I shall ever be able to reciprocate.

Introduction

Someone coming into a strange country will sometimes learn the language of the inhabitants from ostensive definitions that they give him; and he will often have to guess the meaning of these definitions; and will guess sometimes right, sometimes wrong.

> Ludwig Wittgenstein, *Philosophical Investigations* (1953)

Then we came across the Paranopyperewa river. They became enraged again.

- "Firstly we're going to kill. Our enemy is lurking in this dense jungle," they said.

At this point the late Tapi'awa became really angry.

- "I'm going to kill the great enemy before anything else, my kinsfolk, I haven't pierced anyone with my arrows, I haven't yet spent my rage-against-people," he said.

This is a passage from one of the many narratives on war conflicts that I collected during my fieldwork with the Parakanã, a Tupi-Guarani speaking people who inhabit the interfluve formed by the Tocantins and Xingu Rivers in the state of Pará, Brazil. When I began my research I was not exactly looking to study warfare or shamanism. In fact, I was too young and ignorant to know what I was going to study. The only plan I had in mind was to learn anything they might want to share with me. It took me a long time to begin to understand their stories. But as soon as I started to grasp the language, I would keep my tape recorder on; while the hours passed, they recounted long and detailed narratives on past war events or their dreams about enemies. As time went by, my research became focused on understanding why enmity occupied such a central place in their social lives, and how violence, predation, and familiarization could be internal and indispensable to their own definitions of how the world works.

By taking indigenous warfare as its theme, my research inevitably waded into an ethical and political quagmire. The imputation of violence to native peoples was a commonplace strategy for justifying their reduction, expulsion, and extermination during colonial history. Notions such as "just war" and "rescuing captives" played a crucial role in that context, and the specter of anthropophagy served frequently to legitimize the enslavement of Amerindians. The problem, though, is the present, not the past. The image of savagery is still one of the weapons used to attack indigenous rights and lifeways, part of an ideological and practical struggle that continues unabated.

One must be aware of the silent continuities of colonial discourses. From the outset, indigenous warfare made a strong impression on the European imagination. When the Portuguese arrived at what would become Brazil, they encountered a vast Tupi-Guarani population distributed along five thousand kilometers of the Atlantic coast. This population shared the same sociocultural complex, centered on revenge warfare and ritual anthropophagy. The importance of these practices in indigenous social life, reported by Europeans of different nationalities and backgrounds, has been a dominant motif in Western accounts of Amerindian societies ever since. Yet this motif has never functioned in isolation. The European imagination has always swung between the image of the cannibal immersed in a state of chronic warfare and the noble savage living in natural freedom. Although antagonistic and apparently irreconcilable, these motifs eventually combined to define a mental attitude and a field of meanings, generating a schema for classifying and dominating the indigenous populations of the Americas.

The twin images of the noble and cannibal savage do not belong to the past alone. Anthropology is also its producer and product. Innocence and violence, abundance and scarcity, nature and culture, predation and reciprocity, communal sharing and self interest are terms that we combine and recombine on the basis of a single conceptual schema for which the conquest of the New World provided a fertile testing ground. The unease and fascination elicited by indigenous violence and peace are part of a primitivization device triggered by a diffuse but enduring conception that Amerindians are closer to nature (whether natural or human) than ourselves. Anthropology has frequently asked them to act as a measure of our own ways, so we can, as Rousseau put it, discern "what is original and what is artificial in the actual nature of man" ([1755] 1989:41).

Escaping this discourse means rejecting the stark alternative given to the "savage people of America" by Western thought: serving either as phantasmic tokens in a critique of our own values or to reaffirm, by means of contrast, these very same values. In this sense – though in this sense only – it makes little difference which pole is chosen: the noble savage or the cannibal barbarian. Quick to acknowledge the historical damage perpetrated in the name of the latter, we often overlook the effectiveness of the former. Yet there is nothing more paternalist than asking Amerindians to be essentially good, a mindset that turns them into mere victims. Victimization is a form of denying the autonomy of the other, an attitude informing the authoritarian – though supposedly benign – models of relationship between the state and Amerindian populations.

The image of natural kindness can be as corrosive as the stigma of bestiality. Both served the purposes of the colonizers: native violence to justify the war of conquest and enslavement; native innocence to encourage their conversion into members of the flock of God. In our postcolonial world, some strands of anthropology have tried to rid themselves of any vestige of this colonial inheritance. Paradoxically, though, this expurgation is frequently pursued in an equally colonialist form by purifying indigenous social practices, deciding which of them have the right to exist in the non-European world of the past and present. Consequently, native warfare and cannibalism have been reduced to mere figments of the Western imagination or the unfortunate by-product of European expansion.

In the 1920s, Brazil was home to a cultural movement that rejected the dichotomy sustaining this political imagination. Trying to circumvent both nationalist regressionism and Europeanizing mimetism, Brazilian modernism used cannibalism as a positive metaphor, invoking sixteenth-century Tupi anthropophagy as a machine for opening onto the other, devouring the different and producing the new. This Brazilian cultural movement can be seen as a counter-discourse to the surviving ideological legacy of colonialism. Literary anthropophagy captured the deeper sense of literal anthropophagy, namely that of the constitution of subjects through the violent appropriation of principles of subjectification, which are, by necessity, external in origin. Cannibalism seeks to mobilize the other's perspective in order to reproduce the self, expressing the ambivalent interconnection between a centrifugal, heteronomic desire and the need to constitute the self as an internally multiple subject (Fausto 1999a). This is the meaning captured by modernist authors in their attempt to overthrow the romantic depiction of the Indian. By transforming the specter of cannibalism into a positive conceptual machine, the modernists threw an entrenched colonial discourse into complete disarray.

I have no intention of eulogizing warfare and violence in this book. My argument is simply that we should avoid basing any value-laden discourse about ourselves and others on the opposing ideas of innocence and violence. After all, how do we define whole societies, countries, and peoples according to this criteria? Is Brazil more cordial than the United States? Are Germans more disposed to violence than people from India? Or is Chinese society crueler than Iranian society? None of these questions makes much sense. However, the same restraint often fails to apply when we turn to indigenous peoples, whether Amerindian or otherwise. We require them to function as models: of kindness or barbarism. If any counter-discourse is possible, it depends on refusing both a redeeming victimization and a demonizing accusation. This refusal is the necessary condition for constructing less asymmetric relations with the original inhabitants of the Americas, relations based on values capable of founding a social space of dialogue, justice, and peace, which are exclusive neither to ourselves nor to indigenous societies.

On War

In focusing on indigenous warfare, we also wade into a theoretical quicksand, since defining what "indigenous" might mean here is far from easy. Colonization profoundly altered the conditions in which Amerindian populations lived. The conflicts, trade, slavery, epidemics, and catechism transformed native systems, introducing new objects and new relations. The impact of European expansion on native warfare practices was wide-reaching and long-lasting, although they also varied according to place and period (Ferguson & Whitehead 1992; Whitehead 1990). There were wars of resistance, wars involving the capture of enemies to be exchanged for metal tools, others that resulted from the movement of populations in flight, or others still motivated by "traditional" values that took place in now "untraditional" sociodemographic contexts. So what kind of warfare are we actually dealing with in this book?

I confront this problem in two ways: first, through a detailed historical examination of the conditions in which the Parakanã opted for either war or peace during the twentieth century. The Parakanã are a recently contacted Tupi-Guarani people of southeastern Amazonia. My fieldwork started a couple of years after their acceptance of state administration, and I followed them for almost a decade. I interviewed many people who had taken an active part in warfare conflicts, killed enemies, lost relatives, and captured women. Based on this data, I try to identify their motives and the context in which the armed conflicts took place. The result is a description embedded in social history, but also imbued with a deep sense of long-term cultural forms. Thus, I also confront the problem of defining the nature of warfare that I analyse in this book through a comparative analysis of indigenous practices and representations in different contexts and temporalities, looking to identify a complex set of systematic assumptions recurrently associated with warfare behavior and a cannibal symbolic. I focus on this symbolic framework and how it interacted with historical events in structuring the Parakanã-lived world during the last century.

The definitional problem is not limited to the category "indigenous," since defining "war" is no simple matter either. In Parakanã, there is no exact equivalent to this word. The most specific term associated with bellic activity is *warinio* or *warinia*, a cognate of *guarini*, from ancient Guarani, which Montoya translates as "war" (1876). In Parakanã, the term designates the act of seeking out enemies, and it is rarely used. Armed combat is not designated by a specific term. To make war is to "attack" (-pakang) the enemy, and the events are described by a myriad of verbs that indicate the type of violent action involved. What unites these acts is their shared objective: All are forms of killing. The generic verb for this action is -joka, which applies to any situation in which the life of a being is taken, without specification of quality or quantity. Some verbs, employed metaphorically, are applied more narrowly to the killing of human beings, such as -mokajym ("to make lose, forget") or -apiji ("to tie up"), both meaning "to kill." These verbs can receive the suffix -pam, indicating a large quantity or completeness, as in oapijipam, for example, "He killed all of them."

Nevertheless, none of the verbs or any narrative resource enables a distinction to be made between the types of armed conflicts in terms of their scale. Whenever I finished recording a warfare narrative, I would ask about the numbers involved, including the total number of victims and killers. However, the Parakanã focus not on what makes all the adversaries alike and countable, but what distinguishes them: the physical features of each one, their ways of talking, singing, or moving. What matters is not just killing, but appropriating an individual history, even when this is inscribed in the bodily forms observable in a fleeting moment. War is not a question of killing just any kind of other. The other has to exist as a particular subject for the act of killing to prove productive.

The absence of a specific term for war, as well as the absence of any quantitative distinction of the armed conflicts, poses difficulties in terms of defining their precise nature. The anthropology of war commonly distinguishes between two types of armed conflict: on one hand, the use of force by collective, politically autonomous subjects who clash violently over public interests; on the other, a private, almost individual mode of violence between people connected by kinship. The distinction is based on a series of dichotomies – public versus private, political versus domestic, collective versus individual – that gives rise to binary typologies, such as the classical opposition between feuding and warfare (Otterbein 1973:923–4). Most of these typologies fail to allow impure combinations: If and when they exist in the real world, they are transitional and necessarily unstable forms. The problem with using such theories to study so-called primitive warfare is that only transitional and hybrid forms appear to exist.

First of all, we face what Hallpike (1973:453) called the "boundary problem," questioning the functionalist assumption that the limits of societies are unambiguously defined. The distinction between intra and intercommunity violence demands a prior definition of the limits between the inside and the outside – a far from trivial undertaking in the contexts of nonstate sociopolitical formations. In the abstract, the limits are determined by political autonomy, as we can read in Malinowski's definition (1941:522): War is "armed conflict between politically independent units." Identifying these units is the crux of the problem. We tend to veer between identifying them with a localized (though transitory) community and trying to match them to larger population sets whose limits are defined by the presence or absence of conflict. As Langness notes, "the public affair most widely used by anthropologists to define the largest polities has been warfare" (1972:925). Thus war defines the polities, which for their part define what is legitimately taken as war. The circularity is evident.

Second, we face what I call the "public revenge problem." Our typologies are founded on an opposition between war and private revenge. Yet the latter only becomes private where juridical regulation of interindividual and interfamilial conflicts exists; in other words, when there is a state apparatus determining when a type of armed conflict belongs to the kinship domain rather than the public sphere (Vernant 1985:11). Indigenous societies, however, in practicing warfare according to a criteria of scale, may conceive of war as an interminable series of acts of revenge, which are not private but necessarily public and socialized. Such was the case of the sixteenth-century Tupinambá, who thought of their conflicts as public vendettas, although the Europeans saw them as wars.

Third, we face what I call the "collective individualism problem," which reflects the difficulties posed by the individual versus collective dichotomy. Take, for instance, a minimalist definition of warfare such as Mead's: "recognised conflict between two groups *as groups*, in which each group puts an army (even if the army is only fifteen pygmies) into the field to fight and kill, if possible, some of the members of the army of the other group" (Mead 1940:402, my emphasis). How do we know when groups are fighting *as* groups? The limits between individual and collective are far from clear, especially in egalitarian societies characterized by a great degree of personal autonomy. Here armed conflicts are frequently individualized, even in formal situations involving hundreds of people, as is the case of the "ritual battles" in New Guinea (Heider 1991:104, Koch 1974:77). As for the Tupinambá, a sixteenth-century chronicler describes "two or three thousand naked men on either side" fighting "in disorderly fashion with many of them losing control in similar fights because they lack a Captain governing them, or any other military officers whom they must obey at these moments" (Gandavo [1576] 1980:132).

If at this scale there is little coordination of collective actions, and revenge seems to be a basic warrior idiom, what should we make of the raids of one, two, or three dozen archers against an enemy village, a frequent pattern in Amazonia in the twentieth century? This typological swamp – where we find anthropologists classifying the war pattern of one group as intervillage warfare and a fairly similar other as individualistic feuding (Ferguson 1989:182) – shows how the dichotomies of political/ domestic, public/private, and collective/individual are inadequate analytic tools for describing the phenomena of violence in these societies. For these reasons, I use the term war quite broadly throughout this book. I classify as a war event any and all encounters between indigenous groups who perceive themselves as enemies and that results in physical violence, irrespective of the size of these groups or the scale of the violence. In this category I equally include a planned attack on any enemy village or a skirmish between hunting parties in the midst of the forest.

The Book

In May 1999, I returned to the Parakanã village of Paranatinga for the last time. After four years away, I was excited about the prospect of seeing friends and hearing their news. I would have the chance to meet the headman Arakytá again and listen to old and new stories in the *tekatawa*, a place where the men gather every evening to talk. The village, though, was not the same. Half of its population had left and two new settlements had been founded. Arakytá was now blind and the *tekatawa* was a pale memory of the meetings in which I had participated a few years ago. The long silences were broken by fleeting remarks, and the *tekatawa*'s spatial morphology, previously delineating differences in age and patrigroup, had dissolved. My first reaction was one of nostalgia but also uncertainty. Had I deluded myself about this recent past? I quickly realized, though, that the Parakanã sociopolitical forms where in flux, again.

It was not the first time this had happened. More than a century ago, a small Tupi-Guarani group living in the Tocantins basin experienced a conflict over women and split into two populations. These I call the eastern and western Parakanã. For almost a century, the two blocs led parallel lives, only interacting with each other through warfare. When contacted in the 1970s and 1980s, they were markedly distinct in both their subsistence patterns and their sociopolitical organization. The eastern group practiced a fairly diverse horticulture, lived in a large communal house, were divided into exogamic moieties, had an institutionalized headmanship, and had been engaged in defensive warfare only. The western group, on the other hand, were organized into nomadic bands, lacked any horticulture, had neither an established headman nor social segmentation, and were still actively engaged in offensive warfare. In less than a century, the two blocs had assumed quite different social configurations.

How do we explain these changes? Which group – if not both – has transformed and in what direction? What mechanisms produced these transformations? These are some of the questions explored in the first three chapters of this book. My approach is informed by the theoretical concerns with history and social action that marked anthropology from the 1980s onward (Rosaldo 1980, Sahlins 1981). I take up Ortner's challenge, set down in a pioneering article in which she observes that although she had chosen the concept of practice to describe the main anthropological trends in the 1980s, she could have equally chosen another key concept: history. Yet merely historicizing anthropology – "if by history is meant largely a chain of external events to which people react" (1984:159) – would obscure the main question: How do we reintroduce social agency into our descriptions without projecting a voluntaristic and unstructured scenario?

My analysis of Parakanã historical changes is an ethnographic response to this question. It involves a microsociological reconstruction of the mechanisms informing the constitution of two different social systems after the group's breakup at the end of the nineteenth century. I intend to show how these transformations resulted from the intersection of both internal and external factors within particular historical situations, shaping and being shaped by human agency. Rather than seeking an all-encompassing set of determinant forces (the world system, the environment, etc.), I describe how small changes occurring in various areas of Parakanã social life produced cumulative long-term effects and redefined the very context in which agents took decisions. This ethnographic case invites us to rethink the way in which most anthropologists have described processes of change in Amerindian societies after the Conquest of the New World.

This is not, though, a historicist book. As the chapters unfold, the emphasis shifts from the "modes of process" to the "modes of form" (Bateson 1980). One of my aims is to visualize forms in history and the history of forms, without implying that, since they exist in history, forms do not exist at all. Although the cosmology and social organization of an indigenous people emerge from a particular history, they also result from a being-in-the-world mediated by long-term sociocultural forms. Indeed the very fact we can study the flux of Parakanã sociopolitical form is itself a by-product of specifically Tupi-Guarani features, such as the low yield of segmentary principles and the nonmechanical character of their social norms.

The book's passage from process to form is accompanied by a shift from the comparison between the Parakanã blocs to a wider analysis of their relations with the outside permeated by a cannibal symbolic: relations woven through warfare with human enemies, through shamanism with nonhumans, and through a combination of both with whites. In examining this relational field, I turn to one of the major themes of Amazonian ethnological studies: the constitutive role conferred to alterity in the production of Amerindian social life. I do so, however, not to reassert the preeminence of the Other over the Same, but to connect exteriority and interiority within the same economy. My argument is simple: Instead of opposing predatory relations with the outside to productive relations on the inside, I seek to understand how external predation is converted into internal production. Or more precisely, how the consumption of others results in the making of kin.

My goal is to move beyond the opposition between an Amazonian ethnology focused on predation and alterity and another focused on production and identity by converting these analytical foci into different moments of the same analysis. I shift emphasis away from the notion of reciprocity toward the notions of consumption and production in search of a common idiom that can account for both the destruction and production of persons and, in particular, elucidate the movement through which the first leads to the second. I call this movement *familiarizing predation*, the conversion of a predatory relationship into a protective one, employing the Parakanã case and other empirical examples to show how this dialectic is central to the comprehension of Amerindian warfare, shamanism, and ritual life. I thus include warfare within a general economy, which makes it comprehensible as a mechanism for social reproduction.

In the final chapter, I return to the relationship between the Parakanã and the whites, first examined historically in the opening chapter. Now I explore the topic from a different angle, combining the structural analysis of myths with an investigation of events occurring during the contact process. I look to reunite the two dimensions explored by this book: one historical and particular, the other structural and general. I examine how certain enduring representations are actualized in specific sociohistorical contexts to motivate collective actions (sometimes with surprising results, such as the Parakanã asking the Funai agents responsible for "pacification" to disinter dead people in order to resuscitate them). I explore the associations of whites with shamanic power, as well as the ways in which Amazonian peoples have conceived white peoples' capacity for violence, relating it to images of jaguars and cannibals.

The Research

The encounter of an anthropologist with a people is always a mixture of a deliberate search and unexpected chance. Today I recall myself huddled over a map of Amazonia, a list of names of indigenous groups by my side, searching for a people to research. But it was in a bar some time in 1987 that I first heard of the Parakanã, then recently contacted. The latter was music to my ears, since I was looking for an isolated spot where I imagined I would find "real" Indians and an "authentic" field experience.

I arrived at Altamira, in the state of Pará, in February 1988. Altamira is a Janus-like city: part facing the river, the other facing the road. Its port, previously a stopover for boats transporting rubber, waned in importance as it succumbed to the dust and trucks plying the Transamazonian highway. On reaching the city, the Xingu River curves to the right and flows in a narrow channel before sweeping round and flowing toward its mouth. A landscape of green shores still lines its clear waters upriver, dotted with a few riverside dwellings. In the rainy season, the Xingu flows calmly and smoothly, but as the river level falls, porous black rocks, whirlpools, thick growths of sarandi plants, and rapids appear. These shores were once occupied by indigenous peoples. Depopulated during the Conquest, they received a small influx of inhabitants during the rubber boom. When the latter subsided, the region was again abandoned until logging fever erupted in the 1990s.

The journey from Altamira to the Bom Jardim River, a small affluent of the Xingu where the Parakanã then lived, took four days to reach by boat. When I arrived at Apyterewa village for the first time, the Parakanã had accepted state administration four years previously. The only link with the city was the monthly visit of the boat that brought a few trade items, and took away ill people who would bring news from the city on their return. This state of relative isolation would change rapidly in the ensuing years, but this was the atmosphere in which the present book began. The first phase of research took place in this region, where I stayed for eight months between 1988 and 1989. The second phase spanned from 1992 to 1995 when I completed another eight months of research, this time remaining mostly in the Parakanã Indigenous Land in the Tocantins region. I also made two brief visits in 1996 and 1999.[1]

The experience in the Tocantins villages differed from that in the Apyterewa. The Paranatinga village, where the eastern Parakanã then lived, could be reached easily by car from Tucuruí, a town that served as the base for building the hydroelectric dam on the Tocantins River. Along the Transamazonian highway, farms and pastures rather than forest-lined shores dominated the landscape. The four days' travel upriver were replaced by a few hours' trip, including a forced stop at the village (today a town) of Repartimento. The latter is an important reference point for the Parakanã of Paranatinga, who visit the town to sell assai, rice, maize, and chickens; to buy matches, batteries, tapes, and fishing hooks; and to drink guaraná and eat cookies. Relations with the local population were cordial but involved little verbal communication. As the Parakanã had yet

---

1 The Parakanã live in two different Indigenous Land (*Terra Indígena* is the official designation of indigenous reservations in Brazil). The first is the T.I. Parakanã, located in the Tocantins basin in Pará state, with an area of 351,000 hectares. The land is demarcated and officially recognized. In March 1999, the total population was 475 people, distributed between five different settlements, three belonging to the eastern group and two to the western group. The second area of 773,000 hectares is the T.I. Apyterewa, located in the Xingu basin, also in Pará. It was only demarcated in 2007. In May 1999, it had a population of 248 people living in two villages (Apyterewa and Xingu). All its inhabitants are from the western bloc and were contacted between 1983 and 1984.

to learn much Portuguese, interaction was limited to actions, gestures, and a few phrases.

The initial sensation of finding myself in another space-time gradually dissolved, leading me to consider other factors and themes in my research. However, I did not focus systematically on the insertion of the Parakanã in the local and national contexts. Rather I tried to apprehend their relations with the whites from the viewpoint of life in the villages, looking from the inside outward rather than from the outside inward. One of the strongest impressions I retain of the relationship between the old and the new is the contrast between the visual and auditory. Shortly after contact, the Parakanã abandoned their distinctive body markings (haircut and lip adornment), replacing them with clothing and caps. They also adopted new objects: rifles and aluminum pans, not to mention axes and machetes. They ceased constructing a single communal house and spent years trying to persuade the Funai to build them rectangular houses with wooden-plank walls, cement floors, and chipboard roofs. However, when night falls and only people's silhouettes can be distinguished, spoken or sung words fill a previously unimaginable space. This was when I nourished my desire to see a world different from my own everyday reality.

Most of those who have worked with Tupi-Guarani peoples have probably had this experience. Their cultural resilience is not invested in space or in bodily markings, but mostly in speech, music, and dance. The valorization of the aural universe contrasts with a certain disregard for the visual. The forms through which people and things are displayed are not subject to any strong emotional investment or aesthetic pleasure. This frequently bothers white visitors expecting an enchanted visual world and clear communication in Portuguese, two things that the Parakanã cannot offer. Aware of this fact, I strove to learn the language and songs and to participate in rituals whenever possible. This was my entry point into Parakanã life: dancing and singing for men, women, and children. Although my performances were no more than tolerable, people were always generous in their judgments.

In terms of research methodology, I arrived in the field with just two guides: a manual on studying kinship and a vague notion, acquired from reading ethnographies, of what participant observation was supposed to be like. Over time, I developed my own forms of collecting, checking, and systemizing information, adapted to the themes and characteristics of my field research. There is no space here to detail these methods, but I should like to mention one aspect that will help to understand the book's mode of exposition. When replying to my questions about norms ("Do you eat Y?"; "Does X marry Z?") or requests for explanations ("Why are babies carried at the end of the ritual?"; "Why can't a warrior have sexual relations after killing?"), the Parakanã rarely resorted to a universal rule or traditional formula such as "That's our custom" or "That's how our ancestors did it." Sometimes they would narrate a historical event, answering my question through direct illustrations: "So-and-so once did X, which resulted in Y, which is why we don't do X." At other times, they used an expression composed by a morpheme indicating intention followed by a citational form. Hence, the question "Why do people dance with the electric eel?" received the response "To dream, it's said." People did not provide an explanation without marking the response as a viewpoint enunciated by a third person. Combined, these two native formulations (historical and perspectival) led me to avoid a mechanical and normative description of Parakanã sociocosmology.

All the research was conducted in the Parakanã language with some assistance from bilingual consultants in translating narratives and songs from 1992 onward. In the 1980s, there was nobody in the Apyterewa village with a minimal knowledge of Portuguese to help me with the translations. When I resumed my research, I already knew enough to continue collecting data in the indigenous language, which indeed was convenient since my main interlocutors were older people who knew no Portuguese. It would have been interesting to turn more frequently to younger people for help in translating the numerous recordings I made. However, I always resisted paying for this arduous work. I nurtured the hope (and illusion) that our relations were based on mutual empathy rather than mutual interest.

Money and presents were not absent from the research, though. I performed more than once the role of gift distributor, a script born in the first contacts between Europeans and Indians, matured with the Jesuit *descimentos*, and consolidated during the Republic with Marshal Rondon's blueprint for pacification. Repeating these gestures as an anthropologist, I looked to reconcile my research interests, my principles of fairness, and Parakanã expectations. The formula I found was a large-scale equitable distribution of items the day following my arrival, dividing the presents into three categories – for men, women, and children – and ensuring that everyone from each category received the same quantity and quality of objects. In the Tocantins villages where the official policy of the Parakanã Program is to break with this mode of relationship, the accord reached was different.[2] I paid a fixed contribution to the community in money, deposited into the account of the young leaders who made monthly purchases in Tucuruí.

---

2 The Parakanã Program is responsible for the administration of the T.I. Parakanã. The Program was established following an agreement between Funai (National Indian Foundation) and Eletronorte (a subsidiary of the Brazilian Electric company). Eletronorte provides the funds as compensation for the impact caused by the construction of Tucuruí Hydroelectric Plant.

At no time did I live in the Parakanã houses, staying mostly in the buildings at the indigenous posts, except during the hunting trips and the rituals. Traditionally, the Parakanã lived in a single collective house, but this pattern gradually altered with the multiplication of habitations, each containing one or two nuclear families. My spatial separation from the village was a hindrance to a better understanding of intimate life, which I looked to redress through my involvement in practical and ritual activities. On the other hand, this separation allowed me to discuss sensitive issues with people from different factions.

Most of my data was collected in dialogue with men, a dialogue that depended as much on my own male condition as their own. This limitation is not without bearing on the outcome of the research. However, this ethnography is neither that of a generic anthropologist on a genderless culture, nor the result of a dialogue between men closed within a men's world. Every ethnography results from a conversation between the author and multiple interlocutors, a conversation that, in turn, contains other conversations between the interlocutors themselves.

Another important aspect of my research derives from its time frame. It was conducted over a decade, which allowed me a deeper insight into the temporal dimension of Parakanã social processes. I was able to accompany the social dynamics as they unfolded. In addition, the experience of studying indigenous peoples in one's own country demands a constant emotional and political investment, continually tracking events even when one is far from the field.

Acknowledgments

The research on which this book is based was conducted between 1988 and 1995, originally resulting in my doctoral thesis, completed in 1997 at the Graduate Program in Social Anthropology at the Museu Nacional, Universidade Federal do Rio de Janeiro. The work received the prize for best thesis of the year from the Brazilian Association of Anthropology. The research received financial support from the Fundação de Estudos e Projetos (Finep), the Wenner-Gren Foundation for Anthropological Research, the Ford Foundation, and the Federal University of Rio de Janeiro. I also held scholarships from the Conselho Nacional de Desenvolvimento Científico e Tecnológico (CNPq) and the Coordenação de Aperfeiçoamento de Pessoal de Ensino Superior (Capes). I express my gratitude to the Funai staff at Altamira and the Programa Parakanã staff at Tucuruí for their support during fieldwork. Documental research was conducted at the Museu do Índio (Rio de Janeiro), Funai (Brasília), Instituto Socioambiental (São Paulo), and the Library of the Museu Nacional. My thanks to those who allowed me access to the archives and bookshelves.

Some people provided specific contributions to this book. Here I thank Aparecida Vilaça, Boris Fausto, Bruna Franchetto, Cecília McCallum, César Gordon, Cynira Stocco Fausto, Federico Neiburg, Gérson dos Reis Carvalho, Michael Heckenberger, Michael Houseman, Peter Gow, Ricardo Ventura Santos, Ruy Fausto, Sérgio Fausto, and Yonne Leite. My heartfelt thanks to Marcela Coelho de Souza for her careful reading of the original manuscript. My greatest intellectual debt is to Eduardo Viveiros de Castro, who supervised the research. I also thank Marcos Brito de Castro for drawing the maps and Thiago Barros for the images digital treatment. Finally, I express my deep gratitude to all the Parakanã, who kindly welcomed me for such a lengthy period. I particularly thank Iatora, Arakytá, Pi'awa, Koria, Akaria, Namikwarawa, Awanga, Karája, Pykawa, Ajowyhá, Warerá, Ty'é, and Mojiapewa for sharing their life histories, narratives, dreams, and songs. I hope that this work can in some way help redress the Brazilian state's historical debt to the Parakanã. This adventure also belongs to Bruna and Antonio, who provided me with the happiest moments throughout these years. I thank my parents for everything and more besides.

Transcription

My spelling of Parakanã terms is based on Velda Nicholson's phonological analysis (1978) of the language spoken by the Asurini do Tocantins. It differs slightly from the orthography adopted in the Parakanã schools. I have retained the local spelling for the names of the current villages, though. I use the following symbols for the phonemes:

Consonants

/p/	voiceless bilabial plosive (like an unaspirated *p* in English);
/t/	voiceless alveolar plosive (like an unaspirated *t* in English);
/k/	voiceless velar plosive (like *c* in cow);
/kw/	voiceless labialized velar plosive (like *qu* in quantum);
/m/	bilabial nasal (like *m* in English);
/n/	alveolar nasal (like *n* in English);
/ng/	velar nasal (like *ng* in sing);
/j/	voiced palatal fricative (like *j* in justice), manifested as a voiceless alveolar fricative [ts] before /i/;
/r/	alveolar tap (like an unretroflexed intervocalic r);
/h/	glottal fricative (like *h* in English);
/w/	labial-velar approximant (like *w* in power);
/ '/	glottal stop;

Vowels

/i/   high front unrounded vowel (like *ee* in flee);
/y/   central high unrounded vowel (like *i* in fit, though further back);
/e/   mid front unrounded vowel (like *e* as in the initial vowel sound in play);
/o/   mid back rounded vowel (like *o* in ordeal), also manifested as a high back
        rounded vowel (like *u* in put);
/a/   low central vowel (like *a* in father).

Most Parakanã words are paroxytonic: I have accented the exceptions.
All verbs require a pronominal prefix. Whenever I cite the verb in a nonin-
flected form, I replace the pronoun with a hyphen. For example, I write "to
dance" as -*porahai*, whereas "he dances" is written as *oporahai*. All the nouns
possess a final nominalizer *a*. Some of the Parakanã terms transcribed in the
book are segmented into morphemes, though in various cases I have left
this final vowel attached to the nominal word. When analyzing indigenous
words, I use "nom." to indicate that the morpheme is a nominalizer, "excl."
to indicate that the first-person plural pronoun is exclusive (in other words,
a "we" that excludes the interlocutor) and "incl." when it is inclusive.

I have used people's real names in the text, omitting them only when
absolutely necessary. Since in most cases there were no implications for the
actors or any reputations at stake, I decided to give each person credit for
their actions and words.

I

The Matter of Time

History is a nightmare from which I am trying to awake.
James Joyce, *Ulysses* (1922)

The Parakanã call themselves *awaeté*, "real people," in contrast to *akwawa*, a generic term applied to strangers. The name Parakanã appeared at the beginning of the twentieth century, designating an "unknown tribe of wild Indians" (Nimuendaju 1948a) inhabiting the headwaters of the western tributaries of the Tocantins River. They were first sighted in 1910 on the Pacajá River above the town of Portel, and were later identified as the Indians who appeared in the 1920s between the town of Alcobaça and the lower Pucuruí River.[1]

These first reports coincide with a period of increased Brazil-nut and rubber extractivism on the Tocantins. Rubber began to be exploited at the end of the nineteenth century, leading to an increase in the local population and trading activity in the region surrounding Marabá and Alcobaça (modern Tucuruí). The growth was short-lived. Following the crisis in the rubber market, the local economy shrank, a process that lasted until Brazil-nut harvesting was resumed on an intensive scale in 1920. Exploration of these products did not advance across the whole Parakanã territory; instead, they were concentrated in the south, close to Marabá. Nonindigenous occupation of the region in the 1920s was still confined to the shores of the Tocantins River, which, as Ignácio Batista Moura observed in 1896,

... are veritable deserts. Between Alcobaça and Praia da Rainha, along a wide bend of river ... with extremely fertile lands, large expanses of Brazil nut trees and rubber trees, some 165 km distant, you can count less than a thousand inhabitants! This minimum coefficient ... is mostly due to the terror spread by the wild tribes, whose settlements are located deeper into the wilds. Suffice to say that no-one

---

1 Throughout this book, I freely employ the noun "Indian," which has no negative connotations for indigenous peoples living in Brazil. Much the opposite, it is a label that they employ positively in their dealings with national society.

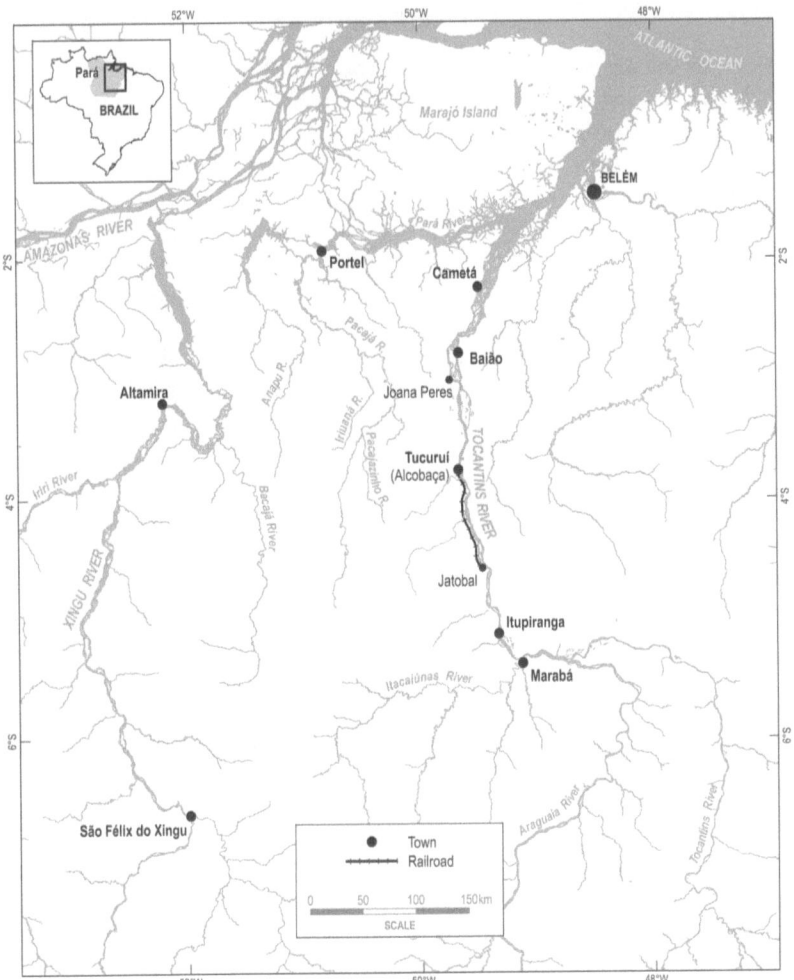

Map 1.1. Xingu-Tocantins interfluvial region before the Tucuruí
Hydroelectric Dam.

knows the Tocantins more than 3 or 4 kilometres inland from its shores. (Moura
[1896] 1910:127)

All the travelers reports from the end of the nineteenth century convey the
idea that the *terra firme* forest to the west of the Tocantins had been preserved from the expansion of the economic frontier. Had this actually been
the case? To what extent had the indigenous groups living in this region
been spared the impact of colonization?

First Reports

The Parakanã are survivors of one of the Tupi-Guarani peoples that had inhabited the region for centuries. Whether they were already there at the outset of European conquest is difficult to say. Intense migrations occurred throughout the region from the sixteenth century onward. Many Tupi-Guarani groups from the northeast coast fled to Maranhão and Pará to escape capture and epidemics. It is also likely that Indians from the Brazilian south had evaded the Portuguese yoke by fleeing north via the Araguaia-Tocantins River system, a route later used by seventeenth-century slave hunters from São Paulo.

The French were the first to explore the Tocantins River. Until the Iberian Union in 1580, Portugal neglected the colonization of the north of Brazil, allowing the French, English, and Dutch to advance into the region. In 1594, when Captain François Rifault armed three ships with the aim of achieving "some kind of conquest" in Maranhão, he could already rely on the good relations forged with a Tupi chief on previous voyages (H. Clastres 1985:9). Two of his ships were wrecked and he abandoned his project. However, one of the shipwreck survivors, Charles Des Vaux, spent a long time among the Tupinambá of Maranhão. Backed by the French crown, he later launched the first attempt to colonize the region, led by the Huguenot captain La Ravardière. Two expeditions were sent to Pará and Maranhão between 1605 and 1609. The French colony on the island of São Luís was founded soon after in 1611, becoming known as Equinoctial France. We owe the Capuchin priests Yves d'Évreux and Claude d'Abbeville for the most detailed accounts of this undertaking.

Both priests describe a native social situation already altered by several decades of sporadic contacts. Portuguese colonization of the northeast coast had provoked inland northwestward migrations (Métraux 1927; Évreux [1613] 1985:254). At the same time, the French had penetrated farther to the west and south even before the foundation of Equinoctial France. Des Vaux, having previously been involved in the wars among the Tupinambá, had set up a trading post at the mouth of the Tocantins, and La Blanjartier had explored the same river in 1610 from its mouth to the Itaboca waterfall (Velho 1981:16). More lengthy incursions were undertaken after the colonization of São Luís island: In 1613, the French ventured up the Tocantins as far as its confluence with the Araguaia. The same year, La Ravardière left São Luís with forty soldiers, ten boatmen, and an army of Indians in the direction of the Pará River, where he traveled up the Pacajá, massacring the local inhabitants (Évreux [1613] 1985:50).

Whereas the French sought control of the region from the north, the first Paulista explorers were arriving from the south in search of slaves.[2] Also in 1613, a *bandeira* made up of thirty adventurers and an equal number of Indians left São Paulo. They reached the headwaters of the Tocantins River and descended as far as the mouth of the Araguaia. Close to the confluence, they encountered seven large villages inhabited by the Caatinga, speakers of *língua geral*:[3]

> Among them we found many tools, scythes, wedges, axes, countless beads, a great number of Rouen shirts, accompanied by many hats; all of which they claimed had been acquired by trading feathers, arrows ... and cotton with the French who they say are located eleven days journey downriver at a fort built there many years ago. (Araújo [1623] 1937:105)

The fortress was probably the French trade post on the lower Tocantins, which controlled upriver traffic. The report gives us an idea of just how important the flow of goods along the large rivers already was. The Paulistas' incursion also showed the feasibility of an inland route linking southern Brazil and the Amazon basin, which the Paulistas wished to use as a pool of slave labor. However, such a venture was expensive, and it only became attractive after the 1640s when the southern Guarani population had been largely devastated by the *bandeiras* (Monteiro 1994:79–80).

The biggest pressure continued to come from the north, particularly following the end of Equinoctial France in 1615. Seizing control of Maranhão, the Portuguese began a new phase of colonization. In 1616, they chose the location for the future town of Belém, which – along with São Luís and a number of *entrepostos* – would serve as a base for "the dynamic that eventually depopulated large swathes of Amazonia" (Monteiro 1992:148). The ensuing three years were marked by bloody conflicts between the Indians and the Portuguese. In 1619, the former attempted a direct assault on Belém, provoking the Portuguese to launch a war of extermination in which they burned villages, captured slaves, and killed many people. The same year, the *sertanista* Bento Maciel Parente launched an attack with an army of 80 soldiers and 600 indigenous archers, sweeping away insurgent forces from Tapuitapera (Alcântara) to Belém (Hemming 1987a:215).

The war induced enormous losses among the region's indigenous populations and an intense territorial upheaval. Shortly thereafter, a smallpox epidemic broke out in São Luís, inflicting further losses on the survivors

---

2 In colonial times, the term *Paulista* designated those living in or around the town of São Paulo de Piratininga (modern São Paulo city), founded in 1554. Largely cut off from the Atlantic slave market, the inhabitants of São Paulo became famous for their slave-raiding expeditions against indigenous peoples deep in the hinterlands of Brazil. These expeditions were known as *bandeiras* and their members as *bandeirantes*.

3 In the sixteenth and seventeenth centuries, *língua geral* referred to either the Tupi language spoken along the Atlantic shore or the Tupi-based lingua franca employed by missionaries and colonial agents in their relations with indigenous peoples.

from the recent conflicts. Depopulation of the regions surrounding the Portuguese towns and *entrepostos* produced a vicious circle already observed along the coast: The growing scarcity of the local native workforce intensified the slave-hunting expeditions, which in turn led to the further decimation of indigenous populations from warfare and epidemics, making the need for new expeditions even more pressing.

Depopulation of the Pacajá-Tocantins Region

The economy of Maranhão and Pará was based on the production of tobacco and sugar, trade in native people, and the harvesting of *drogas do sertão* (Monteiro 1992:151). Poorly connected to the Atlantic slave trade, the local economy relied on indigenous labor until the mid-eighteenth century. This labor pool, however, quickly dried up along the large and medium-sized rivers. An example is the fate of the Tupi-Guarani living on the lower course of the Pacajá River. When Father João de Souto Maior traveled along it in 1656, it was already uninhabited. Forty years earlier,

Paulo da Rocha arrived with 40 canoes to punish a village whose Indians had ignorantly pulled down a cross and some Portuguese arms we had erected there. The Indians gathered and set off to meet us with over 200 canoes, which ours completely overwhelmed, killing these wretches with such efficiency that the river flowed red over a wide area: terrified, those who had escaped our fury fled into the hinterland with their families, which is why the entire river (like the others within our domain) has been deserted. (Souto Maior [1656] 1916:164)

According to Betendorf, this expedition, which tinged the river red with blood and took many Indians downriver, succeeded in "setting up five villages in Cametá, Pará, Serigipe and Tapuytapera" ([1698] 1910:97). By mid-seventeenth century, the Pacajá's once-numerous population had been annihilated or moved to towns and missions. In a dynamic that defined the history of the conquest of Amazonia, the survivors retreated to remote zones. This brutal demographic collapse was witnessed not only on the Pacajá and Pará Rivers and at the outskirts of Belém, but also along the Tocantins. Father Antonio Vieira confirmed this fact in 1653: "The Tocantins river is named after a nation of Indians of the same appelation, who inhabited the river when the Portuguese arrived in Pará: but of this nation, like so many others, the only thing surviving today is the memory and scattered ruins of a small village" (Vieira [1654] 1943:331).

Vieira's expedition navigated the Tocantins from its mouth to above the Itaboca waterfall. On December 30, 1653, a chief from the Tocantins village came to meet them:

This Indian was accompanied by six from the nation we were seeking out.... We have lost no time in declaring His Majesty's intention and our own, in which it seems they are well instructed and have promised us that they would not think otherwise than consider themselves allied with him as sons of the Priests and vassals of El-Rei. I was astonished to discover how familiar the king's name is and how it is constantly on their tongues; when I inquired into what idea they had of the words and of the king, they replied: *Jará omanó eyma*, meaning: *a lord who does not die*.[4] We explained that only God is immortal, but the high conceit which these heathens had of our king meant that, as a reward for the immortality attributed to him, they deserved at the very least that he protect them effectively from so much wanton violence. (Vieira [1654] 1943:331)

Over the following years, new Jesuit incursions ventured farther up the Tocantins, bringing back Indians speaking the *língua geral*. In 1654, Father Francisco Veloso reached the "nation of the Tupinambá," who lived 300 leagues upriver; he returned with more than 1,000 souls to a village near Belém. Four years later, Father Manoel Nunes made a second incursion with a troop comprising 45 soldiers and 450 Indians. They brought back 1,000 Potiguara inhabiting an area of terra firma on the Tocantins, and they also reached the Tupinambá settlement. The colony was then "augmented by more than two thousand enslaved and free Indians." Yet, as Betendorf adds, "even so, its colonists were never satisfied" ([1698] 1910:114).[5]

Although less bloody than the slave-hunting expeditions, the Jesuit *descimentos* pursued the same logic of relocating entire populations, which equally contributed to the region's depopulation.[6] Whether in the missions or in the fields, the Indians were highly vulnerable to the epidemics that devastated the region. In the 1660s, waves of smallpox "spread through the city and Captaincies, so ravaging the Indians that the majority of them were wiped out" (Betendorf [1698] 1910:213). Betendorf visited some villages to anoint those about to die. In some of them, all the inhabitants had contracted the "pestilence," meaning the only people capable of burying the dead were the priests themselves. Betendorf accompanied

---

4 The translation is precise: *jara* means "master" or "owner"; *omano* is "to die," and the suffix *eyma* is a negation. This attribution of immortality to the king was part of a general assumption about whites that survived long after the immediate bloodshed of conquest and that permeated many centuries of interethnic contact. Never, however, would "Their Majesties" provide effective protection to the Indians in reward for the powers the latter attributed to them.

5 The demand for new slaves rose in proportion to the depopulation of Grão-Pará and the economic expansion that occurred during the 1640s. It was in this context that Vieira had arrived in the region, keen to use his influence to curb the enslavement of Indians. The legislation in force since 1611 favored the colonists, but by 1655, Vieira had succeeded in persuading Dom João IV to proclaim a new law conceding management of all Indians to the Company of Jesus (Varnhagen 1959:193). Missionary activities acquired a momentum during this period, yet less than a decade later, the colonists would shift the balance back in their favor.

6 Because most Indians were brought downriver from upland areas, the Portuguese used the term *descimentos* ("descendings") to name the transference of indigenous peoples from their villages to towns and missions.

this mission to Cametá and the Tocantins village, both on the same river, where the smallpox outbreak had inflicted heavy losses. The Indians had fled inland, taking the disease with them. This huge epidemic, the second of the century, reduced the labor supply to such an extent that in 1670, an Indian slave in São Luís fetched almost the same price as an African slave (Varnhagen 1959:199).

During this period, the Paulistas resumed their advances into the region, which increased the competition for native slaves. In 1671, a number of "Aruaquize pagans" arrived in Cametá, having fled down the Tocantins to escape the *bandeirantes*. A counterincursion from Belém ventured upriver as far as the Araguaia and returned with approximately 1,000 Aruaquiz, Caatinga, and Naimiguara Indians (Leite 1943:341–2). In 1673, news of the activities of the Paulistas provoked a new incursion upriver, during which they came across Pascoal Pais de Araújo's troop, who "insulted those Hinterlands ... after having subjected the nation of Guarajuz Indians to unjust captivity" (Berredo [1718] 1849:539).

In 1680, the Jesuits regained the monopoly on incursions through the hinterland, inflicting a short-lived defeat on the colonists. However, the Tocantins River no longer much interested the missionaries, who began to explore new areas of Amazonia. Reports about this region thus become scarce. We know that smallpox struck again in the last decade of the century, spreading out from São Luís. Almost the entire population of the missions from Maranhão to Pará was devastated (Betendorf [1698] 1910:585). It reached Marajó Island and spread from there to the town of Belém in 1695. The epidemic struck swiddens, villages, and sugar plantations alike. It was followed by new infectious diseases – "terrible catarrhs" and a "strain of measles" – that also had a "ruinous effect" (Betendorf [1698] 1910:611).

By the beginning of the eighteenth century, the Pacajá-Tocantins interfluvial area was entirely deprived of any regional indigenous system that might have existed before. The surviving population had fled to upriver zones. Along with the slave captures, the Jesuit *descimentos* helped scour the "red gold" from the green forests of the region: There were approximately 50,000 Indians in the Pará and Maranhão missions in 1730 (Hemming 1987a:413). Across the whole of Amazonia, there were just four small towns and more than fifty villages run by missionaries (Moreira Neto 1988:22). On the Tocantins River, however, there remained the solitary Cametá mission, proof that the region had already ceased being an important source of souls for the priests or slaves for the colonists.[7] Moreover, from the 1730s to the end of the century, Portugal

7 The last incursion involving Jesuit missionaries took place in 1721 and 1722 (Leite 1943:343–4).

prohibited navigation of the Tocantins, fearing that gold from the mines of Goiás and Mato Grosso could be smuggled out of the port of Belém (Velho 1981:21).

Throughout the eighteenth century, epidemics continued to take their heavy toll on the indigenous population. Betendorf ([1698] 1910:ix) mentions an "outbreak of pox" in 1724; La Condamine ([1745] 1992:110) reports that smallpox swept through Belém in 1743, causing the Indians to flee from their villages into the hinterland. Six years later, a measles epidemic erupted, followed in 1750 by a smallpox outbreak. The governor, Mendonça Gurjão, estimated at the time a death toll of 40,000 people in and around Belém (Hemming 1987a:446), whereas João Daniel talks of 30,000 deaths in the missions ([1776] 1976:283). Over the following decades, the epidemics continued to sweep across Amazonia, reaching a peak between 1762 and 1772, and again between 1793 and 1800 (Balée 1994:33).

The People of the Headwaters

As we approach the nineteenth century, depopulation of the Pacajá-Tocantins interfluvial region was already consolidated. There was no longer any regional system in operation. The supralocal networks had been destroyed, leaving only isolated villages with small populations sporadically connected by warfare and alliance. The western shore of the Tocantins from the mouth of the Itacaiúnas to Cametá was then ready for nonindigenous colonization and repopulation. However, the economic frontier would advance slowly.

On the left bank, the village of São Bernardo da Pederneira was founded in 1781, close to the future location of the Alcobaça fort and later a town of the same name (today called Tucuruí) (Baena 1848:88). The fort was conceived as a defense against attacks on the river-dwelling population launched by the Tupi-Guarani living in the terra firme as well as against the raids launched by the Apinajé along the Tocantins in their search for tools (Nimuendaju 1956:2). However, when Ayres Carneiro ([1849] 1910:45) visited the region in the mid-nineteenth century, São Bernardo da Pederneira was in ruins.

Colonization of the right bank of the Tocantins was spurred on by cattle ranching, which had been expanding from Maranhão since the mid-eighteenth century thanks to the discovery of natural grasslands in the Sertão dos Pastos Bons. From there, the frontier penetrated toward the Tocantins and Goiás, with small towns and villages springing up in its wake. Unable to afford large-scale investments, cattle farming depended on the existence of natural fields to expand (Velho 1981:28).

Consequently, the forests on the left bank of the Tocantins between the Itacaiúnas and Alcobaça remained untouched until the height of the rubber boom. This stretch of the river was difficult to navigate; in particular, the Itaboca waterfall posed a natural barrier to river traffic between Goiás and Pará.

Evidence of indigenous occupation of the region during the nineteenth century relates entirely to Tupi-Guarani peoples. Villa Real ([1793] 1848:426) refers to the Jundiaís living on the left shore of the Tocantins, a short distance below the Itaboca fall, the same location given by Castelnau in 1844. Brusque records an Anambé village on the upper Pacajá River with approximately 250 people, which was destroyed in conflicts with the Curumbu in 1874 and subsequently decimated by smallpox. The most frequent designation for Indians appearing on the left shore of the Tocantins during this period is Cupelobo, or *kupen-rob*, a name given by the Apinajé to the groups they attacked during their forays through the region (*kupen*: "non-Timbira Indian"; *rob*: "jaguar"). The location of the Cupelobo matches the territory where the Parakanã were encountered half a century later. Baena (1848:106) states that they lived on the Lago Vermelho, a creek that flows into the Tocantins above the town of Itupiranga. Ayres Carneiro ([1849] 1910:79; 90) describes the encounters of his expedition with these Indians on a beach along the Tocantins and on the Pucuruí River. The final reference to the Cupelobo comes from Moura, who navigated the Tocantins in 1896. The expedition entered the Pucuruí River, passing "before the port of the Cupelobo, the site of an ancient village belonging to Indians of this tribe" (Moura [1896] 1910:160).

The voyages made by Moura, Coudreau (1897), and Buscaglione ([1899] 1901) at the turn of the twentieth century were part of the government of Pará's attempt to open up the Tocantins to colonization. It aimed to stimulate forest extractivism, particularly rubber tapping. Caucho rubber trees (*Castilloa elastica*) were discovered along the Itacaiúnas River, and the extractivist front arrived at the recently founded town of Marabá, provoking an urgent need to solve the problem of the Tocantins's lack of navigability. This breathed new life into the project to build a railway through the region, an idea first mooted in the 1870s. Originally, the project aimed to bypass the stretches of rapids that prevented free navigation as far as the confluence with the Araguaia, thereby linking the middle Tocantins with the grasslands in the north of Góias, where cattle ranching predominated (Paternostro 1945:88). Following the discovery of rubber trees in the region, the railway line was envisaged as a means of transporting production from Marabá to Alcobaça, from where it could be shipped by river to Belém.

The project ended in failure because of a chronic lack of funds, the relentless rains, and the conflicts between workers and the indigenous population.[8] Despite its failure, the railway proved decisive for the contact with the Parakanã and Asurini peoples. It redirected the area of nonindigenous occupation inland, prompting the emergence of small settlements along its tracks. This enabled the Parakanã to consolidate a long-term strategy for accessing nonindigenous goods, breaking with the isolation that had helped ensure their survival thus far. The Parakanã claim that until the end of the nineteenth century, they had no direct contact with the whites, or as they call us, the Toria.[9] They continued to clear small swiddens with stone axes and carefully avoided the lower courses of the Tocantins's tributaries. But then everything began to change.

Crossroads

So far, I have systematized the documental information on the Tocantins region from the start of European colonization to the end of the nineteenth century. From this point on, I turn to Parakanã oral history, which covers the period during which the grandparents of my oldest interlocutors lived. Historical memory coincides here with genealogical memory. Beyond this threshold, we enter a zone in which any reference to the person who witnessed the event is lost. The accounts thus become more precise from the 1880s onward. All of them corroborate the image given by the written records: By this time, the larger social networks had vanished and the region's native population had been scattered into small, isolated local groups. Where relations persisted, these took mainly the form of warfare.

The more devastating effects of colonization had already worked their course. No direct reference exists in Parakanã memory to the epidemics or the violence of the whites. Just one narrative indirectly evokes the diseases that devastated the Pacajá-Tocantins interfluvial region. This tells of a conflict between two great shamans that led to numerous deaths and the dispersal of the survivors, giving rise to the region's Tupi-Guarani peoples. Other narratives suggest the earlier existence of a linguistically homogeneous complex formed by five different subgroups: Apyterewa, Tapi'pya, Marojewara, Wyrapina, and Mykojiwena. However, this complex had already disappeared by the start of the twentieth century. Just two main linguistically related peoples inhabited the region: the Parakanã, who

8 A 43-km stretch was opened in 1908, running from Alcobaça to the site of the future settlement of Breu Branco. In 1914, the railway was extended to 58 km, veering away from the shores of the Tocantins toward the lower course of the Pucuruí River (Paternostro 1945:90). In 1935, two trains per month linked Alcobaça to the 67-km point where the Tocantins Pacification Post had been operating since 1928.

9 Toria is a designation common to the Tocantins-Araguaia peoples irrespective of linguistic affiliation, being found among the Tapirapé (Wagley 1977:311), Suruí, Javaé (Mendonça Rodrigues 1993:14), and Karajá (Toral 1992:ix).

occupied the headwaters of the Pacajá, Pacajazinho, Pucuruí, Bacuri, and Da Direita rivers; and the Asurini, located farther to the north. In addition, there were a few small clusters made up of single extended families or slightly larger groups.

The Parakanã had been living in headwater areas for a long period. No one remembers whether they once knew how to build canoes. At contact, they were unable to swim and had no knowledge of fish species found exclusively in larger rivers. The Asurini, by contrast, had been less isolated; they had not retreated to unnavigable areas and were still able to fabricate canoes (Arnaud 1961:12). The Parakanã isolation allowed them to discover the whites anew by the end of the twentieth century.

The Discovery of Metal Tools

According to the Parakanã, at this time, their grandparents entirely lacked metal tools and their swiddens were cleared with stone axes. Such facts are an indication of their withdrawal, since, as we have just seen, at the start of the seventeenth century, Tupian groups from the Araguaia-Tocantins system already possessed a wide variety of nonindigenous goods. For the Parakanã, however, the first to obtain axes from the whites was a man called Moakara, who is known for that reason as the "first master of the whites" (*Torijarypya*). Moakara lived with his kin group on a tributary of the Pucuruí River and maintained contact with Mojiajinga (White Chest), a nonindigenous Brazil-nut harvester who frequented the lower course of the river.[10] In the mid-1880s, the Parakanã warriors located Moakara's small village and encircled it. They called him to come out into the open and asked him what he had used to clear the swidden from which they had just dug up yams:

- I use an iron axe [*karapina*] to fell the trees, my nephew [Moakara replied to them].
- What do you mean by *karapina*, my maternal uncle? [the Parakanã retorted].
- I mean the axe [*jya*], my nephews. Look, this is what I use to clear the swidden.

Moakara showed them the tool, and they eagerly asked how he had acquired it:

- Who has *karapina* to [give to] you?
- It's the whites who have *karapina*, my nephews. I shout to them from the other side of the river and they bring the axes to me in a canoe.

---

10 According to Coudreau (1897:24–5), Brazil-nut extractors possessed three stations on the Pucuruí River at the time.

The warriors then asked him where they could find the whites, and Moakara showed them the way. Yet a crucial question remained:

- How do you "pay" [-*wepy*] for the axes, my maternal uncle?
- With tortoises, my nephews. I give them tortoises, and then they give me the return gift: axes, tobacco. (Pi'awa 1995: tape 19)

This dialogue can be interpreted in two ways: Either the Parakanã were unfamiliar with the term *karapina* but knew about the tool, or they were unaware of both. This more radical hypothesis would suggest that they had lived for numerous generations without access to metal tools – so long that they no longer recognized the object. This strikes me as unlikely. In the narrative, no surprise is expressed about the object in itself, nor doubts about the whites. Even so, my interlocutors maintain that Moakara was the first to possess a metal axe, whereas their grandparents only used stone blades. None of them, however, not even the oldest, born in the 1920s, reports seeing stone axes being made. So what evidence can we glean from the narrative about Moakara?

Although its structure is similar to that of the maize origin myth (see Chapter 2), the fact in itself – namely, that Moakara owned something they neither possessed nor knew how to possess – seems to me very likely. The story is recounted by both Parakanã blocs, which split apart shortly after this event. It is thus plausible that the death of Moakara set in motion a new phase in Parakanã history in which, after having retreated as far as possible, they attempted to establish direct relations with the whites. The pattern of these new relations coincide with Moakara's advice. In contrast to the Asurini, who took a number of victims in their raids against the nonindigenous population, the Parakanã always looked to avoid conflict, appearing at the homesteads of settlers with their tortoises held over their heads and shouting from the surrounding clearing: "[W]e're going to your house, my father [*miangá*]." They then took everything they could, danced, sang, left their "payment," and departed.

The Split: Western and Eastern Parakanã

The encounter with Moakara added another important twist to Parakanã history. At least eight women and four boys were kidnapped. Three of these were soon killed, because the Parakanã believe that raised enemy men will always desire to avenge their killed parents. The youngest, however, was spared thanks to the intervention of his adoptive father. This boy, called Jarawa, would grow up, marry, and have many children. One of his sons is Arakytá, the chief of Paranatinga village during my research.

Some time later, a conflict over one of the captured women caused the group to split. The conflict erupted in the 1890s and left two people dead.

Following this event, two Parakanã blocs formed: The eastern bloc settled on the upper courses of the Pucuruí, Bacuri, and Da Direita Rivers, and the western bloc settled on the headwaters of the Pacajá River to the west. The split did not result in the emergence of two local groups occupying a shared territory. Instead they moved as far as apart as possible. I shall therefore narrate two Parakanã histories, which only converge during some warfare clashes between the 1910s and 1950s, and more recently when Funai resettled them into two indigenous territories.[11] In this and the following two chapters, I will trace the paths taken by each of the branches throughout the twentieth century, including their adoption of distinct economic and political strategies. The western group extended their periods spent trekking, progressively abandoned horticulture, and intensified both their warfare activity and their contacts with the regional nonindigenous population. The eastern bloc, on the other hand, adopted a more sedentary pattern, more withdrawn from the outside and with a defensive rather than an offensive posture.

Such process of differentiation may already have been under way after the split. Over the next two decades, the eastern bloc remained isolated in their own territory and refrained from any warfare activity, whereas the western bloc relocated to a new territory where they clashed with an enemy group, whom they called Makakawa, today identified as the Asurini.[12] The western Parakanã invaded the latter's territory in the Pacajá River basin, forcing them to move northward. Two consecutive attacks were launched, enabling them to take over the area, where they would remain until the start of the 1910s, when they started venturing again into their previous territory.

Trekking and Fighting

The western Parakanã resurfaced at a former eastern bloc village being used as a hunt camp, located between the Bacuri and Da Direita Rivers. They stole manioc flour and swidden produce. Such pilfering was common as a way of making up for the lack of cultigens during the periods of trekking. After taking the flour, they left, but the eastern Parakanã discovered the theft and set off in pursuit. Rather than clashing violently, what followed was an initially peaceful encounter. Because night was falling, they

---

11 The distinction between the Parakanã blocs does not coincide with the current division of the group into two territories. The western group is found both in the T.I. Parakanã (Tocantins), where they occupy the villages of Maroxewara and Inaxy'anga, and in the T.I. Apyterewa (Xingu). The eastern bloc, for their part, live exclusively in the T.I. Parakanã, in the villages of Paranatinga, Paranowa'ona, and Ita'yngo'a.

12 The denomination *makakawa* is a nominalization of the verb -*pakang* ("touch," but also "kill").

agreed to meet the next day, this time accompanied by the women. The idea was to negotiate marriage exchanges as there was a dearth of marriageable women, and this seemed a great chance to remedy the situation. Another encounter took place the following afternoon. However, a youth had an epileptic attack, which proved catastrophic. His father sparked a conflict resulting in the death of six people from the eastern group and one from the western group. This was the first confrontation between the two Parakanã blocs after their definitive rupture (see conflict 1, Map 1.3). Various other conflicts followed, always with a clear disadvantage to the eastern bloc (see annex, Table A.1).

After attacking their former kin on the headwaters of the Bacuri River, the western bloc raided another group they called the Akwa'awohoa ("big enemy people"), kidnapping three women who spoke an unrelated language. This people may have been the Arara-Pariri, a Carib group that reported having been assailed by the Parakanã at this time, on the upper course of the Iriuaná River, a western affluent of the Pacajá (Nimuendaju 1948a:206). At the end of the 1910s, the western group enjoyed still another military victory, this time against a small group speaking their own language and known by the nickname given to its leading figure, Temeikwary'yma, so called because of his unperforated lip. This time they tried to establish peaceful relations. As they circled the house, they yelled for its residents to come out. Temeikwary'yma proposed for them to take his mother as a wife, as she had no husband. The warriors agreed and left with the woman, promising to return soon. The jubilation was short lived, though: The woman died soon after. The western group returned to deliver the bad news and the atmosphere became tense. Pretending to show Temeikwary'yma how to use a metal axe, one of the western Parakanã men struck him on the head. A conflict erupted in which eight women were captured.

At the start of the twentieth century, contacts were not only rare between whites and indigenous peoples, but also between the latter. Goods circulated at an extremely reduced scale and invariably in hostile situations. Metal axes were one of the main objects – along with arrows, songs, and women – employed in the difficult task of mediating relations between indigenous populations. However, for the Parakanã at this moment, any mediation proved impossible: No gift was capable of linking groups previously separated or never related. The axe ended up being converted into an efficient weapon for close-range combat, and women became targets for predation rather than for reciprocity.

Between 1910 and 1920, eleven foreign women were absorbed into the western Parakanã matrimonial circuit, eight of them bearing children. For a population numbering approximately 200 people at the time, this input had a sizeable impact. This dynamic of warfare and capture would eventually lead to an ideal of generalized polygamy among the western Parakanã, without privileges guaranteed to the oldest men. Such a dynamic was absent among the eastern group who did not kidnap any foreign women after the split. The blocs therefore differed not only in their subsistence strategies, but also in their mechanisms for group reproduction. Whereas the western bloc expanded its theater of operations, launching successive attacks against new enemies, kidnapping a number of women, and seizing goods, the eastern bloc retreated into isolation and defended themselves from territorial invasions. This difference, as will see in Chapter 3, would have great impact on defining gender and political relations among each of the Parakanã blocs.

In the 1920s, the western bloc abandoned the territory occupied since the split and moved farther westward, settling on the upper course of the Jiwé River, presumably the Pacajá, between 4°15' and 4°45' S. Their strategy involved keeping their territorial core as distant as possible from the areas of white penetration while expanding out from this core in various directions. Pursuing a systole-diastole dynamic, the group split into hunting bands that ventured into increasingly remote zones and later reassembled back where the manioc swidden had been planted. This periodic outward dispersal hurled them into new warfare skirmishes, almost always offensive in nature. This would be the pattern in the 1920s, when they launched five new attacks: one against the Asurini, two against the eastern Parakanã, and another two against groups I am unable to indentify.

First they raided a small Asurini band found in a hunting camp on an affluent of the Pacajá River. Some time later, they unsuccessfully besieged the village of the Yrywyjara ("masters of the carnaúba palm"), whom they today equated with the Araweté.[13] Subsequently, they raided two different peoples simultaneously: While one band attacked the Jojywapokytaho-iwa'é, so named because they used assai palm trunks as posts for their cabins, another band headed toward the sources of the Pucuruí and Da Direita Rivers, where they once again confronted the eastern Parakanã (conflict 2, Map 1.3). After this attack, the latter moved to an affluent of the Pucuruí River, building a house walled with lathes of stilt palm (village 4, Map 2.1). Yet it was to no avail. It was precisely through the gaps between these lathes that the western warriors fired their arrows, killing a woman. This event closed the first cycle of conflicts between the two Parakanã blocs. From the 1930s onward, a new series of clashes began that lasted until the

---

13 The Araweté also associate the Parakanã with past enemies, the *iriwy pepa ñã*, or "masters of the vulture feathers" (Viveiros de Castro 1992a:52): One of the distinctive features of Parakanã arrows is the use of vulture feathers for the vanes. Carnaúba is probably *Copernicia prunifera* (Lorenzi 1992:278).

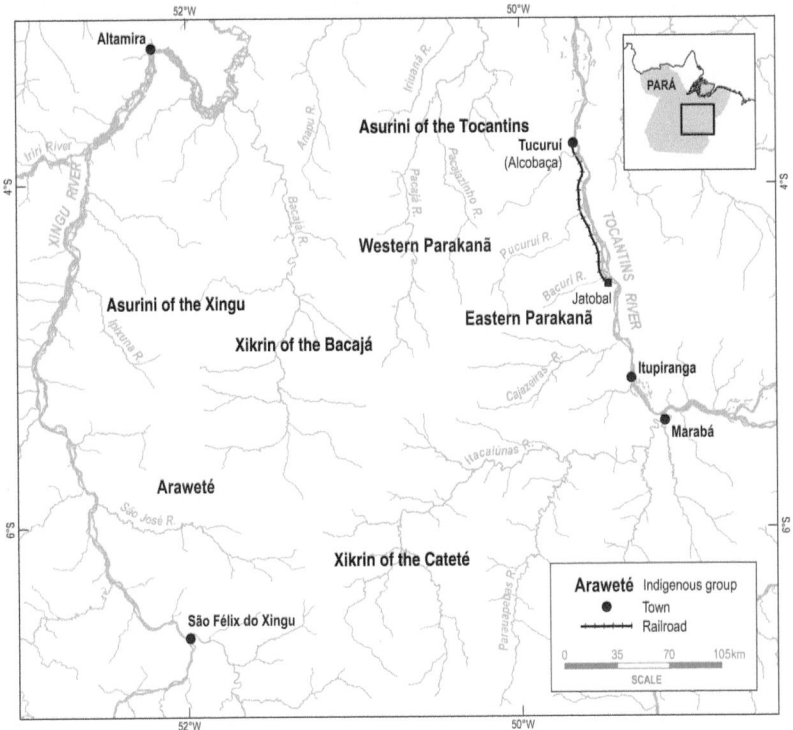

Map 1.2. Location of the indigenous groups of the Xingu-Tocantins interfluvial region in the mid-twentieth century.

1950s, involving increased interaction between them. The eastern bloc, however, never came to know that their assailants were ex-kin.[14]

In summary, during the 1920s, the western group extended their trekking zone from the Bacajá-Pacajá watershed to the west (51°00' W) where they encountered the Yrywyjara, and to the middle courses of the Pucuruí and Da Direita Rivers to the east (49°45' W) where they attacked the eastern group. Pursuing a north-south axis, they wandered from the sources of the Pacajá (5°00' S) to the confluence of the Pacajazinho-Arataú, where they clashed with the Asurini (4°00' S). The constant mobility of their hunting bands was based on a stable territory in which they built their houses and planted manioc and where they regrouped after periods of trekking.

14 Until recently, the eastern group had no idea that they had been confronting the same enemy throughout this time. The western group, on the contrary, were well aware of this, as they knew the territory they were invading. Besides, the captured women also supplied them with information on the enemy group.

The conflicts, though, were not a mere by-product of this subsistence strategy. Although the dispersion increased the chances of encountering traces of other indigenous peoples, they also actively tried to find and raid them. At the turn of the 1920s, however, it was their turn to be caught by surprise in their own territory.

The Kayapó Arrive

In the universe of enemies, the Ge groups hold a unique position. They are associated with the Karajá, protagonists of the Parakanã dream world, representing the extreme embodiment of alterity.[15] Karajá customs and physical features are described as utterly grotesque, but they are masters of a superior form of shamanry (see Chapter 5). Although omnipresent in dreams, the Ge peoples were absent from the area occupied by the Parakanã from at least 1880 until the end of the 1920s, when the Kayapó launched an assault on the western bloc, then camping in a large clearing in the forests of the Pacajá basin.[16] As the terrain was suitable for dancing, the women decided to perform a ritual known as *waratoa*, the name given to the rhythm baton used in the festival (see Chapter 6). The group dispersed: Some went in search of bamboo stems, others went off to kill vultures for feathers to decorate the participants. At this moment, they were attacked by warriors carrying clubs as well as bows and arrows. Caught by surprise, they attempted to organize a retreat: One group left with the women while another advanced toward the enemies, shooting at them. After reaching safety, they counted their losses: one man dead, four women and three boys captured. They first identified their new enemies as Karajá, but some time later gave them a specific name, Ywywa ("Ground people"), after noting that they did not have hammocks but rather slept on the earth like peccaries.[17]

These Ywywa were possibly the Kayapó-Xikrin, who occupied a territory between the Cateté, to the southeast, and the Bacajá, to the northwest during this period. Pursued by the Gorotire, the Xikrin migrated to the Bacajá in the second half of the 1920s, some of them returning to the sources of the Itacaiúnas River a while later (Vidal 1977:30–1;

---

15 *Karajá* is a Tupi-Guarani word. It was used by the coastal Tupi in the sixteenth century to refer to enemies living inland of the Captaincy of São Vicente (Staden [1557] 1974:154) and, since the seventeenth century, has designated a group speaking a macro-Ge language on the Araguaia River.

16 It is possible that Timbira advancing to the north of the Itacaiúnas had clashed with the region's Tupi groups during an earlier period. As we have seen, Nimuendaju (1956:2–3) reports that in the first half of the nineteenth century, the Apinajé made incursions into this region against non-Timbira peoples whom they called *Kupen-Rob*. The Parakanã tell of distant and somewhat fantastic warfare skirmishes with the *Karajá* and the "Kayapó-to-be" (*Ywywoma*).

17 *Ywywa* is probably composed of *ywy* ("earth," "ground") and *awa* ("people," "person").

Fisher 1991:72). Perhaps some of this latter group advanced into Parakanã territory. After the first attack, the Ywywa quickly returned to encircle a western Parakanã encampment but were immediately repelled. These Kayapó attacks, although isolated events – they would only be repeated in the 1970s – refueled the western Parakanã imagination concerning the Karajá, reawoke the potential presence of entirely other indigenous peoples, and announced the existence of enemies whose warlike spirit was comparable to their own. Even today, the western Parakanã admire the Kayapó for their skill, strength, and ability to follow the tracks of enemies in the forest, a quality that would prove fatal for them fifty years later.

During the 1920s, another fact signaled the transformation of the context in which the first postfission generation had lived until then: the foundation of a pacification post on the shores of the lower course of the Pucuruí River in 1928, leading to increased contact with likewise richly imagined figures, also entirely other and equally masters of potent forms of shamanry: the Toria.

The Whites and the Railway

In the 1920s, the region of Marabá and Alcobaça experienced a spurt of economic growth, thanks to Brazil-nut harvesting. Local production expanded more than twenty times between 1919 and 1926, turning the region into the country's largest Brazil-nut supplier for exportation, a position it would maintain over several decades. The center of exploration was located along the Itacaiúnas River and its right-bank affluents. Alcobaça gained prominence as an intermediate port between Marabá and Belém. Development of the region lent a new impulse to the construction of the Tocantins Railroad, and work was resumed around 1927 (Velho 1981:47–57). At this moment, the attacks on workers and settlers along the railway line by indigenous groups began to multiply. Called in to ensure the safety of workers by pacifying the *silvícolas*, the Indian Protection Service (SPI) founded the Tocantins Pacification Post in 1928. This was situated on the 67-kilometer point of the railway on the left bank of the Pucuruí River (see Map 1.4).[18]

Pillaging in the region was the work of two indigenous groups, the Parakanã and the Asurini, who employed fairly distinct strategies: The former sought to obtain goods peacefully, "paying" for them with forest produce; the latter raided and killed the owners of goods. Despite the confusion reigning in the literature until the Asurini were contacted in 1953,

---

18 *Silvícola* means "forest dweller," and it was commonly used to refer to Indians at the time. The *Serviço de Proteção ao Índios* (SPI) was created in 1910 by the Brazilian government and headed by Cândido Mariano da Silva Rondon.

this distinction was quickly perceived by the local nonindigenous population. In the annual report for 1929, the head of the Pacification Post, Alípio Ituassu, already differentiates the "warrior Indians" who attacked in the vicinity of Alcobaça from the "nomadic Indians" who frequently appeared near the Post (SPI 1929). Three years later, he contrasted the "warrior Indians" with the "Indians on the way to pacification," "who are used to visiting us annually . . . always peacefully and with displays of complete comradeship" (SPI 1932).

The hostilities practiced by the "warrior Indians" would become one of the main obstacles to building the railway, making the SPI a necessary (albeit inconvenient) partner in the region's development projects. In October 1929, for example, the "warrior Indians" assailed settlers at the 5- and 7-kilometer points, "killing a man named Acylino so-and-so and slightly wounding Maria so-and-so, his companion" (SPI 1929). The following year, they killed a woman and a boy at the 40-kilometer point, prompting a punitive expedition organized and sponsored by then director of the Tocantins Railroad, Amynthas de Lemos (SPI 1930a). Led by one of the director's henchmen, the posse comprised the local police chief, two soldiers, and around thirty men invited to take part in the action, most of them agricultural workers from the region. They reached an Asurini encampment and killed a large number of the people, including women and children.[19]

In the administrative inquiry into the massacre, the head of the Pacification Post affirmed that he could do nothing to prevent fresh reprisals, given that "Dr. Amyntha de Lemos has publicly stated that he has the State Governor's support to do whatever he wants in Alcobaça," and "inflated by his own act of savagery, he proclaimed he was merely waiting for soldiers and munitions to arrive before embarking on a new expedition" (SPI 1930b). Indeed, in 1933, after the Asurini attacked a farm worker at the 22-kilometer point, they were pursued by a police force, joined by civilians armed with .44 caliber guns and Mauser rifles. The secrecy imposed by the expedition commander prevents us from knowing whether any deaths resulted.

These actions marked the limits to the "pacification" work carried out by an organization that was ill-equipped and underfunded from the outset. The conflict between local interests and the principles of Cândido Rondon, permeated by a moralizing and impotent discourse, is abundantly recorded in the Tocantins Pacification Post's reports as well as other SPI documents.

---

19 After the return of the expedition to Alcobaça, the head of the Pacification Post went to speak with the lieutenant Manoel Francisco, chief of police, who told him: "Mr. Alipio, the stripes on my uniform help feed my family, but I prefer losing them to making another journey for the same purpose as this one now. I've never seen such barbarity" (SPI 1930a).

The texts written by Ituassu, the first and most diligent head of the post, are filled with condemnations of white people's barbarism and the arrogance of those responsible for constructing the railroad. By 1931 he had already concluded that "in the town of Alcobaça ... the civilized people are more savage than the actual Indians" (SPI 1931).

Despite the punitive expeditions, the "warrior Indians" continued to harass the local population and the railway workers. When they began to reappear in 1937 between the 47-kilometer point and the outskirts of Alcobaça, the director of the railway was obliged to request help again from the SPI. In a letter to the SPI's regional inspector, the director asked the employees of the Protection Service to abandon their static mode of operation and set up mobile groups, penetrating the deep forest with the aim of "living with groups of silvícolas, even in indigenous settlements, if necessary" (Federal Railroad Inspectorate 1937).[20] Yet the SPI lacked the funds and staff to carry out its work in the region. Despite setting up the Caripé subpost at the 11-kilometer point on the railway in 1937, which was dedicated to attracting the Asurini, the situation was one of obvious decline a decade after the foundation of the Pacification Post. In a telegram to Inspector Philadelfo Cunha, dated January 1938, Rondon expressed his astonishment at the events in Alcobaça, where the Asurini attacks had provoked the population's exodus; he requested energetic measures to avoid any retaliation against the Indians since a civil force was being formed to hunt them down (SPI 1938).

The situation continued to be tense over the following decade. In 1945, the police chief, Carlos Teles, organized a ferocious expedition against the "warrior Indians," armed with guns, gas bombs, and hand grenades. The expedition failed, and the Asurini continued to hinder colonization near Alcobaça for a few more years. In 1948, they finally ventured down south along the railway, discovering the Pacification Post at the 67-kilometer point. Five years later they were pacified (Laraia & DaMatta 1967:34). Contact was accompanied by depopulation: In one year, flu and dysentery caused 50 deaths among a population of 190 people (Arnaud 1961:8).

The Tocantins Pacification Post

The Parakanã adopted an opposite stance to the Asurini, always looking to establish peaceful relations with the Toria.[21] This contrast seems

---

20 Such a strategy would only be adopted in the 1970s during the building of the Transamazonian highway, with disastrous effects for the eastern Parakanã.

21 This is one of the criteria allowing us to determine which of the groups was involved in the events described in reports from the period. Another important criterion is the area frequented, much smaller for the western Parakanã who appeared only between the 60- and 70-km points and who limited their visits to the SPI base after its creation.

to have resulted from their different experiences prior to the 1920s. The Parakanã had been preserved from the economic frontier, whereas the Asurini were exposed to it much earlier due to the proximity of their territory to the towns of Portel on the Pacajá and Alcobaça on the Tocantins. When the railway began to cut inland through the forests, the Asurini were already immersed in conflicts with the regional population, whereas the Parakanã were considered nonhostile Indians even before the foundation of the Pacification Post. Describing their first visit to the post, Alípio Ituassu writes that although the latter arrived in high spirits, their attitude "didn't seem quite so peaceful as we expected based on the information I had," since they were armed and made a lot of commotion (SPI 1929). He quickly learned that this tumult was a distinctive feature of the Parakanã, along with their insistence on paying with tortoises and captured young animals for the goods received, as Moakara had instructed them. In truth, they were never content with just receiving the goods. They also took the workers' personal objects and raided the few settlers' houses found next to the post.

The western Parakanã visited the Post regularly from its creation in 1928 until 1938. During this period they arrived in large numbers, frequently accompanied by women and children.[22] The fact that they took women and children – something they would refrain from doing on resuming their visits after 1953 – suggests the western Parakanã not only had no fear of physical violence from the whites, but they also did not associate them with diseases. Whites were not thought to practice sorcery, despite being attributed with a potent shamanic power. This lends further credence to the hypothesis that the Parakanã were isolated over a long period, as it implies the absence of any memory of epidemics resulting from contact.

The western Parakanã not only showed no fear, but they arrived in boisterous mood. Ituassu perceived this as a display of uncontained joy, animated by singing, dancing, and nonstop incomprehensible conversation. For the Indians, the visits were festive bonanzas where they acquired a quantity of goods never before imagined. They went from penury to bounty in a couple of years. During this period, one aspect of interethnic contact gained special prominence in western Parakanã thinking: namely, the generosity of the "masters of objects" (ma'ejiroajara), who should not be killed lest one lose access to their goods. The whites came to occupy

---

22 Reports from 1929 to 1934 provide the following estimates of the number of visitors: 25 to 30 men and 15 boys (January 27, 1929); 100 people including men, women, and children (June 19, 1930); 60 men, 10 boys, 30 women, and 15 children carried in the sling (February 5, 1931); 12 men, while the rest stayed camped 1 km from the Post (November 21, 1931); 40 men and boys (September 23, 1932); 80 people, an equal number of men and women, and many children and young infants (September 25, 1932); 6 men and 3 boys (July 31, 1933); absent (1934).

the place of providing fathers in their imagination and until "pacification" would be called *miangá*, a formal term for classificatory father and potent dream enemies converted into pets (see Chapter 7).[23]

According to Arnaud, western Parakanã's visits continued until 1938, when they disappeared "for no apparent reason" (1961:19). The motives for this disappearance are unclear. The author suggests that an outbreak of measles had hit settlers along the railway line earlier in the year and that the risk of contagion had scared away the indigenous visitors. However, my Parakanã interlocutors have never mentioned this fact to me. My guess is that they had already a considerable stock of metal tools by then, and they were now turning their attention to their indigenous neighbors. The Post had been a rich mine of objects: The 1929 report lists thirty-five machetes, eighteen axes, five knives, thirteen hammocks, and three *alqueires* of flour taken by the visitors.[24] Later reports omit the actual number of gifts, indicating simply that they were lavish. A large quantity were said to have been given in 1930, for example, albeit not enough for all the visitors (around 100, including men, women, and children). Between 1931 and 1932, the Parakanã visited the Post four times: The first time, 115 Indians appeared; the last time, roughly 80. On this occasion, they discarded a portion of the gifts they had received in the forest: clothes as usual, but also metal tools (SPI 1932). In 1933, just nine men arrived, and the following year no one came (see note 24).

Between 1929 and 1933, the western Parakanã must have acquired more than 100 axes and possibly double this number of machetes, as well as dozens if not hundreds of hammocks. Almost overnight, they went from a situation in which metal objects were still scarce to one where every adult man owned at least an axe and a machete. What were the consequences of this sudden and abundant influx? Contrary to our expectations, instead of stimulating swidden cultivation, it actually reinforced the shift toward hunting and warfare since it made agricultural work less demanding. It also facilitated harvesting wild food: The simple task of opening a babassu coconut became much less arduous. Individual possession of these tools made them an instrument of autonomy: The axe came to mean for gathering what the bow meant for hunting. From this point on, the atom of subsistence became a man, his wife, a bow, and an axe.

23 This generous view of the generosity of whites also characterized the eastern bloc, who tried to reproduce a similar pattern of interaction. However, they had few chances to put it into practice as they never discovered the Pacification Post. Occupying the middle and upper course of the Bacuri, Da Direita, and Pucuruí Rivers, they only interacted sporadically with Brazil-nut harvesters, rubber extractors, and big-cat hunters who penetrated their territory. These invaders were the only source of metal instruments, since the eastern Parakanã incursions along the lower course of the Bacuri River proved unsuccessful and never represented a consistent source of goods.

24 *Alqueire* is a unit of dry volume corresponding to 36.27 liters.

War in the Forest

During the 1930s, the western Parakanã concentrated on visiting the Tocantins Pacification Post. The acquisition of goods had dominated collective actions, leading to a relatively peaceful period. My chronology suggests that the resumption of conflicts coincided with the moment when they stopped frequenting the post. Hence the "disappearance" of the Parakanã can also be linked to the reappearance of warfare, as though, satiated with nonindigenous products, they turned once more to "goods" that the whites were unable to offer. Between the mid 1930s and the mid-1950s, the western Parakanã undertook ten new offensive incursions, three against the Asurini and seven against the eastern Parakanã.

The first raid of this period occurred in the second half of the 1930s when a band of trekkers reached the headwaters of the Bacuri River. As the western Parakanã knew they were entering alien territory, they left the women camped one day's journey away. A dozen warriors ventured upriver until encountering a dwelling with a nearby swidden. It was a new village that the eastern Parakanã had cleared for future occupation. The swidden was producing crops already, and there was manioc flour stored at the site. The invaders stole it and left to reunite with their wives. As had happened in the 1910s, the theft was quickly discovered and the raiders pursued. The next day, western Parakanã men found themselves surrounded by the eastern group (see conflict 4, Map 1.3). They approached them to allow their women to escape. The encounter was peaceful: The adversaries embraced each other, forming pairs of formal friends and danced until dawn. The following morning, the eastern men invited the western warriors to come to their village and meet their women. They agreed: "[L]et's see our friends' wives," the widower Warepojooa reportedly said, "so they can give me a women who will cook for me."

However, the eastern men led them to an abandoned village where they had hidden axes and machetes the day before. On the way there, tension grew as distrust and fear set in. Dusk loomed as they sighted the deserted village ahead: "[L]et's sleep there, my friends, and tomorrow we'll take you to the women." They left their weapons on the path leading to the encampment. Night fell and with it came sleep. Resolved to kill the invaders, the eastern men stayed awake. One of them, Takorahá, asked his nephew for the *tauari* cigar, inhaled and passed it on to another kinsman, rubbing it on his fingers. This was the signal. Inajokynga saw the crimson ember of the cigar fall and realized what was about to happen. In vain, he tried to awaken his companions, but Takorahá immediately struck Awaparima's skull with an axe. At the same instant, his brother-in-law sliced at Jy'oa with a machete. Two other men from the western group were wounded by knife and machete blows. All of them succeeded in escaping, but Jy'oa

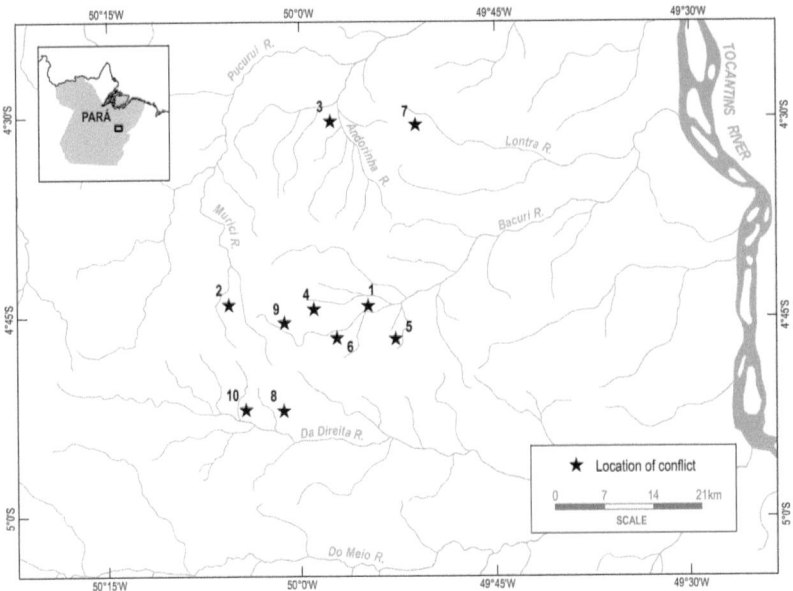

Map 1.3. Location of the conflicts between the Parakanã blocs (1910–1955).

died on the path back. Awaparima was also unable to withstand his injuries and died after reaching the village. After this event, the western Parakanã named their former kin *Amowaja*, the nominalization of the verb *-mowai* ("to cut"), a reference to the killing of Jy'oa by machete blows.

Some time later, once the dead had been mourned and the injured cured, the western Parakanã ventured back into the eastern Parakanã's territory. It was not just a revenge expedition. Although they certainly pondered the idea of avenging the previous deaths, they also envisaged the possibility of establishing peaceful relations. The scarcity of marriageable women among both groups created a mutual interest and the potential for reciprocity. Disposed for exchange and warfare alike, the western Parakanã reached the village where they had previously taken the flour. Since the site had been deserted, they journeyed down the Bacuri basin until they encountered their adversaries (village 7, Map 2.1). They surrounded the village with its single house walled with lathes of stilt palm. Most of the adult men were out hunting. Only three of them had stayed behind with the women and children. A western Parakanã warrior shouted to the people inside: "Have you gone away, my friend?" The response came back immediately: "No, I waited for you, my friend, I stayed here." The responder then asked why they came visiting. "We've come on a whim, we're not angry with you, my brother-in-law. We've just come to see you," one of the visitors replied.

"Oh, that's good to hear, my brother-in-law. I've missed you too. Come over here so we can see you." Some of the visiting warriors stepped out into the open while the others remained hidden in the forest.

Since there was no chance of escaping the visitors, it was crucial to keep the situation under control until the hunters returned. The village women took flour to the visiting warriors on the patio, looking to placate them and, at the same time, ascertain the conditions of the siege. They quickly saw the other men hiding in the woods ready to shoot. An eastern man came to the door to talk about the peaceful relations that could be established through matrimonial exchange. When the hunters began to arrive, the situation almost collapsed into conflict: They had heard their enemies' speech some way off and arrived with their bows at the ready. However, confrontation was not the best tactic. So they resumed talking and danced all night. As daybreak approached, they began the formal partings:

- Dawn's coming, my father-in-law, will you continue to not bare your teeth at me [will you stay calm, not angry toward me]?
- I shan't bare my teeth at you, son-in-law.
- Will you go away and bring me my niece, father-in-law?
- We'll soon bring our daughters for you, brother-in-law.

As usual, the visitors asked for arrows and the hosts duly supplied them. The western warriors left amid promises of a future encounter. The visit had been successful with offers of women on both sides. The first step to establishing peaceful relations had been taken; now it was necessary to advance. The western Parakanã quickly organized a new expedition, this time accompanied by wives and daughters. However, fearing a sneak attack, the eastern Parakanã decided to abandon the village. They relocated to the Lontra creek, a left bank affluent of the Bacuri River, far downriver (see village 8, Map 2.1). Since they had no swiddens there, though, they continued to visit the old village.

When the western Parakanã returned, taking women as promised, they found the site abandoned. They slept there and in the morning they heard the sound of people in the swidden. The eastern group had returned to make manioc flour. The groups met once again, repeating their promises to exchange wives. They danced throughout the night. The next morning, though, the situation got out of control and conflict ensued once again. The eastern group came out worst, with two men and one woman killed as well as two preadolescents kidnapped. On the western side, one man and a young baby also died. The episode buried any possibility of peaceful interaction (see conflict 6, Map 1.3). Fearing pursuit, the eastern Parakanã moved even farther to the northeast, settling on a tributary of the lower Pucuruí River, where they took refuge for some years (see village 9, Map 2.1).

For both Parakanã blocs, the 1940s were marked by new intertribal conflicts and isolation from nonindigenous society. Although then living close to the Pacification Post, the eastern Parakanã remained unaware of its existence. They continued to seek out contacts on the Bacuri River, interacting sporadically with intruders venturing into the forest or settlers living along the railway. These encounters often ended up in conflicts.[25] The western group, for their part, stayed on the Pacajá and did not visit the SPI Post for a while. Instead they headed northward in search of new victims. They set off as a large band of trekkers, hunting and gathering while looking for the traces of enemies. They encountered abandoned villages and swiddens. As usual, the women halted and the men went ahead. As they approached, they ceased hunting and stopped lighting fires at night. Locating the enemy, they advanced in a pincer movement. They ended up surprising the Asurini in a hunt camp, shooting a number of them and kidnapping two women.

Some months later, they returned to the Asurini territory. As they recount it, "the killers-to-be became enraged once more and said, "let's kill enemy people." This time they reached an actual village. Advancing via a swidden, they came across a family digging up manioc and shot a boy. Alerted, the Asurini counterattacked. The western Parakanã recall that they heard a shotgun go off and, frightened, quickly retreated. The shots had the desired effect, leaving the Parakanã uncertain about their enemies' relations with the whites. They decided not to undertake a new raid, and would only confront the Asurini again at the beginning of the 1950s.

In the second half of the 1940s, the western Parakanã went off in search of the eastern group once more, penetrating their territory even more deeply. Memory of the previous visits was still fresh in the minds of the eastern Parakanã, who, foreseeing an imminent attack, had just danced with armadillos to close their bodies against enemy arrows. Good bet. The western group attacked without delay, besieging the village (village 14, Map 2.1; conflict 7, Map 1.3). At nightfall, the eastern Parakanã managed to break through the siege and flee. The following day, however, five women came back to fetch their hammocks and were intercepted by the invading warriors. Night fell. They slept in the abandoned house and left in the morning with their captives, although not before obliging them to toast flour. Some months later, they returned to the locale to check the skulls of their victims

---

25 Three telegrams from the head of the Pacification Post report these skirmishes. The first is dated August 1944 and states that the "Paracanã Indians" had killed three people on the 96-km point (SPI 1944a). The second, dated December of the same year, reports Indians emerging on the Bacuri River: "I verified that they are Paracanã. They asked for material and flour" (SPI 1944b). The last telegram, dated 1945, refers to an attack on the 107-km point (more or less where the railway line crossed the Bacuri River) that resulted in the death of a railroad worker (SPI 1945).

and prepare more flour with the manioc from the abandoned swidden.[26] They then continued to trek through the region. Eventually they discovered new tracks left by the eastern group, this time in the basin of the Da Direita River (village 16, Map 2.1; conflict 8, Map 1.3). They attacked them once again, killing three men, including the headman Ijianga.

At the start of the 1950s, the western Parakanã raided their ex-kin once more, killing a woman in a forest encampment. Some years later, they captured four women on the Da Direita River but were unable to escape with them. Intercepted by eastern warriors, they were forced to retreat. This was the last of a series of ten encounters between the two Parakanã blocs, leaving a toll of seventeen dead and seven kidnappings on the eastern side, and six deaths on the western side.

The Enemies Disappear

After the kidnapping attempt, the eastern Parakanã were finally rid of the western group. Yet this did not translate into a peace dividend. They soon clashed with a small kindred of Ge Indians, whom they named Iawoho-iwa'e ("the long-haired ones"). Later on, at the start of the 1960s, an internecine conflict erupted, leading to the deaths of four people and the exile of one of the killers. The eastern group relocated once more, moving northeast to the upper course of the Andorinha River, the region where they would be reduced to state administration in 1971 (village 27, Map 2.1).

The western group, for their part, experienced an atypical moment in their recent history: After half a century of feverish bellicosity, they found themselves without enemies to attack. They thought the eastern group had moved to live with the whites since they were no longer able to track them down. The Asurini had indeed been "pacified" at the start of 1953, after seeking refuge with the SPI agents following an attack by the western Parakanã.[27] After this pacification, the latter resumed their monopoly of the SPI Post from this date until the mid-1960s, as they had done previously in the 1930s. They returned with a huge thirst for industrialized goods.

---

26 Seizing products from the swiddens of enemies was a common practice among the western group. It indicates the importance attributed to crops and, simultaneously, the little amount of work they invested in producing them. The practice may well precede the fission of the Parakanã blocs since it appears in the narratives describing the attack on Moakara's group back in the nineteenth century.

27 In the report on their pacification, the Asurini chief is said to have invited the SPI agents to visit the village so they could show them "the devastation they had suffered, which was caused by the Indians who were appearing at the 3rd Encampment. They even asked us to help them fight their adversaries" (SPI 1953a). Third Encampment was the name of an advance base in the forest connected to the Pacification Post by an open trail.

In 1953 they appeared countless times, taking everything they could. A telegram from April of that year reports that

Parakanã Indians arrived peacefully on Sunday 3rd, at the third encampment, having met only two workers, who, despite seeing completely unarmed Indians calling them, ran towards the PIA Pucuruí, where all the team members were, including interpreters. The Parakanã took various items from the third encampment, including flour, tools and materials for the domestic use of workers, leaving in exchange two agoutis tied to the leg of the table and some tortoises. (SPI 1953b)[28]

They reappeared throughout the year, twice in May, once again in October, November, and December, creating difficulties for the SPI in replacing the stock of goods. They had spent fifteen years without ample access to metal tools, and most people were keen to acquire them. On these visits, they maintained the same peaceful attitude. They arrived with tortoises and the young of animal prey, yelling, "Are you there, father, we're going to your house." They came in and took everything they could. Two important differences marked this new cycle of visits though: First, they no longer took women and children with them, as they feared the "cough," an illness they quickly associated with inter-ethnic contact; second, the presence of indigenous interpreters injected a new dynamic to the relationship.

The figure of the Indian-turned-white deeply impressed the western Parakanã. Iatora recounted to me a dialogue he had with one of them, whom he called Je'e'yngoa. The latter explained to him how they would be pacified: "You're going to take our flour, then you'll return and take more flour, you'll return again and take flour. Just before pacification, you're going to take it again. Then we'll go after you, pacify you and bring you back here" (Iatora 1993: tape 36). The verb I translate as "pacify" is -mo'yng, but the best gloss would probably be "captivate," with the same ambiguous sense that the word has in English, meaning to subject and to seduce simultaneously.[29] The term also applies to the capture and integration of foreign women, implying a transformation of the person being pacified vis-à-vis the pacifier, a movement of transculturation. It also implies a spatial dislocation in which the patient joins the agent: in this case, the former moving to live with the whites.

28 PIA Pucuruí stands for "Posto Indígena de Atração Pucuruí" (Pucuruí Attraction Post), the new name of the former Tucuruí Pacification Post. "Attraction" was the jargon used by the governmental agency at the time and expressed their strategy of luring Indians into contact and out of the forest through gift giving.

29 Kracke (1978:48) translates the Parintintin cognate -monhyrõ as pacify and Betts (1981:131; 150) as "civilize, tame, bind loosely." The latter analyzes the term as a composite of the factive -mo and the adjective nhyrõ, "tame, docile." Montoya translates the term "pacify" into the ancient Guarani as amoyngatú (-gatú is the modifier "good" or "well") or amo ñyrõ uca.

The western Parakanã preferred to remain autonomous though, only visiting the Attraction Post. At the turn of the 1960s, however, the economic frontier began to reach the core of their territory, which had been preserved until then. Logging activity reached the upper course of the main rivers, whereas mineral extractivism and big-cat hunting penetrated deeper into the forest. Such intrusion threatened their dynamic of expansion and contraction: The place where they planted manioc functioned as a safe port of call, localizing the community at a single point and allowing the centrifugal movement of trekking. The invasion jeopardized this way of life: Departing meant leaving the site exposed, and returning meant running the risk of an undesirable encounter. Until then, they had been in control of their interaction with whites precisely because they were capable of isolating themselves and seeking out contact whenever they wished. In the 1960s, this changed irreversibly. A radiogram sent on November 23, 1962, by the head of the Pucuruí Post tells of the group's unrest: "understanding between civilized Indians (Asurini) and Paracanã; latter asked for their lands not to be invaded and excursions to their villages to be avoided, thereby avoiding continual conflicts" (SPI 1962). During this period, the western Parakanã also suffered their first losses in interethnic contact: Two men were killed when they approached to steal nonindigenous goods from a forest camp. A little while later, another man was similarly killed.

Along with the transformation in the relationship with whites, long-term alterations in the economic base were approaching their climax. The group's mobility had evolved in a crescendo, accompanied by the abandonment of villages and a dwindling in the variety of cultigens planted in their swiddens. This movement was already under way prior to invasion of their territory, but it accelerated to such an extent after this moment that, even before leaving the Pacajá basin, the western Parakanã had abandoned manioc cultivation. At the same time, tension within the group was mounting, partly because of the pressure exerted by the extractivist frontier, and partly because of the absence of enemies. Warfare had not just enabled tensions to be projected outward: It had also diluted tensions inside the group through the steady influx of women. Between 1910 and 1955, more than twenty foreign women had been captured, seventeen of whom later had children. These additions were fundamental to maintaining internal peace. For the generation that reached adulthood in the 1960s, however, there was no alternative: Unmarried men had to vie for wives with their kin. This exploded in internecine conflict, causing the first large fissure among the western bloc and provoking their migration westward.

Last Years of Autonomy

The march west began in the final years of the 1960s and ended with the final contact of the western Parakanã in 1984, in the Xingu-Bacajá interfluvial region, around 250 kilometers from their original territory. This relocation was not undertaken all at once but in numerous trips to and fro.

After the first internal conflict, they divided into three groups. One of them headed toward the Bacajá River, believing the region to be empty of whites, and collided with the Kayapó-Xikrin. They found them camped next to a grove of Brazil-nut trees and promptly attacked them. Next they escaped south, where they were found on a revenge raid a short time later. It was December 1969. The Xikrin attacked during the day. Most of the men were hunting, with just women and children remaining in the camp site. Counting the dead and captured, the western group suffered thirteen losses: four adult women, four girls, and five boys. The attack was devastating. They caught the Parakanã unprepared. For the first time, an enemy had dared to follow their tracks and, also for the first time, had attacked them with firearms.[30] When the survivors managed to meet up again, they decided to take the reverse path back to the Pacajá basin.

Meanwhile, the other western bands were also confronting new enemies, albeit less formidable ones. I have been unable to identify them. The Parakanã insist they were neither Araweté nor Asurini of the Xingu, peoples they had come to know fairly well after settling in the Xingu basin. They spoke an incomprehensible language, were armed with starnut palm bows, and slept in fiber hammocks. The women used skirts while the men wore straw penis sheaths. Neither their ears nor their lips were pierced. The Parakanã called them simply Akwa'awa, "enemy people."[31] One of the western bands surprised them in a hunt camp, killing several people. Six Parakanã women took part in the raid, went into seclusion, and acquired the status of killer (*moropiarera*). Soon after this attack, those who had not participated in the combat launched a second assault on the Akwa'awa. This time, they found only women and children.

After these attacks, the three western bands gradually joined up again. The scars had still to heal, and it was only in 1972 that all of them united again, this time, as they said to me, "by the manioc of the whites." They were close to the swiddens of nonindigenous settlers on the Do Meio River, a tributary of the Cajazeiras, at the southern limit of the eastern Parakanã territory. A little farther north, their ex-kin had just been pacified.

---

30 The Xikrin of the Bacajá had been pacified at the beginning of the 1960s. At the time, the chief of the Funai Post was responsible for organizing the gathering and sale of Brazil nuts by the Xikrin (Fisher 1991:87–9). Apparently, he used to supply munitions for the Xikrin to attack "wild Indians" who disrupted the work. The habitual victims were the Asurini and the Araweté.

31 The Araweté refer likewise to a nomadic enemy tribe, the *o'i woko* ("long arrows"), who lived off hunting and flour from the mesocarp of the babassu palm coconut (Viveiros de Castro 1992a:339).

The "Pacification" of the Eastern Parakanã

The eastern Parakanã kept to their option to remain autonomous for a long time. They withstood the rubber boom, the Brazil-nut boom, and the project for the railway connection between Tucuruí and Marabá. However, they were unable to resist the so-called Brazilian miracle.[32] In the 1970s, the federal government's program for building roads in Amazonia had a decisive impact on colonization and indigenous lands. Funai and Sudam signed a contract to pacify the indigenous populations located along the Cuiabá-Santarém and Transamazonian highways.[33] They feared that the Indians would obstruct construction of the highway system, as they had in the past during work on the railway lines. The new context was unfavorable for the Indians. The government's urgency was assisted by financial backing from sizeable international loans (Davis 1978:89–93). As a result, the recently created Funai, run by military personnel, abandoned the static posture previously adopted by the SPI in the Tocantins and embarked on a "war of pacification," creating four penetration fronts to contact the Parakanã in their own territory (Funai 1971a; Magalhães 1982:54–5).[34]

On November 12, 1970, the first encounter with the eastern group took place on the Lontra River, an affluent of the Bacuri, at a site used as an encampment by loggers. The eastern Parakanã reacted aggressively on this occasion. The man responsible for the operation, Colonel Bloise, contrasted their behavior with that of the "Indians who five years ago emerged on the Pucuruí in search of gifts and food" (Funai 1971a:3), a reference to the visits made by the western Parakanã. The situation now was different because Colonel Bloise's team had instructions to advance as far as the villages rather than wait passively at the base. The eastern group still wanted to repel the invaders but eventually succumbed to the fatal attraction of presents. Over time, relations became closer, and in October 1971 they abandoned their villages and relocated to the front's encampment.

Contact had disastrous consequences for the eastern Parakanã. Despite the financial resources made available by the Brazilian government for constructing the Transamazonian highway, the planning for pacification was wholly inadequate. The recently created Funai had inherited the methods as well as the employees of the extinct SPI, which for its part had

---

32 "The Brazilian miracle" refers to the rapid economic growth during the military dictatorship, especially from 1969 to 1973.

33 Sudam (Superintendência de Desenvolvimento da Amazônia) was instituted by the federal government in 1966 to coordinate efforts for the development of the Amazonian region. Funai (Fundação Nacional do Índio) replaced the SPI in 1967 as the official organ responsible for the Brazilian Indians.

34 *War of Pacification in Amazonia* is the title of a documentary by Yves Billon, which includes scenes from the first contacts with the eastern Parakanã.

evolved from the kinds of interaction with indigenous peoples pursued by missionaries and settlers since the Conquest. Postcontact deaths were seen as an inevitable fate. At the time, no provision was made to use the available funds for professional advice, medical care, or preventive work. The ensuing tragedy was seen as part and parcel of the contact procedures, just as it had been since the sixteenth century. To make things worse, the opening of the Transamazonian highway had made it impossible to confine the contacted group's interactions with non-Indians to the Funai team: The eastern Parakanã pillaged the camps of contractors located next to the highway and sometimes went as far as to pilfer goods from the small town of Repartimento (Funai 1971h; 1971i). This not only exposed them to the typical contact diseases, but also to gonorrhea, poliomyelitis, and hepatitis (Magalhães 1982:56–8; Soares et al. 1994:129).

The demographic collapse over the first year was high. It is difficult to estimate the losses since some of the deaths occurred before sustained contact. My data indicates a population of no more than 150 individuals and a depopulation of around 35 percent (Fausto 2001:91–2). The only certainty is that just 92 people remained by the end of 1971. At the beginning of 1972, they reached their demographic nadir: 82 individuals. After this point they began to recover. I met them for the first time in 1992, and again in 1995 and 1999. On my first visit they numbered 220; their population already exceeded 300 seven years later.

The demographic recovery had begun in mid-1972 and gradually accelerated, especially after Funai's agreement with the Vale do Rio Doce Company (1983) and later Eletronorte (1987). In the period I lived with them, they received reasonable medical and economic support and their lands were demarcated and free of intrusions. Over the thirty years since contact, they have confronted a series of new problems posed by national society. Among the most crucial were the displacement caused by the flooding of part of their lands caused by the construction of the Tucuruí Hydroelectric Plant and the fight to demarcate their lands (Magalhães 1991, 1994). They lost various battles and won many others: Their population has multiplied, they have established a *modus vivendi* with the surrounding society, and they have been led with sagacity by the headman, Arakytá.

The eastern group's initial experience of stable interaction with national society had a profound impact on their bodies, their lives, and their conception of whites. Instead of attributing the deaths to an inevitable outcome of interethnic contact, they blamed them on the sorcery of the "pacifiers," who rather than killing them through warfare did so through shamanry. Initially taken as gifts, the medicines began to be seen as palliatives for the diseases sent by the whites. The eastern group's ambivalent attitude toward the Toria is not limited to health care; rather, it involves a more widespread distrust cultivated after years of promises of every kind, not always fulfilled. Hence, they tend to maintain a reserved and wary attitude toward outsiders, in contrast to the effusive nature of the western Parakanã. Anyone who has worked with the two Parakanã blocs is used to seeing the eastern group as a more closed and distrustful people, although at the same time more hard working. By contrast, their ex-kin are taken to be open and easy going, although also little accustomed to the discipline of work. This contrast between closure and openness not only results from different contact experiences, but also from internal sociopolitical differences, which I will analyze in the next chapters.

The Great March West

One will recall that we left the western group stationed on the Do Meio River, eating the settlers' manioc. The year was 1972. Advised about the presence of Indians, Funai sent a team that made a preliminary contact in May 1972 with sixty Parakanã (Magalhães 1985:29). The team led by the *sertanista* João Carvalho remained in interaction with them for two months. Lacking support from the Pucuruí base and without presents to offer, it was forced to retreat. When they returned the next year, almost all of the group had departed.

The Parakanã had headed southwest via the upper course of the Cajazeiras River, where an adult man was killed by settlers. They decided to continue westward in search of lands not yet occupied by whites. En route, a fresh dispute over women led to the separation of a band whom I shall refer to as "Akaria's group."[35] To avoid the looming conflict, the band fled northwest toward the headwaters of the Anapu River. They arrived there at the end of 1975 and decided to settle. After more than a decade without horticulture, they planted manioc taken from a swidden in the region. However, they had moved too close to the Transamazonian highway and never got to see the manioc grow. In January 1976, they were contacted by Funai and transferred by bus to the Pucuruí Post. They numbered forty people, eleven of whom soon died (Magalhães 1982:87).

Most of the western group, meanwhile, traveled westward, reaching the Xingu-Bacajá watershed. There, they once again encountered other indigenous peoples: the Araweté, whom they called Yrywijara ("masters of the carnauba palm") or Arajara ("masters of the macaws"), identifying

---

35 This group was structured around two siblings (Akaria and Pi'awa) who had ceded their sisters to two men, patrilateral parallel cousins, and married their daughters (that is, their ZDs). The concentration and repetition of these alliances over the following generations led to the closure and isolation of this kindred. For a detailed analysis of the processes of fission and the constitution of these kindreds, see Fausto (1991:253–61).

them with enemies they had fought in the 1920s. Between 1975 and 1976, they launched three attacks, raiding them on the Ipixuna, Bom Jardim, and Jatobá creeks (*igarapés*).[36] They killed eighteen people, captured three women, and suffered just one loss (Viveiros de Castro 1992a:55, 313). More than two decades after hurling the Asurini into the arms of the SPI, they did the same with the Araweté, who, taking refuge on the shores of the Xingu, ended up being pacified by Funai shortly after. The western Parakanã returned to the bellicose life. However, there was another adversary in the region, much more difficult to vanquish. In 1977, they approached the outskirts of the Kayapó-Xikrin village located on the Bacajá River, where they killed a man (Funai 1978). They fled but were intercepted by Kayapó warriors armed with shotguns: Sixteen Parakanã perished and nine were captured.[37]

The attack halted the northern advance of the western Parakanã, forcing them to seek refuge farther south. They tried to resume horticulture, using manioc taken from abandoned Araweté villages. However, new difficulties hindered their settlement in this area. The economic frontier had finally closed the circle begun decades earlier. The project for colonizing the region south of the sources of the Bacajá River was transforming the small village of Tucumã into a pole of economic activity that revolved around timber exploration and farming. At the start of the 1980s, some farms had already reached the left bank of the São José River, and prospecting activity was penetrating even farther, reaching the headwaters of the Bacajá and the Bom Jardim.

Between 1980 and 1982, the Parakanã undertook various raids on the farms springing up in the region (Funai 1982). In response, Funai sent a team that eventually achieved contact with the "Namikwarawa group" in January 1983 (Funai 1983a). Numbering forty-four people, this kin group had separated from the rest a few months earlier after yet another fight over women. They were soon transferred to the T.I. Parakanã in the Tocantins region, joining with Akaria's group in Maroxewara village. Eleven people died in the first six months (Vieira Filho 1983:22–3).

The remainder of the western group fled north, evading contact and the approach of the farmers. In February and April 1983, they fired arrows at the Araweté Post on the Ipixuna, injuring several people. As they retreated, one of the leading warriors was hit by a rifle shot and fell to the ground dead. This event was decisive for the pacification that ensued some months later. The Parakanã realized that they were the only ones still using bows

---

36 *Igarapé* is a Tupian word literally meaning the "canoe's path." In Amazonia it designates streams that seasonally flood, invading the forest along their margins.

37 Funai later rescued the latter, but the majority died during the transfer to Altamira and from there to the Pucuruí Base.

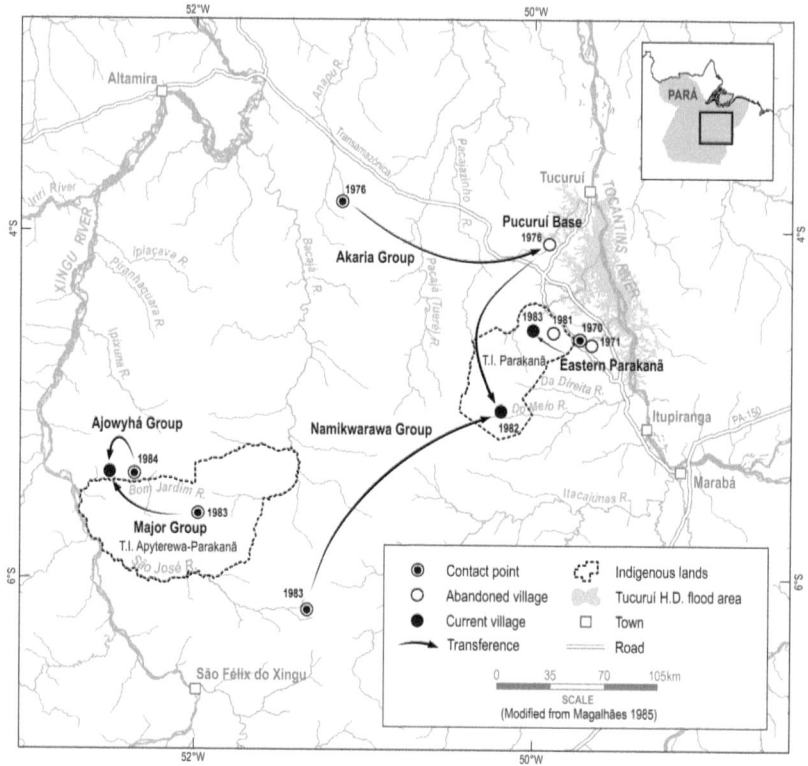

Map 1.4. Parakanã contacts and transferences (1970–1984).

and arrows and they could no longer survive without access to firearms. In May 1983, they appeared at two open mines on the Xingu-Bacajá watershed, taking guns, metal tools, hammocks, and flour. The atmosphere was uncertain, and another dispute over woman led to a new breakaway section, "Ajowyhá's group."

In December 1983, the larger group, composed of 106 people, was contacted by the Attraction Front. A roving team, accompanied by a young Parakanã man from the Namikwarawa group, reached an encampment located between the sources of the Bacajá and the Bom Jardim. Some men wanted to expel them violently, but the women sliced their bow strings, ensuring a peaceful encounter. After a night of dancing, they ended up agreeing to "live among the whites" in the hope of receiving goods and, above all, firearms. The Front then transferred them to the lower course of the Bom Jardim creek. In March 1984, Ajowyhá's group of thirty-one people came to join them.

This was the birth of the Apyterewa-Parakanã Indigenous Post, initially numbering 137 people. It closed the long process that had begun far back in 1928 with the foundation of the Tocantins Post. These last unreduced Parakanã had tried to avoid this fate, but, realizing they were definitively surrounded, they too resolved to accept pacification. Their efforts to maintain their autonomy was recompensed: There were just three deaths in the first year of contact – a demographic fall of around 2 percent, a figure that exposes the calamity of the earlier pacifications. This time there was adequate funding, careful planning, medical care, a team of dedicated workers, and a ready acceptance of medication by the Indians. Contact did not end the western Parakanã's territorial problems, though; it merely gave rise to a new phase. The long migration to the Xingu had allowed them to find an area that was less occupied and devastated than the Tocantins. However, the economic frontier took little time in arriving. Swift and voracious, the chainsaws were soon roaring nearby.

First Years of Dependence

Four years of subjection to state administration had passed when I made my first trip to the T.I. Apyterewa. The Parakanã had rapidly adopted new techniques and tools. They had taken up agriculture again and had already adapted to using canoes and fishing with hooks. Shotguns were still rare, but they would soon become frequent as their clashes with intruders increased. Previously scorned, clothes had become a desired and necessary item. If the habit makes the monk, clothing makes the person ashamed: The Parakanã were already saying that they were embarrassed to be nude. A few Portuguese words were spoken by younger people, but they were still essentially monolingual. Although not a cause of demographic collapse, recently introduced diseases had already marked the experience of these first years of contact. Medications and health care were the main signs of their new dependence, more striking than the objects accepted during pacification. The distribution of medications was a daily ritual, announced in the late afternoon by a bell. It brought a swarm of people to the infirmary where they obtained spoonfuls of sweetened syrup, decongestants, painkillers, and cotton wads soaked in mercury-chrome that were widely used to color the bodies injured in everyday tasks.

Although the diseases made it clear that living with the whites was a path without return, the items they received at the time from Funai gave them the impression that they had made the right choice. In 1988, however, the flow of goods was beginning to dry up, and a preoccupation with how to ensure access to Western goods had already set in. It was around this time that the Parakanã discovered the advance of vegetal and mineral extractivism between the sources of the Bom Jardim creek and the Bacajá

River. In April 1988, they surrounded a logger camp, took two work-ers as hostages, and initiated a decade of conflicts and raids against the intruders.

Although pacification had been an outcome of the expansion of the eco-nomic frontier, it also helped deepen the latter process, since the transfer-ences of the recently contacted Parakanã allowed the extractivist front free access to the Xingu-Bacajá watershed. This front was led by logging on a massive scale, which, advancing from south to north, reached the region in the mid-1980s. The high price fetched by mahogany on the international market had made exploration of previously inaccessible areas not only via-ble but also extremely lucrative. The process was controlled by two large companies, which built a road, slicing through about 100 kilometers of forest from Tucumã to the Xingu-Bacajá watershed.[38] The road built to transport the mahogany became a route for colonization of the region in the 1990s. Centers of colonization and cattle ranches were opened within the indigenous territory (Fausto 1996). In 2007, after a decade of advances and setbacks, the T.I. Apyterewa was demarcated with 733,000 hectares.

---

38 The volume of timber cut in the Tucumã and Redenção saw mills attained extraordinary lev-els between 1986 and 1994. In 1990 alone around 460,000 cubic meters were processed, with mahogany accounting for half of this volume. A large portion of this wood was illegally extracted from indigenous lands.

2

Images of Abundance and Scarcity

Would they therefore be the only ones ... to enjoy the exorbitant privilege of having endured and had no history?
                    Lévi-Strauss, La notion d'archaisme en anthropology (1952).

As we have seen, following the fission at the end of the nineteenth century, the Parakanã blocs began to drift apart. When contacted in the 1970s and 1980s, they were markedly distinctive in both their subsistence patterns and their sociopolitical organization. The former practiced a relatively diversified horticulture, lived in a single communal house, were divided into exogamic moieties, and had a strong headman. The latter, on the other hand, were organized into nomadic bands, lacked any horticulture, and had neither an established headman nor social segmentation. In less than a century, these two branches had assumed quite different social patterns. How shall we explicate this process of differentiation?

The dominant perspective in the literature regarding nonsedentary Amazonian peoples would predict that these changes occurred as the result of a "cultural regression." The more "complex" eastern Parakanã would thus represent the original form, common to both groups prior to the split, whereas the western Parakanã would have devolved into a more nomadic, warlike, acephalous, and undifferentiated form. A reconstruction of actual circumstances through indigenous oral history, though, shows that framing this process as a sequence of cumulative losses is misleading, since social segmentation and the structure of headmanship among the eastern Parakanã developed after the schism. It is therefore necessary to approach the differentiation as a double process of construction, which was the result not merely of exogenous forces, but also of the interaction of these forces with internal processes and decision-making mechanisms.

Moving

The Parakanã term that best translates our concept of village is *tawa*. Traditionally, a *tawa* was a nontemporary settlement composed of a collective house, manioc swiddens, and a space cleared for men to meet some distance from the main dwelling. The village was the synthesis of these three dimensions: house, swiddens, and "plaza." This configuration was common to the two Parakanã blocs during part of the twentieth century, although each space quickly received distinct meanings and emphases. In the 1950s, the western group broke with this pattern, first with the multiplication of houses, then with the abandonment of the swiddens and the disappearance of the plaza.

In contrast, for the eastern Parakanã, the unit constituted by these three domains still represents the appropriate space for sociability. In the past, the whole group sheltered in a single communal house (known as *angaeté*, "true house"), thatched down to the ground. Estimating its dimensions is tricky. We can count only on the guesses of the Funai employees responsible for the pacification, since the *angaeté* was abandoned after contact. The *sertanista* João Carvalho describes one such house: "We were enchanted by the style of the house, which is shaped like a hangar and measures around 25m in length by 10m in width ... and there are somewhere between 150 and 200 places for hammocks" (Funai 1971e). Following this estimate, the communal house's area was 250 square meters, a conservative assessment given that it was occupied then by approximately 145 people. The internal space was uniform, as the head of the Pucuruí Base, Colonel Bloise, notes:

It comprises an enormous area covered by green babassu thatch with 10 different and independent entrances. Its highest point is some 8 metres off the ground and on the outside it is shaped like a hangar. Inside the space is ample and open, divided only by the locating of the hammocks of different families. (Funai 1971d:5)

During the day, the house was a space used by everyone – men, women, and children alike. For part of the night, however, it became a place of female intimacy, since the men met in the plaza. The swiddens were the place where women toiled daily. Men participated in agricultural activities – especially in the felling, clearing, and burning, which spanned from July to October – but women were responsible for most of the quotidian work in the swidden and in processing the manioc. As a space, it cannot be qualified as female in opposition to the male domain of the forest due to the complementarity involved in subsistence production. Men and women were not collectively opposed in the swidden, house, or forest. These spaces are cross-cut by family relations, and the minimal production unit is the married couple.

The strongest opposition was between the house and swidden as spaces for the production of everyday life and the *tekatawa* ("living place") as an exclusively male political space. In contrast to the Ge or Xinguano model, the plaza was not located in the center of the surrounding world of houses.

Instead, it was situated outside, always at a certain remove from the dwelling place – a distance calculated by the need to provide security to those left in the house and the imperative for the men's talk to be inaudible to women. In the *tekatawa*, men learned to speak in public, took collective decisions, and shared the songs to be performed in rituals. As the place where the group was configured politically as a (male) unit, its permanence was seen to be guaranteed by daily practice. The most important function of the leader was to promote these meetings: The headman was the man who, every night, "made the conversation for us" (*oapo morongeta oreopé*).

For the eastern Parakanã, a village is defined by the presence of these three spaces: a relatively permanent house (or houses), manioc swiddens, and plaza. A dwelling place without these elements is a camp site, defined by its incompleteness. A product of dispersion and fragmentation, the camp is a space of more restricted and intimate sociability, where neither the differentiated social morphology or the leadership structure of the village are reproduced. Village and camp represent moments of concentration and dispersion, playing a complementary role in the production of Parakanã social life. However, whereas the former tended to predominate over the latter among the eastern bloc, the western bloc transformed the village itself into a semipermanent encampment. In comparing the two blocs, we need to explain why the camp was an incomplete locus for the former, whereas the village became too big for the latter.

Dispersion and Contraction: The Western Parakanã

During the twentieth century, the western Parakanã prolonged their periods of trekking to such an extent that the village and horticulture assumed a peripheral function in their social and economic life. A continuous movement of hunting and warfare bands across the territory is a feature common to almost all historical narrative I collected. They seem never to stop: After raiding an enemy they would not just come back to the village, but would continue hunting and chasing new adversaries, or would look for whites to "pay" for metal tools. All reunions are said to occur because of their desire for manioc. Let us recall, for instance, the dynamic following the Xikrin assault in the late 1920s. After the skirmishes, abductions, and reprisals, they found themselves without hammocks and traveled many kilometers to take them from the whites, who lived along the Tocantins Railroad. They then returned to the scene of the conflicts: "We followed the war path used by the enemies. There we came back searching in vain for Awajiringa [he had been killed]. So we carried on. The deceased Tamia said: 'let's make manioc flour and eat.' ... There where Akynaria would later be buried, we had planted manioc" (Iatora 1993: tape 50). Manioc appears as the

Photo 1. Koria with manioc stems ready for planting (western Parakanã, Apyterewa village, 1989).

cause for the return to the village and the reunion of the group. After long periods of hunting, they returned "to make manioc." Although swidden products made up a lesser portion of the western group's diet, manioc (along with tobacco) continued to be a highly valued crop, a fact not lost on the *sertanistas* of the SPI and Funai. In all the contacts undertaken from 1928 onward, they offered flour and tobacco to the Parakanã as much as axes and machetes. We can also recall that the "whites' manioc" provided the rendezvous point for the group to reunite once again at the start of the 1970s, after years of crises and fissions. In this sense, the western Parakanã village was as much a place of reproduction of the plant crop as of the group itself. The village guaranteed the continuity of horticulture and the political unity of the group. As Maybury-Lewis wrote (1984:50) vis-à-vis the Shavante base village, this was where the *community* was located. The village was more of a point of concentration for future dispersion than a permanent dwelling place.

The time spent trekking in the past was probably greater than that of other very mobile tropical forest groups, such as the Araweté (Viveiros de Castro 1992a) and the Yanomami (Good 1995a:60–1). The periods spent trekking varied over the course of the twentieth century, increasing in response to warfare and pressure from national society, until reaching their peak in the mid-1960s. They also varied seasonally, though this did not mean the Parakanã were entirely nomadic in one season and sedentary in the other. The village was occupied for part of the dry season, from June to November, so that the swiddens could be cleared and planted. The hunting and gathering excursions became shorter and more intermittent. This period was ideal for long warfare expeditions, though, since the rivers were shallower.[1] Most of the visits to the Tocantins Pacification Post and the Pucuruí Base took place during this season. As the rains arrived at the end of November, the village gradually emptied. With the manioc planting over, the family groups finished toasting the flour to be taken to the forest and departed. The village was deserted for almost all the rainy season, since this was the best period for hunting. Various wild fruits ripen during the rains, attracting normally dispersed animals to known locations. The season is also when game fattens, enriching the dietary intake: Along with the plentiful Brazil nuts from January to March, animal fat partly substituted for manioc flour.[2]

In contrast to the Araweté and Yanomami, who prefer short-cycle crops (maize and banana, respectively), the Parakanã prefer bitter manioc, which takes a year to reach a size large enough to be dug up. Although they also planted other cultigens – particularly maize, banana, yam, and sweet manioc – I never heard them link returning to the village with one of these crops. These cultigens were for sporadic consumption. On the other hand, manioc's long growth cycle localized the community, and its subterranean resistance made it well suited to the lengthy trekking cycle. Processed into flour, it was also ideal for transportation and could be consumed over a relatively long period.

While the western Parakanã settlements were similar to the Shavante base villages in functioning more as a reference point than a permanent dwelling place, their spatial design differed considerably. The semicircular layout of the Shavante village was unvarying and reproduced even in the temporary encampments (Maybury-Lewis 1984:103). The western Parakanã ended up doing precisely the opposite: They reproduced the pattern of their camps in the village. In other words, they abandoned the model of communal house, swiddens, and *tekatawa*, adopting monofamily habitations and shifting the plaza to the patio between the houses. This transformation reflects a progressive fragmentation of the group: Not only did the houses multiply, but the *tekatawa* also gradually vanished. This process was concluded when they left the territory on the Pacajá in the mid-1960s. Two decades of nomadic life ensued. When pacification was undertaken between 1976 and 1984, an entire generation knew nothing of village life or agricultural work.

---

1 The Parakanã are a headwater people, not canoeists, who traversed large areas of forest by foot. The rivers were not seen as routes, but natural obstacles crossed where they narrowed or became shallower.

2 Other sources of food included the flour made from the mesocarp of the babassu coconut, the coconut itself, palm heart, coleoptera larvae, wild yams, and a variety of wild fruits.

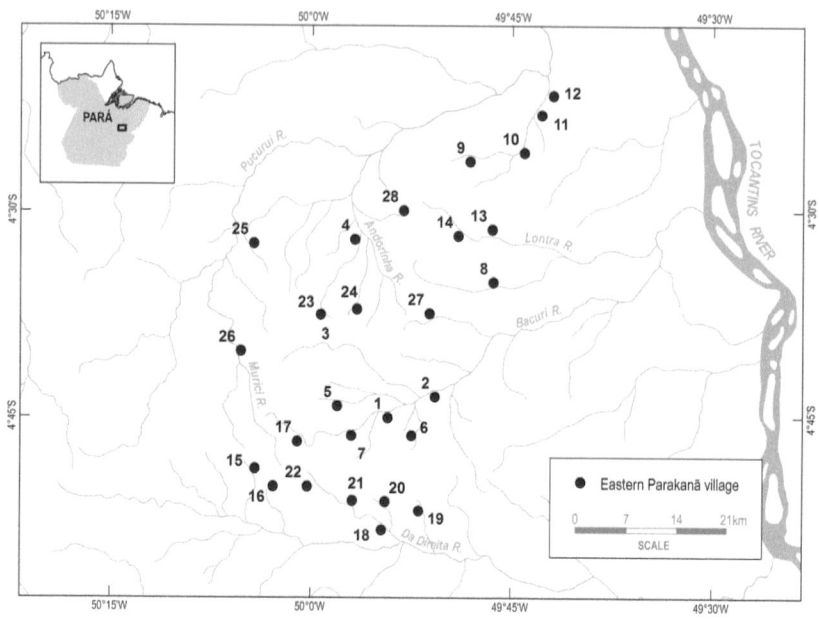

Map 2.1. Eastern Parakanã villages between c. 1925 and 1971.

A Semi-Domestic Space: The Eastern Parakanã

The lesser mobility of the eastern Parakanã when compared with the western Parakanã must be better qualified, since the former cannot be simply characterized as a sedentary people. Between approximately 1925 and 1970, the eastern Parakanã constructed twenty-eight villages (see annex, Table A.2). The average time of occupation is less than two years, being quite short even for interfluvial areas of Amazonia.[3] It roughly corresponds to the period needed for some manioc varieties to fully ripen. Many of the villages were abandoned early for security reasons, a fact that lowered this average.

When one examines the sequence of village occupation, two types of relocation come to the fore: one medium range, the other long. The former resulted from the exhaustion of the manioc swiddens: In these cases, people say they moved "because of the manioc" (many'ywa-rehe) or "after the manioc" (many'ywa-rewe). The latter derived from the need to abandon the

3 A comparable time span of occupation is found among the Araweté, who occupied around sixty villages between 1940 and 1976, with the existence, on average, of four contemporary settlements (Viveiros de Castro 1992a:49). During this period, they were under intense pressure from enemy groups and from whites invading their territory.

site as a defensive measure. The middle range relocations varied between five and ten kilometers, whereas the longer range relocations exceeded twenty-five kilometers. The absence of micro-movements contrasts with the Yanomami pattern described by Chagnon (1973, 1992), with villages moving over very short distances (less than one kilometer) to accompany new swiddens as they were cleared farther into the forest. The western Parakanã opened new swiddens at middle distances and occupied them when the old swiddens became exhausted. Instead of remaining at the same site, therefore, they established a semi-domesticated polygon whose vertices were, minimally, the previous, current, and future villages.

Typically, the group divided its time between the old and new villages for a while until ultimately abandoning the former. Houses were vacated when they began to rot or were razed by fire. Villages, swiddens, and semi-permanent camps formed thus a sort of semi-domesticated area in the middle of the forest, interconnected by trails. It was this spatial distribution – camps with small plantations and shelters, old swiddens where annatto still fruited, one or two more permanent dwellings with manioc swiddens – that the Funai *sertanistas* encountered at the moment of contact, as we can see in the following map (Map 2.2).

There existed, then, two communal houses in usable conditions, the most recent still without swiddens.[4] The closest gardens were located at encampments about three hours' walk from the site. Funai's employees reached them on November 24, 1970:

At 11:30, when we arrived, there was a makeshift straw fence less than 10 metres away. We looked ahead and saw a camp with 23 *tapiris* some 40m away.[5] Some 50 metres further on ... a swidden measuring a little over two *tarefas* [6,000m²] planted with manioc, sweet potato, yam and cotton.... After examining everything carefully, we looked for a path to go in search of them ... but after about 500 metres we found another camp with 33 *tapiris* and a lot of indigenous items ... We noted another clearing and discovered it was another swidden, a little smaller, but featuring the same crops (Funai 1971e).

Following the trails, the front encountered several other camps (the largest with fifty-three *tapiris*, capable of sheltering the entire group). On November 27, the *sertanistas* finally glimpsed a "well-cleared track, over a metre wide" (Funai 1971e), which led them to the shores of a creek; from there they could see a clearing with a house on the opposite shore. The

4 According to Gérson dos Reis Carvalho, who took part in the contact, this house had just been constructed since the straw was still green. The other village was more than three years old and had seven swiddens ready for harvesting and another three recently cleared (Funai 1971d:5).

5 *Tapiri* is a Tupi word incorporated into regional Portuguese meaning "improvised shelter."

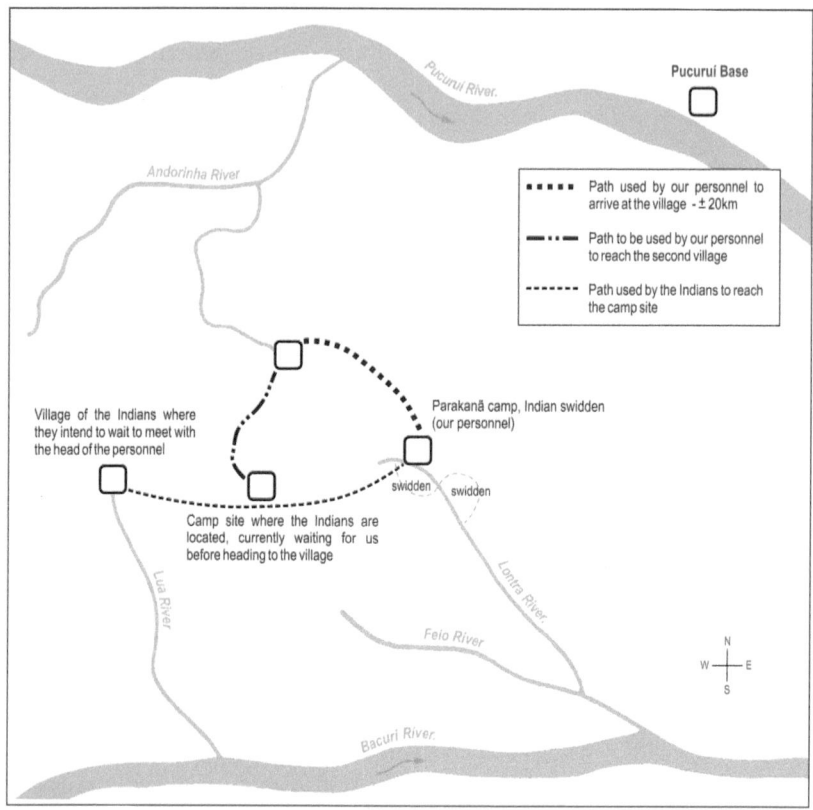

Map 2.2. Penetration front ("pacification" of the eastern Parakanã).
Source: Drawing III - Special Penetration Front - Pucuruí Base. Annex to the memo/
bp/036/71 from the Special Sheriff of the Pucuruí Base to the Director of DGAS,
22/03/1971 (apud Magalhães 1982:66).

village was empty, since the eastern group moved continually to avoid contact with the whites in their dwellings.

At the time of pacification, therefore, there were three interconnected swidden sites forming a triangle of occupation. This cluster resulted from a series of middle-range relocations, revealing that instead of maintaining a fixed settlement area with swiddens cleared from the village outward, the eastern Parakanã built new villages at a distance to which they moved some time later.[6] This pattern is ecologically efficient, especially in terms of game stocks: First, the population moved before the local area was overhunted, relocating to a site beyond the old village's radius of the most

6 See, for example, Map 2.1, which shows the clusters formed by villages 5 to 7, 9 to 12, 15 to 17, 18 to 22, and 23 to 25.

intense predation. Second, the fact the villages were coterminous meant the group was temporarily split and exploited more than one area. Past, present, and future swiddens functioned as epicenters for the group's subsistence activities. Third, the mosaic formed by this set of swiddens and forests in different stages of regeneration favored hunting and gathering, as well as a supply of babassu palm straw for thatch.[7]

Long-distance movements were prompted by an actual attack or the suspicion of enemies close to the village, though never by the presence of whites in the surrounding area. Although these moves implied abandoning the previous semi-domesticated space, this did not mean migrating beyond the known territory: The new villages were built in familiar areas, many of them occupied previously.[8] The long-distance movements revolved around two poles: to the south, the area between the headwaters of the Bacuri and Da Direita Rivers, the core of the eastern Parakanã territory; to the north, the drainage area of the affluents of the Pucuruí and the northern tributaries of the Bacuri, where they ended up being contacted. As Map 2.3 shows, the group shuttled between the two poles during the fifty years prior to contact; around 1925, they moved from the southwest to the northeast, retracing the route in the opposite direction at the end of the decade. They once again moved from the first to the second pole around 1935 and ten years later returned southward, where they remained until the start of the 1960s when they headed north once more.

The long-distance relocations of the eastern Parakanã involved the recurrent occupation of portions of the same territory for defensive reasons. These movements were only possible because of the absence of a multivillage system. Compared with more densely populated regions with an active supralocal system, the Parakanã landscape differs less through the presence of war than through the absence of alliance. In a situation of "social circumscription" (Chagnon 1968), the settlement pattern of the eastern group would have a high political cost and would demand strong alliance relations with neighbors.[9] Had such a context existed, they probably would have been unable to reoccupy previously abandoned areas or relocate the

---

7 Deer, large rodents, and peccaries feed on the domesticated and semi-domesticated plants found in productive or abandoned swiddens (Balée 1994:155–8; Johnson 1983:56). Regeneration areas are rich in babassu palm, one of the first trees to germinate after burning. For a discussion of this anthropogenic mosaic, see Balée (1989; 1994) and Balée & Gely (1989).

8 Nonetheless, reoccupations of old villages were rare within the timeframe in question (c.1925–1971), in which only one instance occurred (*Rokotawa*, built c. 1930 and reoccupied c. 1960).

9 The Parakanã population density (around 0.02 pop/km2) is comparable to highly mobile groups, such as the Kayapó Mekrãgnotí (0.01 pop/km2 – Werner 1983). Among "warlike peoples" such as the Yanomami, it is on average 0.2 pop/km2 (Hames 1983:425), whereas among the Jívaro, this figure varies from a minimum of 0.12 pop/km2 among the Achuar (Descola 1986:49) to a maximum of 0.9 pop/km2 among the Aguaruna (Beckerman 1987:86).

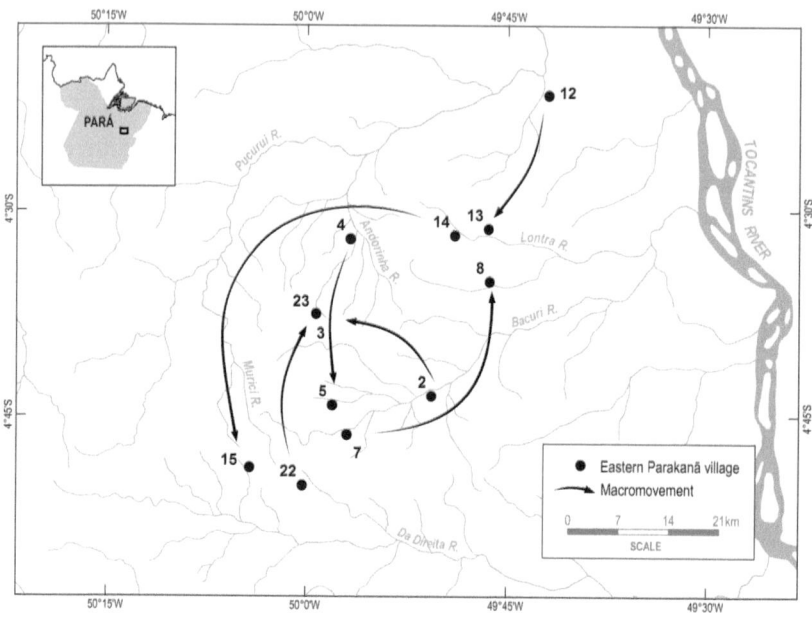

Map 2.3. Macromovements of the eastern Parakanã (1920s–1970s).

village over mid-range distances, a pattern that emulates a multigroup system without actually leading to its formation. In fact, the array of swiddens and habitations formed by a sequence of relocations is like a small-scale multivillage system, except that the group avoids political fragmentation into smaller units.

Two facts thus deserve our attention: the nonatomization of the group and the impermanence of the villages. The first is related to the sociological mechanisms that ensured political unity. Turning to a group linguistically and culturally proximate to the Parakanã, such as the Urubu-Ka'apor of Maranhão, we observe a completely different pattern with the proliferation of small local groups. This model is so deeply rooted that all the attempts made by government agencies to concentrate the population in fewer villages have failed.[10] Why, then, did the eastern group emulate a multivillage system rather than actually adopt one? Why did they not disperse into three or four local groups? I will answer this question in the next chapter.

10 In 1943, the Ka'apor population numbered more than one thousand individuals, occupying twenty-nine villages (on average, thirty-five inhabitants per village). In 1982, they totaled just 490 people, living in fifteen villages. Although the population had halved, the number of inhabitants per village was practically identical (Balée 1984a:82–91).

The second fact, the ephemerality of the villages, results from a *sui generis* compromise between mobility and village life, foraging, and horticulture. The short timescale of occupation was more than a response to warfare: Although attacks by enemies provoked the abandonment of various settlements, the occupation time of any site never exceeded three years, precisely the period over which a swidden is typically abandoned in Amazonia (Beckerman 1987:70–1). The pattern was thus a compromise between the value attributed to village life and to hunting. In this sense, the circulation within the polygon of past and present villages played a role similar to the lengthy trekking of the western Parakanã, allowing them to exploit forest resources in a fairly selective manner. The work involved in clearing new swiddens at mid-range was probably no greater than that involved in felling areas close to the settlement. Metal axes also enabled the work to be done by fewer men and reduced the overall time involved; this meant the group could combine living at one site with opening another. Moreover, the construction of the communal house was a relatively easy task for a population of one hundred or so people.

In sum, the eastern group's settlement strategy appears to have been highly selective. The ephemerality of the villages did not result from any impossibility of increased sedentarization, as could be presumed by the oft-made assumption of a causal association between mobility and resource scarcity. Following pacification, though, the eastern Parakanã settlement pattern changed profoundly, with increased sedentarization, an expansion of the cultivated area, and diversification of the animal-based protein diet. The lower mobility resulted from the growing dependence on national society. The Post and its services – including the school, health post, and store – became essential elements in the makeup of the villages. As this infrastructure became consolidated, the cost of moving grew. On the other hand, new factors started to be taken into account when deciding on the location of new villages, especially ease of access to the regional centers outside the indigenous area.

Village relocations between 1972 and 1983 were determined by Funai employees for logistical reasons or in response to the flooding of part of the Parakanã territory caused by the construction of the Tucuruí dam (Magalhães 1995:30). After demarcation of the indigenous reserve, they settled in the village of Paranatinga, where part of the group still lives today. They have occupied the same area for more than fifteen years, with a much larger population (259 people in May 1995) compared to the moment of pacification. The swiddens are located at some distance, but the group has new means of transportation: some pack animals, canoes, and motorized vehicles. Although not overhunted, the surrounding area shows declines in terms of hunt productivity. On the other hand, the Parakanã diet has become more varied with changes in food habits, the acquisition of new technologies (guns, torches, and fishing equipment), the purchase of some industrialized foods, and the introduction of new crops.

Planting

As we have seen, by the 1960s, the western Parakanã had abandoned horticulture and were living by hunting and gathering, along with the occasional pilfering of crops from enemy swiddens. For two decades, they freed themselves from agricultural work and the consequent restrictions on movement. After pacification, Funai's employees reintroduced horticulture, which had a profound impact on mobility and diet. Large swiddens were cleared with the help of chainsaws and metal axes, and they collectively planted manioc, maize, banana, rice, and beans (yam, sweet manioc, and sweet potato were planted separately by the nuclear families). All agricultural work was coordinated by the head of the Funai Post, who not only decided which area should be cleared, but also established the calendar of activities. In 1989, every swidden at Apyterewa belonged to one of the village's two large factions. The larger group (ninety-six people) worked collectively in one area, while Ajowyhá's faction (fifty-nine people) worked in another. In 1995, I encountered a similar structure in Maroxewara, where there were also two collective swiddens identified with the young leaders Jytyria and To'ia. In both cases, the separation of the swiddens indicated a deeper split that would soon escalate into a fission producing distinct villages.

The resumption of agriculture also redefined the sexual division of labor, since men ended up assuming responsibility for all collective work. Whereas the adoption of new crops often has repercussions on female work, in the case of the western Parakanã, the most significant impact was on men. Aside from doing most of the planting, with the advent of new technologies they also started to assume an active role in processing the manioc. The flour house – with its press, motorized grater, and stoves with iron cauldrons – lent the process a whole new connotation. Some older women continued to make flour in the traditional way, but the men became increasingly responsible for drying, grating, and toasting the manioc pulp.

In the mid-1990s, horticulture continued to be an activity foreign to the western Parakanã. There was no efficient coordination of tasks: Perhaps because it was too collective, the swidden work ended up being assumed by nobody, and it continued to depend on the supervision of a Post employee. Without the latter's supervision, the result was predictable: small, badly burned, and under-planted swiddens. Even in Maroxewara, there was no autonomous structure of production. Although there were young leaders responsible for mediating with national society and, supposedly, for organizing collective work, agriculture continued to depend on the intervention of whites. How can this difficulty in reintroducing horticulture be explained? After all, the technical knowledge is not particularly complex, and there was already a new generation familiar with it. The problem seems to be sociological rather than technical.

Productive Bonds

The plasticity observed among the western Parakanã in adopting a new sexual division of labor and community production is unmatched among the eastern group. Funai tried to promote collective plantations in the mid-1970s, as family swiddens were seen as an obstacle to growing surplus produce (Magalhães 1994:117). The policy, however, failed to achieve the expected results. A compromise was obtained in which "production groups" became responsible for agricultural work, Brazil-nut harvesting, and commercial relations. Each group possess a set of swiddens for growing cultigens such as bitter and sweet manioc, maize, banana, yam, and sweet potato, each family cultivating a patch of land with exclusive access to the planted crops. The groups are structured around two leaders: a young leader responsible for dealing with the whites, and another, traditional leader responsible for internal relations.[11]

In Paranatinga village in 1992, there were five different production groups, whose principle of constitution was clearly patrifiliation, not affinity. Out of forty-six adult men, only six worked with their father-in-law, whereas only four men considered that they worked *for* their father-in-law. Analyzing the links between adult men within the groups, we find fifteen father-son relations from a possible nineteen, compared to just six father-in-law–son-in-law relations from a possible thirty-two.[12] The structure of the production groups thus evinces a principle of collective-work organization and the existence of economic agents broader than the nuclear family among the eastern Parakanã. Patrifiliation as an economic bond unites not individuals but nuclear families, which are the minimal unit of production and consumption. This implies that when a woman reaches sexual maturity, she starts to produce for her husband's family instead of her own family of origin. Agricultural work results from the coordination of female work through marriage and male cooperation through patrifilial ties. In other words, in contrast to bride-service societies in which the son-in-law

11 The young leader's function implies privileged access to the Post's employees and services, responsibility for the production group's bank account, as well as making the monthly purchases in the town of Tucuruí. Although the position allows prestige, it is also demanding. The tasks of intercultural translation are complex. The leader has to navigate between his group's demands and the limits imposed by Funai, without understanding the long web of political-economic facts that define these limits.

12 For a detailed description of each group's composition, see Fausto (2001:130–1).

produces for his father-in-law's family, here a woman works for her husband's agnates.

Comparing this structure with the western Parakanã, one notes that the latter lack such coordination of male work through patrifilial ties. Once constituted, the nuclear family acquires total autonomy. The couple's independence derives precisely from the absence of any economic obligation of the husband to his father or father-in-law. Before marriage, the man provides a kind of anticipatory service to his future wife, providing her with a portion of the game he kills. This helps win the approval of his parents-in-law and publicly marks a relationship that only becomes concrete years later, but it has no economic implications. Likewise, a son does not work for his father, even before marriage; he is expected to work exclusively to support his wife and children. Among the western Parakanã, therefore, the nuclear family is the sole economic agent: It is the cooperation between husband and wife that drives subsistence activities. Neither filiation nor alliance organize production. The coordination of efforts among family hearths generates flexible networks, not groups.

How did this difference in the organization of production come into existence? Was it determined by the objectification of patrifiliation in the form of sociocentric groups among the eastern Parakanã? Before answering this question, we need to evaluate how different the precontact horticulture of each bloc actually was.

Horticulture in the Past

Here the difficulty resides in determining the "traditional" Parakanã form. How do we evaluate the relative importance of village life and agricultural produce in the past? No definitive response exists. We know that among the western group there was a decline in the work dedicated to horticulture in the 1950s, resulting in its abandonment a decade later. However, this is not a case of a traditional pattern suddenly ruptured by pressure from national society. An oscillation in the importance of horticulture may have been typical since the end of the nineteenth century, if not earlier. The settlement pattern of the eastern Parakanã suggests an image of the traditional mode of life halfway between the mobility of trekkers and the sedentarism of permanent horticulturists. Perhaps we could speak here of the mobility of a permanent form of horticulture equally applicable to hunting activities. Today, as in the past, the eastern Parakanã make use of semipermanent camps during hunt excursions, in contrast to the western Parakanã, who are unconcerned with fashioning semi-domesticated spaces in the forest.

The western group's horticulture seems to have been less diversified than that of the eastern group even before the mid-twentieth century. When I asked my oldest interlocutors to recall the cultigens they used to plant in the past, eastern Parakanã men listed twenty-five varieties of six different food species: eight kinds of manioc (one of them sweet), three varieties of maize, one kind of bean, seven kinds of yam, three sweet potato varieties, and three types of banana. The western Parakanã, for their part, cited eighteen varieties of these same six species: five types of manioc (two of them less toxic), two varieties of maize, one kind of bean, four kinds of yam, four varieties of sweet potato, and two types of banana. Of the eighteen terms remembered by the western group, fourteen have an equivalent on the eastern group's list (see annex, Table A.3).

Losses and acquisitions of domestic plants were common in the twentieth century: Of the eight varieties of manioc listed by the eastern group, two were acquired in the 1950s in an enemy swidden. They also lost some cultigens, such as *many'ywarakapá*, which provides the name of a site abandoned hurriedly by the group at the end of the 1920s. Among the western Parakanã, loss was a constant: More than once they were left without any agricultural products. However, their mobility also favored the acquisition of new varieties, and some of the knowledge of domestic plants held by older people is associated with the plundering of enemy swiddens.

Domestic plants for nonculinary uses – such as cotton, annatto, and tobacco – have been cultivated permanently by the eastern group and only occasionally by the western group. When they lacked tobacco to fill their long cigars, made from the inner bark of tauari tree, they used the foliage from a vine known as *ipowyrona*.[13] The same appears to have happened with cotton: The western Parakanã claim they used to sow it in the past, but it soon became a crop restricted to captured enemy women. Cotton was supplanted by plant fibers, in particular by the leaflets of tucum palm shoots (*Astrocaryum sp.*) with which they fabricate an open-weave hammock called *mokajypa*.

The western group's horticulture became impoverished and less intense over time. People born in the 1940s and 50s recall swiddens with a small number of crops, basically manioc and yam. By then, the bond between cultivation and daily work had already been ruptured: left unweeded, the swiddens acquired a semi-domesticated aspect. Manioc was planted and grew far from human eyes: "we didn't see the manioc grow, we liked to hunt," they once told me.

Remembering and Forgetting Myths

Evidence of the place occupied by horticulture in each Parakanã bloc can also be found in their mythology. The eastern group possesses a mytheme on

---

13 Tauari (genus *Couratari*) is the designation given to various species of the Lecythidaceae family, which also includes the Brazil-nut and sapucaia-nut trees.

the origin of manioc unknown to the western group. This episode is embedded in a larger mythic narrative formed by five main themes – the flooding of the earth, the acquisition of fire, the origin of manioc, the acquisition of female work and flour, and the diversification of indigenous peoples. Here I summarize a version told to me by the headman Arakytá in 1992:

The Day They Punctured the Earth

It was during the *opetymo* ritual. The women had left to fetch firewood. When they returned, the men were asleep, so the women beat the sides of the house to awaken them

– They don't want us to sleep, the men said.

The women beat and beat.

– Let's puncture the earth, the men said.

One of the men, the one who would climb up the bacaba palm, left in search of resin [to glue the king vulture or harpy eagle plumage used in the ritual]. He blew very hard and punctured the earth. Water began to gush out.

The great river reached the house and flooded it. They tore the house from the ground and flew away. Later they touched the earth to see if it was hard. No success. They flew again and once more descended. It was still flooded.

– Let's enter the sky, they said.

They touched the sky but didn't enter. So, they descended and discovered that the earth had already hardened. And that's where they stayed.

Meanwhile, the one who had gone to fetch resin climbed the bacaba palm. Two climbed up. Some birds defecated on the men's heads leaving them bald. The lowest of the two descended to drink. He carried water for the other one in his mouth. The water became warm.

– I'm going to drink down there, the water in your mouth is warm.

He descended, slipped, and fell. He was eaten by the jaguar-fish.

Alone on the bacaba palm, the other one saw many game animals pass by. He said:

– Who's going to harden the earth for me?

But the capybara went away. The deer arrived:

– Who's going to harden the earth for me?
– I shall, replied the deer.

The deer stamped around him. He climbed down to look when the deer went away. It had dried a bit. Then he saw the male tapir further ahead. It didn't approach. A while later, it crossed the water and came up to him.

— Who's going to harden the earth for me?

The tapir ran, stamping its hooves. The water disappeared. Then, the blue-crowned motmot said:

— I'm going down to the ground first.

The piranha cut his tail, which is why the motmot's tail is the way it is.

— Then, the tapir said:
— Let's go, come down here.
— Run first so I can see, the man replied.

The tapir ran off and came back:

— Let's go, come down here.
— Run one more time so I can see.

The tapir ran, returned and said:

— Let's go, come down.

He climbed down to the root and touched the earth with the tip of his toes.

— It's a bit soft, maybe. Run once more so I can see.

The tapir ran and came back.

— Let's go, come down.

He climbed down and went away.

This myth is presented as the saga of Wyrapina, the ancestor of the Parakanã. Women try to prevent men from dreaming during the performance of an *opetymo* ritual, leading the latter to puncture the earth. The subterranean water gushes onto the surface, producing two simultaneous vertical movements: While the dreamers lift the house into the sky, Wyrapina and his companion climb a bacaba palm tree. Those that flew away with the house land far away and vanish from the story: People say they became whites. Meanwhile, back on the bacaba palm, our hero acquires an identity by losing his hair, rotted by the bird feces. This event gives rise to his name: a conjunction of *wyra* (a generic term for birds) and the verb *-apin* ("shave").[14] Finally, the tapir dries the ground for Wyrapina and he descends alone into the now-uninhabited vastness.

Among the western Parakanã, the story ends exactly at this point. The eastern version, on the contrary, continues with the incorporation of two small mythemes that connect the flood with a final episode in which the hero acquires a wife and they multiply. The first mytheme is the conquest of fire, in which Máira pretends to be dead so that the vultures descend and

---

14 The Parakanã had a standard hair cut consisting of short trimmed hair with the upper forehead entirely shaved.

Wyrapina can steal the fire from them.[15] The second introduces the story of women who make flour, explaining how the hero obtained manioc. The episode includes a common theme in Tupi-Guarani mythology, namely the sprouting of cultivated plants from the dead (Combès 1992:147; F. Grenand 1982:183–4). Here is how Arakytá continued to narrate the story to me:

At first, he [Wyrapina] grilled fish without a fire.

- Have you fire? Máira asked.
- I grill fish under the sun and eat it.
- Put termites on top of me to make the vultures descend here, then you'll be able to light your fire-to-be, Máira told him.

He covered Máira in termites, so he looked like rotten game. They heard the vultures:

- Get the fire off king vulture, Máira told him in vain.

A lesser yellow-headed vulture came. He took the cinders the bird was carrying under his wings, blew and the cinders burst into flame. And so he acquired fire.

He cleared a swidden for himself. He broke people's bones and buried them like manioc stalks. The manioc grew. He said:

- Who's going to make my manioc for me?

He left to hunt. Someone made flour and manioc porridge for him. He came back from the forest.

- Who made flour for me?

Again, he shouted:

- Who made flour for me?!

Nobody responded. He went hunting again. Next to his house, someone made flour.

- Who's making flour for me?

He shouted, nobody replied. He arrived home, roasted a tortoise and ate it. The next day, he hid. Two women arrived:

- They're the ones making flour for me.

He rushed out and grabbed one of them, the dark skinned one. The white skinned one escaped, Wyrajinga ("white-bird"), the future white woman.

So he made his sons. First he made two:

- These will be *Tapi'pya*, he said.

Then he made another two:

---

15 Máira (with stress on the first syllable) is the Parakanã cognate of the well-known Tupi-Guarani demiurge Maíra.

— These will be *Apyterewa*, he said.

All of them sons of Wyrapina. So he made more:

— These will be *Marojewara*, is what he said.

He made others:

— These will be *Mykojiwena*.

And others:

— These will be *Pa'ametywena*.

And others:

— These will be *Jimokwera*.

These were the last.

This narrative weaves together themes that normally appear in fragmentary form in other mythologies. It is not just any bricolage, though: The themes follow a clear sequential logic. The composition passes from the rotten world to the theft of cooking fire, then to the origin of cultivated plants, and, finally, to marriage and the differentiation of peoples.[16] The story tells us of the loss of an initial sociocultural state and its later recovery. The loss, however, is only for the ancestors of the Amerindians (*ore'ypya*, "our first ones"), since those who fly away with the house, the whites-to-be, continue to possess the arts of civilization. Wyrapina, by contrast, has to rescue these arts from a rotten world.

What is most striking is the absence of the three themes among the western Parakanã: They just narrate independently the history of the flood and the history of the women who make flour. The origin of fire and manioc, along with the birth of Wyrapina's sons, do not appear in their mythology. How do we explain these absences? Since the eastern and western Parakanã formed a single group until the end of the nineteenth century, the differences between their mythologies can either result from recent processes of loss, the creation of a new theme, or the incorporation of stories from other peoples. This last possibility must be discarded since the eastern Parakanã did not capture any outside women or maintain peaceful relations with other peoples during this period. At the same time, given the similarities with the Tupi-Guarani variants, it is more likely to be a reworking than a creation of a new theme. Hence we are left with just two possibilities: a reworking on the part of the eastern group or a loss on the part of the western group. In either case, the significance remains the same: If the forgetting or reworking

---

16 This sequence to a large extent reproduces Lévi-Strauss's analysis in the third part of *The Raw and the Cooked*, with a double absence: the origin of the short life and the stories of opossum. These, however, appear in the maize origin myth that I analyze later.

of myths has some connection with a concrete activity, it is notable that the western Parakanã, who abandoned agriculture, lack a manioc origin myth. It is equally suggestive that the eastern group, with their differentiated social morphology, were the ones to develop the theme of the diversification of peoples.[17]

Fire and horticulture are two dimensions of the same complex, positively correlated to the domesticated sociality of the village and negatively to life in the forest and the jaguar's alimentary code.[18] This is a theme to which I return later. For now, though, I intend to anticipate, in the form of a question, a proposition to be tested over the course of this book: What relation does the absence of civilizing myths among the western bloc and its presence among the eastern bloc have with the way of life adopted by each of them? Does differences in mythology correspond to differences in the way of representing life in society?

The Civilizing Opossum

It is not entirely correct to say that the western group lack an origin myth for cultivated plants. What is absent is an origin myth for manioc, their main crop. Once, while helping to toast flour on the stoves next to the Post, I asked why they had adopted this cooking technique from the whites. They told me that after the flooding of the earth, the Amerindians lost their cultigens, which remained with those who flew away with the house. As a result, whites are "the true possessors of manioc" (*many'ywa-rerekatareté*). Maize is an exception, though. They then told me the following story:

Máira and the Owner of Maize

In the distant past, Máira made his children via the navel of his wife, who carried them next to her belly like an opossum. One day, the owner of maize (Awajijara) saw them having sex. He returned home and said to his wife:

— I'm going to my sister's house to fetch maize.

---

17 As for the fire, the actual loss of it has different implications for each bloc. For the eastern group, its privation leads to a psychic deterioration. People who become lost in the forest and remain alone and fireless become foolish. This is how they explain the mental torpor of a man, more than sixty years old, who had strayed away from the group during the pacification process. For the western group, by contrast, lacking fire merely implies an undesirable state of food loss: After the Xikrin attack in 1977, Karája and his son spent months lost in the forest without fire, but the only thing mentioned about them is their squalid appearance on their return.

18 In this book, I distinguish "sociality" from "sociability." I use the first term to refer to the abstract quality of the social in general, without determining the kind of relation involved, whereas the second term is used to denote a type of sociality perceived by the agents as morally positive.

So he went. As he arrived, he yelled:

- Are you there, brother-in-law?
- Yes, I am, Máira replied.

The owner of maize entered and lay down in his sister's hammock. He quizzed his brother-in-law:

- Why didn't you teach my sister the path?
- Which path? Máira asked.
- Here, via the vagina, via the true hole. It's not tasty for you doing it via the navel. Via your sister's vagina is delicious for me. I'm going to fetch your sister and do it for you to see.
- Okay, fetch my sister and have sex with her. Teach me, brother-in-law, Máira responded.

The owner of maize went out and returned with his wife, Máira's sister. He placed a mat on the ground and they lay down. He spread her legs and penetrated her. Máira watched. They weren't ashamed.

- Wow! Was I an idiot, brother-in-law? I fucked your sister here [via the navel].
- This way it's delicious. Look at your sister's big labia, brother-in-law. Do it here, make my sister have big labia, urged the owner of maize.

Finally, he stood up and cleaned himself. Máira brought maize for him:

- Pound the maize, sister.

She tipped the maize into the mortar, and Awajijara exclaimed in surprise:

- You are using wild banana as though it were maize, brother-in-law.
- It is maize, brother-in-law, Máira replied.
- You say maize in place of wild banana, brother-in-law, retorted Awajijara.
- Bring maize for me to look at.

The owner of maize went to his house and returned with the maize.

- Is this maize, brother-in-law? Máira asked.
- Yes, this is maize, brother-in-law, this is what we call maize.
- What do you plant to become maize, brother-in-law, asked Máira.
- I bury our hair so it turns into maize, brother-in-law, Awajijara explained.

So, the brother-in-law gave the maize to Máira to plant it.

(Iatora 1993: tape 45).

The myth tells of the acquisition of maize and the discovery of sexual pleasure. It describes a scene in which two brothers-in-law exchange sisters: One is the owner of maize, whereas the other is an idiotic Máira who has sex via his wife's navel and mistakes a wild fruit for a domesticated plant. He is said to be like an opossum (*toymya*), since his wife carries their children next to her belly. In South American mythologies, male opossums are associated with unusual sexual practices, suggesting that, in this sense too, Máira occupies the place of an opossum in the myth.

The narrative has resonances with two mythic series: one Ge, the other Tupi. The association of the marsupial with the origin of cultivated plants is omnipresent in Timbira mythology, in which the opossum appears as both the giver of maize and the sign of aging and death – as if death was the price paid for agriculture (Lévi-Strauss 1964:177). In the Parakanã myth, the opossum appears purified of its rotten function: The main association is not with decrepitude, but with sexual pleasure. This emphasis suggests that Máira should not be taken here as a sign of putrefaction, although the association between death and the opossum is very strong for the Parakanã. The narrative thus conserves the "civilizing" function of the opossum in Ge myths, but in reverse (since it passes from giver to receiver of a cultivated plant), and at the same time, it retains the characteristics of the opossum-child from the cycle of Tupi twins, who is stupid but not putrid.

This is the second resonance of our story: the Tupi-Guarani saga of the twins with different genitors, which recounts the adventures of Maíra's son (wise and smart) and Opossum's son (of limited intelligence and foolish), who leave in search of the demiurge who had abandoned their mother. In the Parakanã maize myth, the twins are merged into a single figure: the demiurge himself, who makes children like a marsupial. This Máira-Opossum duality mirrors the twins while simultaneously linking the Tupi series and the Ge series: Although just as foolish as Opossum's son in the Tupi myths, he is also responsible for the acquisition of maize as in the Ge narratives.

His foolishness is the inverse sign of cultivated behavior, just as the wild banana is the negative of maize.[19] As Lévi-Strauss says,

> the opossum personifies a kind of anti-agriculture which is at one and the same time pre- and pro-agriculture. For, in the "upside-down world" that was the state of nature before the birth of civilization, all future things had to have their counterpart, even if only in a negative form, which was a kind of guarantee of for their future existence. (Lévi-Strauss 1964: 190–191)

Following this reasoning, we could say that, after all, we do have a civilizing myth thematizing the transition from nature to culture, precisely what we deemed absent from the western Parakanã mythology. However, the tale is not narrated as an origin myth. Its tone is that of a *conte plaisant*:

---

19 Morphologically, wild banana contains a silky fiber comparable to the hair-like stigmas of maize. It serves as a sign of nondomesticity since the Parakanã distinguish it from domesticated bananas. The Araweté say that wild banana is the "ancient maize of the *Maï*," that is, the gods who represent a protodomestic state (Viveiros de Castro 1986:220).

a sort of joke, with strong sexual connotation, recited with exaggerated gestures that provoke laughter among the audience. In his comparison of myths in which the opossum plays an important role, Lévi-Strauss marks such a distinction:

Origin myths feature gods in human form, but with animal names, while tales depict animals in human form. Opossum performs an ambiguous function in both. A god in the Ticuna myth (M_{95}), he copulates just like the opossum is believed to do naturally. Although an animal in the Mundurucu tale (M_{97}), he is nonetheless a man, different from the other animals. (Lévi-Strauss 1964:181)

In the western Parakanã version, the opossum is a man with a god's name who behaves like the animal. The narrative plays on ambivalence from beginning to end, as though its point were to offer an ironic commentary on the arts of horticulture. Whereas the eastern Parakanã emphasize the acquisition of cooking fire and the staple crop, the western Parakanã tell an anecdote about an uncultured demiurge who learns how to have sex and cultivate maize.

Regressions and Re-Creations

My aim in analyzing eastern and western Parakanã myths has been to look for evidence that their distinct socioeconomic patterns are closely related to different conceptions of the place of horticulture in social life. Given that the "civilizing" myths of the eastern group are unknown by western Parakanã men born in the 1920s, this divergence must have started soon after the split, and was probably consolidated at the start of the 1920s. The question of how this differentiation took place, however, depends on our understanding of the moment before the split. Two plausible hypotheses exist. The first is that the eastern group's subsistence pattern represents the archaic form, whereas the western group's pattern derives from a process of agricultural loss unfolding after the separation. There is some evidence in favor of the latter: namely, the recent nomadization of the western Parakanã, the existence of swiddens at the time of the split, and a stable horticultural tradition among the eastern Parakanã.

The second hypothesis is to presume the existence of oscillations between horticulture and foraging even before the fission. The twentieth century would have seen a double movement in opposite directions: one bloc emphasizing horticulture and village life, the other extending their trekking periods and fragmenting into hunting bands. This hypothesis has an implication: If there was a "year zero" when the ancestors of the Parakanã possessed a solid agricultural tradition, this tradition was already on the wane by the end of the nineteenth century. In addition, it means that processes of losing and reacquiring horticulture may have been much more common than usually imagined. There is also evidence for this hypothesis: Some western Parakanã men refer to a period, at least one generation prior to the split, when their ancestors lacked domesticated plants. According to Pi'awa, many of the plants cultivated by themselves were obtained by their ancestors in raids on enemies.

Although I lack definitive empirical data to decide between these two hypotheses, some suggestions can be made. Here we need to switch perspective from the differences in subsistence and village life to exploring the features shared by both Parakanã economies. We have already seen how the eastern group's settlement pattern seems to occupy a halfway point between the trekking of the western group and the greater sedentarism of other tropical forest peoples. Something else, though, is held in common: the rudimentary nature of the horticulture of both blocs.

Technology was simple, with no specific tools for planting or grating and drying manioc. Such an absence is not unusual among the region's Tupi-Guarani groups. Already in the seventeenth century, the French Capuchin Franciscans describe only two processes of deintoxicating manioc (grating-rinsing and retting) and just one method of drying (squeezing the pulp by hand and drying it in the sun) among the Tupi of Maranhão (Abbeville [1614] 1975:239–40). The same drying method was observed among the Tapirapé (Wagley 1977:58–9) and the Parakanã in the twentieth century.[20] The absence of presses and graters does not necessarily indicate a rudimentary horticulture, since the Kayabi, who possess a wide range of cultigens, make no use of them either (Grünberg 1970:82–6). However, when combined with other elements, their absence indicates a simpler form of horticulture.

Some of the culinary uses of manioc typically found among Tupi-Guarani–speaking peoples, such as *beiju* bread and fermented *cauim* beverages, are also absent. The subproducts of bitter manioc are two types of flour and a sweet porridge made from the grill-smoked tuber. The only fermented beverage is *inata'y'a* ("babassu-nut water"), made from a wild product. Traditional Parakanã cultigens are also much less diverse than those of more sedentary groups. We just have to compare the eight varieties of manioc listed by the eastern group with the nineteen grown by the Ka'apor (Balée & Gély 1989:138), twenty-five by the Tiriyó (B. Ribeiro 1979:119), twenty-nine by the Wayãpi (P. Grenand 1980:310), forty-six by the Kuikuro (Carneiro 1994:207), and more than fifty by the Aguaruna (Boster 1986:430). Some of these peoples live in regions with a higher

---

20 The traditional method of manioc processing among the Parakanã involves immersing the tubers in water for three to five days until they soften. They are then dehusked and the pulp is squeezed by hand, forming small cakes that are placed on a platform in the sunlight. After drying, the cakes are passed through a sieve and the resulting flour is toasted on ceramic pans.

sociodemographic density, enabling a more intense circulation of cultigens and reduced chances of loss. Still, the data indicate that Parakanã horticulture, even before the fission, was indeed rudimentary.

Thus we cannot discard the second hypothesis formulated previously. The strength of the first resides in its simplicity and linearity: One group loses agriculture, the other does not. However, this strength becomes a weakness if we attribute just one direction to all post-Conquest social processes: involution, the loss of superior characteristics (from an evolutionist viewpoint) or the loss of distinctive characteristics (from a culturalist viewpoint). This idea leads to various theoretical-political impasses in terms of ascertaining the status of indigenous groups in interaction with national society and defining the so-called process of acculturation. Here I aim to avoid these impasses by posing a different question: How did Parakanã society transform itself more than once in a simultaneous process of adapting to external forces and internally re-creating its own conditions of existence?

Hunting

Peoples with elementary horticulture are frequently associated in the South American literature with food shortages. The image of Holmberg on the Siriono – "a group of perennially hungry human beings" (1969:xviii) – fighting daily to survive in a hostile environment reproduces an idea of foraging deeply entrenched since the sixteenth century. Its current version is found in the discussion on whether exclusively hunter-gatherer groups could have subsisted in the tropical forest (Bailey et al. 1989; Bailey & Headland 1991; Headland 1987; for a critique, see K. Good 1995b). In this line of thought, hunting and gathering are signs of insecurity and scarcity, whereas agriculture means stability and abundance. Lévi-Strauss repeats this motif in discussing the two extremes of Nambikwara social organization: "[O]n one hand, sedentary, agricultural life ... on the other, the nomadic period during which subsistence is mainly guaranteed by female gathering and foraging; one representing security and alimentary euphoria, the other adventure and penury" (Lévi-Strauss 1955:255). Curiously, the author adds that the Nambikwara speak of the former melancholically and the latter animatedly without pondering the mystery of a people for whom privation stirs a feeling of pleasure and abundance a feeling of sadness.

For the Parakanã, periods of trekking are marked by abundance, not scarcity. When leaving for the forest with their hammocks, they say "we're going to eat" (*orokaro pota araha*). Or more precisely "we're going to have a meal," since the verb *-karo* is distinguished in quality and quantity from its synonym *-'o*, to eat in a generic sense, much as our terms "lunching" or "dining" do not mean eating just anything in any fashion. Dispersal to the forest corresponds to a desire to consume meat in large quantities: When the Parakanã say they are hungry, they are referring to a lack of meat rather than food generically. Not just any kind of meat, though.

The Siriono hunt almost all animals: various primates, innumerable aquatic and terrestrial birds, peccaries, deer, tapirs, squirrels, capybara, paca, agouti, armadillos, caimans, coati, anteaters, turtles, and even the jaguar (Holmberg 1969). This spectrum of hunted animals is comparable to that of another hunter-gatherer people, the Aché-Guayaki, who place no general taboos on any food item, even consuming a large number of carnivores: two species of procyonidae (crab-eating raccoon and coati), two species of wild dog, five felines, and three mustelines. They also eat numerous reptiles, amphibians, and birds, including two species of vulture (Hill & Hawkes 1983:144–6).

This diversity of consumed animals was taken to indicate that foraging in the tropical forest was an inglorious struggle for survival in an area where hunting is neither profitable nor easy (Lathrap 1968:29). The conclusion may appear self-evident – diversity as an outcome of a extreme shortage – yet the quantitative data on Aché subsistence activities fail to support it (see Hawkes, Hill & O'Connell 1982).[21] This data throws into question some of the generalizations made on hunting in the South American lowlands, as well as the relation between horticulture and foraging:

> Since they do so well as hunters, it is not surprising that the Aché have persisted as such in a neighborhood of farmers. The material presented here in no way contradicts the historical observation that refugee populations often remain nomadic because the depredations of stronger enemies make the cost of resettling too high.... Nevertheless, the Aché data dispute the view that all South American hunters have been pushed into environments where they must pursue a demanding food quest. (Hawkes, Hill & O'Connell 1982:395)

The authors' conclusion converges with one of the main points of this chapter: namely, that Lévi-Strauss's thesis (1974 [1952]) of the regressive nature of South American nomadic peoples or trekkers – an argument later generalized by Lathrap (1968) – led to two overhasty assumptions. The first relates to the pre-Conquest native social forms, whereas the second concerns the post-Conquest processes of socioeconomic involution. On the one hand, an antiarchaist illusion was formed in which most

---

21 During the seven foraging expeditions accompanied by these researchers, the average daily per-capita consumption was 3600 calories, with 80% of this total (around 150g per day) coming from hunt game.

contemporary mobile groups are seen as remnants of once firmly sedentary and horticultural societies; on the other, the mobility observed today was attributed to an inexorable process of adopting a less satisfactory way of life. To understand why the Parakanã case contradicts these conclusions, we have now to examine their hunting practices.

Selective Hunters

The Parakanã are hunters specializing in terrestrial animals. Before contact, they disdained most aquatic and arboreal fauna, which constitute the densest populations in the tropical forest. Among the dozens of non-passeriform birds, only two were hunted: a species of curassow (*Crax fasciolata*), and a guan (genus *Penelope*). They avoided various other birds commonly eaten by the region's indigenous peoples, such as macaws and parrots, toucans, and aracaris. Fishing was a supplementary activity. Both blocs claim they seldom ate fish before contact. The catches were confined to a few months of the dry season, when the rivers emptied and the aquatic fauna concentrated in spots ideal for fishing with barbasco.

Most of the protein intake came from mammals and reptiles, but even here we find considerable selectivity. Out of the thirty-nine species of mammals recognized by the Parakanã (excluding rats, opossums, and bats), the western group hunted eight and the eastern group nine (see annex, Table A.4). In most cases, there are no explicit taboos restricting the consumption of the remaining animals: They are either considered too small or simply inedible. They do not even contemplate eating carnivores, anteaters, sloths, small rodents, marsupials, or bats. Among primates, only the howler monkey is deemed to be potential prey: The eastern group considers it edible, although it is rarely hunted, whereas the western group claim that older people can eat it, but recall very few occasions on which someone actually did.

The capybara, the largest South American rodent, which can weigh up to 65 kilograms, is strictly prohibited. It is the only generic food taboo among the Parakanã. This derives from the capybara's close association with sorcery: Eating the animal is tantamount to ingesting the pathogenic agents contained inside it. Other large rodents, such as paca and agouti, are considered edible, although neither prey was especially targeted in the past, particularly among the western Parakanã. For the latter, paca meat was for women, children, and older people, whereas agouti was little appreciated owing to its association with skin diseases. Armadillos were considered old people's food, and even deer was not a favored prey, being considered lean game. The eastern group claim they only ate deer when it was fat, whereas the western group say they only ate its heart.

The only mammals free of restrictions are tapirs and peccaries, which along with two species of tortoise (*G. carbonaria* e *G. denticulata*) make up the preferred game of the Parakanã.[22] The behavioral particularities of these animals have significant impacts on settlement patterns. Both tortoises and tapirs tend to be the first to disappear from the village surroundings due to their vulnerability to predation (Balée 1984a:231–7). Land turtles are slow moving and easily discovered by specialist hunters, whereas tapirs, due to their size and tendency to stick to forest trails, also become easy prey. Peccaries are extremely mobile animals, meaning they cannot function as a regular source of animal protein for a sedentary group, although they provide moments of large-scale food intake (Berlin & Berlin 1983:317).[23] In sum, a people whose diet is focused on these games must possess a very mobile subsistence strategy: The tortoises provide food security that makes concentrating on less dense (such as the tapir) or less predictable (such as peccaries) animal populations a viable option. This was clearly the path taken by the western Parakanã in the twentieth century, but it is also possible that the rotation of the eastern Parakanã villages was associated both with the decrease in large-size mammals and tortoises.

The other mammals consumed by the Parakanã, such as paca, agouti, and armadillos, disappear less rapidly from the area around villages, and tend to be found near swiddens, from which they extract roots and tubers (Emmons 1990:206–7; Beckerman 1980:95; Ross 1978). We can thus surmise that the more mobile they were, the greater the importance of tapirs, peccaries, and tortoises in their diet, and, inversely, the more sedentary they were, the greater the contribution of rodents and armadillos. This coincides with the western and eastern Parakanã descriptions of their precontact diet: The latter impose no stringent prohibitions on the consumption of paca, agoutis, and armadillos (except for the giant armadillo), whereas the former claim that these animals were consumed infrequently and little valued. It remains to be seen whether they actually succeeded in putting this dietary ideal into practice.

Obviously, no precontact data is available. However, information collected at later dates can be used to extrapolate precontact patterns. Milton studied the western Parakanã diet in 1986, in Apyterewa village. Two years after pacification, they possessed only two or three shotguns and were learning to fish with hook and line. Although less mobile than in the past, they continued to trek for long periods, particularly in the rainy season. In

22 River turtles were not part of the diet. As for caimans, the eastern Parakanã eat two of the three species found in the region, while western Parakanã consumption is limited to old people.

23 The white-lipped peccary, for example, weighs between 25 and 40 kg and is found in bands of up to one hundred or more individuals (Emmons 1990:159; Eisenberg 1989).

Table 2.1. *Frequency of Animals Consumed by the Western Parakanã in 1986 (Milton 1991)*

Category	Rainy Season (10/03 to 11/04)		Dry Season (28/07 to 20/08)	
	Individuals (n)	Relative frequency (%)	Individuals (n)	Relative frequency (%)
Tortoise	80	44	22	28
Tapir	1	<1	1	1
Deer	4	2	–	–
Peccary	10	6	2	3
Paca	30	17	12	15
Agouti	4	2	3	4
Armadillo	32	18	6	8
Birds	7	4	5	6
Fishes	5	3	14	18
Larvae	7	4	2	3
Other	–	–	9	2

Table, 2.1, I reproduce Milton's data that only includes the nonprocessed game brought to the village.[24]

First, the table reveals considerable qualitative and quantitative variation between the rainy and dry seasons. In the former, game is more abundant and fish more scarce, whereas the reverse is true in the dry season. Second, the table shows tortoises were the most frequent game during both seasons of the year, followed by paca and armadillos, indicating that after two years of site occupation – even before tortoises became scarce – these mammals were already important in the diet. Agouti, birds, and deer accounted for a small proportion of killed prey. The exclusion of hunt excursions from the data means that tapirs and peccaries are underrepresented in the data. Milton notes that

When family groups left the village to go on hunting treks in the forest (as they frequently did), hunters stated very emphatically that treks were undertaken with the specific intent of hunting tapir. Remains of smoked game brought back to the village confirm that the Parakana generally were highly successful in this pursuit. (Milton 1991:259)

If we consider the relative contribution of prey in terms of weight rather than their frequency, the picture changes significantly. A paca weighs on

---

24 The table presents small errors in calculation, fails to specify the category "other" and counts any returning fish as a single unit. Furthermore, it only mentions the relative frequency of individual specimens without including relative weight.

Table 2.2. *Frequency of Animals Consumed by the Eastern Parakanã in 1996*
(Excluding Fish and Insects) (Emídio-Silva 1998)

Category	Total biomass/day in kg (relative frequency)	Rainy Season biomass/day in kg (relative frequency)	Dry Season biomass/day in kg (relative frequency)
tapir	95.77 (40.5%)	67.09 (44.6%)	28.68 (33.4%)
tortoises	44.44 (18.8%)	33.34 (22.2%)	11.10 (12.9%)
peccaries	42.00 (17.8%)	28.74 (19.1%)	13.28 (15.4%)
deer	36.80 (15.6%)	18.12 (12.0%)	18.68 (21.7%)
rodents	12.63 (5.3%)	0.66 (<1%)	11.97 (13.9%)
caimans	2.15 (<1%)	0.07 (<1%)	2.08 (2.4%)
birds	1.54 (< 1%)	1.28 (< 1%)	0.26 (< 1%)
armadillos	0.79 (<1%)	0.79 (<1%)	–
howler monkeys	0.11 (< 1%)	0.11 (< 1%)	–
TOTAL	236.17 (100%)	150.20 (100%)	85.97 (100%)

average around a third of a peccary and a twentieth of a tapir. This means that the two tapirs brought back uncooked to the village during Milton's research correspond to the forty-two paca or the twelve peccary killed over the same period. If we further include the hunting trips, we can say that after two years of occupation of the same village by a population of around 140 people, the tapir and peccaries represented the largest intake of animal protein. Pacas, armadillos, and tortoises provided the daily diet and, therefore, food security.

We can turn now to the diet of the eastern Parakanã, studied by Emídio-Silva in 1996. His fieldwork was conducted in Paranatinga village, then inhabited by a population of more than 250 people and occupied for thirteen years. Twenty-five years had passed since contact, and hunting was conducted exclusively with guns. The study results confirm the importance of tapir, peccary, and tortoise in the group's diet, as well as the deer that started to be consumed freely after contact. I summarize the author's data (Emídio-Silva 1998:97) in Table 2.2.

As in the previous table, we can observe a clear quantitative and qualitative difference between the seasons, with the rainy season proving to be much more abundant. According to Emídio-Silva (1998:103), the eastern Parakanã ate 329 grams per day per capita of game meat in the rainy season and 188 grams in the dry season (both amounts higher than the WHO recommended minimum). In terms of species, the notable difference is the both absolute and relative growth in the consumption of rodents over the dry season, indicating that they are only hunted when more prized game is scarce. As for deer, consumption in terms of biomass per day remains steady all year, although its relative importance increases in the dry season due to the overall fall in the capture of other species, including a more than 50-percent reduction in the consumption of tapirs, tortoises and peccaries. Globally, though, the latter represented the main source of animal protein, making up 77 percent of the consumed meat, a figure that rose as high as 86 percent during the rains.

Emídio-Silva's data indicate that, even in a present-day situation of lower mobility, the bulk of animal protein derives from the hunting of large mammals and land turtles, the latter representing the main daily source of animal food. We can offer, therefore, a positive reply to the question posed previously: Yes, it is likely that the Parakanã put their alimentary ideal into practice in the past, when they were even more mobile than today. What can we say, then, about the modifications introduced with postpacification sedentarization and the acquisition of new technologies?

Alimentary Changes after Contact

The situation with which I am most familiar is the Apyterewa settlement, where I began my research two years after Milton's study. At that time, the western Parakanã still spent most of the rainy season on trekking, dispersing in bands and living in forest encampments. The village dwindled to no more than a base: Small groups sometimes returned to make flour and then left.[25] During the remainder of the year, the village was far less deserted: The hunting or fishing trips never involved an entire kindred or lasted more than a week. Tortoises were already rare in the village vicinity, and paca had become the most common prey. Seldom eaten during the first two years of contact, deer was increasingly hunted without restrictions. With the introduction of shotguns and torches, they also created new hunting habits favoring the predation of arboreal and nocturnal

---

25 The Parakanã considered the rainy season excellent for hunting since various fruits eaten by terrestrial animals begin to mature and fall. Normally dispersed during the summer, the animals concentrate under the fruit trees, making them easier to find. Moreover, after months of dry weather, the forest becomes bountiful and game starts to engorge, gaining the highly appreciated layer of fat. Some of the main produce gathered from the forest – Brazil nuts, wild banana, wild cacao, cupuaçu, inaja palm, the sapote family fruits, the anacardiaceae (hog plum, cashew) – ripen during this period. This is also the time when the extremely fat-rich palm larvae and coconut borer larvae are abundant. Beckerman (1994:189) states that the dry season is the more productive in terms of hunting for most Amerindian peoples. The author cites just two contrary examples: the Nambikwara-Maimandê (Aspelin 1975) and the Shipibo (Bergman 1980). To these we can add the Tupi-Guarani speaking peoples of the Xingu-Tocantins interfluvial region, such as the Parakanã, the Tapirapé (Wagley 1977:52), and the Araweté (Viveiros de Castro 1986:154).

species. Over the years, the substitution of the bow by the shotgun lead
to an intensification of nocturnal stand hunting and lower mobility, since,
as they generally possess little ammunition, longer expeditions became
less viable.

The growing scarcity in the area surrounding the village was compen-
sated by the predation of two species of deer (*Mazama americana* and *M.
gouazobira*) and by the increased frequency in the consumption of paca (but
not agoutis) and birds (including the razor-billed curassow, previously
interdicted). New technology extended the hunting possibilities as well
as the individual efficiency of each hunter. Yet it was fish consumption
that grew most. By the end of the 1980s, fish were acquiring an increasingly important role in the diet, especially during the dry season, when it
replaced tortoises as the daily source of animal protein. The introduction
of line, hooks, and canoes made fishing a less collective and demanding
enterprise, allowing boys more than eight years old to contribute to the
group's dietary intake. Significantly, the obligatory collecting of tortoises
after the *opetymo* ritual – a form of compensating wives for the four days
without game – were replaced by fishing. All these transformations, added
to the reintroduction of agriculture, counterbalanced the lower mobility
after pacification, even if such changes did not significantly extend the
spectrum of consumed species (except for fishes).

The transformations in the eastern Parakanã's post-contact diet are similar to those I have just described for the western Parakanã, with some
differences that are remindful of past trends. First, horticulture continues
to receive more work investment, including the production of a surplus
for sale in the nearby towns, leading to an increased share of industrialized
foods (such as sugar, salt, and coffee) in their diet. Second, their mobility
continues to be lower: Hunting trips are shorter and longer expeditions
are directed toward semipermanent camps located at some points across
the territory. Finally, fishing lacks the same importance found among the
western Parakanã of the T.I. Apyterewa, due to the lower fish stocks of the
region's rivers.

Archaisms: Subsistence in the Tropical Forest

In the West's imagination, the Amazonian forest oscillates between two
poles: abundance and scarcity. The first is rooted in an Iberian tradition of
the earthly paradise, appropriated nowadays by a certain kind of romantic
ecologism. The second pole, heir to the colonizers' difficulties in adapting to the tropical forest, dominated much of the scientific literature until
recently. This literature aimed at spotting the limiting factor that would
have restricted cultural development in Amazonia, particularly in the interfluvial zones: low fertile soils (Meggers 1954), low animal protein densities

(Gross 1975), or a combination of both (Roosevelt 1980).[26] The Parakanã are typically *terra firme* horticulturists and hunters. Their example shows that a subsistence strategy based on specialized hunting, mobility, and the complementarity of grown and gathered produce can be successful. Rather than a green desert, for the Parakanã the forest and its fluctuating limitations provides a *range of choices*: what to eat and what not to eat, how to live and how not to live. The mobility of both blocs should be attributed to the possibility of moving rather than the impossibility of settling.

Furthermore, the history of the western Parakanã offers an example of a process commonly qualified in the literature as regressive or involutive (Lévi-Strauss 1958; Lathrap 1968; Martin 1969): the transition from horticulture and sedentarism to foraging and nomadism. The usual analyses of this process depends on two main assumptions: First, the transition is seen as a socioeconomic involution, implying the return to an earlier phase of development of the productive forces and political organization.[27] Second, as a loss, the transition is assumed to derive only from negative conditions imposed on the group from outside: Regression is always imposed, never chosen; the fruit of exogenous factors, never internal processes:

[I]f the nomads lack agriculture, this is not because they did not acquire it, but because they lost it. And in this loss it is necessary to read ... the mark of a History which ... they could not escape. What for the Guayaki was the concrete event that announced their history in reverse, their cultural regression? What uncertain natural catastrophe chased them from their swiddens? Rather, a relation of unfavourable forces, a shock of unequal civilizations, in a word, the war of conquest brought by the Guarani, forcing them to seek refuge far from the invaders. They led an almost clandestine life, seeking even to hide ... their meagre plantations: but ... the regression was irreversible and with the insecurity worsening, given the growing pressure of the Machitara, the Aché – in a fairly recent period – completely abandoned agriculture. (P. Clastres 1972:85–6)

This reconstruction of the historical process through which the Aché-Guayaki of Paraguay abandoned horticulture seems to apply *mutatis mutandis* to other Tupi-Guarani groups that until recently did not plant crops, such as the Guajá (Balée 1994), the Yuqui (Stearman 1989), or the

26 For Roosevelt (1987, 1993), this limitation does not apply to the floodplains of the Amazon and Orinoco Rivers, whose soils were suitable for growing grain crops and supporting complex societies. Roosevelt consolidated a new image of cultural development in Amazonia, previously traced in Carneiro's (1973, 1979) and Lathrap's (1970) works. For more recent contributions, see Heckenberger (1996, 1998) and Heckenberger, Petersen & Neves (1999).

27 Balée calls this process "agricultural regression," defining it as "the transition from 'Agraria' to foraging" (1994:210), borrowing Gellner's terminology (1988) for the macrophases of human history. Losing horticulture is remaking history in reverse.

Avá-Canoeiro (Toral 1985). Historical and linguistic evidence indicates that these peoples once practiced agriculture and lost it under the impact of European colonization (Balée 1994:204–23; Balée and Moore 1991). My intention here is not to argue for the historical falsehood of this explanation. On the contrary, this is what generally happened, and we could cite other examples of how the Conquest positively influenced the mobility of Amerindian peoples.[28] The Parakanã case, though, allows us to complexify this model.

Let us presume that the Parakanã are remnants of a large Tupi-Guarani population of the Pacajá region, consistently sedentary, who practiced a rich and diversified horticulture. Let us also presume that they did not exclusively inhabit the headwater zones and knew how to make canoes. This population was then decimated in the first centuries of colonization. The survivors withdrew to less exposed regions, living close to small water courses where they forgot how to make canoes and began to exploit aquatic fauna less intensively. Horticulture declined under the combined effect of isolation (nonrenewal of cultigens), depopulation (the possibility of depending more intensely on hunting and gathering), and, perhaps, poorer soils. Finally, with the balance between game and cultivated produce gradually shifting, the group became more mobile. This was hypothetically the situation of the Parakanã at the eve of the split near the end of the nineteenth century.

Let us now apply the standard regressionist narrative to reconstruct the process through which the western Parakanã became nomads. This might argue that at the end of the nineteenth century, the pressure on the Parakanã territory increased with the expansion of rubber extractivism in the region. A fission occurred and part of the group was expelled from this territory. They tried to settle in a new area, but were confronted by more powerful and well-established indigenous groups, whose territory was also shrinking due to the advancing of rubber exploration. Hunted on all sides, the western Parakanã were unable to remain very long in the same place. They lived in a semisedentary manner, opening small swiddens where they cultivated quick-ripening plants, always ready to depart at the first sign of enemies in the vicinity. From one moment to the next, they were forced to abandon everything they had planted. As time passed, they had little alternative but to renounce horticulture, turning instead to pillaging the swiddens of their enemies.

---

28 This is what Betendorf indicates, back in the seventeenth century, concerning the groups of Marajó island: "since they expected these hostilities [from the Portuguese], these nations chose not to grow food crops, subsisting for the most part of the year on the fruits that the island produces in abundance" and "raiding the crops of settlers and the food of Christian Indians" (Betendorf [1698] 1910:93).

This account seems entirely reasonable: Indeed, the western block abandoned the territory after the split, entered into conflict with various indigenous groups, and stole flour and crops, all at a time when the presence of whites in the region was expanding. However, the narrative is historically false, and its falsehood consists in describing the process as the result of an ineluctable history to which, as Clastres would say, they "could not escape." Let me recall some of the points set out in Chapter 1: The western group were not exactly expelled from their original territory. They relocated to the west, displacing the Asurini from the Pacajá headwaters. Rather than being pursued by enemies, they took the initiative in the majority of conflicts they became involved, attacking adversaries outside their own territory. The main cultigen was bitter manioc, whose slow ripening (at least one year) and processing (requiring around five days) demands time. Manioc was therefore "stored" in the ground for future use, which implied the certainty of returning to the swiddens and also an effective control of the overall territory. Perhaps this explains why they abandoned horticulture after leaving the Pacajá in the 1960s. As a medium-term investment, clearing a swidden meant assuming a certain level of territorial stability, something that they tried to regain in the Anapu River (c. 1975) and on the headwaters of the Bom Jardim (c. 1980) without much success.

Thus, in a sense, the Parakanã "chose" to live as they did. They did not adopt a semisedentary way of life because they had no alternative, but because this was *one* of the alternatives. As Rival notes, "the 'regressed agriculturalists' of Amazonia, in giving up more intensive forms of horticulture, have exercised a *political* choice" (1998:241). What is notable in the Parakanã case is that their extreme dietary selectivity and their intense mobility only became viable because the region had been depopulated by epidemics, missionary *descimentos*, and slave raiding in earlier centuries. Conquest not only made certain choices impossible (such as living on the shores of large rivers), but it also made others feasible (such as adopting one of the most selective protein diets anywhere in indigenous Amazonia).

Let me qualify the somewhat slippery idea of "choice" to avoid taking it as the symmetrical opposite of cultural ecology's determinism, or as the result of a rational process of cost/benefit analysis along the lines of optimal foraging theory. I am not suggesting that, faced by a certain number of possibilities, the group opted to depend less on agriculture; nor am I claiming that the more mobile pattern resulted from the convergence of particular individual decisions taken to achieve the highest possible return in the least amount of time. I call attention to two points: First, regression should not be understood merely in negative terms, as though it were a residue of history, the evidence of a failure; second, like any complex process, it results from the interaction of multiple determinations taking place in particular historical circumstances through the action of collective and individual agents. This implies, on one hand, not interpreting regression as simply the result of an exogenous force that determines a survival strategy, but as the product of the interaction of these forces with internal processes and decision-making mechanisms. On the other hand, it implies shifting the emphasis from subsistence to other fields: The differential mobility of the Parakanã blocs is a fact of political economy rather than pure economics or ecology (Kent 1989:3).

In conclusion, the Parakanã example points to a greater complexity in the transition from agriculture to foraging than the dominant regressive model presumes. If the narrative I constructed previously was convincing but false, we can ask whether similar narratives are not equally questionable. Are we not faced by a less linear and homogeneous social process than the regressive model leads us to believe? The attempt to reconstruct processes of historical transformation implies discovering evidence to fill the lacuna between an initial state and a final state in which the transformation has already occurred. When adequate documentation is absent, this evidence is typically taken to be an exterior force whose introduction can be generically documented. This procedure is risky, though. First, because the initial state may be only a heuristic hypothesis; second, because the postulated force is not always homogeneous over time; and third, because the object (this people, that society) is an object-subject; that is, they are not merely constituted, but they also constitute themselves.

Our knowledge of Amerindian social forms prior to European Conquest is scant. We do not know, for example, the degree of mobility of the Parakanã's remote ancestors, or how sophisticated their agriculture was, or the complexity of their social organization. Likewise, we are mostly unaware of the diversity of social forms existing in the region at the time of Conquest. The supposition that the ancestors of the Parakanã were consistently sedentary, agriculturists, and canoeists in the sixteenth century must be treated with caution. Nothing excludes that they were already trekkers inhabiting remoter regions, which remained less exposed to the wars of conquest and epidemics (see Carneiro 1995:62). Moreover, the external force in question did not always act in the same form, in the same direction, and with the same intensity. Finally, the object (the indigenous peoples) to which this force was applied not only reacted, but acted on the new context, making choices and taking decisions within a sociopolitical field in transformation.

3

Forms through History

And thus one dies of love where the jaguar lives...
Machado de Assis, "Niâni" (1875)

In the previous chapter I described the socioeconomic transformations experienced by the Parakanã after the split at the end of the nineteenth century. I now focus on sociopolitical changes, approaching social form not as a static constant, but as a dynamic structure capable of accommodating the flux of history and social agency. My aim is to understand how, at the moment of contact and almost a century after the split, the Parakanã blocs presented strikingly different social morphologies and political structures. Whereas the western group lacked any kind of sociocentric segmentation or headmanship, the eastern group was divided into exogamic moieties with three patrigroups and a system of dual leadership. Combining this contrast with the themes analyzed in the previous chapter, we are faced, on the one hand, with a socially and politically undifferentiated seminomadic group specialized in foraging, and, on the other, with a more sedentary, horticulturist group with headmanship and social segmentation. How do we explain this remarkable divergence?

In analyzing material life, I argued that we cannot explain the economic transformations as the simple regression of the western Parakanã from a more complex original form matching that of the eastern bloc. Now I likewise propose that there were two different processes that led to the emergence of a differentiated social morphology among the eastern bloc and political non-differentiation among the western bloc.

Producing Difference

The eastern group is divided into three named patrigroups: Apyterewa, Wyrapina, and Tapi'pya. These designations appear at the end of the mythic cycle narrating the loss and recovery of the arts of civilization and social life (see Chapter 2). After the flooding of the earth, the culture hero Wyrapina, who saved himself from the deluge, stole fire from the vulture, planted bones as manioc, and found a woman to make flour for him. The couple had various sons, two at a time, called Tapi'pya, Apyterewa, Marojewara, Mykojiwena, Pa'ametywena, and Jimokwera.[1] The myth, however, narrates the diversification of peoples speaking the same language from a single source, not the origin of a segmentary system. It reflects the Parakanã sense of their own past: Their ancestors, they say, were the Apyterewa and all the other designations refer to enemy tribes speaking the same language and inhabiting the Pacajá-Tocantins interfluvial region. If so, how did they become mixed? We must return to an event described in Chapter 1, the killing of Moakara, whose repercussions were much wider than his contemporaries could have possibly imagined.

The Difference a Boy Makes

Moakara was a *Wyrapina* who lived with two adult sons, his wives and children on an affluent on the left shore of the Pucuruí River. They occupied a small house walled with stilt palm laths, next to a manioc swidden. They maintained contact with whites on the lower Pucuruí, and one of the group's women, Wewytonga, lived for a while with a Brazil nut harverster, nicknamed Mojiajinga ("White Chest"). At the end of the nineteenth century, the Parakanã came across Moakara's single-house village. Surrounding the site, they yelled at the residents. Moakara and his firstborn son came out into the open, dancing and singing, displaying their courage. The two parties began to converse. Moakara wanted to know who had just killed one of his sons. When the warriors fell silent, he asked his wife to fetch water for the visitors, since he knew the killer would refuse to drink. When the gourd was handed to Warehiwa, he refused, saying: "I'm not thirsty." They insisted. "I'm not thirsty," replied again Warehiwa. Conflict became inevitable. The Parakanã killed the two men at close range, splattering themselves in blood: "The enemy's blood will spoil us. Let's wash ourselves, the blood will penetrate us, it's strong-smelling [(*piji'oa*)]" (Akaria 1995: tape 9). So they left quickly. The warriors bathed and returned home eager to show off their victory to their mothers and wives. Shortly after, they returned to Moakara's village but failed to locate the survivors. They set off in pursuit and ended up finding the remainder of the group by the shore of a river. They captured eight women and four boys. Three of the latter were

---

1 The Parakanã gloss *Apyterewa* as "good head" (-'*apytera kato*), a reference to psychic and moral dispositions (-'*apytera* means "center of the head"). Boudin (1966) translates the Tembé cognate *apitérêw* as "bald." *Wyrapina* can be glossed as "hair shaved by birds" and refers to the hero of the deluge myth, whose hair rotted and fell out when the birds defecated on his head. The eastern Parakanã consider the Apyterewa and Wyrapina to be "humans par excellence" (*awaeté*), one of the distinctive features of the Parakanã having been precisely their shaven heads. *Tapi'pya* means "tapir foot," Marojewara "of the little red brocket deer," and Mykojiwena "husband of the small white opossum."

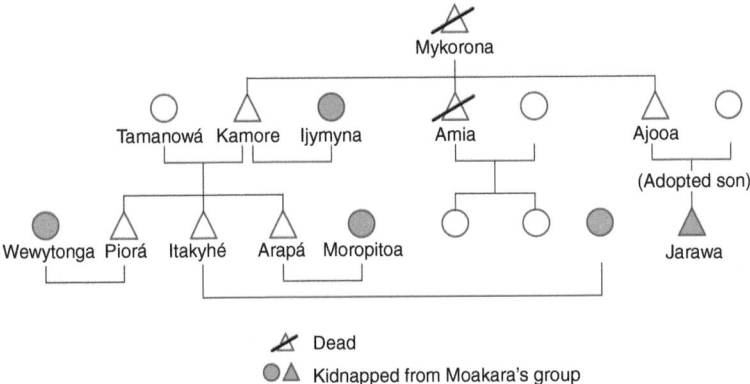

Figure 3.1. The eastern Parakanã after the split (c. 1890).

soon killed, since they feared the boys would become enemies when they grew up. Just one, named Jarawa, was spared. Jarawa was not a Wyrapina like Moakara and his family, but a Tapi'pya. Thus the Parakanã, who called themselves Apyterewa, incorporated a Tapi'pya boy and various Wyrapina women.

It was at this time that the Parakanã split took place. The conflict was provoked by a dispute over one of the captured women: An unmarried man called Wararoa tried to seduce her away from her new husband and was threatened with death in response. Two of Wararoa's nephews came to his defense, provoking a fight in which they came out worse. In the aftermath, part of the group (the future western Parakanã) headed west. Since they had left without cultigens, they returned to take manioc from the swidden but an attempted reconciliation soon collapsed. The separation became definitive.

The group that left was probably both larger and more heterogenic. My genealogy indicates that there were at least four groups of siblings with children among the western group, whereas the nucleus of the eastern group was formed by a single group of siblings joined by the four women from Moakara's group and the captured boy, Jarawa (see Figure 3.1).

The split generated matrimonial problems for the eastern bloc: Except for the wives obtained before the split and the captured women, all the remaining women were patrilateral parallel kin and hence technically unmarriable. My genealogy records only incestuous marriages (according to the Parakanã conception of incest) at the turn of the century.[2] This

2 The four male children of the couple Kamoré and Tamanowá married eight women, comprising six patrilateral parallel cousins and two real sisters.

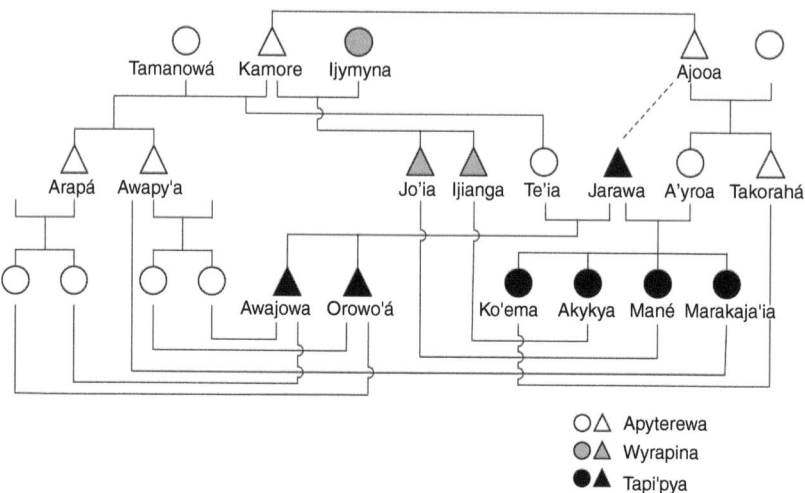

Figure 3.2. First marriages among the patrigroups (c. 1925–1945).

situation only began to change at the start of the 1920s when Jarawa's daughters reached puberty. The captured boy had grown up amid the general distrust of his adoptive kin. As the child of enemies, he could have harbored a desire for revenge; he thus had to wait longer than usual to acquire his first bow. He ended up being incorporated into the group, though. He received one of Kamoré's daughters as a wife, and the couple had four children, all boys. Next he married his adoptive sister and had two more boys and four girls. Jarawa's ten children were born between 1900 and 1925, the two oldest sons being killed by the western Parakanã around 1910.

In the 1920s, therefore, nine Tapi'pya were living among the eastern Parakanã, a significant but still small portion of the total population. During this decade, the system of exogamic moieties started to take shape. Jarawa's oldest daughter, Ko'ema, married Takorahá, Ajooa's son. It was the first marriage of the century to comply with the matrimonial norm: Takorahá had given his sister to Jarawa, who reciprocated with his ZD. Jarawa's other daughters married over the next few years with their MFBSs (that is, their classificatory MBs). In exchange, the sons of Jarawa, received wives from their brothers-in-law (see Figure 3.2).

These marriages constituted the patrigroups as exchange units, providing a new sociological reality to the contrasting Apyterewa and Tapi'pya identities. The exogamic moieties were born as the result of the combination of a patrilineal conception of identity transmission, an avuncular-patrilateral matrimonial regime and a historical event that opened up a field of possibilities for the actors involved.[3] The dualism did not emerge as the simple confluence of preexisting structures and singular events, but as a creative process, the outcome of individual decisions made at specific moments in the group's history. Jarawa's role was not only to set in motion matrimonial exchange, but also to organize the latter into a system of classes. In this way, an internal difference was constructed within a cluster of agnates.

The eastern Parakanã did not limit themselves to creating exogamic moieties. They formed a third patrigroup: the descendents of Ijymyna, daughter of Moakara and the only captured woman to have borne children. This was done, people say, to prevent the Wyrapina from becoming extinct. This exception to the patrilineal transmission of identity is common among the Parakanã, reflecting the prominence given to the exterior in their cosmology: Internally, male identity is valued over female identity, but the latter, when it comes from outside, is valued over the former. As outsiders, the captured women were endowed with a male potency: They brought names, songs and (their own) bodies from the outside, as well as defining the identity of their children.

This is how the system of exogamic moieties and three patrigroups that I was able to observe among the eastern Parakanã in the 1990s came into existence.

The Nature of Social Groups

During my fieldwork, any eastern Parakanã to whom I asked the question "What party do you belong to?" (*ma'é-kwera pa ene*) immediately responded with the name of their patrigroup. But what did belonging to one of these groups mean? Not much if we compare the eastern Parakanã with other Amerindian peoples where social segments are depositories of rights and properties, and are associated with an elaborate symbolism. Parakanã patrigroups are neither corporate in nature, nor part of a totemic system. They just define an internal dichotomy between "us" (*ore*) and "others" (*amote*), in which Apyterewa and Wyrapina are both opposed to Tapi'pya.[4]

The moiety system supplied a sociocentric structure to matrimonial exchange, superimposing a logic of classes over one of relations. The matrimonial rule (a man must marry his "sister's" daughter or his younger cross cousin) acquired an additional stipulation: Apyterewa and Wyrapina men

---

3 The Parakanã prescribe as a man's spouses the daughters of his "sisters" and of his father's "sisters" (younger than himself). I have called this regime "avuncular-patrilateral" (Fausto 1991; 1995).

4 The names of the patrigroups can be classified in a binary mode: on one side, Apyterewa and Wyrapina, both associated with the head; on the other, Tapi'pya, associated with the foot. The names of the Kagwahiv moieties, harpy eagle and curassow, also seem to contain an opposition between above and below (Kracke 1984:101).

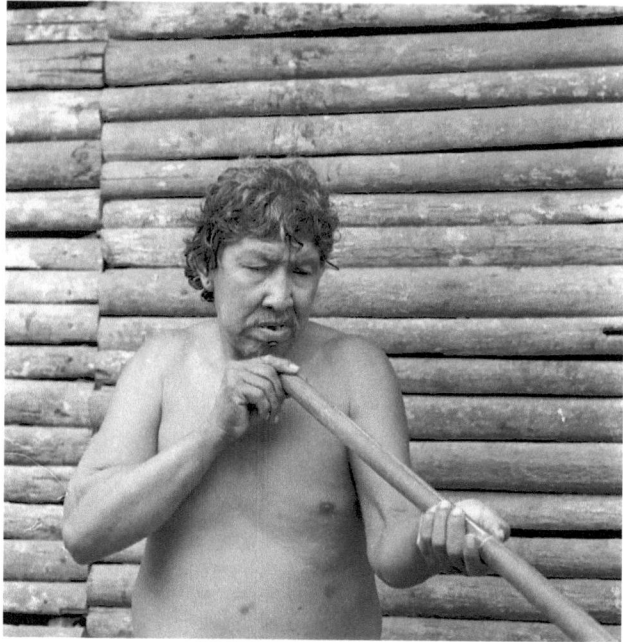

Photo 2. The *Tapi'pya* headman Arakytá confectionates a clarinet
(eastern Parakanã, Paranatinga village, 1992).

marry with younger Tapi'pya women and vice-versa. In the 1990s, political leadership was also structured in accordance with this system. Two
men held the headmanship, one from each moiety. This enabled a degree
of equilibrium and complementarity, though the symmetry was imperfect since Arakytá (Tapi'pya) enjoyed more prestige and authority than his
son-in-law Ywyrapytá (Apyterewa). Despite this asymmetry, most eastern
Parakanã recognized that the currently hegemonic moiety had an external origin, while the other represented the continuity of the *awaeté*, the
"real people." As Arakytá once told me: "we [the Tapi'pya] are enemies
[*akwawa*]."[5]

The layout of houses in Paranatinga village in 1992 also reflected social
segmentation. Residential clusters corresponded to five different patrilines, which in turn formed the core structure of the "production groups"
(see Chapter 2). Much more numerous, the Tapi'pya were divided into

5 This somewhat ironic declaration does not imply that one of the patrimoieties is consistently associated with the outside and the other with the inside, as occurs among the Parintintin (Kracke 1978:40;
   Peggion 1996:46–8) and some Panoan peoples (Townsley 1987:370–3; Erikson 1996:79–81).

three lines, each tracing back to one of Jarawa's sons, whereas the other two lines were composed of Apyterewa and Wyrapina men, respectively. Such layout contrasted with that of the post-contact western Parakanã villages, which were structured according to two different logics: a virilocal and patrilineal one (clusters formed by male siblings and patrilateral parallel cousins) and another one based on repeated affinity (clusters composed of groups of siblings that had exchanged sisters). This second structuring principle lies at the base of the splitting processes observed among the western Parakanã from the 1970s onward: Relations between patrilateral parallel cousins are unstable, since the distancing between two brothers' descendents leads to a weakening solidarity that tends to give way to rivalry over wives (Fausto 1995:100). One of the questions I shall address in this chapter is whether the sociocentric segments of the eastern Parakanã have served to reinforce the ties between patrilateral parallel cousins, thus preventing conflicts over women.

Alliance System: Form and Function

Whereas the eastern Parakanã patrigroups were identity markers used frequently by actors in the 1990s, from the viewpoint of alliance, the system no longer functioned as well as before. From 1930 until contact in 1971, moiety exogamy was observable in 85 percent of cases. Of the sixty-one marriages recorded in my genealogy for this period, fifty-two took place between moieties, and only nine within the same moiety. However, in the subsequent period between 1971 and 1995, the percentage of "incorrect" marriages doubled: Of ninety-one unions, fifty-six (62 percent) were between people from opposite moieties, twenty-nine (32 percent) between members of the same moiety, and six (7 percent) with foreigners.[6]

The gap between the norm of moiety exogamy and matrimonial practice increased over the decades, reaching its peak in the 1990s, when only half of marriages complied with the norm. Analyzing this trend, I suggested in an earlier work that the division into moieties was already failing to produce a true system of matrimonial classes. I predicted that the "incorrect" marriages would have a snowball effect, rendering the segmentation less and less operative in the regulation of alliance. The system would then revert to functioning as a minimal system of deferred symmetrical exchange without groups (as occurs among the western Parakanã). The conflict between a sociocentric logic and a relational logic would be resolved in favor of the latter (Fausto 1995:103). The scenario indicated thus an evolution in

---

6 Here I include all unions, irrespective of whether they were first or second marriages or had produced descendents.

which the moieties would become, to use Kracke's expression (1984), a form without function.[7]

The reason why moiety exogamy ceased to be the main form of regulating alliance is demographic. From the 1950s onward, respecting the exogamic rule became increasingly difficult as the reproductive success of the Tapi'pya was far higher than the other two groups. The Apyterewa had suffered the brunt of the ten western Parakanã attacks: Of the fourteen men who were killed in total, nine were Apyterewa, two Wyrapina, and three Tapi'pya. In addition, between 1930 and 1950, the western Parakanã captured or killed ten women, nine of them Apyterewa. At the time of contact, therefore, the Tapi'pya already represented the largest section of the population, a trend that has intensified further in recent years. In 1995, the 260 inhabitants of Paranatinga village were divided into 165 Tapi'pya, 42 Apyterewa, and 47 Wyrapina (with an additional 3 foreign women and 1 western Parakanã man).

The demographic imbalance made it impossible for the Tapi'pya to respect the exogamic norm, but on the other hand enabled all the Apyterewa-Wyrapina to do so. Between 1971 and 1995, there was just one incorrect marriage in this moiety. The system, therefore, continued to be fully functional for the latter and only partially so for the Tapi'pya, a tendency that can be traced back to the 1950s, as the graph in Figure 3.3 reveals.

The system thus functions in almost 100 percent of the cases for one of the moieties and in less than 50 percent for the other. The fact that the system functions for one of the moieties poses problems for my earlier analysis, since it points to the stability of the norm: Whenever possible, it continues to be followed. At the same time it raises questions about the future implications of intramoiety marriages. As I said, my original hypothesis was that the system would necessarily drift toward a model of non-sociocentric regulation, as the "incorrect" unions would propagate through the generations via the minimal structure of matrimonial reciprocity: A man who cedes a sister acquires the right to claim his niece for himself or for his son. And such a claim was being firmly satisfied: Out of the twenty-eight marriages within the Tapi'pya moiety since the 1970s,

---

7 Kracke proposed the coexistence of three systems that determine marriage among the Tupi-speaking Parintintin: an explicit system of moieties, an implicit system of three patriclans, and an unconscious system of patrilines, the latter the effect of the reiteration of specific matrimonial practices over time. According to Kracke, at the time of his research there was a growing incongruence between the dyadic and triadic models, producing a divergence between matrimonial norm and practice: Despite the ideology of moiety exogamy, the actual alliance structure tended to become bilateral between three patrigroups. This contradiction stems from a historical fact: the incorporation of defeated enemies into one of the moieties. Although they should have behaved matrimonially as members of this segment, they acted as a separate patriline that exchanged with both moieties.

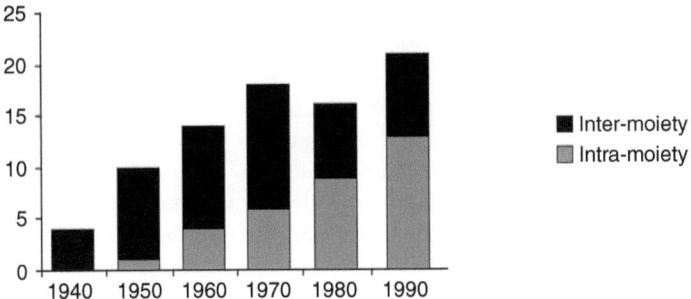

Figure 3.3. Evolution of the marriages of *Tapi'pya* men (excluding marriages with foreign women) (1940–1995).

seven involved a real sister's daughter (ZD) or the daughter of a first degree patrilateral parallel cousin (FBDD), and two involved the daughter of a real father's sister (FZD). In other words, around one-third of the marriages were not only correct from the viewpoint of the logic of relations, but they also corresponded to the most valued forms of matrimonial union (see Fausto 1991:216; 1995:89). How will the accumulation of unions of this type effect the segmentary system over time? What will happen to the moieties, whose existence was always halfway between being the cause and outcome of matrimonial exchange?

Replying to these questions is no simple matter. The best approach is to remain open to the possibility of Parakanã social morphology being transformed again in unsuspected ways through their own actions.

Shadows of the Past

Yet another question needs to be pondered: Did the eastern Parakanã revive an earlier segmentary model that had collapsed under the impact of demographic losses? At issue here is the sociological meaning of the terms Apyterewa, Wyrapina, and Tapi'pya (as well as Marojewara, Mykojiwena, Pa'ametywena, and Jimokwera). What did these designate in the past?

Both the eastern and western blocs assert that these names designated independent enemy peoples sharing a common language but possessing different warfare and dietary practices. According to the eastern Parakanã, the Marojewara used to capture enemies and kill them in the plaza; for the western Parakanã, not only the Marojewara but also the Tapi'pya were cannibals. As Iatora once told me, "we just kill with arrows, which makes us *awaeté* ['real people']. *Awaeté* shoot their prey and then leave" (Iatora 1993: tape 11). People also speculate over who might be the descendents of past adversaries: The western Parakanã, for example, identify the Asurini of the Tocantins with the Wyrapina, whereas the eastern Parakanã muse over whether the Suruí are the Pa'ametywena.

The Parakanã interpretation thus suggests the existence of a linguistically similar set, formed by named, localized, and politically independent groups. Each of these groups would recognize itself as *awaeté* in opposition to all the others who were considered *akwawa* ("enemies") or *ngyngé* ("like-us-enemies"). This system would have already vanished by the mid-nineteenth century since the Parakanã have no historical narratives on conflicts between these groups. Whatever the case, the current eastern Parakanã morphology would correspond to an introjection of an external pan-village system of differences to the level of the village.[8]

Tupi Segmentation Revisited

The Parakanã case provides insights into the nature of segmentary structures in Amazonia. First, it allows us to transcend the opposition between structure and history, which frequently surfaces when it comes to defining social segmentation. Second, it permits us to explore this theme using a generative rather than degenerative model. Third, it suggests that unilinear groups exist as a structural latency within social forms, and may or may not be actualized by particular societies at specific moments of their history. Such groups are not identical institutions or even of the same nature within the spectrum of Amazonian social organizations. They display varying statuses as we shift from the Timbira to the Yanomami, from the Tupi to the Tukano, or from the Tikuna to the Pano. Even so, almost all these formations are permeated by historical references to the formation, transformation, and disappearance of segments. The difference between the various systems primarily resides in the way in which form and process interact in determining groups, segments, and moieties. Let me explore this idea in relation to Tupi-speaking peoples.

Most of the Tupi-Guarani present no kind of segmentation whatsoever. References to segmentation are found only among the eastern Parakanã, Suruí, Tapirapé, Kagwahiv, and Wayãpi. Each of these instances, though, displays a distinct social morphology. The Suruí possess five exogamic patriclans associated with specific ritual functions and activities, with political leadership reserved for one of them (Laraia 1986:118). Among the Tapirapé, there are six named male societies, divided into two unnamed moieties of a primarily ceremonial nature (Wagley 1977:102–3). The Kagwahiv reveal specific compositions according to the group: The Parintintin possess moieties and three clans, the Tenharim just the moieties, whereas the

---

8 For a similar situation, see the Carib peoples of the Guianas, especially the Tiriyó subgroups, whose past existence is equally difficult to determine (Rivière 1969:26–8).

Kagwahiv of the Madeira River were apparently composed of various localized exogamic patrisibs (Lévi-Strauss 1948a:313). As for the Wayãpi, P. Grenand (1982:59–69) suggests the past existence of patriclans, localized as in the Kagwahiv case, although Gallois (1988:29) disagrees with this hypothesis.

What all the examples share is the difficulty of separating social morphology and the historical process behind its formation; Tapirapé ceremonial groups emerged thanks to the influence of the Karajá; Parintintin triadism results from the incorporation of an enemy group; whereas one of the Suruí clans coalesced from the descendents of a foreign captive. The indistinguishability between morphology and event, associated with the fact that the majority of Tupi groups display no form of segmentation, has led most Tupi-Guarani specialists to take positive examples as historical accidents, rather than considering such accidents as the objective possibilities of a structure open to history – a performative structure, as Sahlins would say (1985:xi–xiv).

In an earlier work, I tried to define the conditions that are positively correlated with the emergence of unilinear groups among the Tupi-Guarani, arguing that these should be sought in the alliance system rather than in the concept of descent. I claimed that segmentation is more likely where avunculate and patrilaterate marriages are prominent (Fausto 1991:279; 1995:102). The cumulative effects of a patrilineal ideology of matrimonial exchange, associated with a patrilinear transmission of identity, may lead, under certain historical circumstances, to the formation of a segmented morphology. One of these circumstances seems to be precisely the introjection of external difference through the capture of a male outsider.

If we extend the discussion to include the non-Tupi-Guarani peoples, we discover an inversion in the ratio of the societies with and without segmentation. Evidence of patrilinear groups exists among families such as the Tupi-Mondé (Dal Poz 1991:41–7; Mindlin 1985:47–50), Tupari (Lévi-Strauss 1948b), Munduruku (Murphy 1978:71–96), and Maué (Nimuendaju 1948b). These structures appear in a band across the southern Amazon basin between the Madeiras and Tapajós Rivers and disappear in the Xingu, where the Juruna present no traces of segmentation. Although the patrigroups possess a higher sociological yield in these families from the Tupi trunk, we lack detailed studies on their nature and functioning. More recent works tend to treat patrigroups as principles of classification, without analyzing the ways in which they help structure sociopolitical relations. This tendency probably stems from an overextension of the critique of African models, something we should guard against: The fact that the segments are not corporate entities endowed with rights and duties does not mean they lack a sociological reality or fail to produce consistent social effects.

Table 3.1. *Women Captured by the Western Parakanã (1880–1975)*[9]

Decade	Group	Identification	Captured Women	With Children	
1880	Itakya	same language	2	2	
1880	Moakara	same language	3	3	presplit
1910	Akwa'awohoa	other language	3	2	postsplit
1910	Temeikwary'yma	same language	8	6	
1930	Amowaja	Eastern Parakanã	2	2	
1940	Amowaja	Eastern Parakanã	5	4	
1940	Makakawa	Asurini	2	2	
1950	Makakawa	Asurini	1	1	
1960	Akwa'awa	other language	3	2	
1970	Yrywyjara	Araweté	3	1	
TOTAL			32	25	

Producing Equality

Among the western Parakanã, the segments are entirely absent, but not the denominations. They claim to be descendents of the Apyterewa and say they later became mixed through the capture of women – the sons of foreign women perpetuating the identity of the mother rather than the father. If the versions explaining the origin of the designations and the process of amalgamation are similar, why do we find patrigroups among the eastern Parakanã and only a vague reference to them among the western Parakanã? If the designations were indeed marks of identity by the end of the nineteenth century, why were they not crystallized as social segments in the latter case? Part of the answer lies in the expansion of warfare activities and the capture of women among the western bloc. Between 1885 and 1920, they captured sixteen foreign women, thirteen of them from groups speaking mutually comprehensible Tupi-Guarani languages. From the 1930s to the 1950s, they captured ten more women, seven eastern Parakanã, and three Asurini. Finally, between the mid-1960s and 1976, they captured six more women, three Araweté, and three Akwa'awa (see Table 3.1).

The influx of captured women contributed to dissolving the identities conferred by the designations, not only due to their number but also through succession. For example, what would be the identity of a man whose paternal grandmother (FM) was a Mykojiwena and his mother an

---

9   The table omits those women who died soon after capture as well as those who stayed with the eastern bloc after the split. The final column ("with children") refers to the number of captured women who procreated among the western bloc.

Table 3.2. *Fertile Marriages between Kin and with Foreign Women (c. 1880–1979)*

Period	Between kin (n)	With Foreign Women (n)	Proportion*
1880–1919	04	12	1:3
1920–1959	33	11	3:1
1960–1979	50	07	7:1
TOTAL	87	30	3:1

* calculated to nearest whole number

Asurini? In this case, the father would be a *mykojiwena-memyrera* ("son of a dead Mykojiwena woman") and himself a *makakawa-memyrera* ("son of a dead Asurini woman"). At the same time, the western Parakanã believe that the Asurini are remnants of the Wyrapina, which confuses the situation even further. The eastern Parakanã case is entirely different: On one hand, they operated with a small number of foreign women, since only one of Moakara's kinswomen who remained with them had children and they captured no others after the split. On the other hand, they had a captured boy who combined a double potency: masculinity and exteriority. He supplied a more solid base for constructing an internal difference using the designations. The western bloc's centrifugal movement ended up dissolving potential internal differences, whereas the centripetal movement of the eastern bloc led to their construction.

Capture Makes a Difference

In order to evaluate the impact of the influx of enemy women on the western Parakanã, in particular between 1880 and 1920, a parameter is needed. We have seen that during this period sixteen women were captured, twelve of them having children. What do these figures represent in terms of relative frequency? Knowing how many women were in the group at this time is impossible, but there is a way of making an estimate: that is, determining the ratio of marriages with foreign women and kin that produced children. My data show sixteen marriages resulting in children between 1880 and 1920, twelve of them with foreign women. In the following period (1920–59), the proportion was inverted: thirty-three unions between kinswomen compared to eleven with foreign women, a trend that became more pronounced between 1960 and 1980, when fifty marriages were recorded between kin and only seven with captured women (see Table 3.2).[10]

10 The names of foreign women are perhaps easier to recall. If we count as marriages with kinswomen cases where only the father's name is remembered, the proportion for the first period shifts to 7:12.

Unless we hypothesize a higher fertility rate for marriages with foreign women, the implication of this data is clear: For a generation after
the split, there were few women available within the group, and capture
was a preferential form of obtaining a spouse.[11] The impact of capturing
wives is evident in various fields of western Parakanã life, including certain
lexical variations. Among the eastern group, the term *ngyngé* refers exclusively to enemies who speak the same language as themselves, whereas
among the western group, its primary meaning is that of a set of women
in opposition to men.[12] The shift in meaning is suggestive: For the former
it designates similar others, whereas for the latter it designates women
from the male point of view. The semantic drift corresponds to a historical
fact: Many captured *ngyngé* actually became kin. This was true to such an
extent that even the category "wife" drifted toward the category "captured
foreign women": Western Parakanã men commonly address their wives as
we-akwawa'yn, "my related enemy."

As a matrimonial strategy, capture had a considerable impact on western Parakanã social dynamics, contributing *a posteriori* to strengthening
an antagonistic perception of the matrimonial field – *a posteriori* because
initially it helped lessen the tension existing between adjacent generations. Capture opened up the game of matrimonial alliances for those without wives. However, it created an expectation that could only be met by
resorting ever more frequently to new captures.

The Social Forms of Scarcity

A number of features of the western Parakanã alliance system promotes
male disputes over women by generating a shortfall in the number of potential wives. All men will acquire a wife at some point, but not all mature
men can be married simultaneously. There is always someone old enough
to start a new family who is unable to do so, even when the sex ratio is
equal. The social production of this scarcity leads to clashes between men
over women.

There are four ways of obtaining a woman among the western Parakanã:
through a matrimonial arrangement, through succession after the death of
a husband, by stealing a woman from a kinsman, or by capturing a woman

---

11 Iatora told me that there was indeed a dearth of women at this time. According to him, this was
    due to a conflict in which young bachelors killed the wives of his kin and only a few escaped. The
    narrative may not be actual history, but it expresses well the antagonistic manner in which the
    western Parakanã conceive of the matrimonial game.
12 Interestingly enough, in western Parakanã narratives referring to events that happened at the
    start of the twentieth century (not witnessed by my interlocutors), *ngyngé* still signifies a "like-
    us-enemy." The term appears with this meaning only in direct citations, which implies that such
    citations are repeated as narrative formulas across generations.

from enemies. The first two forms rarely lead to disputes, as they are embedded in the sequence of past matrimonial exchanges. They are conceived as part of a dynamic of reciprocity between kingroups over time and as the actualization of a maternal uncle's legitimate claim over his niece.[13] The other two forms, by contrast, depend on individual action founded not on notions of reciprocity and legitimacy, but on a violent disposition.

Matrimonial arrangements per se do not lead to factional conflicts. Kingroups do not act as corporate groups vying over spouses. Relations are not constituted from the sociocentric viewpoint of a controlled distribution of a scarce resource, but are produced case by case, albeit as part of a sequence of prior alliances (Fausto 1991:220–34). The arrangement itself is conceived to belong to the female sphere rather than the male, as an accord between women who exchange sons.[14] Women therefore perform a double role in alliances: They are the ones who circulate between men, but they also intervene in this circulation to benefit their sons and brothers. This form of negotiation prevents matrimonial arrangements from becoming a locus of conflict between men. Where contradictory and equally legitimate claims exist, men pretend to be uninterested and uninformed. Marital arrangements are indeed relevant to the future evolution of conflicts, but they are never the trigger that sets them off.

There is an aspect of arranged marriages that has a profound impact on future dispositions: the early closure of the matrimonial field. Many of these accords are made before the birth of the child as the outcome of an equation involving avuncular preference, the current strategies of the kingroups involved, and past exchange cycles. Although not every woman's marriage is decided at her birth, she is likely to be allocated a husband while still an infant. In 1993, in Apyterewa village, there were just nine single females from a total of ninety-one: Eight of them were less than five years old, and one was prepubescent. Hence, 90 percent of women and 99 percent of those older than five were unavailable, as shown in Table 3.3.

A woman's original civil status is married, meaning there is a man behind every woman. Prepubescent marriage is not a kind of engagement. No gradation is conceived to being married: One either is or is not. True, marital arrangements may include some comings and goings, since

---

13 For the Parakanã, the uncle's claim derives from the bond between "sister" and "brother," which forms the basis on which alliance is constructed. A sister is a credit for the future, a guarantee for one's own marriage.

14 This is particularly true in the case of a man's first marriage. He receives a wife when he is approximately ten years old. The arrangement is brokered by the couple's mothers, who in an ideal situation are mother and daughter. If the baby is a girl, the mother of her future husband picks the newborn off the ground and passes her to the mother: She "picks up" (-pyhyng) the child for her son.

Table 3.3. *Married Women Apyterewa and Maroxewara Villages*

Village (year)	Total Women (n)	Married (n)	Percentage	Total ≥5 Years (n)	Married ≥ 5 Years (n)	Percentage
Apyterewa (1993)	91	82	90.1%	67	66	98.9%
Maroxewara (1995)	66	56	84.8%	47	45	95.7%

new events may reshape them. However, the rearrangements always occur within an environment where the allocation of women is at each instant entirely given. Except for cases of widowhood, the only way a single man can obtain a wife for himself is by stealing one from somebody else.[15] Every divorce represents a subtraction: The lover is said to have "extracted" (*-ekyi*) the wife from her husband.

The closure of the matrimonial field thus implies an equivalence between the two strategies available to a bachelor to obtain spouse: capturing an enemy woman or stealing the wife of a male relative. The system is always opened up by an act of expropriation. The equivalence results from the fact that the matrimonial field is also closed externally; there is no supralocal village system where one can find a spouse. In such a limited universe, highly susceptible to demographic vicissitudes, the tension surrounding each person's marital destiny tends to increase.

There is still another element that intensifies this potentially conflictual scenario. Due to the avuncular-patrilateral regime, husbands tend to be much older than their wives. This means that each sexually mature man must wait some years before cohabiting with the wife he received through arranged marriage. In Apyterewa village, in 1993, the average age difference between spouses in their first marriages was ten years, the difference being equal to or over a decade in 56 percent of cases. More than half of the men began to cohabit or would cohabit with their wives after the age of twenty-five. Thus there is always a certain number of sexually mature young men without mature wives in a context where all the other mature women already cohabit with their husbands. Hence the sexual satisfaction of these youths depends on married women and any

---

15 The death of a married man makes his widow available again for marriage, but the situation is less conflictual, since some men are recognized to have a more legitimate claim over her. The most common forms of succession are: marriage to the brother, first-degree patrilateral parallel cousin or dead husband's son (HB, HFBS, and HS). Moreover, widows are less desirable as wives, either because they are older, and/or because they already have children who will have to be raised by the new husband (Fausto 1991:202).

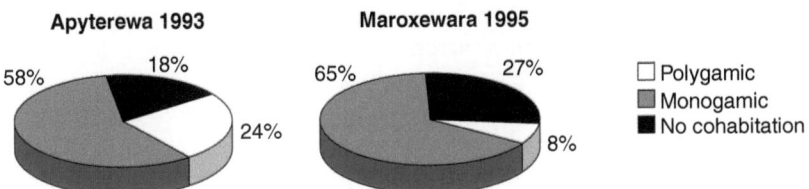

Figure 3.4. Forms of cohabitation of mature men in Apyterewa (1993) and
Maroxewara (1995).

more long-term affective ties are inevitably impeded by another, older
man. This scenario becomes more critical as a result of polygamy, which
produces a social scarcity of women even when the sex ratio is balanced.
In 1993, in Apyterewa village, this ratio among adults was slightly tilted
toward the female side (96 men:100 women), yet 18 percent of men
were not cohabiting with a woman.[16] In Maroxewara, where the sex ratio
among adults was 119:100, more than 25 percent of mature men were
living without a wife.

In Apyterewa village, 24 percent of men were cohabiting with more than
one wife, whereas 18 percent lived without any; in Maroxewara this ratio
was 8 percent to 27 percent (Figure 3.4). Polygamy marks out and accentu-
ates the only difference possible between men in this society. Among this
extremely egalitarian people, polygamy is conceived not as a privilege of a
few, but as an ideal pursued by every man. There is no social restriction on
attempting to acquire multiple wives, nor is there any guarantee for those
men who obtain them. On the contrary, it encourages wifeless youths to
contest the only significant asymmetry between men.

This tension tends to surface when a man's second wife reaches puberty
and there is a group of youths wishing to compete for her as a way of
anticipating their own matrimonial fate. For her part, when she reaches
puberty, the second wife in a polygamous marriage also has reasons for
avoiding consummation of her prearranged marriage, since she may see
little advantage in giving up her coetaneous lovers for a husband twenty
years her senior. Second marriage also instigates another dynamic between
cowives. When the balance tilts toward the youngest, as commonly happens, the older wife seeks out the company of bachelors. This produces a
situation with four structural actors with irreconcilable desires: Young
men seeking sexually mature women; pubescent girls who would like
to choose their partner; husbands who have waited many years for the
wife's first menses; and married women who fear being pushed into the

16 By adult, I refer to women ≥ 13 years and men ≥ 15. The global sex ratio was 113 men:100
women.

background. The question here is determining the structural consequences
of the interplay between these actors.

Hungry for Women

What sort of asymmetry does marriage produce between men? Why is
the bachelor's condition so difficult to bear, especially among the western
Parakanã? The model of the marriage relation is the swapping of game for
cooked food. The lack of a wife implies hunger, an association that repeatedly appears in narratives on the capture of foreign women. On seizing a
girl, the old Warepojooa said to his war partners: "Let's take my enemy, my
grandchildren, I suffered greatly living alone. I kept thinking: who's going
to roast tortoise liver for me?" (Iatora 1993: tape 38) For men, the suffering experienced in bachelorhood is expressed as a hunger for special parts
of game, such as the tortoise liver roasted by a wife as soon as the hunter
arrives from the forest. This is a selective hunger, an absence of privileged
access to certain kinds of food that symbolize the reciprocity of services
and affects found in marriage. Women also feel hunger: In polygynous
unions with a marked asymmetry between the wives, the preferred woman
receives the favorite parts of the animal game. Widowhood is also associated with hunger. A woman once told me that she had become a widow at
a young age, but had refused to marry again for some time while she still
pined for her dead husband. I asked her why she had eventually remarried:
"I was hungry," she answered.[17]

As the extended family is not an organic unit of production and consumption, a single person ends up living on the fringes of nuclear families, depending on the good will of their sisters or brothers to eat properly.
Marriage implies a greater autonomy as the couple comes to constitute a
new productive unit. Among the western Parakanã, sons-in-law do not work
for their fathers-in-law, and there is a very low coordination of economic
efforts.[18] Marriage thus produces a marked asymmetry between men with a
wife or wives and those without, and between cowives in polygamous unions.
Hence, the motivations of our actors: Men *and* women want to establish
a relation by exchanging services and constituting a new productive unit.

---

17 Although it remains true that the basic image of the relationship is the exchange of raw game for
cooked food, the wife also takes part in hunting expeditions and gathers wild foods with her husband. The heightened mobility of the western Parakanã not only led to a convergence of male and
female activities, but it also cut the time women spent cultivating and processing manioc.

18 The service provided by the husband before the wife's first menses is a service-*for*-the-bride, which
anticipates the male function of the conjugal relation. His only obligation is to supply her with
part of the game or fish he occasionally kills. He is said to be "nurturing" (-*pyro*) his wife, the gift
of food functioning as a public reaffirmation of a matrimonial arrangement whose consummation
remains some years in the future.

However, although any marriage is a sufficient condition for male autonomy, some marriages produce the only asymmetry possible between women. Cowives compete for their husband's preference, just as men compete for wives.[19] Polygamy is valued by men more as a way of guaranteeing autonomy than as a means of political differentiation, a response to the fear of losing what makes them equal. If possessing a mature wife marks a critical difference between men, it also defines what they are willing to fight over.

All this explains why young men may be eager to marry quickly, young girls may want to escape their older husband, married men may fight to keep their wives, and older married women may not wish to share their husbands. But under what circumstances do these wills turn into reality, and what are their consequences? As we have seen, there are just two types of second marriage for an adult: one implying an act of expropriation, the other involving an act of succession. No third way exists, since a woman is always the wife of someone. There is no divorce – a woman only abandons the home when another man is willing to "steal her." Female autonomy is curtailed by the cultural impossibility of remaining single.

At the same time, no man will "extract" (-ekyi) a woman from someone else against her will. A convergence between male and female desires is needed for a dispute to be generated between two men. The intensity of the clash depends on the circumstances and the husband's attitude. The least dramatic situation involves the theft of an older woman from a polygamic man. In this case, the husband is unlikely to risk an escalation of the conflict. However, when a younger woman is involved, the situation tends to deteriorate: As well as beautiful and desirable, pubescent girls allow a man to initiate a new reproductive cycle. In these cases, the husband will not let others take his wife without a fight, unless he is at a clear disadvantage. When the correlation of forces is unfavorable, the best option is to abandon the village.

Les Fleurs du Mal

From the end of the nineteenth century until the 1960s, no internal conflict ruptured the fragmentary unity of the western Parakanã. Although dispersed, they continued to represent themselves as a unit. In the 1960s, though, this cohesion evaporated. A dispute over women led to two deaths and several injuries. Pressed by the influx of whites and the lack of enemies, they abandoned the Pacajá territory. Thereafter the group's unity was threatened various times: Kingroups opposed each other, attacks were

---

19 Men say it is difficult to satisfy two wives and they often end up fighting. Some women try to prevent their husband from marrying again or treat the younger wife so badly that she will desist from the marriage.

planned and almost executed, kin became enemies, and the separations multiplied. This was the mood reigning in the years prior to pacification and indeed continued after. Understanding this process means answering two questions: What were the general reasons for the outbreak of conflicts? And what were the underlying mechanisms that determined their form?

Here we can recall some of our findings from Chapter 1. Between the end of the nineteenth century and the first half of the 1950s, the western Parakanã carried out more than twenty attacks against enemies and captured more than twenty women. Warfare allowed most men to become killers. During the turbulence of adolescence, men went on war raids, entered posthomicide seclusion, and, in some cases, acquired an enemy wife. Warfare offered young men a way to develop into adults, an alternative path that did not necessarily involve marriage. Being a killer and passing through ritual seclusion was not a necessary or even sufficient condition for a youth's social maturation, but it was one of the ways for them to become adults. Between the mid-1950s and 1960s, however, the Pacajá-Tocantins interfluvial region was devoid of enemies. All the warpaths had petered out for the 1940s generation.[20] No war also meant no influx of women to alleviate the bottlenecks in the Parakanã matrimonial system. This was part of a long-term trend: From the beginning of the twentieth century to the end of the 1920s, eleven women had been captured; between 1930 and 1945, another nine were taken. From then until the mid-1960s, only one captive was incorporated into the group. The framework sustaining the warfare practice of the western Parakanã during the twentieth century was starting to crumble.

Moreover, the whites were moving ever closer. They approached the group's territory, threatening the core that had allowed them to combine expansion and contraction. Their dispersed unity depended on both the centrifugal movement toward warfare and a common reference point. The manioc swiddens were perhaps less important in dietary terms than in marking the group's unity and continuity. Thus as the 1960s began, the western Parakanã found themselves at a crossroads: If there were no more enemies, warfare, and capture, trekking was also threatened by the possibility of no longer being able to return to a shared starting point, making their previous "unity in dispersion" less and less viable. It was in this context that the conflicts over women turned critical and their escalation became unavoidable.

The largest of these conflicts occurred in the mid-1960s, when they were already beginning to abandon the Pacajá territory. It was the dry

20 The remaining alternative was to kill the whites who were starting to infringe on the group's territory. Yet we had been always imperfect victims: On one hand, shooting us causes "softness" (*tawera*) and "stupefies" (*-moawaipam*) the killer; on the other hand, it seemed unwise to kill us if we were the ones giving them the commodities they wanted.

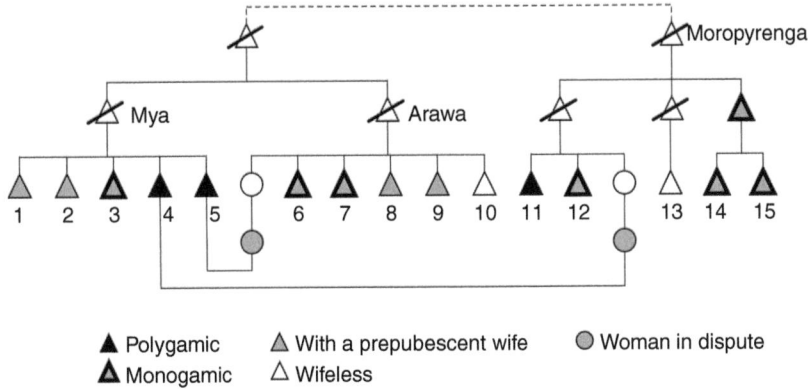

▲ Polygamic   △ With a prepubescent wife   ◯ Woman in dispute
△ Monogamic   △ Wifeless

Figure 3.5. Marriage situation on the eve of the conflict.

season. Almost the entire group was united in a forest camp for the bamboo clarinets festival. The ritual has a strong sexual connotation associated with (usually inconsequential) extramarital affairs. This time, though, events took a different course. A young bachelor's desire for a pubescent girl acquired collective proportions, since, at a deeper level, it amounted to the climax of a long-running unequal process of allocating women: A sibling group (Mya's sons) had been much more successful matrimonially than their first- and third-degree patrilateral parallel cousins, thanks to their affinal relationship with another patriline.[21] These affines had yielded Mya's sons a number of women, which were not reciprocated, thus creating even another unbalanced matrimonial situation (see Figure 3.5).[22]

This was the state of the alliance network when two of Mya's sons' wives entered into puberty. This set the explosive context for what I have previously described in structural terms: Some older men were in polygamic cohabitation, while other, younger men remained unmarried. This situation was aggravated by the genealogical position of the girls: One of them was ZD to one of the bachelors (m10); the other was FBDD to the other one (m13).

The crisis was looming when the kingroups gathered in the mid-1960s. The plan already hatched, the killers invited their victims to go hunting: M10 accompanied his cousin (m3), and shot him through his shoulder.

---

21 The patrilines are informal lines, unnamed, and noncorporate, formed by groups of male siblings from different generations linked by patrifilial ties. They are the epiphenomena of a marriage network with limited colateral reach and shallow vertical depth, but which may function as exchange units (Fausto 1991:220–49).

22 This unmatching was the result of a series of historical and structural facts, which I have fully analysed in Fausto (2001:212–15).

The victim managed to flee. Not so lucky as his brother, m1 was shot dead by m14. M2 was wounded by m12 and fled into the forest. He was pursued by many men and was killed by a volley of arrows. The attackers broke camp and departed westward, taking five of the seven wives of Mya's sons. The surviving sons returned to the site of the killings, buried the dead, and left in pursuit of their kin. They recovered their own wives, but not those of their dead brothers. The plan was successful. The attackers managed to steal three women, including the two prepubescent wives of the killed men. Men 10 and 13 acquired wives, whereas m11 obtained a second one. There was thus a forced transfer of wives from Mya's patriline to their patrilateral parallel cousins, reequilibrating the allocation of women.

The Parakanã preference for marriage at a minimum distance and the nondispersion of alliance sometimes leads to a very short cycle that ends up isolating certain patrilines, forming an endogamic nexus within the group itself. This is a way of guaranteeing the maternal uncle's right over his niece, since it avoids the separation between brothers and sisters in a virilocal regime. Thus the very structure of alliance leads to an isolation of certain agnatic lines, which compete with each other for the most advantageous affinal relations. In the case at hand, the line of rupture fell between very close ties, splitting first-degree patrilateral parallel cousins. This fact corresponds to a specific moment in the development cycle of the patrilines, extending across three generations: When one or both of the grandparents (mutual brothers) has already died and the matrimonial fate of the grandchildren begins to be defined, the tension between FBSs grows. It was precisely at this moment that the capture of foreign women intervened, enabling older brothers to acquire wives for their younger brothers or for their sons. The abductions served to open up the matrimonial system and quelled potential conflicts. Political unity depended thus on a matrimonial dynamic that was basically sustained with a constant influx of foreign women; the group had been formed by capture and had made it an essential component for its own continuity as a political unit

The Public Sphere

For the western Parakanã throughout the twentieth century, dispersion of kingroups was a mode of social organization as much as concentration: It served the objectives of hunting and warfare, and it also allayed internal tensions. In the absence of institutionalized mechanisms for mediating conflicts, intimidation and separation were the only alternatives. Thus although the concentration of alliances between patrilines was the long-term process that determined splits, and although the social scarcity of women was the immediate cause behind the irruption of conflicts, their form and outcome were linked to the absence of broader institutions organizing society according to principles other than kinship. All politics was focused on determining marriage as there was no political sphere separated from kinship. This, however, was not the case among the eastern Parakanã. What then had happened to them in the hundred years following the split? How did they manage to mediate conflicts in order to stay together as a single political unit?

Making Conversation

The answer to this question lies in a historical process in which a public sphere was constituted in close association with headmanship and women were clearly excluded from public affairs. The locus of such process was a singular and unique space: the *tekatawa*, the "living place," which functioned as the group's political center, albeit spatially off-center. The *tekatawa* is a cleared area, without any construction, positioned at some distance from the dwellings. The physical separation is taken as a function of the opposition between the men and the women. The distance ensures women cannot hear the men's speech and songs. The emphasis is on hearing since there is little to see: It is not the movement of bodies that animates the *tekatawa*, but the voices. It is the place for conversation, the speech-work performed by the headmen, or, more precisely, enabled by them, who are defined by the eastern Parakanã as those who "make conversation for us" (*oapo morongeta oreopé*).

During my fieldwork, just after sunset, the Tapi'pya headman, Arakytá, then aged seventy, would walk out of his house silently, shotgun in hand, winding his way through the narrow alleys toward the *tekatawa*. His son-in-law Ywyrapytá, the oldest Apyterewa, would soon follow. Little by little, other men arrived, gun in hand, looking for their places. Each man occupied a predetermined space according to their moiety and their age. The men formed into a rough circle: The Tapipy'a sat on the east side, the Apyterewa and Wyrapina on the west. The dualism was also represented in the leadership: The oldest man from each moiety occupied a central position in the *tekatawa*, facing the north with other senior men (*moro'yroa*) behind him.[23] Clustered immediately in front of them were the youths (*awarame*) with or without children. Finally, at either side of the headmen

23 It is not entirely clear when this pattern of dual leadership mirroring moiety segmentation emerged. After the split, headmanship fell to an Apyterewa man called Ajooa. Subsequently it was occupied by Ajooa's brother's son, Awapy'a, an Apyterewa, who was killed by the western Parakanã at the end of the 1930s. Ten years later, the same fate befell Ijianga, a Wyrapina who occupied the leadership after the death of Awapy'a. In the beginning of the 1950s, Orowo'á, one of Jarawa's son, gained prominence, and I suppose it was at this moment that the dual pattern emerged. Orowo'a prestige grew over the following years, reinforced by the demographic success of his agnates. After his death, the leadership finally fell to Arakytá.

were the full adults (*awaramekwera*). The meetings lasted until almost midnight. Nobody left the locale before Arakytá stood up and said: "peje, jaken" ("let's go and sleep"). He was responsible for sensing the moment when the conversation had died down and the group wanted to disperse.

The *tekatawa* layout expressed the symmetry between moieties and the asymmetry between age categories. This internally differentiated assembly was conceived of as a male collectivity prohibited to women. Auditory secrecy was essential for constituting such a unit, through which men appropriated the representation of collective actions and relations in such a way that the group appeared as a single male collectivity, eclipsing all cross-sex relations. In the *tekatawa*, the group was posited as a totality through the exclusion of women, who could only be present through their absence.

What was the secret that the men keep? What did they talk about in the *tekatawa*? They talked about everything, except women. Seemingly chaotically – with voices overlapping in a discourse collectively composed on the skill of the headmen – they recounted the day's events, swapped information on hunting, discussed the sales of produce in town, and talked about the need for joint work. The tone oscillated between joking banter and guarded talk, depending on the occasion. Sometimes the group fell silent to listen to a myth narrated by one of the headmen. The *tekatawa* had such pedagogical function: It was conceived as the appropriate place for the collective transmission of the group's historical, mythical, and ritual knowledge. The role of the headman was to crystallize a collective memory and retransmit it. The difference in prestige was based on the leader's capacity to accumulate memory and present it in spoken form. It is not enough to be *moro'yroa* (old) in order to be a *moro'yroa* (headman): One needs to contain knowledge and be capable of animating this content through the flow of words.[24]

Thus although both Arakytá and Ywyrapytá were recognized as headmen, it was the former who had the qualities needed to perform the task, lending him an additional authority. During my research, whenever I asked a question my interlocutor was unable to answer, he would say: "the *capitão* knows."[25] Generally, this was true: not only because Arakytá was actually a knowledgeable man, but also because the others could not know as much

24 There is no specific term for headman. Moro'yroa can perhaps be analyzed as *moro* ("relating to humans") and *yroa* ("container"). Among the eastern Parakanã, the term designated both a leader and men and women with grandchildren. For the western Parakanã, the term did not connote prestige, meaning simply "old." When the western Parakanã wanted to transmit the idea of authority (for example, when they referred to the president of Funai), they used the term *moropetenga*, meaning "one who strikes people," equally applied to great warriors.

25 The introduction of the Portuguese term *capitão* (captain), applied exclusively to Arakytá, dates from the time of contact.

as him. This social division of mnemonic work founded a political economy of memory. Arakytá knew the genealogy of the group from after the split, knew the narratives and the most suitable way of narrating them, remembered many songs of the past, and so forth. His speech was distinguished by its form as well as its content. Indeed, only older men knew how to "speak well" (-je'engato), and they continually corrected the younger men. The construction of generational asymmetry, as well as the tenuous political hierarchy, was rooted in this capacity for verbal expression.[26]

A headman had a few privileges, which included a special access to game meat and wives. Polygamy was not exclusive to headmanship, but its occurrence did comply with a logic of prestige: The headmen and their sons had more chances of acquiring another wife than those without a leadership role. Hunters, for their part, used to give a portion of the killed game to the headmen. In Arakytá's house there was a constant flux of meat that benefited his family and those of his sons. This privilege was seen by the younger men as a fair exchange, the necessary price for a tekatawa to be possible. Given the obligation to hold the meeting every night, the headmen should not be involved in subsistence activities. There was thus a close association between headmanship and the tekatawa, whose functioning depended on gender and age asymmetries.

The description of how the tekatawa functioned among the eastern Parakanã in the 1990s holds some lessons for understanding the political life of Amazonian indigenous peoples in general. The Parakanã case enables us to glimpse the historical process through which a public space was institutionalized and turned into a device for countering political factionalism. Such space was neither the mere continuation of a solidly established tradition nor a purely out-of-the-blue invention. The tekatawa as a ceremonial space and a space of male sociability is found among other Tupi-Guarani peoples in the region, but without the functions observed among the eastern Parakanã. The Asurini, for example, use it exclusively on ritual occasions, since political decisions "are taken in the sphere of the houses, without the village being activated as a whole unit. Politics is produced in dispersion" (Andrade 1992:48). This seems to have been the case too among the western Parakanã in the past: The tekatawa was a male space used to prepare for rituals. The nocturnal meetings followed the ceremonial calendar and were primarily linked to the transmission of songs heard in dreams by the older men. The eastern Parakanã potentialized these features and conferred a new meaning to the tekatawa, moving back and forth from song to speech, from ritual to political life, and from the asymmetric

26 Arakytá had been trained by his brother Orowo'á, a man twenty years older who had led the group for two decades and died soon after contact. Arakytá never attributed his knowledge to ancestors or tradition: The source was always his brother. He never tried to sacralize or dehistoricize it.

relation between song-givers and receivers to that between the headmen and their followers.

In constituting the *tekatawa* as a political arena, the eastern Parakanã institutionalized a social space focused on internal relations. Traditionally, as a space for transmitting ritual songs, the *tekatawa* was constituted in the relation between interiority and exteriority, enabling the external politics of ritual life. Even today, everyone goes to the *tekatawa* armed, since this is still a place for linking the inside and the outside. The eastern Parakanã, however, added to it a further feature: that of being a point of internal articulation. They made it into a public sphere of debate, founded on a discursive modality opposed to the intimidating speech of warriors.

The Parakanã oppose two forms of verbal interaction: "conversation" (*morongeta*), which seeks to convince, and "strong-speech" (*-je'engahy*), which looks to bend the will of others by intimidation.[27] The eastern Parakanã conceive the *tekatawa* as the space for conversation par excellence, citing it as the reason for their internal peace. In claiming this, they project an image of violence and discord onto all those peoples who fail to hold meetings – in particular, their ex-kin.[28] They did not model the headmanship on the war leader, but rather on the figure of the mediator, the person who enables dialogue. The transformation of the *tekatawa* is part of a wider political process that aims to build an internal consensus founded on a decentered sharing of arguments.[29]

If this was the way the eastern Parakanã came to deal with factionalism and conflict after the split, what can we say about the western Parakanã political form? Do they simply lack an instance for presenting the group as a totality, or did they actively work to exorcise it? In the decades following the split, the *tekatawa* as a differentiated physical space was progressively diluted, becoming merely a virtual setting in which rituals are prepared. Its decline saw the disappearance of a neutral space, equidistant from the

27 The suffix *-ahy* indicates intensity and efficacy. The verb *-je'eng* ("to speak"), even without the suffix, may have the connotation of a harsh interpellation. *Morongeta* is the nominal form of *-porongeta*, "talk." The term is composed of the suffix *-moro*, relating to human beings, and the verb *-mongeta*, which can be glossed as "speak-tame." When a person needs to be calmed and pacified, this taming speech is used; when the need is to impose oneself on someone else, strong speech is employed.

28 The eastern Parakanã were highly sensitive to any kind of discord expressed in the *tekatawa*. In 1992, I witnessed a brief debate concerning which production group would have priority in using the rice-planting machinery. At the time, it seemed to me an appropriate discussion for the nocturnal meetings. After all, would this not be the place for each group to put forward their claims and reach an agreement? The following day, though, a youth came to tell me: "We messed things up in the *tekatawa*" (*oromoron tekataipé*). I replied with the laissez-faire typical of the western Parakanã: "That's the way it is" (*einon-té*). But he replied emphatically: *einon'y'ym*, "That's not the way."

29 I call it "descentered" to avoid conflating it with the liberal-democratic model of interaction between rational agents in the public sphere. The *tekatawa* is based on other discursive practices and implies another conception of the person (see also Graham 1993 for the Shavante).

dwellings and family groups, that had once served as a place for men to gather and welcome visitors. As the group gradually unraveled throughout the twentieth century, the positing of a legitimate sphere of representation for collective actions became a remote possibility, which the social actors today look to recover in their political practice.

Soon after contact, the Funai Post started to be used as an alternative *tekatawa*. In the western Parakanã's Apyterewa village, every night the families drifted toward a covered area flanked by a half wall. Women and children remained outside, while the men talked among themselves and with the Funai employees inside. The younger men quickly perceived that the challenges imposed by the surrounding Brazilian society required presenting themselves, internally and externally, as a political community. They asked the head of the Post to help them build a house in a supposedly neutral location so they could hold nightly meetings. Another covered area with a half wall and electric lighting was built between the Post and the village. The effort was in vain. Nobody met there, because the place was associated with those who had taken the initiative to construct it. In the mid-1990s, some young men who could speak Portuguese began to proclaim themselves "*cacique* assistants," naming an adult from their kingroup as "*cacique*."[30] However, although their wish was to represent the community vis-à-vis the whites, they were unable to assume internal leadership and complained about the failure of people to turn up to the meetings: "The elders," they told me, "don't make the conversation for us."

Defusing the Timebomb

The incipient hierarchization and centralization of the eastern Parakanã contrasts with the transformations seen among the western group. The unity in fragmentation, the dispersal of the trekking groups and the village's waning importance were accompanied by the disappearance of any generational or political asymmetries. The *tekatawa* itself, where the men gathered occasionally to hear the speech and singing of the elders, gradually vanished as a defined physical space, surviving today merely as a provisional space between the houses used while preparing for rituals. The sociability of the encampments was projected onto village life: The village became an aggregate of hunting bands, an informal set of kingroups. This shift also had repercussions for gender relations by reducing the political and economic asymmetry between men and women. All the asymmetric relations founded on kinship became deemphasized, leading to a growing equality in

---

30 The term *cacique* comes from a sixteenth-century Taino word that served to designate their chiefs. It was generically employed by Spanish conquerors to name all political authorities (chiefs, headmen, leaders) among South American indigenous peoples.

all sectors of social life, a change that was accompanied by a reduction in the opportunities for public recognition, prestige, and authority.

Among the eastern group, the sociopolitical transformations were also accompanied by changes in gender relations, but in the reverse direction. Male and female capacities and work became more sharply distinguished. At the same time, male solidarity was carefully constructed, less from an ideal of hypermasculinity associated with warfare and more from an effort to avoid internal conflict and gain greater control over female work. Social segmentation, leadership, and the *tekatawa* performed a key role in shaping these dynamics and preventing the group's fragmentation. Factionalism did not threaten the eastern Parakanã's unity at any time during the twentieth century. So how did they deal with the problem of allocating women without making recourse to capturing foreign women? How did they defuse the time bomb in their alliance system?

There was a practical and ideological deemphasizing of the rivalry between men over women, which today appears as a discursive veil, a semiconscious mechanism for denying the reality of competition. This veil is even projected over the past and the interpretation of historical facts. None of my eastern Parakanã interlocutors admitted that the nineteenth-century split had involved the dispute over a woman, something that the western Parakanã always told me. They explained the clash as a sort of collective frenzy provoked by homicidal action: Moakara's killers had "lost their minds" (*-pikajym*), treating their kin like enemies. The same deemphasizing of male competition for women occurs in relation to actual marriages. As we saw, among the western Parakanã divorce is represented as an act of expropriation: A man inevitably takes the wife of another. The reference to the ex-husband is obligatory since the verb "to take" requires two arguments. Someone takes something from someone: *oekyi* [female name] *ijohi*, "he took [x] from him." In contrast, the eastern Parakanã say that the husband "threw away" (*-etyng*) the wife – that he dispensed with her – without the connotation that she was taken by a third party. She is neither taken nor given, but abandoned. In both groups, the initiative is conceived to be male, but in inverse ways: For the western bloc, men dispute and steal women; for the eastern bloc, the husband relinquishes a right, he loses interest. Whereas the former manifest the antagonistic nature of marriage, the latter deemphasize the involvement of an external agent in the rupture of the matrimonial relation.

Attitudes concerning adultery also differ. Among the western Parakanã, any measures taken in response to a spouse's love affairs are slight, since extreme action may lead to a lethal clash between men. Day-to-day infidelities are widely tolerated. When the betrayed husband wishes to express his anger and discomfort, he cuts the cords of his wife's hammock. Yet women sometimes respond the most violently, slashing their husband with a knife or a bamboo blade. The scars covering a man's skin bear witness to his amorous adventures. Among the eastern Parakanã, the opposite occurs: A husband's violent intimidation of his wife, which sometimes leads to physical aggression, is generally tolerated. The most frequent response is to cut off tufts of her hair with a machete. This injures her scalp and leaves her too ashamed to wander around in public. To hide the scars, they – usually recently married girls – wind cloths over their heads until their hair grows back. Responsibility for the adultery is attributed to the woman, thereby eliding the involvement of the other man. The husband's violence is channeled toward his wife and away from the relationship between men.

In practical terms, two elements dampen male rivalry over women among the eastern Parakanã. On one hand, the matrimonial field is relatively open compared to the western Parakanã case: Only a minority of the girls between four and twelve years old are married.[31] On the other hand, unequal access to women is mediated by other kinds of asymmetries based on age and political factors. These asymmetries are reflected, for example, in the distribution of polygynous marriages. In 1995, there were four men with three wives (all adult) in Paranatinga: Arakytá, the headman and the oldest Tapi'pya; Ywyrapytá, also a headman and the oldest Apyterewa; Inataijona, the second-oldest Wyrapina man; and Ja'e'oma, the son of the deceased headman Orowo'á. These were followed by six men with two adult wives, including two sons of Arakytá, and two sons of Orowo'á. Finally, there were three men with an adult wife and a prepubertal one, all of them considered young leaders of the production groups. The allocation of women was determined by the structure of prestige, benefiting not only the headmen but also their descendents. The privilege of headmen's sons depends, though, on exercising authority effectively. Hence the political predominance of the Tapi'pya over the last four decades explains the fact that only one Apyterewa man and one Wyrapina man were polygynous.

Nothing similar is found among the western Parakanã. First, it is rare to have three adult wives simultaneously, and impossible to keep them for

---

31 Two factors combined to generate this contrast: the first is mobility. In an avuncular and virilocal regime, one of the key questions is how to ensure the maternal uncle's privilege; i.e., how to ensure that a spatially distanced sister becomes the source for a future marriage. This was less of a problem for the eastern Parakanã, but for the western Parakanã, mobility created a greater distance. During periods of trekking, brothers-in-law were often in different bands, meaning that a brother and sister could live much of their lives apart. Under these conditions, prepubescent marriage was an extra guarantee of the future return of a wife. The second factor is a response to this problem. Anticipating marriage is a way of recovering "credits" in a deferred system where no other kind of compensation is available. The anticipation manifests the desire to shorten the temporal hiatus involved in avuncular-patrilateral exchange: When a sister leaves her birth home, she is already able to produce a daughter and wife. Prepubescent marriage seems to function as a way of regulating a system involving deferred exchange and virilocality but no sociocentric segmentation. Among the eastern Parakanã, this regulatory function was performed by the exogamic moieties.

Table 3.4. *Matrimonial Situation of Men over 14 Years Old in Each of the Blocs*

	Polygamic	Monogamic	Wifeless	Total	Sex-ratio 1	Sex-ratio 2*
Western Parakanã	14 (17.1)	50 (61.0)	18 (21.9)	82 (100)	113	105
Eastern Parakanã	10 (17.2)	33 (56.9)	15 (25.9)	58 (100)	99	92

* sex-ratio 1: entire population; sex-ratio 2: men (≥15;) and women (≥13).

very long. Second, polygamy is not based on a hierarchy of prestige; rather, it depends on the composition of the sibling group. The initial condition to polygyny is to have sisters who produce wives (and brothers who help keep them). As an example, we can take the matrimonial destiny of the sons of Jy'oa, killed by the eastern Parakanã in the 1930s. Awokoa and Koria had no sisters and were therefore forced to try their luck in warfare: The first was married to an Asurini woman whom he captured himself in the 1940s. At the start of the 1970s, he gained a second wife, a widow no longer able to have children, but his first wife was killed soon after by the Xikrin. Koria, for his part, married three foreign women in succession (all eastern Parakanã), and at the end of the 1970s, he adopted an orphan girl to "nurture" (-*pyro*) and become his wife. In 1993, after fifteen years of waiting, this girl gave him a daughter. Sisterless, Koria and Awokoa had to make their own fate through capture, depending only on their individual capacity to acquire and keep wives.

Among the eastern Parakanã, on the contrary, the insertion of polygamy in a hierarchy of prestige limits the rivalry between men over women. The competition is shifted to another field, which confers legitimacy to the inequality in the access to wives. This explains how different sociopolitical dynamics were produced within the two blocs, despite the similarity in the matrimonial situation. As it can be see in Table 3.4, the distribution is fairly similar in relative terms. The eastern Parakanã situation is potentially more prone to conflict, though, given that the population has a higher percentage of adult men without a wife, a greater concentration of women in polygamous marriages, and a more favorable sex ratio. Nonetheless, the matrimonial asymmetries among them do not result in disputes between men over women and are not expressed as open conflicts. Although polygamy in this case too produces a social scarcity of wives, it is socially sanctioned and legitimated.

We also need to consider the young bachelors' perspective: Why are young eastern Parakanã men not in a rush to get married? Three factors help explain the differences in motivation. First, the matrimonial field is not completely closed by prepubertal marriages. There are various girls approaching their first menses who have yet to acquire a husband and who could, therefore, marry the bachelor. Second, young people are introduced into the productive structure, which is independent of marriage, since boys make up part of the production groups and participate in economic life. Other incentives derive from insertion in the monetary economy through the sale of swidden produce and Brazil nuts in the nearby towns. Having the money and power to purchase commodities is an important stimulus for young men, even bachelors, to take part in economic activities.

Finally, young men take part in the universe of male relations, organized by an asymmetric logic based on differences in age and knowledge. Intimidating a rival to steal his wife would involve throwing into question the male solidarity woven in the *tekatawa* and the very authority of headmen to mediate conflicts. Being married or unmarried is not the only possible asymmetry in this society, meaning that it does not define what people are willing to fight over. The rivalry for women is not conceived as the main reason for conflicts, even when they are effectively involved. It is the structure of prestige that organizes and confers meaning on the asymmetry found in marriage, and not the contrary.[32] The defusing of matrimonial rivalry is linked, therefore, to male solidarity expressed in the *tekatawa*, where individual conflicts are converted into relations mediated by the male collectivity. This was achieved by excluding women and correlated with a heightened distinction between male and female activities, which is manifested at all levels of eastern Parakanã social life.

When we compare the two Parakanã blocs, it becomes clear that there is a strong affinity between the transformations taking place in gender relations and those unfolding in the economy and politics. The western Parakanã show a greater plasticity in terms of gender. In the productive sphere, this is connected to the low importance of agricultural work and the production of manioc flour, which freed women, allowing them to accompany men and take part in the hunting trips. The dispersion of the trekking groups, for their part, led to a more intimate and less formalized sociability in the encampments. The *tekatawa* was gradually incorporated by the dwelling space until it became located, as today, between the houses. The aural secrecy that surrounded the ceremonial space was abandoned. Previously solely male, the rituals acquired a female version that, although held less frequently, comprise the symmetrical inversion of those performed by men. Women actually became incorporated into warfare, accompanying warriors to the outskirts of the enemy village or even handling bows and arrows and becoming killers, as occurred at the end of the 1960s in one of the attacks on the Akwa'awa.

---

32 Here and in the preceding section, I build my argument in contrast with Collier and Rosaldo's (1981) article on politics in brideservice societies. For a closer look, see Fausto (2001:201–10), and for a similar argument in another ethnographic context, see Kelly (1993:415–525).

The eastern Parakanã took an opposite path, leading to less plasticity in gender-marked activities, an increased asymmetry between the sexes, and the institutionalization of a sphere of sociability barred to women. The emergence of a political arena where ritual knowledge is transmitted ended up excluding women from it. Ceremonial life became concentrated in male hands, and the possibility of a rite being held from the female perspective, as occurs among the western Parakanã, is inconceivable. In the economic sphere, patrisegmentation, combined with virilocality, reinforced the asymmetry between the sexes, allowing a group of men united by filiation to exert greater control over women's work. Finally, there was an exacerbation of sexual antagonism, expressed as a diffuse ideology on the virtues of masculinity.

To better explore the effect of these transformations on the dynamic of internal conflicts among the eastern Parakanã, I turn now to three historical events.

Conflicting Dynamics

The first conflict occurred in the 1920s and is associated with sorcery accusations. The second took place at the beginning of the 1960s, when Kynyjoa, brother of the then chief Orowo'a, killed two men. The third concerns the ambition of a young leader who at the start of the 1990s tried to ascend the ladder of prestige and authority, in the context of Arakytá's succession. I analyze the cases in chronological order.

In the 1920s and 1930s, the system of exogamic moieties was taking shape. Jarawa had received two women from his captors and eventually reciprocated with his own daughters. The enemy boy had become the pivot of a series of affinal relations. However, it was impossible for him to satisfy all seven brothers of his wives, since he had only four daughters, which provoked a dispute between brothers (real and classificatory). One of these men demanded one of Jarawa's daughters, but was passed over in favor of his youngest brother. Jarawa died soon after, struck down by a sudden fever. His death was attributed to the man who had "spoken strongly" with him, asking in vain for a wife. Jarawa's sons did not seek revenge, though. On the contrary, they sought to assuage the tension by distributing meat to their affines, thus reconstituting their alliance.

I call attention to two points. First, although the conflict involved a woman, it was channeled by the relation between affines (rather than between agnatic kin) and organized by the opposition between moieties. Second, the hostility did not lead to an open clash between the opponents, but rather to sorcery accusations. Here such accusations have a higher sociopolitical yield than among the western Parakanã: On one hand, it is a form of engaging in politics without the use of material weapons; on the other, by becoming absorbed into a dualist logic, the politics of sorcery acquires a greater impact than when dispersed into multiple perspectives. The accusatory politics of sorcery is the hidden face of the politics of conversation in the *tekatawa* and of the male consensus.

The second moment of discord, occurring in the 1960s, has distinct features and provides other lessons. The context is different: The moiety system was fully operational; the Tapi'pya had ceased to be a minority and were politically dominant. They were then living near the headwaters of the Bacuri River in a village later known as Kynyjoa'atawera, "the village from which Kynyjoa departed." Kynyjoa was also Jarawa's son and, along with his three brothers, Awajowa, Orowo'a, and Arakytá, was part of the most prestigious kingroup at the time. One day, he picked up his bow and fired a lethal shot at A'ia, a Wyrapina. Then he attacked Wajomaré, the headman Orowo'a's son, killing him too (see Figure 3.6). He subsequently escaped, accompanied by three of his sons. The young men wanted to pursue Kynyjoa, but the older men told them to wait. At the end of the rainy season, Orowo'a allowed them to leave in search of the killer. And so they left. It was Wajomaré's brother who found them: "We first came across traces of them. I then went on alone. I walked along the river shore, still alone. One of my small children had just died and this had left me fairly wild." He spotted them near the headwaters of the Paranatinga River. He killed two of them, but Kynyjoa and one of his sons managed to escape. They then abandoned the eastern Parakanã territory, settling far to the west on the sources of the Bacajá River. It was there that Kynyjoa met his death at the end of the 1970s, killed by western Parakanã warriors.

Comprehending the motives behind the conflict is far from easy. Why on earth did Kynyjoa suddenly kill his ZS, A'ia, and his BS, Wajomaré? People answered this question in two ways. The most frequent version referred to the special condition of the killer's psyche: Kynyjoa had killed many enemies and, affected by these deaths, had become prone to violence, including against his own kin.[33] The second answer was that women had lied to Kynyjoa, gossiping about the infidelity of his youngest brother's wife. In this version, Kynyjoa had only intended to kill A'ia, an affine, but ended up losing his mind (*-pikajym*) and shooting Wajomaré too.

Even without elucidating the precise reasons for the conflict, there are some points to observe. The first concerns the explanations given. Once more there is a woman involved, but this fact is not clearly explicated. Either Kynyjoa's behavior is attributed to his condition as a killer, or it is admitted that something else is involved, but this something is "women's lies." The second point refers to the structure of the conflict in which the

---

33 Kynyjoa's life history was indeed shaped by warfare. Two of his wives and a daughter were captured by the western Parakanã, and his firstborn son was killed by the same enemies.

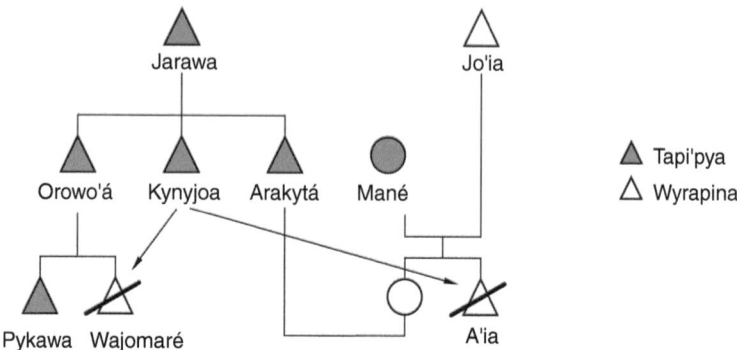

Figure 3.6. Internal conflict among the eastern Parakanã.

primary opposition is between affines: As in the previous example, Kynyjoa first attacked a wife-giver. Finally, the dynamic after the killings is remarkable: The community does not split into kingroups but exiles the killer. The outcome might have been different had Kynyjoa not killed Wajomaré, a Tapi'pya like himself, making the support of his agnatic kin unviable. In all events, it is the group as a whole that takes a stance against the killer and organizes the revenge, which falls – not by chance – to another Tapi'pya. This dynamic depends on the existence of the *tekatawa*, a space where the community is represented as a political unit.

The third situation I wish to analyze is more recent. It concerns the role of young leaders and Arakytá's succession. As we saw in Chapter 2, among the eastern Parakanã, work is organized in production groups centered on an older man and represented by a younger leader. The latter is responsible for mediating with the agents from the Indigenous Post and employees housed in the town of Tucuruí. The category *líderes*, hierarchically inferior to that of *capitão*, resulted from the crystallization of preferential relationships with young men who acted as linguistic and cultural mediators at the start of pacification. Through this experience, some youths rose in prestige within the group.

In 1992, despite the existence of five different production groups, only two men aged around thirty years old were recognized – by the whites and the group alike – as prominent leaders. One of them was the headman's son (m1), the other was the grandson of the former headman (m2). For a while, they maintained an equilibrium between them. However, the rapid rise of m2 began to create problems. In 1989, his production group was formed by nineteen individuals (DAM 1989); three years later, there were thirty-two. His group had grown by around 70 percent compared to the 20 percent increase of m1 group. Aware of his strength, m2 looked to extend his capacity for liaising with the exterior, sponsoring the first-ever visit by the western Parakanã and the Asurini to Paranatinga village. For this, he counted on the support of the Parakanã Program as well as the group's approval. They built houses for the visitors and organized an intense program of football games, dancing, and singing.

The Program's truck brought the visitors. The activities were frenetic: dancing all night, football under a blazing sun during the day. The politics of alliance pervaded all the activities, and parents sought out foreign sons-in-law from whom they could extract services. Local leaders such as m2 planned to build alliances with men from other villages, offering their daughters in marriage in order to consolidate supportive relations. However, none of these attempts bore fruit. Instead, the main outcome of the visit was the deterioration of the relation between m1 and m2. The latter worked intensely to feed the visitors, but food was scarce and the visitors numerous. In these circumstances, the Asurini ended up leaving earlier than planned. M2 saw his projects thwarted and blamed m1, since it had been up to the latter to look after the Asurini. Given the tension between the two leaders, it was decided that the matter should be discussed in the *tekatawa*. Late afternoon, m2's son-in-law came to advise me that I should not go to the nocturnal meeting because they were going to "make a mess." Next day, the village awoke empty and remained quiet virtually all day. At dusk I met m2's son-in-law again. I asked him what had happened. Good humouredly, he replied in Portuguese that the community had decided to collect 200 tortoises for m2 and 100 for the *capitão* for them both to distribute. I never found out what happened in the *tekatawa* that night, nor do I know if there had been any distribution of tortoises afterward. Nobody mentioned the subject ever again.

The political process continued its course. M2 voiced his desire to found a new village. M1 insisted that they should not separate, because if they did so they would be unable to gather everyone in the *tekatawa*. When I returned in 1995, m2 had relinquished the leadership. Pressed to adopt tougher positions in relation to the whites, he ended up clashing verbally with the white employees. His place was taken by one of the sons of the Apyterewa headman Ywyrapytá, strengthening the two kingroups that formed the nucleus of power in Paranatinga. The goal was to lessen the inequalities in prestige existing between the moiety headmen, since the dual organization functioned to keep factionalism in check, subjecting each of the five production groups – which coincided politically with what we would call factions – to a symmetric complementarity.

However, the capacity for maintaining this unity reached its limit. At the end of the 1990s, the eastern Parakanã had swelled demographically to an unprecedented size, and Arakytá was quite old. The population density began to demand more of the structures for political mediation. M2 and his paternal uncle, the son of ex-headman Orowo'a, therefore aired the possibility of opening a new village where the latter would assume the task of "making conversation" while the former would mediate with the whites. In 1997, Paranowa'ona village was created on the shores of the Pucuruí River, formed almost exclusively by Tapi'pya men and their wives. The split occurred along the agnatic ties between patrilateral parallel cousins, a tendency also observed among the western Parakanã. The political dynamic was different, though: First, the object of the dispute was not women but prestige; second, the aim was to avoid open conflict at all costs. Despite the diverging interests, the process eventually took the shape of a consensual decision and ensured the continuing relationship between the different villages.

At the end of 1998, having seen the successful experience of Paranowa'ona village, a group of approximately seventy people under the leadership of Ywyrapytá's kingroup abandoned Paranatinga to found the Ita'yngo'a settlement on the shores of the Bacuri River. This time it was Apyterewa and Wyrapina men who abandoned their affines. These divisions appear to represent the end of the dual system built up over the course of the twentieth century. In its place, a new multivillage reality has emerged with, perhaps, the extroversion of the difference between patrigroups onto the plane of locality. It is also possible that we are witnessing the actual dilution of the segments: Paranowa'ona today is a Tapi'pya settlement composed of kindreds that, as well as being related by patrilateral parallel ties, exchanged women and became affines. What will happen, then, to the eastern Parakanã's social morphology? The process of transformation is still under way and the answer remains in the future.

Revisiting an Enduring Dualism

In this chapter, I have analyzed the processes of differentiation in the social morphology and political organization of the two Parakanã blocs. To conclude, I turn to the distinction between domestic and political spheres, a topic that has received close scrutiny in anthropology, especially in works inspired by feminist analysis. Despite all the theoretical refinements, however, we continue to oscillate between rejecting the dichotomy and unavoidably reviving its specter. It would be reassuring to abandon its use once and for all. Here, though, I cannot do so: The dichotomy is not only important for understanding the difference between the Parakanã blocs, but also pervades the main analytical models of Amazonian ethnology.

Let me provide a minimal definition of what I understand by political and domestic. In the Parakanã case, I am equating the first term with the space of sociality of the *tekatawa* and the second with other areas of

Parakanã social life. In a certain sense, the opposition is between two forms of sociality as suggested by M. Strathern (1988:93–7), who contrasts collective action (based on shared objectives and identities) and particular relations (based on the difference and interdependency between people). However, this contrast does not really abandon the classical formulation of the dichotomy, despite reformulating it as a heteroclitic comparison between actions and relations. Founding the collective on an abstract identity that implies common ends, and the particular on a difference that implies interdependence, essentially restitutes the classical Greek dichotomy – relations between equals in the *polis* and relations between unequals in the *oikia* – albeit attributing a more positive value to the latter and rejecting the equivalence later made between the political and the social.

This eternal return to the image that inspired Fortes (1978:14) seems to imply that either the dichotomy is inescapable because we are so impregnated with it that we find it in every corner of the globe, or it corresponds to an objective and widespread mode of constituting society. In other words, the conclusion is either entirely negative (the dichotomy is nothing more than the projection of our ideology onto other cultures) or entirely positive (the dichotomy is a universal abstract, varying superficially according to the society in question). Is there an alternative to this aporia? I suggest we focus on the relation between the terms rather than their content. What defines the political sphere is the appropriation of collective actions and relations *to the exclusion* of other areas of social life, which are thereby represented as subsumed by the former. The contrastive and pluralized formulation of the second term – "other areas of social life" – indicates that what matters is not its objective content, but the fact that the position of a political sphere implies, by exclusion, a representation of the remainder as that which is encompassed or exceeded. Hence the act of constituting the political sphere produces the representation of a totality and, complementarily, of the particular. It is only at this moment that factional politics appears in opposition to the political, becoming associated with dissent and the concealed discourse of gossip.

By defining the political domain as the constitution of a totality that excludes other domains in the process, I am not suggesting that it is a false appearance, since the collective is only posited as such insofar as it is appropriated by a specific sphere of sociality.[34] The *tekatawa* is the form through which the group presents itself as a totality – a provisional and relative totality, which is already presupposed but needs to be posited by

34 Analyzing the relationship between political and domestic among the Kayapó, Turner claims that "It is not simply that the collective institutions 'reflect' a pattern of weighting that is already there ... in the structure of the household. It is only through the embodiment of that pattern by the system of collective institutions that it comes to exist as such" (1984:343).

the very act that constitutes it. Without the *tekatawa*, there is no effective totality, only a presupposed one (for example, in the localized unity of the group or in its relations with the outside).[35] The equation between a sphere of political sociality and the collectivity, with the consequent exclusion of the domestic, is the form of presenting the group as a political community. This form, however, is partial, because it is exclusive: The posited community is no longer the community, but – in the Parakanã case – a male collectivity. It is a part posited as a whole. The same-sex relations in the *tekatawa* totalize the community, meaning that collective relations appear as relations between men to the exclusion of women, and men present themselves as the architects of relations beyond the family.

How does this approach to the political and domestic dichotomy simultaneously avoid an entirely positive reading (the dichotomy as a universally posited objective reality) and an entirely negative one (the dichotomy as false appearance)? In two ways: First, by arguing that the positing of the political (and therefore of the dichotomy) is necessarily negative. The political sphere is the place for positing a totality affected by its own negation. It constitutes itself – and constitutes the encompassed element (the domestic) – by exclusion (see Lefort 1983:68). Second, by emphasizing its existence *in potentia*: Where it is not posited – and this is the western Parakanã case – it is presupposed, existing as an objective (but not necessary) possibility. In these terms, it could be said that it is both universal (as a presupposition) and not universal (as a position). The notion of an objective modality allows us to understand why Clastres's political anthropology is not opposed to Lefort's: "Primitive society" does not ignore the division, since where it is not posited, it exists as a possibility inscribed in the object (Lefort 1987:191). Moreover, this notion implies, as R. Fausto notes (1987:191), a dialectics of constitution, which differs both from the teleological conception of political evolution and from the radical particularism dominant in cultural anthropology.

35 I borrow the concepts of positing (*Setzung*) and presupposition (*Voraussetzung*) from modern dialectics. This distinction is heir to the one between act and potency employed by Aristotle to tackle the problem of contradiction. Here I focus, on one hand, on its pertinence as a discourse on the object and, on the other, on the fact that a presupposed object "is not an object of pure actualities. . . . The world also contains the non-existent existent" (R. Fausto 1987:155).

4

The War Factor

Do I tell you, Sir? I shot, my turn. Then I caught my breath. Have you ever seen a war, Sir? That one, thoughtless, we stumble upon and wait: wait for their answer.

Guimarães Rosa, *The Devil to Pay in the Backlands* (1956)

Over the previous chapters I have examined how the eastern and western Parakanã came to develop distinct social configurations after the fission at the end of the nineteenth century. In describing this process, I have sought to avoid the double mistake of conceiving Amerindian societies to be alternately subject to an autonomous natural history or to determinant external forces initiated by the discovery of America. I have examined the changes among the Parakanã as an outcome of the interaction between internal and external factors, which, through various forms of positive feedback, eventually produced the distinct economic and sociopolitical configurations of the two blocs. In reconstructing these changes, I have looked to emphasize the place of practice and events in my analysis. In the case of the eastern Parakanã, I have shown how the emergence of a segmentary morphology and the structure of headmanship was a date-able event resulting from decisions taken in specific historico-cultural conjunctures that proved determinant over the long run. In the western Parakanã case, I emphasized that mobility did not result from a lack of choice: They were not confined in an ecologically degraded territory, nor were they hunted by powerful warring groups. Rather, they expanded into an area that had become depopulated after the Conquest. In a sense, they "chose" mobility, and the question was how to describe this choice without falling into a voluntaristic explanation. Finally, we have seen that the differences between the two blocs were systemic, in the sense that they were well articulated and clearly expressed across all fields of social life, including the relationship with other indigenous peoples. In this chapter, I shall focus precisely on the relations with human others through warfare.

The Ways of War

From the split until contact in the 1980s, the western Parakanã were involved in violent actions against a variety of Amerindian peoples. In less than a century, they participated in thirty-three conflicts, almost all of them offensive. On average, they confronted adversaries every three years. By contrast, the eastern Parakanã settled in the area drained by three affluents of the Tocantins and only warred with groups that made incursions into their territory. From the end of the nineteenth century until 1971, they suffered ten attacks from the western bloc and clashed with other adversaries invading their lands another five times. On average, they confronted enemies every five years. If we exclude the clashes between the two Parakanã blocs and take an equal period for both – between the split and the "pacification" of the eastern Parakanã (1890–1971) – the difference becomes even more striking: The conflicts occurred on average every sixteen years for the eastern bloc compared to every five years for the western bloc. This contrast is also manifested in the diversity of adversaries: The western Parakanã confronted eight distinct groups, whereas the eastern Parakanã clashed with just four. The scale of the conflicts differed too: The eastern Parakanã fought with individuals or small families rather than groups, whereas the western bloc faced much more numerous enemies. There is no way of calculating the exact size, but the Araweté villages raided during the 1970s, for example, were inhabited by approximately sixty individuals (Viveiros de Castro 1986:170). The Asurini villages attacked in the 1940s were bigger, since at the time of contact in 1953, the total population numbered 190 people, divided into two local groups (Arnaud 1967:60). The difference in scale is reflected in the number of captured enemy women: The western Parakanã caught more than thirty women, whereas the eastern Parakanã caught none. The question, then, is twofold: How do we account for the aggressive behavior of the western bloc and, simultaneously, the withdrawn stance of the eastern bloc?

Speech Modalities

From the dominant viewpoint in the anthropology of war, the second question makes no sense: There is no need to explain the eastern Parakanã "pacifism" given that, in the demographic and sociopolitical situation in which they lived, there existed few motives for the emergence of conflicts. After the fission, they became the sole occupants of a vast tract of forest; there was no contiguity between their territory and that of other indigenous groups. The Xikrin do Catete were located to the southeast, separated by the areas of commercial exploration of Brazil-nut trees on the Itacaiúnas River; the Asurini occupied an area to the northwest and never entered the region to the south of the Pucuruí River. Only the western Parakanã were located nearer, but their trekking zones did not overlap the area exploited by the eastern bloc. Hence, the lack of bellicosity among the latter could be merely an unmarked behavior: They simply wanted to live in peace, satisfying their needs in an extensive, depopulated territory. However, this strategy was not actually the most adequate from a military point of view. Between 1910 and 1955, the eastern Parakanã suffered heavy losses during attacks by the western bloc: Seventeen people were killed and seven women captured. Were they cornered and thus forced to adopt a defensive posture?

The eastern Parakanã description of themselves today carries no indication of impotence. They consider themselves no less warlike than the western group. They attributed the offensive mode of the latter to their erratic wandering – which they disdained – and believed it pointless to pursue people without villages and swiddens. From the 1970s onward, when they were obliged to share the same indigenous reserve with the western bloc, they began to censure the latter for not making the *tekatawa*, not being serious enough, and for wanting "to become whites" (-*jemotori*). The impression they give when speaking of the past is that of a strong and autonomous nucleus, capable of defending itself from territorial invasion by nomadic people. There is another reason for believing that the lower bellicosity of the eastern group did not result from their simply being cornered. The pressure exerted on them by the western Parakanã between 1935 and 1955 was much greater than that imposed on the Asurini, a much more overtly warlike and numerous groups. Whereas the Asurini eventually sought refuge with the Indian Protection Service in 1953, the eastern Parakanã never abandoned their territory, nor did they seek out the protection offered by the whites.

The eastern Parakanã defensive posture therefore seems to be part of a more general reconfiguration of the social field, one that I have described in the last chapter. An important indication of this fact is the abandonment of a warfare practice typical of the region's Tupi groups: shooting arrows at the corpses of war victims in order to multiply the number of people who entered seclusion as killers. The eastern Parakanã did this for the last time at the start of the twentieth century after killing two Amerindians on the Bacuri River. Soon after they abandoned the practice, claiming that "it brings bad luck" (-*momoraiwon*) for the warrior. This abandonment reflected the growing ambivalence in relation to the killer, who, affected by the enemy's perspective, may turn against his own kin.[1] It also reflected the

---

1 People say that "his adversaries made him lose consciousness" (*howajara omopikajym*), or "go crazy" ("*ficar doido*") as the Parakanã translate the expression in Portuguese. Among the eastern Parakanã, the stative verb -*pikajym* also designates the state of unconsciousness produced by tobacco intoxication. The nonpossessive form of *howajara* is *towajara*, "the one who is on the other side," a classic Tupi-Guarani term.

development of asymmetries in the social system and the nongeneraliza-
tion of certain attributes. The chances to become a *moropiarera* ("killer")
had narrowed: Only those who had shot a living enemy could now go into
seclusion.

These transformations are linked to the strengthening of an alternative
model to warfare, founded on a political arena where the prevailing discursive modality was "conversation" (*morongeta*) rather than the intimidating
speech of war leaders. Knowing how to "talk tough" (*-je'engahy*) is a capacity
few possess: Only the *moropetenga* ("people hitters"), the great killers, have
the requisite strength and courage to do so. As a discursive mode of relating to others, this speech is admired and necessary, but when projected onto
relations among equals, it conduces a shift from amity to enmity. There are
only two possible responses to imperative speech: It either "provokes fear"
(*-moky'yje*) or "provokes rage" (*-momirahy*). In a society where the means of
production and destruction are distributed equally, fear or anger do not lead
to subservience or revolt, but to flight or murder. This is why headmanship
among the eastern Parakanã could not be based on the warrior's speech, but
had to use the opposite discursive mode. The *tekatawa* became the space par
excellence for building consensus through a collectively produced speech,
of which the headmen are simultaneously precondition and outcome.

The opposition between these two modes of speech – one aimed
toward building internal consensus, the other aimed at the destruction-
appropriation of the other – expresses a structural contradiction. Both are
associated with male maturation and the capacity to relate with the outside and produce on the inside. The same qualities expected in the *tekatawa* are linked to homicide, insofar as the latter is a determinant event
in the maturation of male capacities. The question, therefore, is how
to domesticate *Homo bellicus* without completely neutralizing him. The
killer's ambiguity expresses the contradiction inherent to cosmologies in
which the *dynamic* is founded on a predatory potential directed outward,
and the *static* on containment of this potential in order for sociability
to be possible. The predatory potential is a principle of movement and
growth, yet, uncontained, it casts a shadow over the very possibility of
communal life.

The solution pursued by the eastern Parakanã was distinct from that
of the small endogamic local groups of the Guiana Shield (Overing
1993a:204–8), where internal differences are minimized in order to project
an image of an undivided community. By realigning their social life during
the twentieth century, the eastern Parakanã instituted a series of differences
that in conjunction afforded a new sociability: They formed patrigroups,
fixed alliance in a sociocentric moiety structure, and constituted a political
sphere based on a discursive pragmatics in which the headman's function
is distinct from that of the war leader. By doing so, they reinforced village

unity, neutralizing the conflicts over women as well as the factionalism between kindreds.

Centrifugal Vertigo

In claiming that the internal political process helps explain the low level of warfare activity among the eastern group, I am not presuming that the warfare fever of the western group corresponds to a "normal" pattern of conflicts. Evaluating the intensity of native warfare in relation to a supposed norm is an undertaking doomed to failure. Even if we accept that warfare is a paradigmatic form through which Amazonian indigenous societies relate with the exterior, this fact in itself tells us nothing about the intensity and scale of war.[2] I have no interest in determining a supposed original warfare behavior, nor any intention of distinguishing the nature of a culture and its history. I just wish to investigate the reasons behind the western Parakanã appetite for war at a specific historical moment. Can we identify a determinant cause for this warfare impulse, one that was simultaneously absent among the eastern group?

Let us begin by the capture of enemy women. Despite its importance, I do not think it was the primary motivation for war. First, capture only took place in eleven of the thirty-three conflicts. This was not merely a question of opportunity, as more than once women who could have been captured ended up killed. The clearest example is the attack in 1969 on a Akwa'awa group, when just one woman was taken. I asked one of the participants why they had not captured the others: "Because everyone already had a wife," he replied. In fact, the youths seem to have preferred victims to wives on this occasion, since it was the first opportunity in fifteen years for them to become killers.[3] Second, in the war narratives, capture emerges as a secondary motivation compared to homicide and the acquisition of *moropiarera* status. Finally, the eastern Parakanã also experienced a shortage of women after the split, as shown by the incestuous marriages among them, but they did not adopt an offensive posture to obtain them.

Let us consider, then, territorial conquest as a determinant element. Did the relocation after the split make it necessary to create an inhabitable space through force? The first conflicts with the Asurini at the end of the nineteenth century were related, in effect, to the relocation of the western Parakanã to a new area, as were the clashes with the Xikrin and the

2 See the polemic surrounding Yanomami warfare, especially on whether or not its intensity is "an expression of Yanomami culture itself" (Ferguson 1995:6).

3 It is interesting to compare this decision with the inverse choice made by the eastern Suyá, who after suffering various losses in an attack at the start of the twentieth century decided to avoid homicide and favor the capture of women (Seeger 1981:168).

Araweté from the 1970s onward, when the group invaded the headwaters of the Bacajá River. In both situations, occupation of the new territory was followed by a decline in warfare activity. This lull, however, was only temporary. Ten years after settling in the Pacajá basin, the western Parakanã began to expand their range, unleashing half a century of conflicts in enemy territory. At the time, there was no supralocal network in the region, and the different communities were living in near complete isolation; only offensive warfare prevented the total absence of relations.

One piece of evidence of this sociodemographic dispersion is the extremely selective and specialized diet of the Parakanã. It may be tempting to argue that their bellicosity stems from the need to ensure an extensive hunting area. However, once again, the eastern Parakanã diet was virtually identical to the western group's. Warfare activity was connected to subsistence in another sense. Constant trekking allowed monitoring of an extensive area and the western Parakanã always adopted an offensive policy: If they found enemy footprints, they employed every means to locate the strangers, penetrating areas far beyond the known territory. This was an efficient strategy, given that the low demographic density made it difficult to track them following the attack: The only reprisal they suffered took place in the 1970s in the Bacajá River region.[4] There was also a practical consonance between the subsistence and warfare activities. Procedures for the latter were no different to hunting, demanding the same skills in tracking and in the handling of a bow and arrow. The mobility of the hunting groups accustomed young people to long periods in the forest and trained them to survive without cultivated foods.

If there is no causal connection between warfare and subsistence, can we attribute the western Parakanã war fever to the fluctuating and unequal circulation of metal tools, as Ferguson suggests in the Yanomami case? Ferguson makes two predictions in relation to the time and direction of violence: First, he claims that outbreaks of violence follow changes affecting the availability of industrialized goods in a determined area; after a one- to three-year period, a new political equilibrium emerges, and, if there are no new changes, the war comes to an end; second, he claims that attacks are executed by those farthest from the sources of industrial commodities against those with better access to these goods (Ferguson 1995:56). These predictions do not apply to the Parakanã case. On one hand, the direction is reversed: The attacks were conducted by the western Parakanã, a group with greater access to manufactured commodities. On the other hand, the order of events differs: Political equilibrium occurred as a temporary interruption

---

4 From the quantitative point of view, offensive raids (excluding, therefore, the losses incurred during the Xikrin attack in the 1930s) were fairly successful: Between 1910 and 1955, they suffered six losses and captured twenty-one enemy women.

to the conflicts for the purpose of acquiring more commodities. The periods of relative peace coincided with more frequent visits to the Pacification Post. The western Parakanã did not need to monopolize this source of goods, since there was no competition for its control: The eastern Parakanã never learned of its existence, and the Asurini only frequented it for a brief period between 1949 and 1953. Furthermore, the cessation of visits to the Post at the end of the 1930s suggests that commodities possessed a diminishing marginal value, and that they did not serve, in this context, to mediate relations between groups. The pursuit of Western goods thus cannot account for the western Parakanã warfare dynamic.

In fact, there does not appear to be a single explanation for their centrifugal movement. It was the product of a set of internal and external factors, both structural and conjunctural in kind, that shaped actions and were simultaneously shaped by them. To gain a better understanding of its meaning, we need to provide a denser description of the events that I have been calling "warlike." Above all, we need to include warfare within a general symbolic economy that makes it comprehensible not only as a successful strategy, but also as a mechanism for social reproduction. Before that, however, let me introduce some Parakanã categories of identity and alterity.

The Enemies and Us

When examining categories of identity, the first question is whether a self-denomination exists. The western Parakanã often use the term Apyterewa in response to questions like "What kind are you?" (*ma'e-kwera pa pehe*) or "What's your self-designation?" (*mo pa pejenoinawa*). However, inquiring further, we soon discover that only the ancestors were truly Apyterewa, since those living today are mixed. The eastern Parakanã, for their part, use the term even more narrowly, as it designates one of the patrilineal segments in which the group is divided. Apyterewa is thus currently a name indicating "what we were" or "what some of us are."

There is another designation that is commonly given the status of a self-denomination: *awaeté*, which we can translate as "true humans" or "humans par excellence." The word *awa* can function as a deictic, an interrogative pronoun, or a noun.[5] As a noun, it means man or human, depending on whether the relevant distinction is man/woman or human/nonhuman. In the first dichotomy, the opposite is *kojoa* ("woman").[6] But *awa* and *kojoa*

---

5 As a deictic, *awa* refers to nearby and standing people or things with a vertically elongated form. As a pronoun, it occurs in interrogative sentences precisely like "who" in English and is distinguished from *ma'é*, which in interrogative phrases means "what."

6 Both occur in a series of composed terms such as *awarame* ("now-man") and *kojarame* ("woman-now"), respectively male and female pubescent. Many names are formed by these roots, which mark

do not cover the same semantic field: The former is only applicable to humanity, whereas the latter can be applied to human beings and animals alike. In the latter context, *kojoa* is opposed to another word, *akoma'é*, as "female" to "male." When asked about the sex of a child or an animal, there is only one pair of terms with which to respond: *kojoa* or *akoma'e*. The term *awa* is never used in this situation. We have, then, three categories for two oppositions: one that applies to the sexual distinction of animals and humans (*akoma'e/kojoa*) and another that refers solely to the gender of the latter (*awa/kojoa*).

In its wider sense, the category *awa* designates human in opposition to nonhuman. Animals are not *awa*, although in dreams they "can make themselves human," *-je-mo-awa* (reflexive-factive-human), which means they can appear in human form. Human enemies are also *awa*. An euphemistic expression used to ask if someone is a killer is precisely "did you see humans?" (*ere'ejang pa awa*). Although all those who possess or acquire a human body can be called *awa*, not all of them are *awa-eté*, "true humans." When suffixed to stative verbs such as "he is really strong" (*hato-eté*) or "he is very good" (*ikato-eté*), *eté* functions as an intensifier. When suffixed to a nominal syntagma, though, it acts as a modifier to indicate perfect belonging to a class or greater representativity as a member of a category (Lakoff 1987:44). The *awaeté* are, then, the most perfect examples of the *awa* category.

As Viveiros de Castro (1998) notes, the translation of *awaeté* as "true humans" should not lead us to presume Amerindians think that humanity ends at the strict limits of the local, tribal, or ethnic group. *Awaeté* are the prototype of a wider class, just as some varieties of cultigens are taken to be more representative of their category: There is a "true manioc" (*many'yweté*), a "true maize" (*awajieté*), a "true potato" (*jytyngeté*) without implying that the other varieties are not examples of the categories of manioc, maize, or potato.[7] The same principle of categorization applies to *awa*: All those possessing a human body are *awa* (kin and strangers) or are in the condition of *awa* (animals and spirits), though only some are human in a stricter sense.

The category *awaeté* has a variable range of applicability, expanding and contracting according to context. Its minimal extension is not the kingroup (*te'ynia*), but all those who share the same language, customs, and body markings. When listening to a narrative of a war event, if I asked what enemy they were talking about, I often received the reply, "*awaeté*." The

---

the person's gender: *Awa-namia* ("ear-man"), *Awa-pinima* ("painted-man"), *Awa-tawa* ("soft-man") or *Koja'orywa* ("happy-woman"), *Kojo-jinga* ("white-woman'), *Kojo-hona* ("dark-woman').

7 Another example: Shotguns are called *tatayroa* ("fire container"), but also, like bows, *ywyrapara* ("curved stick"). When the intention is to differentiate them, however, *ywyrapareté* ("true bow") is used for indigenous bows, and *ywyraporohoa* ("great bow") for guns.

two reasons most frequently used to explain this remark were "it's the same language as our own" (*oreje'engimo*) or a reference to the type of lip-plug used. In its maximal extension, *awaeté* can be used, today, like the Brazilian category "Indians," when wishing to distinguish indigenous peoples from whites. This widening of the term's range results from post-contact political experience, although the dichotomy was already present in the contact experience itself, at least from the 1950s onward, when the SPI began to use interpreters in the attempt to pacify the western Parakanã. In the narratives of the visits to the Pucuruí Post, these interpreters appear as recently pacified *awaeté*:

As we were leaving, he [the interpreter] asked if we would come back. We said yes. He told us how many nights we should wait before returning, since they wanted to pacify us. He asked whether we were scared of them. We replied that we were not:

– We're brothers, he said.

He was *awaeté*:

– We're brothers, which means we should not fear each other.

He was an *awaeté*, *apyterewa*, who had been pacified.

– They pacified us, he explained.

He had not abandoned his language and so he spoke to us in this way. He told me that at first he had a bow and only later acquired a gun. He told me that they had killed the whites [Toria] with arrows:

– We shot them with arrows. So they [the whites] said: the *awaeté* are going to finish us off. So they pacified us.

We said to him:

– Why did you shoot the Toria, just get along with them.

That's what I said to Je'e'yngoa [the name given to one of the interpreters]. I don't know why he didn't use shorts. Well, the Toria had just recently brought him. He wore a shirt only.

(Iatora 1993: tape 37)

Je'e'yngoa was not Asurini, since the visit narrated by Iatora happened before the pacification of this people in 1953. He was probably Tembé or Ka'apor, a speaker of another Tupi-Guarani language, meaning he was able to communicate better with them than the whites. In this context, the interpreter – who had a perforated lip but did not use a lip-plug – appears as an *awaeté*, though already in a process of transformation. Note the attention Iatora gives to the absence of shorts: Je'e'yngoa had a shirt and gun, but only half of him was dressed as a white. What interested the Parakanã about this process was the possibility of acquiring distinctive characteristics of the whites, which index their special capacities. Pacification implied the transmutation into an other – a transformation manifested among the Parakanã soon after contact in the 1970s and 1980s with the rapid abandonment of lip piercing and the adoption of clothing.

Bodily metamorphosis marks not only the transformation from an indigenous to a nonindigenous condition, but also that from one indigenous condition to another. Both are conceived as a gradual process of adopting new body markings and dispositions, as well as the capacity to communicate adequately. The Parakanã narrate, for example, the history of the Jotaywena ("husbands of the jatobá tree"), who dwelt in tree hollows and fed on fruits. Incorporated into the Apyterewa, they gradually turned into humans: "After a while, they became a little bit human (*ojemoawa ere*). Later, they definitively grew accustomed to their new life and became true humans (*awaeté-ramo aka*). Then, [the Apyterewa] made them dance the *opetymo* ritual" (Pykawa 1992: tape 11). This transformative process was repeated after each capture of women over the course of the twentieth century, even though the Parakanã have always preferred to seize women who were already *awaeté* and had their doubts concerning the practical viability of pacifying a Kayapó woman.

Awaeté, in sum, is not a proper noun, but an identity category whose extension alters, and it applies in varying degree to human collectivities. If minimally it designates a set wider than the socially distinct grouping to which the enunciator belongs, this is because another category exists to indicate this "us." The most frequent term to designate "those from this side" (*kakatywara*) in opposition to those from another band, the *towajara* ("those from the other side"), is *te'ynia*. The warriors referred to the collectivity to which they belonged as *wete'yi*, "my kin" (vocative form):

– They [the enemies] already know that we're here, *wete'yi*, let's go and shoot them now. (Iatora 1993: tape 38)
– Someone tore apart our grandparents' house: They were the Asurini, *wete'yi*. (Pi'awa 1995: tape 19)

The translation which Montoya (1876) gives to the ancient Guarani cognate *teiî* closely matches this usage: "*manada, compania, parcialidad*" ("pack, company, faction").[8] Those from "my faction" are "my kin," *jere'ynia* (referential form), a category that also varies in scope. In its narrowest

8 There are various cognates of *te'ynia* in other Tupi-Guarani languages: for example, *-e'yj*, "kin, member of the same moiety," in Parintintin (Betts 1981) or *hey*, "my companion," in Tembé (Philipson 1946:24). Also see the cognates of the Tupinambá *anama* or the Guarani *anã*, glossed as "kin," "kindred," or sometimes as "from one's own faction" (Stradelli 1929). For an analysis of these terms, see Fausto (1991:73–5).

sense, it denotes ego's siblings, but it can also be applied to all cognates, that is, to everyone recognized as having a common origin. And here, in contrast to what happens among the Suya (Seeger 1980:127–32) or among the Wari' (Vilaça 1996:288–91), the exchange of substances does not make people kin. Hence the ambiguous status of the captured enemy women: The latter are kin because they take part in the universe of relations marked by sharing and exchange, but they never cease to be foreigners, *akwawa* – or more precisely, "daughters of *akwawa*." The category *te'ynia* has, then, the double meaning of "common descent" (cognation) and "member of the same collectivity." This explains why the western Parakanã can state that the eastern Parakanã are "kin" (*te'ynia*) and "ex-kin" (*te'yiwera*) at the same time, although between one and the other classification an enormous practical distance exists. In our own conception of kinship, people who possess a shared remote ancestor are said to be distant kin, and the relation is indeterminate in terms of the system of attitudes. In the Parakanã case, on the contrary, an ex-kinsperson is necessarily an *akwawa*, and the relation is marked by enmity.

Akwawa is the main category of alterity. It is the generic form to classify all those humans who do not belong to the same faction as ego, as well as all those beings – human and nonhuman alike – who appear in dreams. The central attribute of the category is enmity: the *akwawa* is not just an "other" (*amote*), but an enemy. The categorization implies a relational schema in which predation is the default value. In the dream universe, though, things happen differently. The interaction between the dreamer and an *akwawa* is not modeled on hunting, but on the familiarization of animals: The oneiric interlocutor is conceived as the dreamer's pet (see Chapter 5).

There are no prototypical *akwawa* – or *akwaweté* – to match the *awaeté*. We can, though, distinguish four macroclasses of human enemies: There are the Toria (the whites), the *karajá* (generic designation for any Ge group), the enemies who are *awaeté* (called *ngyngé* by the eastern Parakanã), and those that are simply *akwawa*, without any additional specification. Each of these macroclasses potentially defines distinct forms of social interaction and modes of appropriation. Later in this chapter, I shall analyze the relations involved in warfare predation, focusing on those *akwawa* that are *awaeté*. In Chapter 5, I shall discuss another mode of relation with enemies, familiarization, focusing on the dreamt Karajá. Finally, in Chapter 7, I shall return to the relation with the Toria.

War: A User's Guide

Offensive war is not launched with a single decision after public deliberation. Its initial dynamic depends on mobilizing individual volitions: it is necessary, as Florestan Fernandes says, "to stir up the already polarized emotions against the enemy" (1970:70). In order for each individual to pass from providing for life to a collective undertaking towards death, psychic forces need to be directed towards a common objective. Hence the question: how can people be persuaded to act in an egalitarian society like that of the western Parakanã?

Stirring Desires

Among the various conditions for setting a war band in motion, one stands out in all the narratives that I collected: the idea of an enragement, without which – even where practical reasons exist – there will be no subjective motivation. For warriors to act, they need to "become enraged against the enemy" (-jemamai akwawa-rehe). The verb -mamai (or in the reflexive form, -je-mamai) defines a passion with a well-defined scope: The gloss provided to me was not "to become intensely angry," but "to want to kill an enemy."

Rage (mirahya) is a powerful feeling in Parakanã ethnopsychology. To say that a man is angry (-pirahy) implies that a lethal act of aggression may follow. For this reason, the Parakanã are very attentive to small demonstrations of anger. Once I became vexed over something and showed my annoyance; people immediately ceased doing whatever they supposed was the cause of my irritation and kindly pressed me to return to conviviality and conversation: "Are you angry?" they asked, forcing me to resume talking and, above all, to laugh. Laughter is the antidote to anger, which always festers in silence and isolation.[9]

Anger cannot always be controlled, though. Critical episodes produce violent reactions. When a kinsperson dies, for instance, men are filled with rage. Unable to take revenge for the death, they kill pet animals, fire arrows at the house thatch, and shoot in the air. These are forms of "expending" (-mongy) their fury, which would be better spent killing an enemy. During the 1976 contact, an old man died. His son became furious (-jemamai) and picked up his bow to kill the Funai officers: "to exact my revenge," he said, walking toward the whites. The young interpreter Mojiapewa calmed him down by speaking to him of the human condition ("That's how it is with people, only the rocks truly last") and the whites ("Don't take revenge, they are the ones who will cure us when we're sick") and advising him: "Kill the dogs to get rid of your anger."

---

9 Clastres (1972:169) describes what he calls a "ritual of reconciliation" when the allied Aché bands meet. After a simulation of warfare, the men search for a partner. Embracing in pairs, they begin to tickle each other to provoke laughter.

The rage produced by the death of a relative could also recall the memory of past adversaries and revive the desire to make war and kill enemies. One of the expeditions against the eastern Parakanã in the 1920s followed the death of My'a's son. When My'a himself died at the start of the 1940s, they decided to leave in search of the Asurini, a people they had last confronted twenty years earlier. Projecting anger outward was a way of avoiding internal conflicts. As we have seen, until the mid-1950s, war played an important role in maintaining the dispersed unity of the western Parakanã, not only because of the substantial influx of captured women, but also as a mechanism for sublimating the anger directed at kin and reaffirming the unity of the group.

Some narratives directly associate war events with the avoidance of internecine fights.[10] The attack on the Yrywijara, in the 1920s, followed a dispute between kin. My'a tried to shoot his patrilateral parallel cousin, Tama, provoking a split. A while later, the assailant's brother went to meet Tama's group to attempt a reconciliation, but they were intractable. Subsequently, two women decided to try to pacify them through conversation. They were successful and the western Parakanã reunited again. They then decided to go in search of enemies, discovering tracks left by the Yrywijara. Disputes over women could also be sublimated by going to war, as Iatora tells in describing the incidents leading to an attack on the Asurini in the 1940s:

The now-dead man had become jealous of his younger brother over a woman. For this reason we went [to war], and I killed Kaiaré [name of the victim].

[Afterward] they became angry again. I was lying down, some distance away.

    – What did my younger brother say? I asked the now-dead woman.
    – "We're going to kill enemies!" I think they said.

Later, Kojaitá came to speak to me:

    – "Will you go with our kin?" Your grandfather told me to ask you, my grandson.
    – I shall stay with you, grandmother.
    – Yes, let's stay, my grandson, these people know how to use a bow. . . . . You killed an enemy just recently, she said to me.
    – Okay then, I'll stay with you. I've got a skin infection on my arm.

10 After pacification, this role was assumed by ritual, in particular by the homicide drama of the tobacco festival. In 1989, performance of this ritual was prompted by a quarrel between brothers-in-law. A man had become furious with his sister's husband after he heard it said that the latter had threatened to kill her. To placate his anger and avoid a confrontation between two allied kingroups, he asked his maternal uncle to begin preparations for the festival in which he would dance. Lacking real enemies to execute, they killed dreamt enemies.

They went. We stayed. So, the now-dead woman came back:

- — "Aren't you going with me?" your uncle asked, nephew.
- — I don't know aunt, I replied.
- — Let's go with your uncle, she insisted.

So I stood up and said:

- — Father, I'm going with our kin.
- — Make sure you know the forest you're walking in [that is, be careful], my son, he replied.
- — I'll know the forest, dad, I'm going to kill the Makakawa [Asurini].
- — Who will come back to tell me about your deeds? he asked.
- — Perhaps I'll kill for our kin, dad, I replied.

(Iatora 1993: tape 47)

Iatora's narrative forges a link between jealousy and the initial acceleration of passions: One person's anger transforms into a collective rage. For this to happen, the desire to kill needs to spread to other people – something the narrator resists at first. This conflict of wills is described by the interposed speech of the women, which also contains the speech of other men: "You killed an enemy just recently," one of them says to Iatora, but he yields to the demand of others who speak in the name of their husbands: "Aren't you going with me, your uncle asked." The women appear here as mediators of the relations between men in the context of war. They commonly performed this function as spouses and sisters, bringing together brothers-in-law, particularly those who were originally maternal uncle and nephew. The arrows used by young men in an attack were either given to them by their fathers or by their maternal uncles via a sister. Pi'awa tells that prior to an attack against the Asurini, while he was preparing his arrows, his classificatory sister brought him one more: "My late sister brought the killer-to-be [referring to the arrow]: 'Use this to hit them,' your maternal uncle said, my brother" (Pi'awa 1995: tape 29).

Viveiros de Castro (1986:300–1) has elegantly described the epidemic nature of collective actions in a politically acephalous society. Rather than the outcome of formal decisions taken by some in the name of others, actions become concerted through a social process of contagion. Nobody tells anyone else what they should do, but rather suggests what he himself will do. Initiating a joint undertaking depends on harmonizing unrestrained wills. To achieve this aim, it is necessary for someone to initiate the action, dispelling the general inertia. In warfare, this function was assumed by those whom the western Parakanã call *moropetenga*, "people hitters."[11]

---

11 *Moropetenga* is also the name of a kind of ant, whose bite is not painful but extremely itchy.

The term designates people who are capable of persuading others to act, since they are unashamed to speak strongly to their kin and enemies alike. Eloquence promotes action. In the following dialogue, taken from a narrative, Arawa incites the youths to leave for war after the death of his older brother:

The late Arawa provoked us:

- You lot are going to run from those wretches, children, he said.
- They don't scare us, so we won't run, we said to him.
- Humm, I have no faith in you youngsters, he told us.
- Humm, you're bragging emptily, when the enemies approach, you'll run, we said.
- Humm, say you're going to run, he said.
- Humm, I say that my victim will fall screaming, I said to him.
- I'm the one who'll kill those wretches for you, he said.[12]

(Pi'awa 1996: tape 29)

Arawa became widely missed. The young men who in the 1990s were looking to build a leadership capable of dealing with the postpacification challenges felt the absence of someone who knew how to catch people's attention with words. In the first decades after contact, the Parakanã living in the Xingu basin left the task of coordinating collective actions to the head of the Funai Post. By the mid-1990s, however, the situation had changed. A younger generation began to search for ways of improving their control over the relations with whites. This new context awoke something in them that, to my knowledge, had not been present in previous years. For the first time, I saw them recall the *moropetenga* with nostalgia. This qualification started to be attributed to various men from the past, those reputed as great killers capable of persuading others through harsh speech.

The incitement to go to war depended on these men: They were the warriors who went in front, the *tenotara*. The war party, which varied in size, did not contain different functions: there was no war leader responsible for organizing the actions. The level of collective coordination for an attack was minimal: The incursions did not require the formulation of any prior strategy. The only preparation required was the production of

---

12 Arawa's taunts pale in comparison to the harangues of the Tupinambá *mborubixa*. According to Léry ([1553] 1980:185), these could last over six hours, though they had the same purpose of stirring people's desire to confront the enemy. The social process of enragement among the Parakanã is more of a decentered conversation than a speech, involving short phrases pronounced by various people almost simultaneously. Some of these phrases are standardized expressions and possess a different rhythm and intonation to those of everyday speech.

new arrows and, sometimes, a new bow to avoid the risk of it breaking in the heat of battle.[13] The oldest and most experienced led the way, while the youngest, very often still adolescents, followed behind. In this context, the term *moro'yroa* is employed with a connotation of prestige normally lacking among the western Parakanã: The youths say that the more experienced warriors were "leaders to us" (*moro'yroa oreopé*).

Whereas some men had the charisma to arouse people's rage, others served as shamanic "telescopes." Given the difficulty in locating enemies in the forest, the Parakanã resorted to a sort of ritualized public dream called *wari'imongetawa*.

Shamanic Telescopy

Everything vanishes into the depths of the forest. The horizon is limited by thick trunks, dense undergrowth, and the convoluted network of vines. Staring into the distance means facing a monotonous green continuum. Only a microscopic gaze is capable of perceiving details and small transformations, which are invisible from a panoramic viewpoint. Tracking enemies is never easy. It demands the ability to read the slightest hints. Such anxieties can also be reversed, because if the prey is elusive, so too are any attackers: When they are perceived, it may well be too late. Faced with these problems, the Parakanã respond with a shamanic practice that aims to free vision from the limits imposed by the forest environment.

Wari'imongetawa is the nominalized form of *-wari'imonge*. The verb *-monge* signifies driving into a closed space: It is used, for example, in the phrase "the dogs drove the agouti into a burrow." *Wari'imongetawa* therefore means something like "cornering *wari'ia*." I am unsure what *wari'ia* signifies.[14] The person with this ability is called *wari'ijara* ("master of *wari'ia*") or *wari'imongetara* ("the person who *wari'imonge*"). The practice is triggered by a dream. Iatora narrated one such experience to me:

Some time ago, in the middle of sleep, the great blue macaw came to me.

– What's up? it said.
– Enemies are going to attack us. How can I see them? I asked.

---

13 The arrows of the western Parakanã possess spearlike tips that vary in size according to the type of bamboo used. They average 50–60 cm long by 4–6 cm wide at their widest point. The concave side is painted black, and the convex side is covered with graphic patterns. The shaft is about 85 cm long with two half-feathers fastened to its end, taken from the king vulture or harpy eagle. The bows are made from the wood of carnauba or pati palm trees.

14 This is probably a variant of the word *warinia*, which designates the act of "searching for enemies" (see Introduction). Unfortunately I never tested this hypothesis during my fieldwork.

– With this you'll be able to see the enemies arrive, partner, it said.

It brought me a large black cigar.

– Come on, inhale it. You won't see anything if you don't inhale.

It blew the smoke over me.

– Ready, partner?
– I can see a little, partner, I said.

It blew some more smoke, and then:

– I can see, partner.
– Come with me, I'm going to put you in the blind (*tokaja*), partner, the macaw said to me.

In the blind:

– Come on, see your enemies, partner, take a good look at your foes.
– Are these the enemy, partner? I asked.
– Yes, they are, partner. Are they not coming to you, partner?
– They're not coming, partner.
– So, your adversaries will not join up against you, partner? the great macaw asked.
– No, they won't join up.
– Take a good look, partner, so you can see your foes when they're arriving, it said to me.

Then it said:

– Now look in the other direction, partner.
– Which way should I turn, partner? I asked.
– Turn this way, partner. Look at everything, look at the whites (Toria).

Over there you can see the Indians (*awaeté*), over here the whites. So, are the whites coming towards you?

– No.

It insisted:

– Look well, very well for us, partner.
– The enemies are not coming over to our side, partner, there are just tapirs over here, I said.
– Only the tapirs are gathering for us, partner. Deer, armadillo, paca, agouti. They're gathering for us. Our food, partner.

I returned from it [the macaw] and awoke.

– Humm, did I really tele-view [*awari'imonge*]? Did I tele-view a little bit? I said as I lay. I'm going to look at the forest.

(Iatora 1993: tape 41)

In his dream, Iatora brings a blue macaw in the belief that they will be attacked by enemies.[15] The macaw makes Iatora inhale the smoke and he begins to see at a distance. He is then put into a blind where he can peruse the territory. The dialogue takes place between himself inside the blind and the macaw outside: "Come on, see your enemies, partner, take a good look at your foes.... Your adversaries will not join up against you, partner?"[16] Iatora recounts what he sees. Then he turns to the other side to see the whites, like a telescope focusing on a new target. They too remain at a distance. There are only game animals nearby. At the end of the dream, the macaw starts to identify itself with the dreamer, no longer asking about *his* adversaries, but about "*our* enemies." The change in the point of view announces the second moment of the dream, its public realization.

On awakening, Iatora tells "his formal friend" (*ipajé*) that he saw the enemies in a dream and he decides to place him in the blind. They go to a location some distance from the encampment and construct a small cabin from inajá palm straw. Seated next to his -*pajé*, Iatora inhales the long cigar made from the inner bark of the tauary tree and tobacco, having spent the day fasting to avoid vomiting. Then his paternal uncle says to him:

– Go, my son, perhaps they are already talking.

I stood up and listened. So, I heard their conversation. That's how it works, the *wari'ijara* stands up and listens to the talk between those who he is about to see. I went inside [the blind].

– Look carefully for us, partner, Ji'awa said to me.

Iatora did not see them this time: "Was it just a [false] omen, partner?" Ji'awa asked him. "Maybe. Perhaps our foes made an omen for us." Omen translates the term *moraiwona*: a negative presage, an announcement that something bad is going to happen. Unusual events – such as fledglings falling from their nests, a victim that remains standing, shot animals that fail to die, bamboo flutes that are played but make no sound – are *moraiwona*. Certain dreams may also be signs of negative events, just like the song of some birds. The concept implies more than just a signal, since people can be contaminated by bad luck: Contact with the enemy's blood -*mo-moraiwon*, "makes-portend," dooming the killer to a tragic fate. As I mentioned

---

15 In the *wari'imongetawa*, the oneiric interlocutor is always a bird. Of the four telescopies on which I have detailed information, three were initiated by a dream of a blue macaw and one of a formicarid bird known as *ty'eja*. I don't know how to explain the association with the former; as for the latter, its song is taken to be an alert against the forest's dangers, since *ty'eja* is said to "know" the predators.

16 I translate the vocative *tywa-kwai* as "partner." It is a form of reciprocal address between human and animal, which appears in mythic and dream narratives.

earlier, the eastern Parakanã explained their abandonment of the practice of shooting the corpses of victims precisely because it *-mo-moraiwon*.[17]

The public rite repeats the dream scene, and the *wari'ijara*'s kin assumes the role played by the blue macaw: They place Iatora in the blind and listen to him narrating what only he sees. The dreamer's experience is mainly visual, whereas that of the assistants is auditory. Before entering the blind, though, "the owner of the *wari'ia* hears the talk of those whom he will see." Only he can hear them: "Go, my son, perhaps they are already talking," his paternal uncle says to him. This is the signal to enter. From this point on, the *wari'ijara* will be called by different vocatives to those used in everyday language, such as *tywa-kwai* ("partner") or *weporo'yro* ("my old man"). These are forms of address used only in a ritual context or in mythic narratives.

The conception that the *wari'ia* owner hears the talk of the enemies, which resonates from the blind, suggests that in addition to functioning like a telescope, the *wari'imongetawa* is an encounter with the adversaries inside the small shelter (*tokaja*). A *tokaja* is not just a screen that allows the hunter to see the game without being seen himself; it also designates a cage used to hold land turtles and the offspring of wild animals. In the *wari'imongetawa*, the former meaning is dominant, whereas in other Tupi rituals the latter prevails. In the *maraká* festival of the Asurini of the Xingu, for example, the shaman attracts his spirit familiars inside the *tukaia*, where he interacts with them (Müller 1990:135–49).[18] In the Parakanã case, where "spirits" do not strictly exist, the *tokaja* primarily functions as a telescope that allows the person inside to see the prey without being seen by them. Moreover, what is seen are not images or doubles, but what is actually happening at that moment. Inside the blind, the *wari'ijara* sees real enemies made from flesh and bone. "What does he see?" I asked Pi'awa. "He truly sees their skin (*ipira*), he sees their real skin (*ipireté*)," he replied. This is the difference between the vision in the dream and the vision while awake: The former involves the "enemy's double" (*akwawa-ra'owa*), but the latter involves "his true skin" (*ipireté*).

The *wari'imongetawa* is reminiscent of a Tupinambá ceremony in which a shelter was constructed: A hammock was hung up and large quantities of food and drink placed inside it:

With everything ready, the people gathered and their prophet was led to the cabin. . . . Once inside and alone, everyone else having left, the shaman lay on his

---

17 For a similar concept, see the Wayãpi *morawan* (Gallois 1988:239–40).

18 The Tupi concept of *tocaia* as a cage or container for spirits is not limited to the form of a shelter. The flute ritual performed by the Asurini of the Xingu features a large pan called *tauva-rukaia* into which the supernatural entity Tauva is attracted (Müller 1990:124). The maraca can also be conceived as a *tocaia* in its double function of attracting spirits (through sound) and containing them (through its enclosed spherical form).

hammock and began to invoke the malign spirit.... At the end of these invocations, the spirit arrives, revealed by the sound of chirps or whistles.... The spirit is asked about the wars against their enemies. They always ask it whether they will achieve victory.... (Thevet [1576] 1978:118)

The reference to a cabin where the shamans divine the fate of warriors reappears in numerous authors from the period (Fernandes 1970:74–7). Staden describes one of these rites, claiming that, at the end, the diviners ordered "them to leave for war to capture enemies, since the spirits inside the maracas are eager to eat slave flesh" (Staden [1557]1974:174). Anchieta, for his part, claims that one day before entering into combat, they offered "a sacrifice to their sorcerers in a little house constructed for the purpose, questioning them as to what would happen in the conflict." (Anchieta [1554–94] 1988:51).

The Parakanã *wari'ijara* do not enjoy the same prestige as the sixteenth-century shamans, and its performance does not differentiate between the great dreamers. In the 1990s, few were left who had practiced the rite. One of them, Pykawa, had performed it during pacification. The Funai officer João Carvalho describes Pykawa's telescopy in his diary:

It was just after 6 P.M. when they called us.... Arakitá said that we were going to the swidden, then I saw that everyone was armed with bows and arrows.... We arrived at a manioc swidden where there was a cleared area with a kind of blind in one corner, so we all sat down, and Pikáua with his enormous cigar began to blow smoke on the straw, rubbing the cigar in the latter which scattered embers everywhere. After speaking for some time, pronouncing words to scare away the enemy ... everyone twanged their bow cords and roared ... saying the same things that they had said to use on our first encounter, that is, we will kill all of them.... [T]he worst bit was that they invited myself and Lourival to help them with our guns to kill them all, and asked us to bring rifles for them as they would be better for killing. Afterwards they put down their arrows, holding just their bows and remained pulling the bow cords the whole time; this lasted about 3 hours. I then asked what direction these ruapara [probably, -*rowajara*, "adversaries"] lay; the chief showed me the direction and that there were three since he pointed in different directions. (Funai 1971f: 12–13)

This event occurred on June 25, 1971, when contact had already been established. The day before, some of the Parakanã had used a rifle for the first time and began to solicit them from the Funai team. The invitation to João Carvalho to watch the *wari'imongetawa* was partly a ploy to obtain the guns. However, the rite itself was not a simulacrum: Pykawa is said to have really seen the enemies, especially the western Parakanã. They thought that, were they able to locate them, they would finally emerge victorious with the help of the whites and their guns. João Carvalho's description adds an important fact concerning the audience: They were all armed as if going to war. The interaction with the *wari'ijara* is an interposed mode of relationship with the enemy.

The *wari'imongetawa* was performed during moments of uncertainty. Shortly before contact in 1971, the eastern Parakanã had held another telescopy, and the *wari'ijara* announced: "The whites will get us." There is a sense of foresight present in this speech, echoing the interpretation given by the chroniclers of the Tupinambá rites in which the shamans are very often called diviners. The idea of foreseeing future events is not foreign to the Parakanã rite: According to Mojiapewa, the *wari'ijara* would tell who would become a killer, who might be killed, and so on. In the narratives recorded by myself, though, there are only predictions on success in hunting.[19] In all cases, television always concerns a sort of present-future tense: Although it foresees what has yet to happen, this is achieved not only through knowledge of the future, but also through knowledge of what is already happening.

This aspect of the rite takes us to the problem of the truth status of the *wari'ijara*'s speech. One time, Mojiapewa, speaking of a man who had performed various telescopies, told me that in some "he lied" (*itemon*), in others "he knew" (*okawaham*). Although the stative verb -*temon* is normally used in the same sense as "to lie," here it has an involuntary character: It is a failure rather than a fraud, applying to shamanic visions that involve practical consequences that fail to materialize. The person is said to have "lied," but this does not mean he/she did not actually see what he/she claimed. The reason for the failure is located between the vision (which is factual) and its realization. The lie occupies this interval and rather than implying falsity, it indicates the nontransition from potency to act. As a possibility it remains objective, as an act it comprises a lie (and people can suggest the reasons or circumstances that – during this space-time interval – prevented its realization). The *wari'imongetawa* is thus a public narration of actual events rather than a form of divination, although it always implies a condensation of present and future.

Pi'awa told me about two telescopies that preceded an attack on the eastern Parakanã in the 1940s, when they captured five women (including his future wife). His father was then placed in the blind:

Then he saw:

– The enemies are still there for us, that's how it is, Tewenga is still there.
– Where, my old man? I asked him.

---

19 Once again, the association between hunting and warfare is reminiscent of the sixteenth century data. Although the primary theme of the divinations was warfare, some passages suggest that the abundance of game was also important. The Tupi interpreted Anchieta's nocturnal prayers as a tête-à-tête with the spirits and asked him both about war ("Didn't God tell you something about killing them?") and about hunting ("Make God order all the game from the hills to fall into my traps") (Anchieta [1554-94] 1988:236-7).

- There, my son, all of them remain still. Let's encounter them.
- You're right, let's encounter them, my father, I replied.
- The Amowaja are all there, Tewenga is still there, Joropehe, Namijawa.[20]
- Look carefully, look carefully, my old man, I insisted.
- Let's find them, my son, you're going to cross their path. They're traversing a river.
- You're right, my old man.
- They're returning home, before us, they're going to dance the *opetymo*, my son.
- You're right, they're going to dance the *opetymo*, my father. Let's wait for them to dance so I can speak to them. I'll speak to them, so that they'll give me my future wife, so that she can give me drink, I said.
- Okay, let's call them, if they attack us, we'll run.
- Okay, my father, I replied.
- They're still there, they're performing the *opetymo*, there where they just planted manioc. They are close to the headwaters, they're leaving the area and heading downriver.
- You're right, my father.
- They're going to fetch eagle down, then those who will dance in the *opetymo* will return. Go and call them during the ritual.
- What should I say to them, my father? I asked.
- "What type of people are you, my maternal uncles (*miatyrange*)?" Ask them this and wait. If they reply, then say to them: "Give me your daughter, my brother-in-law."
- Okay, my father.

He came out of the blind.

- And so, my father?
- The enemies are there, we should go that way.

(Pi'awa 1995: tape 5).

The *wari'ijara*'s utterances lack past tense markers: The actions that unfold in the vision are in the present and point to future developments. In the blind, the *wari'ijara* sees what is happening: "They're crossing a river"; "They're returning home"; "They're performing *opetymo*"; and he indicates the actions that should be undertaken by his son.

The telescopy over, the warriors headed in the indicated direction and arrived at an abandoned swidden, followed by a house in ruins. Once again, they had to decide which direction to take. Pi'awa's mother, Mere, asked another woman to place her in the blind. She made the screen from inajá

---

20 These are nicknames given to eastern Parakanã men: Tewenga ("Belly") for Orowo'a, and Namijawa ("Mangy Ear") for Ijianga, the headman at the time. As we have seen in Chapter 1, Amowaja is how the western Parakanã call the eastern Parakanã.

palm leaves: "Perhaps they are already talking." Mere entered the blind and dialogues similar to those previously described transpired: "You're right, my old woman, take a good look at the enemies for us," the assistant said. "I'm not lying, my children, let's encounter the enemies," she uttered from the blind. Finally, Mere indicates the path to follow. Dawn arrived: "Let's go, my children, so you can see the path." The Amowaja were caught by surprise.

Once, while narrating one of the various attacks on them by their ex-kin, the eastern Parakanã headman, Arakytá, asked me: "How did they manage to get so close without us hearing their voices?" He himself replied, "Owari'imonge": shamanic telescopy, a technology for locating enemies in the tropical forest.

True Enemies, Untrue Friends

Once the forces have been mobilized and the target located, the next phase is to advance toward the enemy. The warrior band could include as many as four dozen armed men as well as the women who frequently accompanied their husbands until the group neared the enemy target. The women remained camped about one or two days from the location of the attack, where they kept the fires alight and looked after the warriors' hammocks. After this point, the warrior band continued onward, carefully surveying the enemy territory. Leading the way were the most experienced the *tenotara* ("those who go in front"), also called *makakarow-ypya* ("those who will attack first"). The youngest stayed in the rearguard: They awaited the combat at a distance or sometimes surrounded the enemies in the company of an older warrior, waiting for the enemies to retreat in their direction so they could shoot them more easily or capture any fleeing women.

As they advanced, the warriors split into couples, ideally pairs of "formal friends" (*-pajé*), since these should always be together: *ojoko'a-rehe ojowerekai* ("they walk buttock to buttock"). "Friends" typically hunt, take part in rituals, and go to war together. Parakanã war narratives contain stereotyped formulas to express this cooperation: When shooting an enemy, the killer turns to his *-pajé* and says, "You for me, my friend," to which the other replies, "I for you, my friend" and then releases his arrow. The friendship can actually be constituted on the basis of this war partnership, as Pi'awa told me when narrating an attack on the Asurini:

So my future friend arrived, my late maternal uncle.

– Where are my victims talking, my nephew?
– Look, in the river, my uncle, your victims are in the water.

So we cooperated (*oromotywa*). We went together.

   – I'll go ahead of you, my nephew, I'll kill the enemy alone. Wait for me here.
   – I'll go too so I can shoot for you, my uncle.

So we went together.

(Pi'awa 1995: tape 30)

After the collaboration in the war expedition, the asymmetric relation between maternal uncle and sister's son is substituted by a symmetrical relation between friends. In order to understand this substitution we need to specify the meaning of the term *-pajé*. As I have shown elsewhere (Fausto 1991; 1995), the Parakanã have no specific terms for cross-cousins. The latter, when older than ego, are equated with the mother's siblings (*totyra* for a male alter, *-'yra* for a female alter) and when younger, with the sister's children (*tekojara* for a male alter, *-tejomemyna* for a female alter). The classification of cross-cousins is thus inflected by a parameter of relative age, which pushes older cousins up a generation and younger cousins down a generation. Strictly speaking, there are no cross-cousins, although other kinds of symmetrical affines exist.

In addition to the terms for in-laws, the western Parakanã possess ten reciprocal pairs for male egos and alters, plus five for female egos and alters, all of which may replace kinship terms. Most of these terms substitute the pair *totyra-tekojara* (between men) or *'yra-tejomemyna* (between women), but some of them can also modify relations between classificatory siblings. In both cases, they aim at avoiding the asymmetry of the relative age distinction. Some reclassification terms seem to offer an ironic comment on this asymmetry by appealing to the absurd: there are, for example, affines that call each other "parrot," "husband" and "wife," "women's brother," and so on (Fausto 1991:158–71).[21]

Among the eastern Parakanã there are just two terms of this kind: *-pajé* and *-tywa*. The *-tywa* is a sort of *-pajé*, but whereas the latter relationship is ideally established in ritual, the *-tywa* relationship results from the co-participation in the death of an enemy: *tywa* are those who *ojopotywo akwawa-rehe*, who "help each other seek out the enemy," and thus *ojomotywa* ("made themselves into *tywa*").[22] The eastern bloc is also more restrictive in the use of these reclassifiers: Nobody can have more than one living *-pajé*

---

21 The use of relational terms taken out of context or words belonging to other semantic fields was also observed among the Tupinambá. The priest Leonardo do Valle describes the meeting between two chiefs in 1562, whose peace accords were sponsored by the Jesuits: "The one from Santo André [the host] began: You have come, my wife. This is a way they two great friends have of calling each other by a certain name like this, or my teeth, or my arm, or any other part of the body, and this remains fixed between them forever just as much as a spiritual kinship contracted by sacrament." (Navarro et al. [1550–68] 1988:376). See Léry ([1578] 1980:283).

22 For cognates of *tywa* in other Tupi-Guarani languages, see Viveiros de Castro (1992a:357).

and one living -*tywa*, while among the western bloc there are people with as many as three -*pajé*. This difference is probably linked to their distinct sensibilities in relation to social asymmetries. The proliferation of reclassifiers enabled the western Parakanã to abolish all asymmetries in same-sex relations.

The most productive term is -*pajé*. Most of the reclassifications occur during the *opetymo* ritual, which is ideally executed by pairs of "friends," mirroring the structure of the war band. The -*pajé* relationship comprises thus a form of ceremonial friendship, although without the formalized character observable among the northern Ge, as Parakanã friends interact freely, share food, and visit each other. However, it always implies alterity. The essential meaning of the relation is that of a symmetrical opposition between same-sex contemporaries, as is the case of the Trio *pito* (Rivière 1969:77–81).[23] In contrast to the latter, though, the Parakanã category applies to a minimal genealogical distance: Twenty percent of the thirty-eight occurrences among the western Parakanã, and thirty-five percent of the nineteen cases registered among the eastern group were first-degree cousins. This difference in the use of -*pito* and -*pajé* expresses an important sociological distinction: The Parakanã do not produce a social field in which affines and affinity are masked by a cognatic veil, expressed in etiquette, teknonymy, and the reclassification of coresidents. There is nothing similar to the Guianese fiction of the endogamic monad, which aims to elide the explicit content of affinity between spatially proximate kin. On the contrary, the Parakanã reclassifications reinforce the character of opposition and alterity. A -*pajé* is always and necessarily an "other" (*amote*).

This Parakanã category traverses the inside/outside dichotomy designating both a close affine and a distant enemy: The default form for addressing a non-Parakanã is, precisely, "my friend" (*wepajé*). This is quite common in Amazonia, where categories translated as "friend" are often used as a form of addressing strangers. The Krahô, for example, use the term *hõpin* ("formal friend") for "strangers with whom one wishes to mark friendship or simply good will" (Carneiro da Cunha 1978:75); the Trio trading partners (*ipawana*), who live far apart, call each other *pito*; whereas the Araweté use the vocative *tywã* to address whites whose name they do not know (Viveiros de Castro 1986:391). In all three cases, "friendship" is a device for connecting different levels of sociality, enabling the passage from kinship to politics, domestic to public, inside to outside. There are

---

23 Some people are "friends" from a very early age: Cross-cousins whose births are separated by a short interval are defined as -*pajé* before they even begin to speak. However, there are also "friendship" relations between people of different age groups. In these cases, the category functions like the out-of-context terms.

differences, though: Whereas formal friendship among the Ge possesses a high internal sociological productivity, linking groups that divide up the same village unit, among the Carib peoples of the Guianas it mediates relations between distinct residential and/or ethnic groups. Among the Tupi, we find an intermediate form in which formal friendship structures relations within the local unit and, at the same time, comprises the mechanism for its opening.

In the Parakanã case, the category also defines a partnership relation that can be forged between enemies. When two groups meet and look to avoid a confrontation, each warrior seeks out an adversary and embraces him, becoming his "friend." The embrace is a way of neutralizing the adversary through bodily proximity. In four of the ten occasions in which the Parakanã blocs confronted each other, this is precisely what occurred. As we have seen in Chapter 1, the first of these encounters took place in the 1910s, when the western Parakanã came across an unoccupied village and stole flour. The theft was discovered and the eastern Parakanã left in pursuit of the invaders. They managed to surround them while still in their territory. They did not attack them, though: "Let's just talk to them." They spoke to each other at a distance. At first, the hostile bands treated each other collectively as potential "friends," expressing a generic relation of friendship: "Go there," a western Parakanã man is reported to have said to his son, "and give these arrows to our friends, so they can take them to their wives."[24]

The long-distance talk ended. The eastern Parakanã sang to the invaders, who replied with another song. They then left, arranging to meet again, this time accompanied by their women. The eastern Parakanã wanted to exchange wives since, as they told me, "there were no women to marry" (as we have seen, they were marrying "sisters" during this period). In all likelihood, the western Parakanã had the same idea.[25] Hence after they returned to the encampment where their women were waiting, they immediately left to reencounter the eastern group. The next afternoon, they arrived at the rendezvous site. Each group announced their arrival while still some distance away, initiating a stereotyped dialogue of good will: "Are you going to have a truly good talk with me, my great brother-in-law?"; "Let's have

24 The translation "our friends" fails to capture the collectivized form of the expression used: *jene-pajé-toa* (1pl.-friend-collective). Swapping arrows is a sign of a peaceful disposition. Formal friends swap them at the end of the tobacco festival, when meeting after a long time apart, or simply when they leave together to hunt.

25 The narratives always include reported speech that explains why they initially accepted a pacific relationship: "Let's go to see our friends' wives so that they'll give me my future wife," or "Let's shout for our friends to give me my future axe." In the case of the western Parakanã, this reported speech is always followed by a lament that the enemy had not been finished off immediately. The formula is a direct citation of a warrior stating: "We were foolish not to have killed the enemies."

a good talk with each other, my *pajé*"; or "I came for no reason, I don't get furious with people" (Iatora 1993: tape 12). They sang and danced until dawn. When first light approached, the eastern Parakanã invited the others to accompany them to their swiddens. On the way, the western group stopped near a low-lying area, which they had surveyed in the morning and which seemed a good location were a conflict to break out. Each warrior hugged his enemy *pajé* and took him there. They spread out over the area in pairs but were extremely tired and decided to sleep. As they slept, the conflict erupted leading to the death of six eastern men and one western man.

In the 1930s, a similar situation had an unfavorable outcome for the latter. Caught stealing flour once more, they were pursued. The eastern warriors encircled them and after preliminary dialogues at a distance, advanced into the open and embraced their adversaries in pairs. They danced and sang throughout the night and in the morning invited them to go to the village where their wives were staying. A dozen western warriors accompanied their "friends." As evening approached, they arrived at an abandoned village where the eastern group had hidden axes and machetes. The partnership between enemy-friends demands constant bodily proximity – they should even urinate together – making a bow and arrow useless as a weapon, hence the need to have a means of killing at close range should one decide to finish off one's "friends."

Tired, the western Parakanã allowed sleep to overcome them.

– I'm going to sleep, my friend, my uncle said.
– Why don't you sleep, my friend? Look at me. My bottom is soft [that is, I'm calm], he replied to him.

Sat down, he opened his legs for my uncle:

– Lie down here between my thighs, I'll wake you in the morning.

He lay down, the late My'a also slept between the legs of his friend, my grandfather Te'a'y'yma also slept between the thighs of his friend. They slept.

(Iatora 1993: tape 4)

This is how enemy-friends are made. When one of them wants to sleep, the other should cradle him between his legs in a protective attitude. The "friend" should shield the partner to prevent the others from killing him. But if one group decides to kill the other, it will be up to the partner to kill his "friend." Hence the -*pajé* is not only the guardian, he is also the executioner. Indeed, this is what happened. When the western Parakanã had fallen asleep, their former kin began the killing, each warrior attacking his own -*pajé* by striking him with an axe or a machete.

Friendship is as intimate and ambiguous as the relationship between the killer and his victim. "My friend" (*wepajé*) is either "my future victim" (*jeremiaroma*) or "my future executioner" (*jeropiaroma*). This applies not only to enemy-friends, but also to the friends connected by kinship. When a faction decides to kill someone during an internecine conflict, it is left to his *pajé* to undertake the task. Two of the three internal assassinations that occurred among the western Parakanã were perpetrated by the victim's friend. Indeed, in one of these cases the killer used the victim's own arrow: He invited him to go hunting, asked him for the arrow, and ambushed him a little farther on. The ambiguity of this relation, split between proximity and distance, companionship and treachery, is always present. During the 1960s conflicts, after killing one of his "friends," a man went to meet his other "friend," who was likewise a "friend" of the victim, in order to tell him what he had done with a mixture of boastfulness and sorrow: "I just killed our great friend, my friend.... I took him from us" (Karáya 1993: tape 46). One hundred years after the split between the Parakanã blocs, the attitude of Iatora's grandfather was still evoked: He had refused to take part in the killing that caused the split since "he was too attached to his friend."

The ambivalence of the *-pajé* category is reminiscent of the Tupinambá *tobajara*, a term meaning "the one from the other side" that was applied to both enemies and brothers-in-law. In fact, Parakanã friends are frequently real affines: During the period of my research, 50 percent of friends among the eastern group and 20 percent among the western group were also brothers-in-law. Whereas kin-friends can be brothers-in-law, enemy-friends are potential brothers-in-law, since if alliance becomes possible, they will exchange women.[26] Friendship among the Parakanã therefore spans from minimal to maximal distance, from first-degree cross-cousins to strangers, modeling one relation by the other and crossing the amity-enmity divide. In contrast to other Amerindian peoples who reserve "friendship" for relations between people who are genealogically, socially, or geographically distant, the Parakanã turned it into a tool for linking the near and the far, and across the whole range they preserved the protection-predation ambivalence as its defining feature. Underlying intimacy and protection is the fact that the *-pajé* is necessarily an affine, an other, the nearest enemy, the prey close to hand.

Captivating Women

The hostile encounters between the eastern and western Parakanã in the first decades of the twentieth century highlight the virtuality of alliance as well as its failure. Both groups attempted an approximation,

---

26 In war narratives, the most frequent mode of addressing adversaries is, precisely, "brother-in-law." The term *-pajé* is reserved for a single individual or for the group as a whole (in the collectivized form, *-pajetoa*).

defined their relation through the institution of friendship, and agreed to exchange women. A few angry sparks, however, sent the peaceful overtures up in smoke. Yet even after these deaths, a new attempt was made. Still in the 1930s, the western group reached the eastern village. They surrounded it and one of them shouted to his -pajé: "Have you really abandoned me, my friend?" "No," he answered, "I'm waiting for you, my friend, our talk isn't over." Trying to clear the way for a new interaction, the western warriors made several declarations of peaceful intent: "We've come for no reason [in peace]"; "We're not angry"; "I've no teeth for you"; "I was missing you." As recounted in the first chapter, most of the eastern Parakanã men were in the forest at that occasion, and the few that remained in the village shut themselves within the communal house. At a disadvantage, the eastern Parakanã had to be adroit to avoid a confrontation: Women offered manioc flour to the visitors, men offered songs, cigars, Brazil nuts, and, above all, good conversation. At the end of the day, the hunters returned. They spoke again about exchanging women: "I'm going to bring my daughter for you, so you can kill tapir for her, my son-in-law"; "Bring my niece to me quickly, my father-in-law, so I'll have you truly in my heart" (weywyraparipé, literally "in my bow"). They danced and sang until dawn and bid farewell with well-intentioned words. The western Parakanã returned soon with their women to concretize the promises of marriage. Another night of dancing and singing ensued. As first light approached, though, a new conflict buried the chances of an alliance: three deaths on the eastern side, two on the western side. This was the end of the attempts at peaceful interaction. Until the mid-1960s, the western Parakanã attacked the eastern group another four times, killing nine people and obtaining several women.

The kinds of situation described here were not confined to the cases involving the Parakanã blocs. Every armed conflict could imply a more or less extensive interaction. Contact was frequently sought first, the success of which depended on linguistic comprehension. Talking to the enemy, asking his name, qualifying him, were important aspects of warfare. Rather than being turn into generic and quantifiable objects, their victims had to be subjectivized and individualized. The ideal victim was someone whose songs and names were known to the killers, enabling an expanded appropriation of the homicide. In Amazonia, there is an "optimal distance" (Taylor 1985) at which warfare practices are more productive: The definition of this sociogeographical interval varies according to the people and the system in which they are inserted. This optimum is a function of the equation between a maximal distance (in which difference becomes indifferent) and a minimal distance (in which identity encompasses alterity). This interval provides an ideal space for the cross-flow of identities, trophies, immaterial goods, and so on.[27]

Tupinambá anthropophagy enabled precisely the construction of this optimal distance, rather than taking it as given. The captive – whether French, Tapuia, Tupi, or Portuguese – ended up learning the behavior, speech, and disposition needed to enact a beautiful death. During his captivity, the victim produced what would later be remembered by the killer and the group as a whole. In their interactions with enemies, the Parakanã also sought to capture fragments of alien memory: Even today, the western and eastern groups recall the songs and names they heard from each other.[28] However, the most efficient method for appropriating alien memories was to capture enemy women: These women brought not only their bodies – their capacity to work and reproduce – but also their knowledge.

Capturing women was one of the motives for going to war. It was frequently up to the younger men, accompanied by someone more senior, to ensure the women were caught, encircling the enemy village so as to intercept them as they fled. This is what happened, for example, in the mid-1940s when the western Parakanã attacked an eastern Parakanã village on the upper Lontra River. They fired various volleys of arrows and retreated at dusk, anticipating that the eastern group would strike back. In vain. Paringa, a *moropetenga*, approached the village to provoke them: "Your head is going to whistle on the ground covered in ants," he yelled. Nothing. They then realized that the eastern Parakanã had escaped in the dark. Some women, though, had been intercepted by the younger men while they tried to flee: "We're just going to take you so that you can make food for us." In general, whoever caught a woman took her as a wife or, if he was already married, gave her to his son or younger brother. Foreign women enabled the matrimonial destiny of some men to be anticipated, without annulling any right they might have over a prepubescent wife. A father's concern to give his son a wife could be expressed in a striking form, as happened during the sharing out of the five women captured in this attack. This is how Pi'awa tells the event:

The late Tapaia arrived:

- You caught a wife, younger brother, he said to me.
- Yes, I caught one, older brother, I replied.

---

27 See, for example, the distinction between vendettas and head-hunting among the Jívaro (Taylor 1985) or tooth-hunting and unruly warfare for the Yágua (Chaumeil 1985), or again, in another ethnographic context, between *wim* and *soli* war for the Jalé of Papua New Guinea (Koch 1974:79–80).

28 Various enemy names (*akwawarenwera*, "ex-name of enemies") were actually used to name the new generations. Some of these terms are not proper names, but nicknames given to the enemy in response to a distinctive physical feature. The Parakanã nicknamed the victim to take the sobriquet from him later.

— What sex are her children?
— Two girls.
— Let's share them, younger brother, he said to me.
— I'm going to keep one of the daughters, my older brother. You can have the mother so that she can make food for you right away, I suggested.

So, the late Jakaré arrived and also asked for a woman. We were all unmarried. My wife was a child still. Mororé [the foreign woman] already had mature breasts.... So, we met up with the others again. My uncle Arona took Porake'ia [another of the captured women].

— Give a woman to my son, give him a woman, he's truly unmarried, if not I'll kill them all, Tato'a said.
— We're going to kill them, said Ywy'yra.

So, Iatora obtained a woman:

— Come on, give me my future wife, my maternal uncle, this one, Iatora asked Arona.
— Come on, my son-in-law, if not I'll kill them, said Tato'a.

So, Arona turned to his older brother and said:

— I'm going to give a woman to our true nephew, "give her to me," he said to me.
— You're going to give the woman I caught, younger brother?
— Yes, older brother, our kin said they'll kill her.

And turning to Iatora:

— Come here and get her, my nephew.

(Pi'awa 1995: tape 11)

Tato'a's insistence was understandable: His older son, Iatora, then in his early twenties, had lost his first wife during labor. Unless he captured an enemy woman or stole the wife of a relative, he could spend more than a decade unmarried. For this reason, Tato'a pressed his son-in-law Arona, who was married to Iatora's sister. Arona was forced to anticipate the return for the wife he had received by giving him a captured woman. All the men who caught enemy women on this occasion were in an uncertain matrimonial situation: Jakaré and Pi'awa were married to girls younger than five years, whereas Koria and Tapaia had no wife at all. As we have seen, the negative perception of bachelorhood, combined with the closure of the matrimonial field and the scarcity of women, made capture not only a side-benefit of warfare, but a means of alleviating the internal conflicts over women.

After sharing out the foreign women, the warriors returned to the eastern Parakanã village, which, as everyone had fled, was empty. They stayed

Photo 3. Kojaitá, an eastern Parakanã woman kidnapped in the 1930s (western Parakanã, Apyterewa village, 1988).

the night there in the company of the captured women, who toasted flour for them. Swidden produce was especially coveted by the western group. Very often, they stopped in the plantations before an attack to roast and eat yam or sweet potato. They also searched for tobacco, hammocks, small baskets, and metal tools. Yet the most precious wealth they took from the enemies was their women, whom they had to captivate through a mixture of fear and talk.

The Parakanã preferred to abduct young women, as the older ones were more difficult to "pacify" (-mo'yng) and sometimes resisted capture. Those who had male children presented an additional problem, since the Parakanã feared that in the future the grown boy could want to avenge their dead kin. Escaping was a risky venture whose success depended on the complicity of the captor's wife, who might be willing to help her so as not to have to share her husband. Normally, though, the women of the group maintained a close watch over the recently pacified foreign women. Ararona, the oldest woman from the group captured in the episode described previously, tried to flee a few days after arriving at the western Parakanã village, taking two of her children with her: a girl and a boy, who had so far been spared. When they discovered the escape, the women went after the men, who were hunting for tortoises, and alerted them: "The enemy women have gone. Go after them, my brothers, and kill them." Ararona and her son were killed, but the girl was brought back to her husband.

The women were not just held captive by fear, though. They also had to feel newly at home, "becoming completely accustomed" (-jepokwapam).

People say that they displayed no anger or revolt over their condition, but cried a lot, meaning they had to be persuaded to overcome their sadness. After returning from the expedition, they entreated them to remain: "Menstruate among us," they would say, convincing them that they would be treated well: "Look, you were hungry before and now we'll give you game." This opposition between hunger and abundant food is central: Marriage is founded on the exchange of services between husband and wife, swapping the work of hunting for cooking food. Accepting food and eating with their captors signaled consent and a willingness to enter the game of kinship. After intercepting Ararona, one of the killers admonished her son: "I told you to eat the tapir that I had hunted, that's what I told you in vain" (Pi'awa 1995: tape 12).

The initial moments of integration were marked by singing and dancing. On arrival at the camp or village, the captives were handed over to the killers' sisters or mother, who took them by the arm and led them to dance a "bringing women" song (*kojoa-rero'awa*). The captives were expected to perform the music of their kin, in particular the "victims' ex-songs" (*temiara-je'engarera*). The warriors retributed by presenting themselves to the foreign women, now referred to collectively as "the victim's ex-wives" (*temiara-ratykwera*). The captives carried a musical memory of the enemy, which was transmitted to the captors in a public performance.[29]

After the killers' seclusion, a clarinet festival was performed, incorporating the foreign women in the game of matrimony and infidelity. In this ritual, some women are forced to enter the circle of dancers, where they must embrace a man other than their husband, connoting a relation between lovers. In the case of captives, they were expected "to place their hearts into the bamboo tubes" and thereby spend a long life among their captors. Their social condition of brotherless wives was gradually transformed with the arrival of children and the constitution of kinship ties. Some of the foreign women even achieved a certain prominence due to the stories they recounted, the names of ex-kin they enunciated, or their shamanic abilities.

This process of pacification and kin making, involving both fear and seduction, was not always successful. Success depended not only on the captive's age, but also their origin: The chances were higher when the captors and captives shared the same cultural and linguistic code. Pacifying older women with different speech and customs was considered an arduous task, and, in the case of Ge women, they even thought it pointless to capture them. This selectivity contrasts with the Kayapó's confidence in their capacity to acculturate the captive. Verswijver (1992a:150–3) relates that,

---

29 These songs, however, were not incorporated into ritual life, for reasons that will become clear in Chapter 6.

between 1915 and 1968, the Kayapó Mekrãgnotí captured sixty-three people (forty-six women and nineteen men) from ethnic groups as diverse as the Panará, Juruna, Tapirapé, Munduruku, and even the regional non-indigenous population. The Mekrãgnotí's mechanism for incorporating captives differed from the Parakanã's. Whereas among the latter the captured woman or girl immediately became the wife of someone, among the Mekrãgnotí children of both sexes were initially adopted by the war leader, who could keep them for himself or hand them over to his mother, sisters, or children (Verswijver 1992a:151–2). Thus in contrast to the Parakanã, whose captives were appropriated individually as wives, among the Mekrãgnotí they were incorporated collectively by a leader, who could redistribute them among his kin, constituting ties of adoptive filiation.[30]

Moreover, most captive women did not become legitimate wives but proxy wives: women of the *kupry* category, linked to a men's society whose members had sexual relations with them throughout the long period of postnatal seclusion of their wives. From this point of view too, the foreign women were also appropriated according to a logic of group. Capture did not guarantee an individual's marriage, but rather the existence of a surplus of single women in a monogamic society (Verswijver 1992a:153–4). Among the Kayapó, uxorilocality and the centrality of the transmission of name and ceremonial statuses across generations made a captive woman an incomplete wife. Without brothers or father, she did not enable an adequate social inclusion for her husband or the couple's children. Among the Tupi, by contrast, the absence of affines makes marriage through capture desirable: It is a form of escaping bride-service, likewise marriage to a niece, though at the opposite extreme. Marrying very close or very distant are strategies for freeing oneself from the yoke of the wife-givers and affirming one's autonomy.

The oppositions between individual and collective, dispersed and centralized, alliance and filiation, intransitive and transitive express global differences between the Ge and Tupi sociocosmologies, which are reflected in their distinct ways of absorbing outside values. Not only do the modes of integrating captives differ, but also the forms of incorporating the knowledge brought by them. Among the Kayapó, the appropriation of material and immaterial goods entails their inclusion within a system involving the horizontal and vertical circulation of transmittable properties and prerogatives. Names, songs, dances, ritual themes, and items of material culture are collectively appropriated, transmitted between

---

30 The Ikpeng provide a midway example. They captured only children (of both sexes) for adoption. The captor, however, did not keep the captive for himself but transferred the child to a person of his choosing, frequently in compensation for the death of a relative. Passing on the captive was obligatory but strictly individual (Menget 1988:67).

generations, conserved by groups and traded in a system of loaning prerogatives. They become "wealth items" (*nekrets*) that are accumulated, circulated, and transmitted.[31]

Among the Tupi, by contrast, foreign material and immaterial goods are not incorporated into a system of circulation where prestige is based on the transmissibility of honors. They circulate in restricted form and, if transmitted, do not in themselves contain a distinctive value or acquire additional value by being transmitted publicly in ritual (such as the Kayapó "beautiful names"). This intransitivity implies the need to produce value incessantly, which means capturing names, songs, and people continually from the outside, since there is no feedback internal to the system. This is what gives the Tupi dialectic between interiority and exteriority – as formulated by Viveiros de Castro (1986) – its distinctive character in relation to the Ge systems, and not the contrast between open and closed to the outside, as some authors have erroneously claimed.

Seeing People

Captives and songs, names and axes were important ingredients of Parakanã warfare. But the main theme was the killing. The most frequent reason cited for departing on a war expedition is simply the desire to kill enemies. Each participant wanted to become or confirm himself as a *moropiarera*, a predator of humans, one who "sees people."[32] In the Parakanã case, this objective was not subsumed to a discourse of revenge, as in other Amerindian warfare contexts. Their wars do not seem to emerge from that "absurd and gratuitous feeling of revenge" (Thevet [1576] 1978:135) that the chroniclers identified as the primordial reason for the Tupinambá conflicts. The warrior's drive did not depend on a network of vendettas and the need to "pay" for the killing of a relative.[33]

---

31 The incorporation of enemy names among the Kayapó is residual, though. The large majority is classified as ancestral names (Lea 1992:133). Enemy songs and ritual routines, on the contrary, play an important role in ceremonial life. According to Verswijver (1992a:155) four of the eleven Mekrãgnotí naming ceremonies are considered to have a foreign origin. Items of material culture were often appropriated as "wealth" belonging to individuals and as a privilege of their maternal residential segment (Verswijver 1992b:81).

32 Literally, "ex-killer of people" (*moro-*, "of people," *-ropia*, "killer," *-rera*, contraction of the agentive *-ara* with the past tense marker *-kwera*). The potential or future form is *moropiaroma*, and the neutral form *moropiara*. Among its cognates, we encounter *moropi'hã* in Araweté, *brupiare* in Aché (Viveiros de Castro 1992a:369), *rupiara* in ancient Guarani (Montoya 1876) and *marupiara* in Nheengatu (Stradelli 1929), all with the same meaning.

33 There is a specific verb meaning "to avenge:" *-ajongepyng* (western bloc) or *-ajomepyng* (eastern bloc), which some of my interlocutors glossed as "to pay [the deceased]." The verb *-wepy* ("pay," "offer a return") may indeed freely replace "to avenge" in many contexts.

There is no way of calculating the number of victims in all the western Parakanã attacks. In the confrontations with their ex-kin, they killed seventeen people in nine raids, an average of two people per conflict. This average increased in the three assaults on the Araweté: six deaths per combat, although by then one or two warriors were already using firearms. There were various elements that limited the lethalness of the conflicts: The number of arrows each person could carry, the difficulty of hitting an adversary in the forest, as well as the individualized mode of combat and the loose coordination of the actions. Besides, even a small number of victims could produce various killers, since all those who underwent posthomicide seclusion were considered *moropiarera*. Entering seclusion was not dependent on having actually killed an enemy. On one hand, any injured individual was treated as a victim (even if it was later discovered that s/he had not died, the seclusion already performed was still considered valid). On the other hand, those who had not shot a living enemy looked for the corpses of adversaries in order to shoot them. Young men frequently underwent their first seclusion as "corpse shooters" (*teewera-'ywonara*), the enemy bodies being provided by more experienced warriors.[34]

There were certain limitations, though: It was better if the corpse had not yet gone cold, but above all that it had not become putrid: Its smell had to be of blood (*-pyji'o*), since seclusion is linked to the killer's impregnation by the smell of the victim's blood. On one occasion, they went as far as to dig up the body of a recently buried enemy: Various men, including experienced killers, shot the corpse with arrows, although some had declined to do so since they thought the body had cooled completely. Those who did shoot claimed that it had not rotted and that it still "smelled truly of blood" (*ipyji'oeté*).

Shooting corpses was one way of multiplying the number of killers and socializing the homicide. The idea that it is desirable to expand the number of people involved in the killing of an enemy is widespread in Amazonia. The Kayapó attacked injured enemies, meaning that the killing was rarely an individual endeavor. All of those who took part in the attack were considered killers and received tattoos in the postwar ritual (Verswijver 1992a:179). Among the Wari', a Chapakura-speaking people of Rondônia, one victim was enough for everyone to enter seclusion (Vilaça 1992:98). The Yanomami also shot the enemy after death (Lizot 1989:109), and all those who caused some kind of injury went into seclusion (Albert 1990:559).

---

34 I have information on thirty-one of the thirty-six western Parakanã men alive in 1993 who were at least twenty years old at the time of contact. Thirty of these had undergone posthomicide seclusion, twenty-two of them having shot at least one living enemy and eight having shot only corpses. Only one man, virtually blind since childhood, had not become a killer.

Killers among the Arara, a Carib people of the middle Xingu River, tried to capture the injured enemy alive so that their war partners could shoot him (Teixeira-Pinto 1997:115). These customs were part of a wider set of practices that worked to amplify the symbolic operations following the killing of an enemy.[35]

Among the Parakanã, the socialization of the homicide act did not imply the absence of a distinction in prestige. Although those who shot a dead body were also considered *moropiarera*, this was less prestigious than hitting a living adversary (*tekowé*). The focus of the contrast is on the inertia of the former and the movement of the latter: Only the *moropetenga* who goes at the front of the war expedition has the chance to kill a *iatahowa'é* ("one who walks"). Fearful individuals stay in the rearguard, having nothing but lifeless bodies to shoot. War narratives are interspersed with dialogues in which the vanguard is disputed: "Let me go ahead of you, my older brother, I've never shot anyone"; "Let me go first, my younger brother, I'm more experienced." Or: "Let me go in front of you, my nephew, I'll go alone to kill the enemy"; "Let me attack him for you, my uncle, you were already shooting them when I was a child."[36]

Only those who have killed a living enemy may boast to their kin, or "tell about themselves," as the Parakanã say. Warriors returned with the desire to narrate their successes to women: "Let's tell about ourselves to our wives," they would say. In contrast to ritual contexts in which the actions are directed toward sisters, here the wives (and, in the case of bachelors, the mother) are in focus: "I killed a true great enemy, my mother" or "I killed that which is no longer a human, my niece-wife," the killers would brag. This impulse to share glory had a coalescing function in the past, conducing the reencounters between the trekking bands. War included the movements of dispersion and contraction. The first focused on enemies-men and the second on kin-women.

The distinction between those who merely shoot the corpse and those that kill a living enemy had no overall sociopolitical consequences. The

---

35 This multiplication of the number of killers on the battlefield is linked to the absence of a strong hierarchy of warfare merit. In societies in which this hierarchy exists, there were some restrictions on these practices. Among the peoples of the Chaco, for example, only those who killed and scalped the enemy, bringing the latter back as a trophy, could become a *caanvacle* (Clastres 1982:222; Sterpin 1993). Those who did not wish to obtain this status, however, were not obliged to take the scalp and could relinquish their victim to a companion. In the much more rigid Aztec system, ceding a captive to another warrior was a crime punished by death (Clendinnen 1991:116). In both cases, though, ritual continued to socialize the effects of the homicide, albeit under the control of a warrior and/or priestly elite.

36 There is a supplementary distinction between shooting an uninjured enemy (-*marony'ym*) and collaborating (-*potywo*) in the killing of an adversary who has already been hit by one's war partner. The one to hit an enemy first in an attack is called *makakarerypya*, "the one who touched first."

same even applied to the difference between being or not being a *moropiarera*. While this condition brought some recognition, it did not necessarily translate into political or matrimonial advantages. A man's marriage and his transition to adult life did not depend strictly on the death of an enemy. Although timidity often attracts the interests of rivals and can jeopardize the continuation of a marriage, there are also frequent cases of people successful in war but unsuccessful in love. The absence of internal asymmetries and the strong antihierarchical ethos of the western Parakanã seem to have neutralized the political meaning of warfare prestige.

Among the eastern Parakanã, on the other hand, where a certain hierarchy of prestige does exist, this was constituted, as we have seen, in contraposition to the discourse of war. The headman was not modeled on the war leader. His authority was based on the combination of age and a politics of memory and speech: The headman is an enabler of conversation and an artisan of the word. He cannot be excessively focused on warfare, given the ambivalence of the figure of the obstinate killer. The eastern Parakanã abandonment of the practice of shooting corpses at the beginning of the twentieth century did not lead to a warrior hierarchy, since its main aim was to restrict the number of men predisposed to violence, rather than limit the status of killer to a few valorous men.

If the *moropiarera* status did not translate into any great political-matrimonial advantage, why did western Parakanã men actively look to acquire it? True, a warrior reputation was an important ingredient in the construction of the male personality, but was it enough for them to dedicate themselves so intensely to warfare activity? Here another factor gains prominence: Homicide is a technique for acquiring a long-lasting life. As Koria explained to me, "killing an enemy makes one persist" (*akwawa-jokatawa omoteka*). Becoming a killer does not guarantee a privileged posthumous fate, as in the Tupinambá conception of the warrior's exclusive access to the "beautiful gardens beyond the high mountains" (Léry [1578] 1980:207) or in the non-devourment of Araweté killers by the gods (Viveiros de Castro 1986:578). There is no definitive victory against the forces of death and decay, since the Parakanã do not believe in the soul's immortality and know nothing of the existence of a garden of delights. Homicide does not qualify the killer for a future life, but for persistence in *this* life. Killing and living long, obtaining victories against enemies and against death, are two sides of the same coin.

Posthomicide Seclusion

After killing an enemy or shooting a corpse, the *moropiarera* should walk round a rock and sit down on it, "so that I'll persist," says the killer.[37] Human perishability is contrasted with the solidity of the perennial rock: "That's what people are like, only rock truly persists" (Mojiapewa 1992: tape 1). The killer can also sit on a jatobá trunk (*Hymenaea sp.*), a hard and resistant wood, "so I don't become weak," he says. These are the first steps in a series of actions to be performed after the killing, designed to control the transformations being experienced by the killer. In Parakanã, the verb "to enter into seclusion" only occurs in reflexive form, *-je-koakom* ("to seclude oneself"). It applies to the *couvade* and to the posthomicide interdictions. In both instances, we find a set of negative prescriptions concerning the consumption of foods, sexual relations, and the practice of some other activities. In the former case, though, most of the restrictions are respected by the parents on behalf of the newborn child, whereas in the latter the killer abstains for his own benefit.

During the initial and strictest phase of seclusion, the killer remains in the house, lying in his hammock. For four days he drinks no water, consuming only a bitter infusion of the inner bark of box tree (*marawa*) or cinchona (*inajarona*).[38] The properties of these infusions derive from their bitterness (*-ram*) and function as neutralizers of the victim's blood that contaminates the killer. Some say that the killer is full of "the enemy's ex-blood" (*akwawa-rowykwera*), but the contamination does not require contact with the blood itself; the focal point is its smell. Blood is classified in a specific olfactory category (*-pyji'o*), which is distinct from the smell of rottenness and excrement (*-nem*), the acrid smell of sweat and fermented drink (*-kajing*), the aroma of burning firewood (*-pirem*), and above all the perfume of things that smell good (*-pi'e*). All spilled blood *-pyji'o*, "has *pitiú*," although the emphasis is on human blood.[39] Game animals used for food are not usually said to exude this smell, as otherwise they would be inedible. The handling of game does not demand any notable precautions, unlike menstruation, birth, and homicide. During postnatal seclusion, a wife cannot cook for their husband, since she smells of blood and can contaminate her partner via the food. The killer, for his part, places his wife at risk, meaning she should not share his food or use his bowls.

37 As I noted in the Introduction, the Parakanã, when asked about the meaning of a custom, use this citational formula with the affixation of morphemes to the verb indicating that it is aimed at doing something. The question "Why does the killer sit on the rock?" receives the reply "So that I persist, he says" (*tajetekane oja*).

38 I owe the identification of these trees to Gérson dos Reis Carvalho. Both are from the *Aspidosperma* genus of the *Apocynaceae* family (Lorenzi 1992).

39 The term *pitiú* was incorporated into Portuguese as an Amazonian regionalism, describing the stench exuded by the capybara when its hide is removed. In a number of Tupi-Guarani languages, cognates of the term are also associated with the smell of blood and raw meat.

Among some indigenous peoples, the transmissibility of an olfactive quality is associated with an immaterial principle that passes from victim to killer. Among the Guarani, we find the cognate *pichua*, "the soul of raw meat," which can induce physical and mental disturbances (Cadógan 1965:7). Among the Juruna, "the smell of blood is a conductor of the blood's soul, which swells the killer's belly" (Lima 1995:203). The Parakanã do not postulate any "soul" or "spirit," and prefer to explain this idea as contagion through smell: *Pitiú* is just the odor of blood outside the body, someone's ex-blood that places others at risk.

Contamination through the stench of exogenous blood affects the spleen (-*pere*), making it swell: It "makes someone have spleen" (-*mo-pere*). The symptoms of the illness are tiredness, swelling of the abdomen, and anal bleeding. The remedies are the infusions of box tree and cinchona, which provoke the disappearance of the organ. One man suggested to me that women do not suffer from this ailment because they do not shoot arrows. A woman, however, told me that the wives of killers in seclusion also feel tired and "have spleen." They avoid certain foods and drink bitter infusions, because they feel contaminated by the enemy's ex-blood given their proximity with the killer.

One of the *moropiarera*'s distinctive features, which will stay with him for the rest of his life, is that his mouth stinks of blood: Killing "makes the mouth have *pitiú*." The idea that any homicide is a form of hematophagy is widespread on the continent, and is found among peoples from different linguistic families and geographical areas.[40] Posthomicide precautions normally focus on the expelling, neutralizing, and/or transformation of the exogenous blood. The Parakanã are mainly concerned with neutralizing the smell of blood by means of bitter infusions, and at the same time potentializing its effect through tobacco smoking. During seclusion and throughout his life, the *moropiarera* will smoke in order to perfume his mouth. The cigar is said to neutralize the taste of blood but not its attributes associated with the capacity to dream. The close association between dreaming and homicide is one of the elements that explains why the Parakanã conceived the latter as a technique for obtaining a long and productive life. It opens the way for shamanism and curing: The enemy is killed "for the sickness;" that is, to avoid illness.

It is not only hematophagy that is life-enhancing. The killer's body during seclusion undergoes a process of maturation that hardens him. One

---

40 For example, among the Yanomami (Albert 1985:341–81; Lizot 1996), the Wari' (Vilaça 1992:107–13; 1996:121), the Matís (Erikson 1986:194–7), the Araweté (Viveiros de Castro 1992a:240), the Juruna (Lima 1995:203), the Nivakle (Sterpin 1993:43), the Kayapó (Vidal 1977:156–7; Verswijver 1992a:194–201), and the Timbira (Carneiro da Cunha 1978:103–5; DaMatta 1976a:85–7).

kills "so that I can dry-harden completely, people say." Before becoming resistant and rigid, like a jatobá trunk, the killer passes through a phase in which his body is labile. This makes it necessary to control the food that he ingests. While still in seclusion, he can only eat a very specific part of the meat of the yellow-footed tortoise (*Geochelone denticulata*), considered totally inoffensive.[41] He can also ingest small quantities of babassu coconut and a flour made from manioc toasted with its husk called *manimé*. Breaking this abstinence leads him to acquire the qualities of the consumed food: Eating tapir causes him to walk heavily, white-lipped peccary causes snoring, collared peccary makes the testicles swell, agouti causes him to grind his teeth, and so on. Some plants are also harmful: Huskless manioc flour makes the killer bony, unripe babassu coconut leaves his beard white, and yam causes his buttocks to thin. Other foods do not affect bodily form and disposition, but produce internal disturbances, sometimes lethal. Certain honeys and some fish species are included in this category. There are also foods from which the killer should ideally abstain for the rest of his life, since "they make him have spleen": above all, banana and tortoise eggs, but also curassows and armadillos, which should be eaten by nonkillers such as women and children as well as older men considered "ex-shooters of people."

The lability of the killer's bodily forms and dispositions is similar to that of the newborn child, who needs to be shaped by the parents' hands in order to acquire human form, distinguishing the baby from the animals whom nobody shapes (and who therefore have narrow backs and imperfect buttocks). The danger for the *moropiarera* is not simply assuming animal characteristics, but effectively becoming one. This is exemplified in two myths in which the killer in seclusion leaves to hunt and is taken by his prey, becoming one of them. The first tells the story of Pajejinga, a man who had killed an enemy and was forced to hunt because his kin failed to give any meat to his son. Aggrieved by the crying of the hungry child, Pajejinga set off into the forest. He encountered a band of peccaries and began to shoot at them. When his arrows ran out, he climbed a tree but fell out of it; carried off by the animals, he became definitively one of them: *ojemotajahoeté*, "he made himself truly white-lipped peccary." The other myth tells of the killer who went to hunt vultures for their feathers. He built a hide and used rotten meat as bait. When the birds descended for the feast, he began to shoot at them. After killing a number, he struck the king vulture. Furious, the vultures advanced on the man and carried him to the sky, covering him with the feathers of his victim.

---

41 This is precisely the species prescribed by the Urubu-Ka'apor to women during menstruation (Balée 1984a:227).

During seclusion, the killer is in a process of maturation, and any deviation can lead him to animality instead of granting him longer life. This maturation seems to be conceived as a form of rotting.[42] The Parakanã use the same term to designate the killer's final state of maturation and the decomposition of the corpse: -kwe-pam (where the sufix -pam means "completely"). The term refers to the end point in a process of transformation that involves the passage from a state of humidity and softness to one of dryness and solidity. The corpse -kwepam when it loses all traces of flesh, leaving only a skeleton. The killer -kwepam when he hardens-dries completely, like manioc flour at its toasting point. The Parakanã do not specify the precise amount of time involved in this process. Some prohibitions are said to last for months, such as the avoidance of sexual relations. Failure to observe the latter would lead the killer to die from violent dysentery, caused by a coral snake penetrating his anus. There are also gradations: mature-corrupt a little (-kwepaw-ere-pipi), more or less (-kwepaw-ere), and definitively (-kwepaw-eté). In all events, there is a parallel between the time of seclusion and the time involved in the victim's decomposition. When the corpse is judged to be done, the killer announces that he will take part in the opetymo ritual: "I'm going to dance for you, my sister, and make the ex-hair of my victim fall out."[43]

Viveiros de Castro interprets the process of the killer's maturation-decay as a death in which the perishable portion of the person is subtracted. The Araweté state that a killer never dies, meaning he avoids being devoured by the gods in the sky and does not produce a specter. The author compares this motif to the Guarani conception of perfectibility in life: "We can thus see that the Guarani concept of kandire, the state of the 'non-decay of the bones,' is attained ... by the hubris of the killer, not by the ascetism of the shaman.... After all, the killer has already rotted" (Viveiros de Castro 1992a:247). The parallel with the Parakanã data is clear: Seclusion is a maturation through decay, a cooking through putrefaction. At the outset, the pure smell of raw blood; during the process, metaphors of the putrescence and lability of bodily forms and dispositions; at the end, a rigid and resistant person. The sequence is likened to producing flour: raw tuber, retted manioc dough, toasted flour. Both the killer in seclusion and the flour in the pan become hard-dry and have a long life.

42 The Araweté explicitly affirm that the killer feels like he is rotting, hearing the buzzing of wasps and beetles and the hovering of vultures over his body (Viveiros de Castro 1992a:240).

43 This opetymo for leaving seclusion was the second such rite undertaken by the killers. The first was performed soon after the end of the strictest period of seclusion, which lasted four or five days. According to the eastern Parakanã, the dancing was intended to "disguise oneself from the victim's spirit." Painted and covered in feathers, the killer deceived the spirit of the dead enemy and avoided his vengeance. Although the western Parakanã do not believe in the victim's revenge – "the enemy's spirit does not come after the killer," Pi'awa assured me – they also held the ritual after the first five days of seclusion.

The Misfortune of the Warrior

There is still an another preeminent idea about the warrior's seclusion among the Parakanã: that of a contagion by a "magical substance" from the victim, which produces an indelible propensity toward violence in the killer. This contagion causes a profound psychological alteration, and an inclination to repeat the homicidal act. In such condition, the killer may enter into a wild rage and spare no one, not even his relatives. He therefore needs to be controlled through seclusion, a period in which he will "cool down completely."

Arriving back at the village, each killer, including anyone who shot a corpse, must stick his bow in the ground and abandon it: It has become unlucky and useless for hunting. During seclusion, his kin will come to take away his arrows and any other bow he may have. These are requested by the *moropiarera*'s sisters on behalf of their husbands. Iatora describes the dialogue with his sister Waka'ima, then married to their maternal uncle:

— Give your bow to our uncle, my brother, so he can bring me tapir head to eat, she said to me.
— That's how I am, I kept it [the bow] for nothing. Our uncle has no reason to be afraid of me, my sister, I said to her.
— He will be fearful of you while you have the bow cord, she said to me.
— I'll give my bow to our uncle, my sister, so he can bring a piece of tapir for you to eat, I told her.

(Iatora 1993: tape 24)

The maternal uncle-wife-taker fears that his nephew-wife-giver will come to kill him, since the unpaid matrimonial debt engenders the possibility of predation between affines. This is a recurrent theme among Tupi peoples, one that found literal expression in Tupinambá anthropophagy, in which a wife (frequently a sister or daughter of the future executioner) was given to the captive who would be eventually eaten. Among the Parakanã, the figure of the wife-taker is coextensive with that of the maternal uncle. The temporal hiatus between receiving and reciprocating means that marriage is seen less as an exchange and more as an extraction of women from junior cross-kin. Thus, a maternal uncle is always a taker, the nephew always a giver. The maternal uncle becomes the main focus for the danger posed by the killer, and the sisters emerge as mediators of the relationship: "Those who attack people always carry their bow open with the arrow raised above their head. So my sister made me close my bow. That's why I gave my bow away and no longer picked it up," Iatora explained to me.

The killer does not just threaten his affines. All kin are potential targets of the will to kill, because when enraged he loses consciousness and can see friends as enemies. This proclivity stems from his contamination by another immaterial substance from the victim called -*kawahiwa*, which I translate as "magic-fat."[44] This is not a vital principle that passes from the victim to the killer; only the killers possess it. It is always "the magic-fat of someone's victim" (someone-*remiara-kawahiwa*). It only exists in this form: The victim himself has no -*kawahiwa*, although he makes the killer have it (-*mo-kawahim*). Not all the victims, however, produce this effect. The Parakanã classify them into three categories: *awohoa* (man-augmentative), *haty'ohoa* (wife-augmentative), and *ta'yrohoa* (son of man-augmentative). Killing an adult man makes the killer acquire a lot of -*kawahiwa*, whereas killing children leads to very little. Women are located halfway: The killer is filled with hunger rather than anger, causing him to be selfish with his relatives, since, believing that he will grow thin, he no longer distributes game meat. These distinctions are reflected in the duration of the seclusion; when the victim is a woman or child, the killer soon resumes eating.[45]

Kawahiwa causes an alteration in the killer's psyche, making him unstable and disposed to violence. The eastern Parakanã say that the killer becomes crazy, "loses consciousness" (-*pikajym*), whereas the western Parakanã say that he enters into a state of morbid unconsciousness, similar to someone with fever: "He is unaware of the sun" (*ma'é okwaham ara*). The danger resides in him seeing kin as potential victims, altering his point of view.[46] Such confusion is only one aspect of a general tendency to see everyone as prey. The killer wants to repeat his act, he wants "to expend" (-*mongy*) his -*kawahiwa*. The warrior who becomes enraged will say: "I'm going to kill enemies, my kin, I haven't yet exhausted my desire to become enraged with people, I haven't expended my magic-fat" (Iatora 1993: tape 30). And there is only one way of expending it: killing again. But this is also the way of acquiring it, meaning that "the killer's anger is endless" (*ma'e opam moropiarera-pirahya*). The killing cycle in which the warrior becomes entangled is also the condition for his strength and longevity.

The killer is not the ideal Parakanã man but an ambivalent person. This is what the -*kawahiwa* doctrine is all about. The -*kawahiwa* makes the person wild and dangerous, prone to treat his own people in domineering

---

44 The term can be analyzed as -*kaw-ahiw-a* (-fat-?-nlz). The morpheme *ahim-* (in the nominal form, -*ahiwa*) appears in key concepts of Parakanã shamanism, such as *karahiwa* (song), *ipoahiwa* (dream), *temiahiwa* (dream interlocutor). In some contexts, it also means "bad" or "wild." This is the sense of its cognates in ancient Tupi-Guarani: *mbaé aíba* meant "a bad thing" (Montoya 1876). The Parakanã -*ahiwa* implies immateriality and ferocity, which, as well as danger, implies potency and fertility. Something -*ahiwa* is dangerous but also creative. I translate it here as "magic."

45 The same difference in the duration of seclusion marks the distinction between shooting a corpse and shooting a living enemy.

46 Here we reencounter the theme of other-becoming, the killer's alteration through his identification with the enemy. The Nivakle of the Chaco conceive this process as a struggle: The period of seclusion was a trial for the killer, who had to tame the victim's spirit but was subject to being tamed by it, "losing consciousness," and offering himself to the enemies (Sterpin 1993:44).

fashion. The young Tajywa was killed by his kin in the 1960s. "Why?" I asked his killers decades later. Well, they explained to me, he had just killed a white man and the *kawahiwa* of his victim "made him cease to be a person" (*-moawaipam*). The unequivocal positive moral values are those that involve living with others and are founded on the sharing of words and food. These capacities are not acquired in warfare but in the peaceful relationship with kin. And the Parakanã are normally very peaceful among themselves: Children never fight with each other, nor adults. Parents refrain from hitting their children, who wander around freely without admonishment from anyone. Neither are children trained to become bellicose: There are no trials of strength or stamina, and there is no institutionalized competition between peers. Belligerence is *not* "systematically instilled in males as proper behavior from a very young age," as Overing (1989a:85) states about the Shavante.

The values of warfare prowess and a predatory disposition are diffuse rather than being the object of systematic teaching. The environment is non-competitive: Nobody claims to know more than the other, to be stronger, or a better hunter or warrior. The overall tendency is to keep a low profile and avoid attaching responsibility for an action to oneself. Some youths occasionally do so – the recklessness of adolescence. Here the Brazilian folk expression applies, "A monkey that jumps a lot wants to be shot," since all men – even the weakest – know how to handle a bow and possess an equal capacity to kill. Consequently, it is better to know how to act and speak: Avoid being domineering, never speak harshly, and raise one's voice only in jest. Provoke laughter, never anger. Avoid walking in the village like someone advancing quickly on prey. Do not awaken the *-kawahiwa* that the killers keep within. As for the latter, they should listen to the advice of experienced warriors. As Iatora's father told him: "A killer of people isn't good. Listen to what I tell you: I killed people and I'm not wild. Killing too many people makes you have a lot of *-kawahiwa*. People don't have little *-kawahiwa*. Don't wait for the *-kawahiwa* of your victims, follow my example" (Iatora 1993: tape 25).

In advising the youths, Iatora's father emphasizes the misfortune of the savage warrior: His destiny is not to be loved, but feared and abandoned like the eastern Parakanã Kynyjoa. Although a headman's brother who could have become a headman himself one day, he was too valiant and met a tragic fate. The many enemies he shot eventually ruined him. Losing his sense of judgment, he killed his own and became exiled in the forest, where he lived in isolation until his fate was complete: He killed once more and was finally killed himself. The notion of magic-fat evokes precisely this asocial fate that besets killers. It provides a critical commentary on the limits of war and the vanity of glory. *Awaropiarera naikatoi*: "A killer of humans is no good." Authority cannot be based on glory in warfare; the chief cannot be modeled on the figure of the predator of humans.

This perception seems fairly widespread in lowland South America, expressed in the distinction between war leader and peacetime leader (P. Clastres 1978:23). The Parakanã do not often celebrate great leaders of the past for their power and aggressiveness. As we have seen, the younger western Parakanã remember Arawa as the kind of authoritative figure they seek out today to deal with Brazilian national society. He was a *moropetenga* ("people hitter") who only ever used "strong speech" to motivate people to attack the enemy, persuading them more by issuing a challenge than a command. He knew that in everyday life this speech was useless and even dangerous. Useless because it would face the silent and heterodox resistance of autonomous wills; dangerous because it would expose him to the destructive equality that the universal possession of the bow imposes. This perception underlies the definition of the headman among the eastern group not as a warrior but as a maker of conversation, who enables a collectively produced linguistic interaction.

In sum, there is an evident contradiction between the discourse on the warrior's virtues and the doctrine of -*kawahiwa*, which highlights the danger inherent to bellicism, namely, the return of violence into the community of kin. This contradiction pervades Parakanã social life, as it does the majority of Amerindian peoples, who locate the creative power of their societies in the predatory relation with the outside. Matrimonially self-enclosed, many Amazonian communities conceived of themselves as islands (albeit historically unstable) of a sociability at once secure and sterile (Overing 1981, 1993a). Confined to themselves they produce merely bodies, not persons; objects, not meanings. The representation of such inner sterility underlies the opening up to the exterior on the plane of shamanism and warfare. In order to conclude, I shall now outline a model for understanding these relations based on creative predation.

A New Approach to Amazonian Warfare

My starting point is that we should treat Amerindian warfare as a form of productive consumption. The suggestion derives from a double requirement: First, it is essential to free warfare from its reduction to the discourse of reciprocity; second, it needs to be integrated with the theme of the production of bodies and identities as a principle of social structuration (Seeger, DaMatta & Viveiros de Castro 1979).

Revenge and Reciprocity

One of the central problems in Amazonian ethnology is defining the social units relevant to analysis. In those areas where wider networks were not completely torn apart by the Conquest and colonization, we find more or less open systems with more or less defined ethnic boundaries formed by a multiplicity of local groups, very often unstable and fluid, weaving multifaceted relations among themselves. In these contexts, the construction of the object of analysis involves choosing between different levels of inclusion: the local group, the set of allied groups, the set of groups (allied or otherwise) speaking the same language, and so on. In defining a particular social formation, the author must explain the relations that structure it. In some regional systems, such as the Upper Xingu and the Upper Rio Negro, peaceful exchanges (matrimonial, ritual, and politico-economic) interconnect wider networks of sociability. In other cases, though, hostile relations perform this role. An important theoretical problem therefore emerges: How can one explain social systems that are structured on a relationship that seems to be the very negation of sociality?

Replying to this question implies thinking of warfare as a positive social relation, and not as a simple negation of sociality. Lévi-Strauss already pointed in this direction decades ago. Speaking of the essential place of anthropophagic rites in Tupinambá culture, he argued that a different image of war became evident, no longer negative, but positive:

... not exposing necessarily an imbalance in the relations between the groups and a crisis, but providing, on the contrary, the regular means destined to ensure the functioning of the institutions; placing the different tribes in psychological and physical oppositions, undoubtedly, but at the same time establishing *the unconscious bond of exchange* between them, perhaps involuntary, but nonetheless inevitable. (Lévi-Strauss [1942] 1976:327 – my emphasis)

Although the first part of this passage retains a functionalist flavor, the final sentence anticipates the way in which a structuralist-oriented ethnology would later deal with Amerindian warfare. By subsuming war to reciprocity, Lévi-Strauss positivizes the phenomenon as a *relation* rather than, in the manner of functionalism, a mechanism of social cohesion. Warfare thus appears as one of various kinds of relationship that constitute supralocal social networks. The structuralist inversion of the dominance between terms and relations was a fundamental step for reconceptualizing Amazonian social systems. It emphasized the spaces of mediation, highlighting the complex dialectic between exteriority and interiority, alterity and identity that shapes the region's diverse sociocosmologies. This move provided a way out of the confusion between local and global by forcing us to focus on the nexuses that constitute wider social networks.

At the same time, this structuralist contribution was accompanied by an encapsulation of warfare by the concept of reciprocity, or, more precisely, by its reduction to the synthetic formula of the gift. In this sense, Clastres's criticism that Lévi-Strauss takes warfare to be entirely negative ignores the deeper and more ethnographically productive meaning contained in his analysis, which implies thinking of warfare not as the negative of exchange but *as* exchange. War is positivized by its subsumption to reciprocity, which functions as a transcendental principle in structuralism insofar as it corresponds to an a priori condition of all human experience. In turning from this transcendental principle to empirical analysis, however, we observe a tendency to reduce war to a specific modality of exchange: balanced reciprocity (Albert 1985:380; Lizot 1989:109–10). Such reduction poses some problems for interpreting the ethnographic data. Journet states:

> Either warfare was a non-normative phenomenon for the Curripaco, a pure and simple state of affairs, and in this case it is hard to understand the use that can be made of reciprocity in this setting, or it needs to be admitted that there is no immediate relation between the Curripaco logic of revenge and the axiomatic of reciprocity as a norm of extinguishing the debt, and that a particular, culturally defined conception of managing violence needs to be brought to light. (Journet 1995:185)

The problem here involves reconciling the discourse on symmetrical exchange with a conception of interminable, projective, and nonrestorative vengeance. To a large extent, the domestication of war as a variant of reciprocity turns on the issue of revenge, whose native categories were seen to elucidate the true nature of war, just as the *hau* served in the understanding of the gift, by allowing a synthetic apprehension of the exchange-based reality of primitive violence (Lévi-Strauss 1960:xxxvii–xl). Amerindian notions of revenge, however, pose difficulties of two kinds to such an analysis: First, the meanings common to them refer to a form of exchange that approximates economic transactions and are better translated as payment, return, or compensation. Journet (1995:189) notes, for instance, that among the Curripaco, the expression *pauma pakuada* ("want your return") "applies particularly to revenge and to negotiated transactions such as, for example, marriages with compensation." In Tupi-Guarani languages, the cognates of the verb *tepy* (Montoya 1876) signify both "to pay" and "to avenge." Among the Kayapó, the term *pãnh* is translated as vengeance, payment, compensation (Verswijver 1992a:173), whereas the Wari' translate the pursuit of revenge into Portuguese as "paying a dead kinsperson" (Vilaça 1992:96).

Among most Amerindian peoples, we find a distinction between the notion of "avenging-paying" and the notion of exchanging in the classic sense of the gift. This is not in itself an impediment to analyzing warfare as exchange, since the literature on reciprocity has already shown the interconnection between different modalities of exchange (Humphrey and Hugh-Jones 1992; Thomas 1991). One could also resort to the model of concentric spheres proposed by Sahlins (1972): Revenge-payment would be located somewhere on the continuum between balanced reciprocity and negative reciprocity. Payment in goods and services would tend toward the former pole, whereas payment in lives would tend toward the latter. Furthermore, as Harrison notes (1993:19), what Sahlins calls negative reciprocity cannot be taken as a zero degree of sociality but rather as a definite mode of sociality. Nonetheless, there is a second difficulty concerning Amerindians' notions of vengeance. Their meaning as payment, return, or compensation implies the idea of equivalence, of settling a debt. So, for example, in the case of the Jivaro:

> The exchange of goods and the vendetta – that is, the exchange of deaths – are indeed governed by identical principles; the same term, *tumash*, is used in bartering to designate the obligation to give an object of equivalent value to the one received, and in conflicts to define the situation in which the killer finds himself compelled to pay for the life that he took from another with his own life or with a shotgun. (Descola 1993:172)

The practice of extracting revenge coincides here with its linguistic expression: It is actually a return in kind for a preceding death. Deaths cancel each other out, and the movement of revenge emerges as an exchange of quantifiable and comparable acts of violence. This only applies, however, to revenge within the same dialect group, and not to head-hunting between different peoples. Moreover, even in the case of vendettas, the reduction to the synthetic formula of the gift raises another problem, since it annuls the political dimension of warfare by ignoring a basic phenomenal difference: In the exchange of goods the giver wants the return, but in revenge the killer has no wish to be paid, nor is he obliged to receive the payment (that is, his own death).[47] As Descola states, "mutual predation is the unintentional result of a general rejection of reciprocity, rather than a deliberate exchange of lives through bellicose intercourse" (1996:90). It is precisely this rejection that produces among the Achuar the aggregation of local groups in war houses commanded by a big man (Descola 1993:319–20). It is within the temporal interval separating the exchange of deaths, so to speak, that the political power of a leader is asserted.

The temporality resulting from the nonreciprocity of perspectives produces distinct political phenomena from those generated by the peaceful flow of goods and people. Would it be just a question of recognizing the structural temporality of the gift and applying it to the notion of revenge (Bourdieu 1972; 1980:167–89)? I do not think so. This would not enable us to solve another ethnographic puzzle: In most Amerindian societies, the

---

47 It may be objected that in some contexts of competitive exchange – such as the potlatch of British Colombia or the *moka* of Papua New Guinea – a chief who has surpassed his rivals in a festival may also not wish to receive any similar return. In contrast to the killer, however, he is obliged to accept the retribution of his rival when the latter sponsors another festival.

linguistic expression of revenge does not correspond to its practical reality, since it appears to operate in perpetual disequilibrium. Journet (1995:188), for instance, argues that translating the concept of *kuada* by terms taken from the domain of transactions (such as compensation or return) fails to comprehend the predominant asymmetry of Curripaco warfare. Sterpin affirms that although the Nivakle notion of revenge is "formulated as a 'debt,' [it] is in reality a 'credit' that maintains the system in perpetual movement" (1993:58). Carneiro da Cunha and Viveiros de Castro (1985) also called attention to the infiniteness of Tupinambá vengeance and its projective nature.

In sum, either the notion of payment-vengeance lacks the sense of set-tling a debt, or the native discourse on revenge fails to correspond to its practice. Whatever the case, I suggest that at this juncture we need to dis-tinguish between predation and reciprocity. To do this, we need to find a new language to speak about indigenous warfare.

Warfare as Productive Consumption

I propose we shift away from the emphasis on revenge and reciprocity and turn to explore the concept of productive consumption. In his study of Melanesian economies, Gregory (1982) resituates the problem of the relation between production and consumption, reworking concepts from Marx's *Grundrisse* ([1857]1973:90–4). There we find a contrast between two modalities in which consumption and production compose a dual unity: productive consumption (the expenditure of material and energy for the production of objects) and consumptive production (the consumption of food through which human beings produce their own body). Gregory refers to the production-productive consumption set as an "objectification process" and to the consumption-consumptive production set as a "person-ification process." In gift economies, he says, "the principles governing the production and exchange of things as gifts are to be explained with refer-ence to control over births, marriages and deaths" (Gregory 1982:101). By applying the notion of productive consumption to indigenous warfare, I am suggesting that in gift economies the production of people belongs to the productive sphere rather than the sphere of consumption.[48] In this sense, the symbolic ingestion of the enemy, which provokes bodily and spiritual

48 This inversion marks my distance in relation to authors such as Overing (1989b, 1992, 1993b), McCallum (2001), and Gow (1989; 1991), who also foreground the production of people in Amerindian societies. This distancing results from different approaches to the domestic-public dichotomy, which leads us to focus on distinct aspects of the process of producing persons: Whereas they emphasize everyday intersubjective relations through which the subjectivity and social capac-ity of the child are constituted, I concentrate on the more public forms, ritualized or otherwise, of engendering and developing personal capacities.

transformation in the killer, should not be compared to the consumption of food for the physical development of the workforce, as it occupies a place equivalent to productive expenditure in capitalist societies.

The concept of productive consumption allows us to highlight some of the distinctive features of primitive warfare while simultaneously avoiding the problems inherent to the *échangiste* model previously cited. First, it makes clear that war involves consumption, expenditure, and loss, and not just transference and circulation. In tackling the theme of war, anthropology seems to have emptied it of everything that evokes destruction. In Amazonia, the discourse of reciprocity allowed the phenomenon to be treated with a certain wariness – a justifiable caution in our political context – just as functionalism did in other parts of the world (Knauft 1990:261). An important dimension of warfare was lost though: the disassemblage of the person into different material and immaterial constituents, which generates processes of consumption and production. If "corporality is a focal symbolic idiom" as Seeger, DaMatta & Viveiros de Castro (1979:3) state, it is not limited to the construction of persons and the fabrication of bodies insofar as the destruction and consumption of the latter are a part of the same productive process. This is why we need to reintegrate production with consumption and avoid reducing warfare to circulation.[49] Flesh and names, skulls and souls were consumed prior to being used to mediate relations between allies.

The second term of the concept also has a precise intent: Consumption is not just loss, but productive expenditure. Back home, the enemy's death produces bodies, names, identities, and virtualities of existence. Death fertilizes life, not necessarily as a closed circuit of energy exchange, but as an open and asymmetric circuit.[50] To be productive, consumption cannot be the pure negation of the other; the enemy cannot be reduced to the condition of object or raw input. In the anthropology of war, it is commonplace to say that enemies are objectified or animalized as a way of reducing the psychological impact of the act of killing. Although this may be true in modern war, it certainly is not so in so-called primitive warfare.

---

49 I have no wish here to replace the Maussian concept of the gift with the Marxist concept of circulation. As Gregory shows (1982:42), exchange in a gift economy differs from that in a commodity economy inasmuch as it establishes links between subjects as subjects. Exchange in these societies is thus "subjectifying" and part of a social process aimed toward the production of persons. Here I am distinguishing two ideal schemas of social reproduction: one based on appropriation and the other on circulation, one on subjectifying predation and the other on subjectifying exchange. Both are figures from the world of the gift, as it were.

50 Some authors have suggested that, in Amazonia, "a model of circling and finite energy" (Menget 1985:139) underlies certain warfare practices ("energy" is a shortcut for a set of immaterial elements deemed to be scarce: identities, souls, vital force, etc.). In such cases, we would encounter a closed zero-sum circuit.

One of the distinctive characteristics of the latter is, precisely, the enemy's subjectification: Predation is a social relation between subjects (Viveiros de Castro 1993:186). This is not simply a question of recognizing the subjectivity of the enemy; warfare practices aim to qualify it, extracting this subjectivity from indifference in order to be able to consume its difference.

Numerous examples exist in which the sociogeographic spaces of predation are differentiated according to a logic of quality. Once again, we can refer to Jivaroan head-hunting, in which only the heads of those who spoke the same language – but not the same dialect – were taken (Taylor 1985); or Yagua tooth-hunting, in which only the teeth of ethnic groups that participate in an interethnic exchange system were extracted. These practices involving the capture of trophies occurred at an optimal distance between the identical same and the indifferent other. Perhaps this was also the case of the Munduruku, whose trophies mostly came from other indigenous peoples such as the Mawé, Apiaká, and Parintintin, but not from whites or from their own group (Menget 1993:314). The same logic underlies the Mekrãgnotí's distinction of war goals according to the kind of enemy: vendetta against other Kayapó groups; the appropriation of exotic artifacts as ceremonial wealth from non-Ge indigenous peoples; and pillaging of material goods from white people (Verswijver 1992a:171). The determination of an optimal distance for warfare activities results from an equation between the work involved in subjectifying the enemy and the production of symbolic value through its destruction. The preferential enemy is one who demands less work of socialization and from whom one obtains the greater sociocosmic productivity.

There are groups in which this determination of distance is replaced by a greater attempt to qualify enemies irrespective of their ethnic origin. This was the case of the Tupinambá, who although showing a preference for Tupi-speaking victims, had no problems with killing and eating Tapuia captives or Europeans, since the prisoner's long stay in the village allowed meaning to be conferred to a sometimes excessive difference. Another example is that of the Pirahã, a small people of the Madeira River basin who practiced a form of warfare nomination that involved careful observation of enemies before killing them. Based on physical similarities, the killer-to-be would attribute a deceased kinsperson's name to his future victim, only to recover it for himself or for his group after the homicide (Gonçalves 1993:66).

The subjectification of the enemy is a necessary condition for capturing identities from the outside that enable the constitution of persons on the inside. This does not simply entail the capture of something singular belonging to the victim – his/her soul, his/her names, his/her head. The enemy is a support for a productive operation at a larger scale. The logic of productive consumption does not involve the transference of equal units from one party to another, but the multiplication of effects from a single cause. This logic is expressed in various phases of the warfare complex. Initially, in the socialization of the homicide, which allows the number of killers who will enter seclusion to be increased. Later, in the multiplication of the immaterial goods that the killers become capable of obtaining and transmitting. For the Tupi-Guarani, the killer's hyperproductivity is expressed in his function as a name and a song giver. Among the Araweté, the victim's soul enunciates names and songs to the killer at the end of seclusion, giving him the capacity to set ritual life in motion and to confer singularity to newborns.[51] Among the Parakanã, this association is indirect: the killing and seclusion lead to the development of the capacity to dream, which is the means through which names and songs are captured.

Finally, the multiplicative logic is realized in the transition from ontological work on the killer to the public ritual. The capture of trophies is a classic example of socializing the consumption and digestion of the victim beyond the war party. The trophies are the substrates for a series of ritual operations that enable the effects of the enemy's destruction to be collectivized even further. This helps explain why the idea of the victim's subjectification is not at odds with the mutilation of his/her body; the apparent cruelty of indigenous warfare practices does not entail the objectification of the other. Filling the corpse with arrows or dismembering it are modes of expanding the production of social life from a limited number of killings.

The Tupinambá cannibal feast is an extreme case of trophy capture: Instead of arriving with inert body parts, the warriors brought back entire living persons. Everyone consumed the enemy's flesh, except for the killer, who was deemed to have consumed something else. Moreover, the entire ritual apparatus enabled others aside from the killer to obtain a name from the captive. Abbeville ([1614] 1975:231) suggests that both the warrior who subjugated the enemy on the battlefield and the one who had captured him in the ritual recapturing that preceded the execution acquired "a title from their prowess." Women also benefited from their exploits. Staden ([1557] 1974:170) states that the wives of killers took "as many names as the slaves killed by their husbands," and Monteiro ([1610] 1949:411) writes that those women who welcomed the captive with blows and insults were also renamed.

The anthropophagic complex made every individual event associated with the death of the captive hyperproductive. The goal was not to kill

---

51 It is not just the killer who receives these songs: "One dead enemy teaches several songs to his killer, and even to other people: everyone who had any sort of close contact with the enemy (exchanging shots, inflicting or suffering wounds) receives songs, such that the *pirahë* dance festivals involve the collective and unanimous enunciation of diverse melodies woven together sequentially" (Viveiros de Castro 1992a:241).

the largest number of enemies but to extract a surplus value from a single death. This capacity to extract so much from so little is a general fact of Amerindian war, differentiating it from the warfare of extermination (Whitehead 1990:160). This explains the Tupinambá indifference to scale, something that astonished the sixteenth-century chroniclers who observed them traveling hundreds of kilometers only to capture a handful of adversaries (Staden [1557] 1974:129; Anchieta [1554–94] 1988:55). The logic of quality predominates over that of quantity. Indigenous societies seem to have put less intellectual effort into increasing their military efficiency than into expanding warfare's ritual efficacy: The work of war was focused less on multiplying the victims than on multiplying their symbolic effects.

This does not mean that we should reduce Amerindian warfare merely to the cognitive operation of consuming and producing meanings. This is not a theater of ideas, but of bodies that are destroyed and fabricated. In contrast, though, to the war of conquest aimed at the appropriation of bodies as abstract workforce and wealth, Amerindian warfare focuses on the enemies' bodies as substrates for the fabrication of persons and not as means for producing goods. The "idealism" displayed by indigenous war in Amazonia is linked to the restricted value of material objects in the region, insofar as they scarcely mediate social relations between groups.

I do not mean by this that the circulation of objects is – or had been in the past – irrelevant. Evidences exist on the functioning of vast exchange networks from the first centuries of colonization, particularly in northern Amazonia and the pre-Andean region (Renard-Casevitz 1993), networks that Lathrap (1973) claims to be of pre-Colombian origin. However, although we find consistent information on the trade routes linking the upper and middle Amazon to the Guianese coasts (Butt-Colson 1973; Boomert 1987; Dreyfus 1993; Arvelo-Jiménez & Biord 1994; Porro 1996; Whitehead 1993:294–6), there are very few references to a trade system on the Brazilian coast during the sixteenth and seventeenth centuries.[52] Furthermore, we do not know to what extent the flow of objects served as a basis for the constitution of political alliances. Perhaps they circulated on the fringes of the political field by means of the famous trading partners: nodes of a dispersed and decentered network who enabled the to-and-fro of goods and information, very often between belligerent ethnic groups. The flow of material goods such as luxury items (stones, feathers, collars, etc.) and utensils (scrapers, curare poison, axes, etc.), linked over large distances

---

52 The sixteenth-century chroniclers merely mention occasional exchanges between peoples of the coast and the interior, based on luxury goods for the manufacture of adornments (such as bird feathers and green stones) (see Fernandes 1963:96–8). Although Balée (1984b) has suggested the possible existence of trade relations involving goods for consumption, we have no empirical evidence to support this hypothesis.

by dyadic relations between partners, was immersed in a political space constituted less by commercial trade relations than by the flow of bodies and immaterial goods dynamized by marriage and warfare: sons-in-law and wives obtained at a minimal distance; and captives, names, songs, and trophies captured at a medium distance, between the minimal alterity of the real affine and the inapprehensible alterity of the unknown other.

In contrast to some Melanesian regions in which the circulation of wealth items strongly mediate relations between groups, in many areas of Amazonia this mediation is primarily realized by enemies and their attributes. The Tupinambá captives, the Jivaro head trophies, and the Parakanã enemy-songs weave relations that extend beyond kinship, congregating villages, local groups, and allied bands. These relations are mediated less by objects than by persons and constituents of persons. These Amazonian systems are geared toward the production of persons by means of persons in a particular way, one in which the destruction-consumption of the enemy has a central and fertilizing role. In the classic world of the gift, for its part, the productive consumption of warfare is complemented by an entire other sphere of circulation of goods "strongly linked to the person ... [which] are the vehicle for their 'mana,' of their magical, religious and spiritual force" (Mauss 1960:157).

5

The Master and the Pet

- Why the rope yoked to the neck,
  like a cow led to graze?
- Why lashed to the leash so meek, following the trail, so unfazed?
- The rope serves no real purpose,
  neither dragging him down or detaining.
- It shows merely that this man
  was once a man, was once.
- The rope is to show that already
  he has become less than a person.
- Not a person, but a domestic pet
  who accepts the rope without fret.
- Wild animals are never to be tethered.
  They want to show this clearly.

J. Cabral de Melo Neto, Auto do Frade (1984)

In describing war as productive consumption, I aimed at inserting it within a generalized economy – an economy in which, as Almeida argues (1988:221–2), surpluses are both material and symbolic, control of the means of production involves relations with the supernatural, and production concerns bodies and people as well as objects. Instead of taking indigenous warfare as a mere response to environmental or social stress, I propose to analyze it within a wider sociocosmic field. In this chapter, I will explore the articulations between warfare and shamanism, and will advance the hypothesis that a single schema, which I call *familiarizing predation*, underlies both activities.

A Shamanism without Shamans

In order to understand what Parakanã's shamanism is about, one has to face a crucial and singular fact: There are no shamans among them. There are no specialists who fulfill the public function of shamans or any people attributed with a permanent curing power. At the start of my research, I thought that shamanism had waned due to the success of Western medicines in treating infectious and contagious diseases. Familiar with the term *karowara*, a common category for pathogenic agents among the Tupi-Guarani, I used to ask them naively: "Who knows how to remove *karowara*?" "Nobody, we can't see them," they would immediately reply. "But what do you call those people who can?" I insisted. *"Moropyteara,"* they explained. The term is the nominal agentive form of the verb *-poropyten* ("suck people"), which describes the traditional method of curing through suction. I soon realized that this designation was more of a stigma than a mark of distinction, and I began to explore shamanism via the accusations of sorcery.

Affliction and its Agents

In Amazonia we commonly find two macrocategories of illness: those caused by the introduction of a pathogenic object into the body, and those resulting from the exteriorization of a vital component (Perrin 1992:101; Gallois 1988:243). Treatment of the former involves removing the foreign object from the patient's body, whereas the latter demands recovery of the soul and its refixing in the patient's body. Among the Parakanã, however, the theme of soul loss is absent. Both the terms for illness – *ma'e'ahya* ("pain-thing") and *jemonara* – refer to bodily affections of a strictly physical nature.

A third category of illness is also commonly found in Amazonia, referring to afflictions caused by contact with a nosogenic immaterial substance. Among the Parakanã, this category is associated with the liver (*-py'a*), and is called *my'ahya* ("liver pain"). Its symptoms are similar to those of diarrhea and are treated with aromatic resins. This notion of contagion also applies to the transmission of infectious diseases introduced after contact with nonindigenous society. Finally, there is a fourth category: the illnesses resulting from noncompliance with some taboo associated with a critical transition in the person's life. In the Parakanã case, this category is focused on another organ, the spleen (*-pere*), which is affected by the smell of the enemy's blood. The prescribed remedies are not the sweet-smelling kind (*-pi'e*) but bitter-tasting (*-ram*).

Among various Amazonian peoples, the failure to respect a food taboo or a rule linked to hunting leads to revenge by a spirit, often that of an animal. Among the Parakanã, however, almost all diseases are caused by human actions: the sorcery of the living or the aggression of the dead. Breaking abstinence directly affects the body in mechanical form. There is no need to postulate a nonhuman entity endowed with intention and volition. The absence of counter-predation to hunting activity is even more notable when compared to the specialization of the diet: The list of species hunted by the Parakanã is one of the most restricted in indigenous

Amazonia, and yet this restriction does not translate into an ethics involving the relationship between humans and animals. There is no code imposing moderation, respect, or compensation for the predatory act.[1] Neither is there any shamanization of the game to make it edible. It is predation between the living that obsesses the Parakanã.[2]

The sicknesses that cause most concern are those produced by the introduction of a foreign object and that result from the action of a sorcerer, a *moropyteara*. These pathogenic objects are divided into two classes: *karowara* and *topiwara*. These concepts are common among the Tupi-Guarani. The first designates a category of cannibalistic spirits linked to the production of illness and often associated with the *anhanga*, an anthropophagic being of Tupi cosmologies;[3] the second refers to the shaman's auxiliary spirits, who are frequently animal spirits.[4] Depending on the group involved, the shaman may possess control over one or both classes of spirits, but the second class tends to be that of the better tamed pets, almost like adopted children, with whom a stronger identity is established. Accordingly, they are often glossed as familiar spirits.

Among the Parakanã, *topiwara* and *karowara* are not properly speaking spirits, but rather pathogenic agents controlled by sorcerers. Hence nobody admits publicly to seeing them in their dreams: Those who see *karowara* are considered strong candidates for sorcery. No one calls him or herself a "master of pathogenic agents" or even dares to describe their characteristics,

1 The only restriction applies to any dreamer who attracts white-lipped peccaries during sleep to be hunted the next day. He can only eat certain parts of the game: the trotters, chest, and liver, with an strict interdiction on the animal's head.

2 The animal that could occupy an agentive position in the system is the capybara, considered the owner of pathogenic objects. However, although its meat is prohibited, there is no interdiction on killing it.

3 Among the Asurini of the Xingu, the *karovara* are aquatic spirits that penetrate the sick, cutting up their insides (Müller 1990). For the Wayãpi, *karuara* is both a synonym of *anhanga* and one of the offensive weapons used by shamans, cutting the victim's flesh from within (Gallois 1988). Among the Araweté, it is a cannibal spirit of the forest (Viveiros de Castro 1992a), whereas among the Tenetehara it is the general term for supernatural entities (Wagley & Galvão 1961). The Tapirapé designate both thunder and the shaman's rattle as *kanuana* (Baldus 1970). The protoform seems to be *karuguara* (Viveiros de Castro 1992a:348), which can be analyzed as *karu-guara*, composed of the root "to eat" and a suffix marking agency. The translation conforms to its characteristics: *karuguara* is "that which eats."

4 Among the Wayãpi, the *õpi-wan* are minute creatures perceived by shamans in human form but physically manifesting as caterpillars. They are fed with tobacco and dwell inside the shaman's body (Gallois 1988). For the Kayabi, *rupiwat* are the shaman's auxiliary spirits, responsible for seeking out the *mama'é* in order for them to cure (Oakdale 1996). Among the Parintintin, a shaman controls various *rupigwára*, although he maintains a particular relation with a specific one, since each shaman is held to be the incarnation of an animal spirit (Kracke 1990). This association with animals also appears among the Tenetehara, for whom the *piwara* comprise animal spirits (Wagley & Galvão 1961), and in the Guarani concept of *tupichua*, which the Kaiowá identify as the animal alter-ego possessed by every human (Cadogan 1965, 1966).

since this would display suspicious knowledge. Consequently, we can only apprehend Parakanã conceptions of these entities through sorcery accusations and through comparison with the Asurini of the Tocantins. These latter have specialist shamans, whose power resides in the control of the *karowara*, which are not conceived as spirits but as animated nosogenic objects possessing a single intent: to devour raw meat. They are faceless animated teeth that shamans can absorb and keep hidden between their own teeth and gums.[5] *Karowara* is the omophagic power of the shaman, the representation of shamanism as a form of cannibalism.

The Parakanã distinguish this cannibal principle from its material form. The physical objects capable of being *karowara* are called *topiwara*: capuchin monkey teeth, certain beetle species, thorns, stingray stingers, sharp bones. In fact, any small and pointed object can be a *topiwara* in the hands of someone with the magical knowledge to animate it. This knowledge is acquired in a dream experience with the "master of *karowara*" (*karowarijara*), who transmits the pathogenic agents to the dreamer. Transmission occurs by sucking the *karowara* from the body of their owner, which is as a jaguar among the Asurini, and a capybara, a bat, or even a bony anthropomorphic being among the Parakanã. Power is acquired by learning how to suck, an act conceived as an extraction of blood: Those who obtain *karowara* in dreams have, like the killer, the taste of blood in their mouths.

Acquiring shamanic power therefore involves an oral conjunction with blood: A sorcerer is someone who absorbs exogenous blood and acts in a predatory form against his own kin. Among the eastern Parakanã, people say that such a person "has shamanic power," *ipajé* (whose nominal form is *ipajé wa'é*, "one who has *pajé*"). Nobody, however, admits to possessing it. Among the western Parakanã, -*pajé* also occurs in the verb -*paje'an*, "to lose power," meaning to lose the capacity to dream. Everyone who dreams has a little -*pajé* and some knowledge of curing. However, no one is ever a shaman. Any claim of special powers would make the person an easy target for accusations. In a society in which predatory human action is the cause of all illnesses and in which there is no supralocal system to impute these attacks to a neighboring community, the sorcerer is always a kinsperson.

Among the western Parakanã, the accusations are numerous and reflect a pervasive factional logic. Some people, normally dreamers with a small kingroup, possess a more widespread stigma. Having few kin means being unable to impose one's perspective on part of the group. Thus the majority

---

5 As a prelude to the shamanic initiation ritual, the Asurini shaman makes the *karowara* with teeth taken from collared peccaries, coati, or catfish. These are polished on a stone until they become paper thin. Next they are perforated and strung on a cord: "Then it's already *karowara* ... it moves by itself," in other words, it begins to chew compulsively. The *karowara* is then placed in the cigar to be smoked in the ritual (Andrade 1992:107).

of sorcery accusations were leveled at an Asurini woman captured in the 1940s and killed by the Kayapó in 1977. There were various reasons for this: First, she was married to a man with just one brother; second, this man's father was said to have the powers of a sorcerer (there is a vague conception of the patrilineal transmission of this capacity); third, she was a foreigner and, moreover, an Asurini woman (member of a group that possesses a positive theory concerning the *karowara*). She not only knew and said more about the theme than the Parakanã typically admit, she also went as far as to practice cures, removing *topiwara*. Finally, she was a dreamer, and women should dream seldom, or never, as they are particularly disposed toward sorcery. As Iatora once told me, "Women extract a lot of *karowara*, they obtain too much. Men, though, do not have *topiwara*." A great dreamer may be respected without attracting suspicion, but a woman who reveals her oneiric powers exposes herself to stigma.

The dream activity of women is carefully controlled, making its public manifestation more sensitive. Underlying this gender politics is the idea that women are already, by themselves, beings who smell of blood (-*pyji'o*). The acquisition of shamanic power would be a hyperconjunction making them especially powerful and dangerous (explaining why the dream activity of older women is more accepted). The topic in ellipsis here is female fertility, a dimension explicitly elaborated by other Amazonian groups. The creative function of the Parakanã killer and dreamer is associated with acquiring the smell of blood, something that women obtain through their own biological maturation. In mythic times, female menstruation also had an exogenous origin. In the beginning it was men who menstruated, but when the naked-tailed armadillo (*Cabassous unicinctus*) shot the moon with an arrow, the blood dripped onto women, who had not heeded the advice to stay inside their houses. Menstruation and female fertility therefore result from the incorporation of the moon's blood, just as the "musical fertility" of men is associated with the blood of enemies killed in war.[6]

Among the eastern Parakanã, sorcery accusations are not concentrated on individuals from small kindreds, but on the more prestigious members of the opposing moiety. The moiety system organizes the imputations: Each side incriminates the other. One of the most important accusations concerns the death of Jarawa, which, as we saw in Chapter 3, is attributed to one of his affines. People say that his affine had asked him for a wife and, angered by the refusal, he had killed him "by means of *karowara*" (*karowara-po*).

---

6 This mytheme occurs within a longer narrative that tells of the organization of the world as we know it: the separation of sky and earth, the departure of the demiurge Topoa (Thunder) to the sky, the differentiation of the species according to habitat, and the definition of human reproduction. However, the myth does not elaborate the consequences of the gender inversion for the power relations between men and women.

The son of the dead man made no attempt to avenge his father's death. Instead, he tried to restore the network of reciprocity between the moieties, offering a large quantity of game so as to avoid an escalation: "I'm afraid of you," he told the affine, "because sickness (*ma'e'ahya*) killed my father." As I suggested in Chapter 3, the outcome of this episode was fundamental to the consolidation of the moiety system and to the later rise of Jawara's son to the headmanship.

There are no cases of people killed because of sorcery accusations. Nobody dares kill a supposed sorcerer out of fear of his or her *-pajé*. The transition to death is a delicate moment, comparable to an altered state of consciousness, and favorable for sending sicknesses and avenging any aggressors. Sorcery accusations are part of Parakanã politics, although less productive than in other parts of Amazonia. They function more as a form of dissuasion than as an effective form of intervention in factional politics. They signal: We have secret weapons, we do not show them, but we can use them. Stigma and fear function, like the *kawahiwa* doctrine, as a strong disincentive to any accumulation of power founded on shamanic practice.

A Taste of Blood

The cannibal compulsion is a risk faced by anyone following the path of hematophagy, whether through homicide or through knowledge of the *karowara*. The conjunction with exogenous blood makes us eaters of raw meat, like jaguars. However, without predation we are condemned to sterility: There are no cures, names, songs, or rituals. Although the hyperconjunction of blood can lead to wild predatory behavior, the absence of contact with blood is negative, inasmuch as homicide is a means for developing dreaming capacities. The western Parakanã say that the victim's magic-fat "makes the killer dream intensely" (*-mopoahiweté*). The smell of blood also has this effect. One of the practices designed to develop the capacity to dream is the ingestion of selected parts of the giant otter (*Pteronura brasiliensis*), an animal deemed to stink of blood.[7] The association between this smell and shamanic power also informs the idea that white people's medicines make a person lose his or her *pajé* by neutralizing the taste of blood. In sum, hematophagy is a condition for both legitimate and illegitimate dreaming activity. No disjunction exists between sorcery and shamanism, since both are founded on the same capacity.

We can now turn to the positive side of shamanism: curing. We can identify a continuum between the three Tupi-Guarani groups of the region: At one pole are the Asurini, where shamanic practice explicitly involves controlling the *karowara* cannibal principle. Midway we

---

7 The giant otter is named *jawataranga* ("torn jaguar") and is considered a kind of aquatic feline.

find the eastern Parakanã, among whom nobody admits to a permanent relationship with the *karowara*, though some admit to having performed cures by sucking out these pathogenic agents. Each admission is accompanied by the claim that the cure took place in the past and that the curer has since lost this power. There is no institutionalization of a shamanic position, although the function may be performed circumstantially. Finally, at the other pole, we find the western Parakanã, among whom nobody is recognized to have ever seen or removed *karowara*. Even on the rare occasions when a man can be observed smoking and sucking the spot where the patient feels pain, the act is considered ineffective. The pathogenic agent cannot be extracted by a kinsperson. Every cure is undertaken by the interposition of a dream enemy. The true shamans of this people – owners of songs, names, and therapeutic techniques – are enemies domesticated in dreams.

The World of Dreaming

The Parakanã verb "to dream" is *-poahim* and the term for dreams is *-poahiwa*. Once again we encounter the suffix *-ahiwa*, which is a modifier indicating immateriality and magical potency. The dream is an altered state of consciousness in which the physical body is inert and activity is assumed by a component of the person called *-a'owa*, which I translate as "double." *-A'owa* is not a spiritual component residing in the body, but an epiphenomenon of the capacity to dream, a form of existence only manifested in the oneiric experience.[8]

Although everyone sleeps, not everyone dreams. If a teenage boy is asked "Do you dream?" the answer will probably be negative or that he only dreams a little or forgets his dreams on awakening. Women also deny having a oneiric life: Only the oldest admit to dreaming. The difference between boys and women, however, is that the former should acquire the capacity to dream, whereas the latter should not dream, or at least not excessively. Accordingly, all the propitiatory techniques are assigned exclusively to men. These include: inhaling the cigar of a great dreamer, eating the snout of the giant otter, dancing with a living electric eel, drinking the honey of a stinging bee inside the hive, and dancing with a dead jaguar on one's back. Of the practices stimulating dreaming, women only have access to the *opetymo* ritual (and, even then, only among the western Parakanã). Shamanism is ideally a male activity, although this is not an

---

8 In Wayãpi, dreaming is *-poau* and dream *-moau* (F. Grenand 1989). These are cognates of the Araweté *mo-a'o*, which means "to feel longing." Both contain the Tupi-Guarani protoform for incorporeal states [*a'uva*] (Viveiros de Castro 1992a:208). In Parakanã, we have the expression *-ejang-a'om* (see-*a'om*), meaning "to have longing for someone."

absolute, as even among the eastern Parakanã women are remembered to have possessed shamanic power.

Yet what is a dream? What does it mean to say that some people do not dream? The kinds of dreams that I shall examine here can be called "cultural dreams" (Price-Williams & Degarrod 1990:279). On one hand, their secondary elaboration (transformation into narrative) is strictly codified and standardized by native theory; on the other, this theory seems to operate on dream memory in a form that selects not only *what* is recalled but *who* should or should not recall.[9] Cultural regulation of the individual's oneiric experience should not surprise us. In societies where dreaming is a specific form of knowledge with its own cultural uses, we can expect a restrictive theory determining what counts as a dream and how it should be interpreted.

Mastering Enemies

Oneiric experience is a way of relating to everything outside the universe of "kin" (*te'ynia*). Dreams are always of "others" (*amote*); a person only dreams of kin who are dead or absent. These experiences are an expression of yearning and are negative: Dreaming of the dead is a premonition of one's own death, whereas dreaming of someone faraway provokes melancholy. Socially productive dreams are always of enemies: Everything that is presented to the dreamer and interacts verbally with him is an *akwawa*. Their minimal structure is that of the relation between two subjects in a communicative context: the dreamer and his interlocutor. People dream of astral bodies and natural phenomena, real and imaginary enemies, animals and artifacts, wild and cultivated plants. These interlocutors do not necessarily appear in human form – they do not have to make themselves into "people" (*awa*) – but they are endowed with attributes that define the human condition: They possess names, intentions, and speech. In the dream world, a universal communication is constituted between humans, animals, artifacts, and natural objects. The Parakanã language becomes the Esperanto of everything that is.

No universal animic essence is posited, though. The Parakanã are economical in postulating the existence of souls or spirits, attributing them not even to animals or to prototypical representatives of them, such as animal masters. They distinguish between waking and dream interactions through the opposition between two modes of presentation of the self: the

9 Whenever I speak of "theory," I am not presuming the existence of a systematic, exhaustive native model without internal contradiction that applies deductively to the facts, but to a set of interconnected assumptions, which inform and are informed by social practice, and which present a reasonable degree of internal coherence and interpretative flexibility.

real entity and its double – or in native categories, *ipireté* ("its true skin") and *ha'owa* ("its dream double"). This opposition is not that between body and spirit, but between skin and double. The Parakanã systematically corrected me whenever I used the term *-eeté* ("true body") to describe wakeful interactions, since the entities in dreams are not strictly speaking incorporeal or simply two-dimensional images like a photo or a shadow (both called *-'onga*, like the vital principle). What they lack is skin, conceived as clothing, but that is active and a locus of affections.

Nor can we translate the distinction between dream and waking experience as an essence/appearance opposition. The dream is neither a form of access to a world of Platonic truths hidden behind the mask of appearances nor another space-time parallel to our own. It is a place of experience in which beings without "true skin" are capable of unrestricted communication and can interact peacefully. Predation is excluded from productive dreams – that is, those leading to the capture of names and songs. Predatory dreams have the character of an omen: Dreaming of being killed by an enemy or accepting sexual relations with a woman predict one's own death, whereas killing animals indicates success in war.

There are two terms to designate the position of the dreamt enemy: "pet" (*te'omawa*) and "magical-prey" (*temiahiwa*).[10] These designations imply that the enemy is kept under the dreamer's control, an idea that the Wayãpi emphasize by describing the invisible threads (*tupãsã*) connecting the shamans to their auxiliary spirits (Gallois 1988:303). The relation is asymmetric: the reciprocal term of *te'omawa* is *-jara*, meaning "owner" or "master." The dreamer is the master; the interlocutors, his pets.[11] Owners have a greater volitional power than their pets, since they have them under their control, as the verbal form of *te'omawa* indicates: *-e'omam*, "to be completely forceless," which applies to someone about to faint or die.[12] The pet is "that which lost its force" or "its consciousness" (meaning its own perspective). Among the Nivakle of the Chaco, the killer must make the victim's spirit *nitôiya*:

The term *nitôiya*, translated into Spanish as "manso" [tame] is the negative of *tôiyi*: "good (persons), right, ferocious, wild (animal)." ... These apparently contradictory

10 Here the suffix *-ahiwa* combines with the term *temiara* ("prey"), replacing the agentive *-ara*. *Temiara* means "someone who suffers an action," that is, a "patient."

11 In almost all the dream narratives I collected, both the dreamer and the main dreamt enemy were men. I therefore use the male pronoun throughout this section.

12 The word is formed by *e'o* plus the suffix *-pam* ("completely"). *E'o-* is a cognate of the Tembé *hē'o*, which means "to be crazy," "to have fits" (Boudin 1966:59). Other possible cognates are *teõ* ("death") and *teoá* ("faint") in ancient Guarani (Montoya 1876), as well as *te'õ me'e* ("dead thing"), one of the terms for the corpse in Araweté (Viveiros de Castro 1986:495). All these cognates convey the idea of a loss of vital force or consciousness. In Parakanã, we also find the more common cognate for "pet" in Tupi-Guarani languages, *mimawa*, but it is seldom employed.

Photo 4. Pi'awa holds his pet (western Parakanã, Maroxewara village, 1995).

glosses become intelligible when we consider that *tôiyi* derives from *tôi*: "to have consciousness, knowledge, power, be self-aware, remember." Thus, a "right" animal is one that "has consciousness" of what it is: it appears *tôiyi*, wild and ferocious. A *nitôiya* or captive animal is an "unconscious" animal. (Sterpin 1993:59–60)

The *nitôiya* animal does not recognize itself as an animal, just as the enemy captive no longer recognizes himself as an enemy. However, although tamed enemies are kept under control, they remain powerful. Parakanã dreamt enemies are superior to their masters in terms of shamanic knowledge. They are neither nourished nor protected by the dreamer; on the contrary, they are the ones who protect and feed the latter with songs and names. This explains why the dreamer does not address them as adoptive children, as occurs among many other Amazonian peoples, but rather as nonaffinal relatives of ascendant generations: "my grandfather," "my father," "my paternal uncle" (the exception being the jaguar, who is addressed as "my maternal uncle").

In sum, Parakanã dreams involve an interaction between a dreamer and domesticated enemies, who are under the former's control but are superior to him in shamanic science. Once captive, this enemy does not act as an enemy since he gives everything to his owner, demanding nothing in return – a one-way flow that does not lead to predation. Dreaming is the symmetrical inversion of warfare and hunting, substituting the dead-bodies for songs-names and predation for familiarization. To paraphrase Dumont (1983:167), dreams are an island of domesticity in an ocean of predation.

Cannibal Melodies

The main gifts of dreamt enemies are songs, which always come in pairs. These ensure the legitimacy of a dream and its social productivity: Dreaming is equivalent to obtaining songs. If someone claims to have dreamt but is unable to reproduce the music he heard, he did not dream – he is lying. I once suggested to a young man that I had brought the peccaries killed by a hunter in a dream. I resisted all his attempts to prove me wrong but, when he asked me to sing, I was unable. This proved to him that I was lying. Songs are not the outcome of personal imagination. Creativity is a product not of the individual's internal mental activity, but of an interaction with others posited as subjects. There is no *ex nihilo* creation: Everything that can exist already exists; the new is that which is captured from the outside (and reciprocally, that which is captured from the outside is new and possesses creative potency). Nothing is created, everything is appropriated.

There are various designations for songs. The generic term is *je'eng-ara* (speech-agentive nominalizer). This is a verbal art endowed with agency: The song contains a potency extending beyond its acoustic materiality. The agentivized word acts upon the world. The song is more than beautiful or sublime; it does not act just on the individual's inner world, entrancing and enrapturing. It produces effects that go beyond inner states, since Amerindian melomania relates to the soul's actions rather than passions. Consequently, only humans and dreamt entities (others posited as subjects) have songs; birds and animals in their ordinary condition merely talk.

Another general term for song is *jawara*, "jaguar." Like the dreamt enemy who intoned them, the jaguar-songs are the pets of the dreamer, whose epithet is, precisely, "master of the jaguar" (*jawajara*). Shamanic science involves becoming the master of a tamed enemy, who gives a pet without asking for anything in exchange. These jaguar-songs have a socially productive destiny, but they do not immediately enter the public domain. They must initially follow their own path through the network of social relations until being executed on some occasion in which dance and song are associated. The most important such moment is the *opetymo* ritual. During preparations for this festival, the *jawajara* give their pets to those set to dance. This new act of giving is imperative; the song owner cannot perform it, but must offer the song to a third-party, who will be its executer in a literal sense. The act of singing-dancing is a homicide: The verb used to designate the ritual performance is "to kill" (-*joka*) and the jaguar-song is said to be the singer's "great prey" (*temiarohoa*). The absence of predation in the dream universe is the preamble to the public execution of a "jaguar" that takes the place of an enemy.

Only after being executed do the songs enter the public domain – they will be sung on the return from hunting trips, before sleeping, and during visits to friendly groups, but they cannot be reused in the ritual. Dead, they are now incapable of reflecting the complex dialectic between exterior and interior, which, in dream and ritual alike, involve a dreamt enemy, a dreamer, and a relative through two acts of giving: the song given to the dreamer by the *akwawa* and transferred from the first to a relative who executes it in public. The reproduction of ritual life therefore depends on a continuous appropriation of new songs that are neither a fixed stock nor transmissible. They are pure history, the outcome of furtive nocturnal encounters whose origin and enunciator are known. Every ritual song is someone else's song. Through it, a memory of self is left, a memory of who killed the song ritually, not who heard it in a dream.

Songs executed in the *opetymo* are called *pajé-pewara* ("of the [locative] *pajé*"), since in addition to denoting shamanic power and formal friends, the term *pajé* designates the ritual itself. There is, however, another genre of vocal music, also captured in dreams, but whose fate is not to be killed in the tobacco ritual. These are the *mipá*, songs collectively danced by men, whose performance is linked to reencounters between separated kingroups or welcoming strangers. Danced by groups and sung in unison, these aim to instill a feeling of solidarity and express joy. By contrast, in the *opetymo* each performer dances alone, representing the enemy who gave the song, an act that promotes the maturation of the person's agentive capacities. In summary, the *mipá* oppose the *opetymo* songs as collective to individual, the iterable to the unique, the production of solidarity to the representation of difference.

Finally, there are particularly powerful jaguar-songs called *karahiwa*. The western Parakanã considered these to be the "true jaguars" (*jawareté*), being especially important for curing, although they may also be executed in the *opetymo*. Among the eastern Parakanã, *karahiwa* are strictly linked to therapeutic action: They are songs "for sickness" (*jemonara-rehe*). The term *karahiwa* is a cognate of the Tupinambá *caraíba*, which in the sixteenth century designated the great shamans and by extension the Europeans.[13] It can be compared with other shamanic songs such as the Apapocuva ñeen-garaí (Nimuendaju 1987:36). However, unlike the solemnity of Guarani songs, which refer to the celestial part of the human soul, the Parakanã karahiwa relates to the person's predatory part. The song is literally a jaguar, an eater of raw flesh. Whereas the ñeengaraí stresses the encounter of men and divinities through asceticism, the karahiwa centers on the encounter with a dreamt enemy through predation and familiarization.

The Work of Dreams

The Parakanã have deinstitutionalized the shaman function. Among the eastern group, it may be performed provisionally: The therapeutic act produces the shaman, but nobody *is* a shaman. Shamanism is the science of the past or the future, but never of the present. Among the western group, it is a science only others can possess: the whites, some captured women, and dreamt enemies. This means there is just one way of ensuring therapy in times of affliction: controlling powerful strangers, that is, acquiring dream pets, whose main gift are songs. If effective therapeutic action involves removing pathogenic agents and if the conception of illness is physicalist, how can mere sung words cure? For the western Parakanã, every cure derives from a dream resulting in songs, but the pet-enemies' therapy is strictly physical, just like the work of the surgeons who extract tumors. For this reason, they distinguish two moments of the dream experience according to the ontological status attributed to them. I am not referring here to an opposition between real and illusory but to two distinct planes of the same world, which implicate distinct components of the person.

The Deepest in Enemies is the Skin

Some dream experiences are conceived to be composed of two phases: an initial dream, in which the individual meets an *akwawa*; and a subsequent experience, while awake, of interaction with the previously dreamt enemy. During the first phase, the person's "double" (-*a'owa*) is foregrounded. It is the dreamer's -*a'owa* that interacts with the *akwawa*. During the second phase, the dreamer is already awake and the encounter takes place

---

13 Let me suggest a hypothetical etymology for *caraíba* (or *caraí* in Guarani). The Parakanã suffix -*ahiwa* corresponds to the -*aiba* or -*aib* of ancient Tupi-Guarani, and connotes danger and magic potency. Montoya (1876) translates the term *cará* as cunning, skill. *Cara'íba* would be, then, magical cunning, the skill practiced by shamans. In the same vein, among the Chiripá, the term designating the singer-shamans is *oporaíva*, a word composed of the verb -*poraí* ("sing, dance") and the suffix -*aíva* ("magic") (Cadogan 1966:113; 1968:134).

between subjects in their "true skin" (-*pireté*). These dreams are called *akwawa-rero'awa*, "bringing the enemy." Its development is conceived in the same way as the dreams of "bringing peccaries" (*tajahoa-rero'awa*), in which the dreamer attracts the animals to be killed in an actual hunting trip. In both, two stages are conceived with distinct statuses. For the Parakanã, the stage of physical cure – which for us is merely dreaming – has the same existential density as the hunting of peccaries.

I present here some of the narratives of "bringing enemies" in summarized form. I begin with a dream event whose repercussions I was able to witness. It was in 1988 when the old man Koria suddenly recuperated after several days of sickness. His grandson quickly came to tell me what had happened, saying that his grandfather had been taken away by his pets, the Karajá, who had removed *karowara* from him. I was confused. I had already heard rumors about the presence of Karajá close to the village, but had put the story down to my poor comprehension of the language. I asked the boy to explain the events in more detail; he insisted that Koria had been cured by enemies called Karajá, and that there was even a bloodstain on his shirt exactly where they had extirpated the *karowara*. I was still none the wiser about the meaning of the story.

Some months later, an *opetymo* was performed and Koria gave a "jaguar" to Itaynia to perform. This is what he said:

A'ekyita tene weha	I shall remove
Amoteohoa no	Another again
Kaohoa a'ekyita	This here I shall remove
Kaohoa a'ekyita	This here I shall remove
Kaohoa a'ekyhekyita	This one I shall remove with the machete
Kaohoa a'ekyhekyita	This one I shall remove with the machete

On learning that the song was a *karahiwa* sung by the Karajá for Koria, I realized that I should further investigate the topic. There could be no doubt concerning the veracity of the event: First, there had been a cure; second, there had been songs (and names, as we shall see). Almost a year later, I went to Koria's house and asked him to tell me the dream. Despite being a man of few words (and many songs), he did so in detail, as though the vividness of the experience had impressed itself indelibly on his memory. He told me that *karowara* had killed him, and he had slept and dreamt. He awoke to a noise. He thought it was the Funai nurse who had come to medicate him, but discerned an *akwawa* approaching:

The moon shone brightly.

– Is he an *akwawa*?

So I knew. I listened carefully. He approached and spoke to me:

- Let's go.
- Where are we going? I asked.
- We're going over there, so they can see you. There we'll find "those who make people arise" [*oporomopo'omoho wa'é*]. That's where we are flying.

He grabbed my hands and carried me away.

[Koria describes the aerial journey and the arrival.]

Finally, we heard the grunting of peccaries. He said:

- Look, the great Warynga is coming, he's arriving, he's coming towards you, rejoicing.

Warynga approached grunting and rattling the bones of his victims:

- Who's that arriving? the great Warynga asked.
- He sickened [replied the one who had brought Koria].

Great Warynga was inside a blind. Another man came out of a house shaking his long hair, scattering his head lice.

- Who is this? he asked.
- Our grandson became sick.
- From where did you bring him?
- From far away, he was in a village.

They were arriving. They carried warclubs like the giant otter's tail. We were in the middle of the houses. They gathered and sat down.

- Bring Warynga to remove *karowara*. Look, there's the one who removes *karowara*, bring him here.
- Our people are going to bring Warynga to cut you, they told me.

So Warynga stood up and walked towards me:

- Where does it hurt? he asked.
- Look, here, I pointed.
- Kneel down.

So he stuck his cutter into me, it looked like the "mosquito killer" [Koria is referring to the spray gun used to combat mosquitoes]. He plunged and extracted, plunged and extracted. He sucked up my blood as it flowed out, he consumed it all. He cut me again. He consumed everything. He removed his small cutter. Once more, he stuck it in and removed it. Then he sucked for the last time. He blew.

- Let's go, get up.

I stood up.

- This is why you came to meet us, so we could cure you, he said.

He walked away. He vomited my ex-blood. Then he said to his sister:

- Bring me water so I can wash my mouth.

She brought a tall jug. He drank the water and let it spill, he spilled it, perhaps spilling all the stench of my blood. Then he drank properly.

. . .

They began to dance their songs. They sang well. They were all kin. Ka'apirohoa was there.
  – You came to my house, my maternal uncle? he asked me.
  – Yes, I came, my nephew, I replied.
They talked standing up.

. . .

The people were arriving. They spoke to me:
  – How many children do you have?
  – One.
  – Wives?
  – Just two.
They talked among themselves. They spoke to Kwanokynga.
  – So what do you think, Kwanokynga?
  – What?
  – Should we keep him?
  – I don't know, you decide.
  – You're the one who knows.
  – I'll keep my maternal uncle.
He picked up a worm and ate it.

. . .

I looked as he ate another. He sat eating fish with flying-flour, red colored, like manioc beer that makes you fly. He went to a termite nest and came back carrying termites. He ate them. They talked. They spoke again to Kwanokynga:
  – Let's take him away, his daughters must be crying.
  – Okay. Take him and set him down near to his house.
So they took me. [Koria describes the return journey.] We saw the houses and landed near a rock. The cockerel crowed.
  – Is dawn arriving? he asked me.
  – Yes, father [miangá], I replied.
It was starting to dawn.
  – I'm going, he said.
  – Okay.
(Koria 1989: tape 3)

The story begins with Koria being awoken by someone approaching. This is the clue to understanding that the narrated events occurred while he was awake. Here the preliminary actions of the double are not recounted, passing directly to the events involving people in "their true skin."[14] The account is rich in details concerning the ways of the Karajá. He refers to their physical features (long hair full of lice and small mouths), artifacts (warclubs similar to otter tails, percussive instruments made from human bones), and gastronomy (worms, flying-flour, termites). The Karajá are characterized as a monstrous people, who feed on eaters of decomposing matter and whose manioc flour is like beer. The relation that they establish with the patient, though, is one of protection. Here, unlike most narratives of this genre, the dreamer is treated by kinship terms that denote his seniority. Only the one who comes to fetch him in the village is called *miangá* by him, a formal vocative for father or paternal uncle. This unusual fact indicates that Koria is old and has a well-established oneiric capacity.

The dreamer is taken to Warynga, who performs the cure. He cuts the patient with an instrument resembling the nozzle of an insecticide spray gun (frequently used to control malaria outbreaks). He inserts it into Koria's body and removes it numerous times. He then sucks the blood pouring out, sucking it up until he extracts the *karowara*. He moves away and vomits, asking his sister to bring water so he can rinse his mouth. The therapy applied by the Karajá in the waking dream is physical. It is not a spiritual operation, but a mechanical act.[15] It is only after removing the pathogenic agents that the Karajá sing the *karahiwa*. The songs are not part of the therapy: They are not curing words, but, as we shall see later, words that convoke. The narrative continues with sketches that set the scene and provide information on the lifestyle of the Karajá, whose consistency with the usual depictions of these enemies confers verisimilitude to the experience.[16] Finally, we encounter a dream theme that is repeated in almost all the narratives of "bringing enemies": the controversy among the *akwawa* over whether they should take the dreamer back to his kin. Here what is weighed is filial love and the desire of the enemies to keep Koria among them, indicating the possibility of the pets acting as captors, thereby inverting the relation of familiarization.

14 There is no grammatical mark distinguishing dream narratives from others, nor is there for the two stages of the dream of "bringing enemies." There is nothing similar to the evidential *ra'uv* in Kagwahiv (which also means "soul"), used to mark the oneiric status of an account (Kracke 1987; 1990). Koria uses here the evidential for the witnessed nonimmediate past, *rakokwehe*, which opposes the nonwitnessed past, *jekwehe*.

15 That helps explain why the western Parakanã accepted, from the outset, Western-style surgical interventions. After all, what the whites do is to cut the person and extract the *karowara*, no more and no less.

16 Hence the reference to Ka'apirohoa, the firstborn son of Pi'awa, who became sick in the 1950s in a forest encampment. They sang *karahiwa* to attract the Karajá and abandoned him. He disappeared. Since then, people assert that these enemies took him away.

In other narratives emphasis falls on the enemies' intention to make the patient change his point of view, switching to see his kin as adversaries. Thus in one dream therapy experienced by Iatora, a Karajá said to him: "Come to my house so we can live together. Perhaps it's your kin who are hurling ensorcelled objects at you." This motif appears ostensively in a narrative by Awanga, in which he tells of his encounter with the Ywywa (Kayapó). Awanga had been shot in the leg by Kynyjoa, the exiled brother of Arakytá, in a chance clash in the forests of the Bacajá River. In the dream, he meets the Ywywa, who ask him slyly:

— Was it your kin who killed you?
— An enemy killed me. The lone-enemy [Kynyjoa] killed me, I replied.
— Tell us where your kin are so we can finish them off.

During the entire encounter, the Kayapó try to convince Awanga to blame his own kin. At a certain point, he appears to give in to the honeyed words of the dream enemies:

I was in the midst of them:

— Was it your kin who shot you?
— Humm. *Akwawa* killed me, I replied.
— Tell us where your kin are so we can finish them off. Let's go after your kin.
— Okay, let's go, I said, unaware of what I was saying.[17]

The narrator soon realizes what was going to happen and ends up leaving alone, though not before hearing the enemies tell him, "We shall return to take you with us. Perhaps we'll return when your kin kill you again" (Awanga 1993: tape 42).

This narrative was recorded in 1993, but refers to a twenty-year-old dream. The context at the time explains the emphasis on the alliance with enemies against kin. The dream happened to Awanga in 1970, soon after an attack by the Xikrin of the Bacajá. During the raid, some women managed to escape but became lost. Searching for them, Awanga ended up struck by an arrow shot by Kynyjoa in a chance encounter. The *Ywywa* then came to cure him. The dream's basic operation is converting a predatory relation with the enemy into one of familiarization. As for the *Ywywa*'s recurrent claims that the dreamer's own kin had been the ones to shoot him, we should recall that Awanga's kingroup had headed toward the Bacajá River after an internal conflict that had resulted in the killing of two men. The dream expresses the general climate of distrust and the narrator's own action against one of his kin.

---

17 Literally, "not being a person" – *jeaway'yma* (3p-people-neg). The term *awa'y'yma* also designates dead males and is used as our "the deceased."

We can see just how ambiguous the position of the dream pets is: tamed enemies who do not lose their power and appear to control the dreamer, rather than being controlled by him. From the viewpoint of kin, the dreamer is a master of the *akwawa*; from the viewpoint of enemies, they are the masters of the relation. This is where the *karahiwa* enter the picture: They function as a convocation – not of the spirits, as usually found in Amerindian shamanic rites – but of concrete enemies. This is why one sings for a sick person; whereas a patient-dreamer can bring the *akwawa* in a dream, his or her kin can also call it through the *karahiwa*. The songs are an instrument of mediation between the enemies and ourselves.[18]

The following is an example of this use of the *karahiwa*. In the narrative, Iatora recalls how he was cured by the Karajá while still a youngster:

I was lying down. I heard them singing *karahiwa*. The victim of *karowara* can hear *karahiwa*. I woke up.

   – Are you resting? they asked me.
   – Yes, I decided to lie down, I'm weak.

I could hardly speak. Soon after, I fainted. My sister Waka'ima came to us.

   – Did he faint?
   – He fainted.

She picked me up and carried me to her house.[19] Then I heard just a little *karahiwa*. "Are my kin still beside me?" I wondered.

They stayed until dawn [singing *karahiwa*]. As night fell, the late Paringa arrived bringing peccaries. Everyone decided to hunt peccary.

. . .

They all went off. I remained lying down, watching them leave. Only Pi'awa remained with me. I told him to go and lie down too. Dawn arrived. How did the *akwawa* come, how did they know about me? [Iatora asks himself].

They surrounded the place and two of them approached. Then the late Morejiarona woke me up.

   – I'm going to sleep, she said to me.
   – You can go.

She went. I was alone, lying down. The fire went out. Then they came after me. They shook me until I woke.

---

18 Interestingly, Montoya (1876) translates the term *ñeengara* from ancient Guarani, a cognate of the Parakanã *je'engara*, as "mediator," thus characterizing the function of the Virgin Mary: *Tupaçi ñanderí ñeengara* ("the Virgin is our mediator").

19 When referring to the actions of his kin while he was unconscious, the narrator uses the nonwitnessed evidential *jekwehe* instead of the witnessed evidential *rakokwehe*.

— What's wrong? someone asked me.
— Is it you, Morejiarona? I asked. Did you wait for me?
— It's us. Us.

They shook me. I awoke.

— What's wrong? someone asked me.
— Is it you, *miangá*? I asked.
— It's me. What's wrong with you?
— What was it that killed me?
— We told you to behave yourself.

He always spoke strongly.

— Let's go, sit up.
— How can I sit up, *miangá*?

He helped me sit up in the hammock with my legs open.

— Where is the thing that is killing you? he asked me.
— Here, in my anus. What thing is eating me completely, my father [*wetom*]?

. . .

Morning came. So I thought: "*Akwawa* is going to take me far away from my mother."

— You came here, my father, I said to him.
— We came, we knew, that's why we came here to see you.
— What thing is devouring me completely? Perhaps it's eating my flesh.
— Let's go away, morning is arriving. I shall return to take you, he said to me.
— Okay, I replied.

So I stayed sat on the hammock with my legs open.

— We're going away first, he said. Keep away from us my grandfather, or else we'll perforate his head and eat his brains.[20]
— Wait a while before coming back, my father, so that I can send my uncles away from me, I replied.

They started to leave. Just one of them danced next to me with an enormous ankle rattle, he stamped like a tapir. The rattle woke my late uncle.

— Who's there? What grandiose-thing is this? he asked. It was the great ankle rattle. They are dancing. This is what also happened long ago. They shook the great rattle, [so as] to cure the child, he slept truly.[21]

---

20 The enemies refer to the dreamer's ascendant kin as "grandparents," indicating that they – called "father" – are actually the dreamer's children.

21 Grandiose-thing refers here to the dream *akwawa*. When wishing to know who sung a song, a person asks: "What grandiose-thing sang for you?" (*ma'eohoa pa rakokwehe o'a'ang neopê*); or "What grandiose-thing did you see for it to sing for you?" (*ma'eohoa pa ere'ejang to'a'ang neopê*). The augmentative is typically employed in dream and warfare narratives.

Then Paringa, the true *moropetenga*, spoke:

> – I grew truly. So I'm going to make people lose themselves [that is, I'm going to kill].

So the late Arakoria said:

> – Where did they go? They went that way dancing with the great rattle. Perhaps they went away.

I knelt down watching them leave. My late mother came over to me.

> – Where did they go? She asked me.
> – I don't know, I didn't hear anything.
> – Your uncle said that *akwawa* made the great ankle rattle resound.
> – I didn't hear anything, my mother.

I then asked her:

> – Has it dawned already, mother?
> – Completely.
> – So go away from me, keep away from me. All of you go away, I shall lie down alone.
> – Why should we all leave you?
> – Go hunting. Take my father. I'm going to stay alone in our house.

The men came over to me. Jakaré, Inajokynga, my late friend (-*pajé*).

. . .

> – Go away from me, my -*pajé*, leave me alone lying in my house.

. . .

Everyone left. Ajikia was the last. I turned around and thought: "The *akwawa* made me send away my kin from their things; the *akwawa* are going to take the things of my kin." I searched for my bow. I stood up, but I was trembling. So they arrived and took me:

> – Let's go.
> – How shall we go? I asked.

They picked me up and put me in a basket. "Are they going to kill me?" I wondered.

This section of the narrative tells of the arrival of the dream enemies. Iatora sickens and his kin sing *karahiwa* for him. They spend the night singing until morning comes. The next day, some men arrive from a hunting trip and announce that a herd of peccaries has been sighted. The village starts to empty. He sleeps another night, and in the morning Iatora sees the *akwawa* approaching but is woken by a woman who fails to see them. This is the moment of transition: The vision is a dream, since nobody else notices; what follows, however, is perceived consciously. This state becomes evident when the narrator's uncles wake up, certain that they have heard the sound of the ankle rattle. By introducing this occurrence, the narrator assures his audience of the veracity of his experience.²² The departure of his kin enables the encounter with the *akwawa* and highlights an important point: The master-pet relation is exclusive since the enemies pose a danger to the dreamer's kin.

The idiom of the affliction is once again bodily. In their blind compulsion for raw meat, the *karowara* eat the sick person's flesh. The only cure is to extract and bury it:

So I understood everything completely.

— Stand up, my son, he said.

I stood up. He rubbed *janya* [a fragrant resin] on my shoulders and legs.

— Where does it hurt?
— In my anus, what is eating me, my father?

So he fetched a cigar and smoked it.

— Okay, kneel down.

He sucked, he sucked until he extracted it, leaving it in his mouth.

— What did I remove? It bites a lot.

It was a large capuchin monkey tooth. He spat it out.

— Look, was it this that was killing you, my son? he asked me.

He dug the ground and buried the tooth. He sucked me again.

— Is that enough? he asked me.
— Perhaps so, my father.

So he made me stand up. I stood up a little, I was trembling. Then I stood up firmly. He came and fetched me. They began to dance, performing the *karahiwa*.

A metonymy of the devouring jaw, the capuchin monkey tooth bites the shaman's mouth. Its movement is repetitive and unintentional; once animated, it acts mechanically. This is why the shaman should spit it out. "This operation," Andrade states (1992:150), describing the therapy among the Asurini, "must be done quickly, since the *karowara* provokes pain in the shaman." Presented to the patient as proof of the effectiveness of the treatment, the pathogenic agent must then be buried immediately.

---

22 Iatora told me the dream in the presence of various people, including Karája, another experienced dreamer. Hence despite the freedom to fabulate allowed by the fact that most of the people mentioned in the narrative were dead, there were still constraints on constructing its verisimilitude. Iatora therefore established a complicity with his main interlocutor, which was not myself but Karája. For example, he put a phrase in the mouth of the latter's dead father, Paringa, and called him *moropetengeté*, a war leader. This is not an illusionist trick, but rather the transformation of a subjective experience into a shared fact, which implies the construction of its truth conditions for others who did not experience it.

Interaction with the dream *akwawa* is modeled on the protective relation between father and son. In this case, which occurred when Iatora was
a boy, he addresses his curer as *miangá* or *wetom* ("my father"), making
evident the inversion of the relation of familiarization, which was not so
clear in Koria's dream. The curing episode is followed by the dispute over
whether the dreamer should be sent back to live with his kin:

> — My mother must be hungry, *miangá*, I said.
> — You have a mother?
> — A father and mother.
> — Come with us and you'll eat potatoes, yams, banana, maize, flying-flour,
>   he said.

He took out a bit of flour and ate it.

> — Should we take him? he said [to his companion].

Finally, they bring Iatora back, although not without warning him of the
possibility of his kin casting sorcery spells: "If something happens to you,
shout for us so we'll hear and we'll come to see you." This phrase expresses
the special relationship that develops between the dreamer and his protec-
tor-pets, a necessary condition for a long and productive life. The narrative
closes as it began, assuring the veracity of the experience.

I returned. I bathed in the river to remove the fragrant resin. I lit my mother's
small fire, which had gone out. My late maternal uncle arrived with my maternal
aunt, who was bringing tortoise liver for me.

> — You awoke, my nephew.
> — Yes, I awoke, aunt. I'm going to get up, I'm feeling a little better already.
> — You've been cured for us, my nephew. Which *akwawa* healed you?
> — Which *akwawa* would it be, my aunt? I don't know. "We cured you," they
>   said.
> — Did they all go away?
> — They all went, my aunt. None of them stayed.

I then ate a piece of tortoise liver, lying in my hammock.

[Iatora's father arrives.]

> — Did they all go? my father asked.
> — Yes, they went. Come close, dad, I said.
> — You are Moakara, he told me. In the past, Kajomaria also killed Moakara
>   with an arrow in vain. He got himself cured by the Karajá. Did the *akwawa*
>   sing?[23]

---

23 Iatora's father is referring to another story in which Moakara is said to have been mortally wounded
    by his son-in-law Kajomaria, but when his kin went to bury him, he was raised from the grave,
    thanks to his Karajá pets. The death-resurrection is equated to a sickness-cure.

– Yes, they sang, I replied. [The narrator sings.]

– My kin, they sang. Let's search for them.

They searched for them in vain, they could not find them.

(Iatora 1993: tapes 5 and 6)

The cure is the first evidence of the *akwawa*'s actual presence, but it is the songs that guarantee its veracity for others, so much so that on hearing the *karahiwa*, the patient's kin go in search of the enemies' tracks in vain.

The Raw and the Rotten

In the therapeutic dreams of the western Parakanã, the most frequent figures are the Karajá, a generic category for Ge Indians. Next appear the Ywywa (the Kayapó), who assumed a larger space in oneiric life following the war conflicts over the course of the twentieth century. There are also other enemies, such as the Jotaiwena, a people who lived inside jatobá trees.[24] These human-others are usually called fathers by the dreamer, whereas nonhuman enemies are called grandfathers or partners (*tywa-kwai*), as in the case of Awararijá, a mixture of man and bird who possesses a long beak with which it sucks out the heart of its prey. There are also two animals that appear in oneiric therapies owing to their ability to suck blood and extract pathogenic agents: the vulture and the jaguar. Let me briefly describe two additional dreams.

Karája's son fell from a hunt platform, where he had been waiting for toucans. He was brought to the village and placed in the health post. At night he stayed there alone. His father dreamed of vultures:

Sleeping, I went in search of the vultures.... This is why I made the vultures descend, when they brought Karamoa back all broken, so they could eat all Karamoa's ex-blood.... They smelled the stench of his blood [*ipyji'oa*]. So they came and landed behind the health post.

– What happened? they asked me.

– Your grandchild broke himself, my grandfather, I said to the vulture.

– Where is he? Show me.

They came round the back and stopped at the door to the infirmary. They looked at him for a while. His ribs were swollen.... They entered. Then the vulture sucked up the ex-blood, eating it all. And so Karamoa recovered.... They smelled the stench of his blood {*ipyji'oa*}, that's why they descended to meet me. During the night, they ate all his ex-blood. I awoke shortly before dawn. I saw them fly away. Only the yellow-headed vulture remained alone in the vicinity when it truly

24 I know of no examples of cures performed by dream enemies speaking a Tupi language, as if their women were good to capture but not their songs.

dawned. I left the house and went to look. The vultures were hovering above, looking down on our houses, after getting Karamoa to rise.

Karája's dream reiterates the association between cure and hematophagy. There are no *karowara* to extract – since it was an accident – but the curing procedures are similar. It may seem strange that necrophagic birds had smelled the blood of Karamoa, since the meat which they relish stinks of putrescence (*-nem*) rather than blood (*-pyji'o*). The distinction between eaters of the raw and eaters of the rotten, however, is unmarked among the Parakanã and the Asurini of the Tocantins. Among the latter, the decisive experience in shamanic initiation is the encounter with the jaguar, who – rather than being a powerful feline – is a sick old man, surrounded by corpses and rotten flesh, whose body is being devoured by the *karowara*. He asks the dreamer to extract these assailants from him, but first subjects the novice to an ordeal – that is, to eat raw-rotten meat, full of blood. Many initiates fail at this moment and wake up vomiting. He who passes this stage is ready to suck one of the *karowara* from the jaguar, which he will then keep as the source of his power (Andrade 1992:132–7). Shamanic initiation among the Asurini implies eating like the jaguar and absorbing a cannibal potency. Significantly, though, eating like the jaguar means eating raw-rotten blood.

The jaguar is also an important persona in Parakanã waking dreams, appearing in two forms: as a shaman who assumes human form (*-jemoawa*, "turns into a person") to cure the dreamer, or as a skin that the dreamer wears in order to metamorphose. These forms may comprise different stages of the same dream event: the dream of the jaguar and its later arrival as a "true skin." Such dreams possess two distinctive features. First, two vocatives seldom found in the dream narratives are employed: *wepajé* ("my formal friend") and *wetotyn* ("my maternal uncle"), both connoting affinity. The jaguar always appears as a wife giver capable of imposing uxorilocal residence on the son-in-law, contradicting the group's virilocal norm. The second distinctive feature is that predation remains strongly thematized. As an example, I cite the beginning of a narrative recounted by Pi'awa, which describes how a jaguar cured him of a pain in his neck. The feline says:

- He said that he would fetch a [human] husband for his daughter, which is why Awajanya [name of a jaguar] came to you and you killed him. Who killed Awajanya, my grandson? he asked me.
- It was my nephew, when he [the jaguar] went for his maternal uncle, I replied.
- But did Awajanya really attack him?
- He got up. Only the predator, the jaguar, died, I replied.
- And he was only after his daughter's future husband ...
- But he attacked my nephew ...

— How exactly did Awajanya try to capture him? Did they shoot him first? he asked me.

— They didn't shoot. The jaguar attacked unprovoked.

The interlocutors discuss a recent actual event: A jaguar had attacked one of Pi'awa's relatives and they had killed the animal. In the dream, the jaguar explains that the dead feline had only come to find a human husband for his daughter. Pi'awa, in reply, claims that the jaguar had indeed attacked his relative, and asks the jaguar to establish peaceful relations with him:

— Don't be angry with me, my grandfather. Since when I'm scared of you, I can't leave in search of tortoises. That's why I'm thin.

— Okay, let's not fight, my grandson. I came in search of Awajanya, in vain. That's why I came. I wondered: "Could he still be there?"

— Our kin killed him, my grandfather. That's why I'm scared of you all. Talk with your people. Say to them: "Let's hunt over that side only."

— Okay, I'll tell that to my people, my grandson. We're going to hunt over there.

— Tell them: "Our grandson is going to waste away, he's scared of us, he only opens babassu coconuts" [he only eats babassu kernels]. Go on, say this to them.

— I'll tell them, my grandson.

(Pi'awa 1995: tape 31)

Here, the dreamer's interlocutor is called grandfather. The plot, however, is set by the desire of a jaguar to become a father-in-law to a human. Misunderstanding the jaguar's intentions (or understanding them at a deeper level), the humans kill him, and Pi'awa has to pacify the deceased animal's relatives in order to avoid their revenge. In the final part of this narrative, Pi'awa told me that he brought his dreamt interlocutor to the village, but on waking was unable to transform himself into a jaguar.

The verb designating this metamorphosis is *-jyromonem*, "to place oneself in a container"; its antonym is *-jyroekyi*, "remove oneself from a container." The first action applies to the act of wearing clothing, the second to removing it. Metamorphosis into a jaguar is a interspecies cross-dressing (a transvestment) that implies the acquisition of the animal's dispositions and capacities. Once again, we have two episodes with a distinct status: the bringing of the jaguar and the subsequent transformation into the animal. In Pi'awa's dream, the second part fails to occur. Iatora, on the other hand, tells us that he brought the jaguar to himself while convalescing. On awakening, he goes to meet the jaguar and wears his "clothing":

— It's me, my maternal uncle, I cried.

— Is it you, my nephew? Why did you follow our trail?

Then the younger brother [of the jaguar] came over to me:

- Who are you, my maternal uncle? I asked.
- We, well my nephew, we.
- Tell me your name, I asked him in vain.
- Why did you follow our trail, my nephew? What's wrong with you?
- My back, what thing is eating me completely? I said.

He put down his long arrow and spread his hands over me.

- Let's go, my nephew, so your grandfather can see you.
- Where is his house, my maternal uncle?
- Look, way over there ...

They go to the house of the jaguars. As they near the house:

- Don't be scared, my nephew.
- I won't be scared, my maternal uncle, I replied.

We went, he whistled and the *akwawa* began to arrive:

- There he is, my nephew, your maternal uncle is coming to see you.

He came walking at the front:

- Who's there? he asked.
- Our nephew followed our trail, my brother.
- Is it an *awaeté*? An *awaeté* coming after us, following our trail? What made him to do this? Did he fall ill? he asked.

The talk continues. The figure of the jaguar-father-in-law surfaces: "Wait for your father-in-law to return, my nephew. He left to hunt white-lipped peccary." He returns with the game and welcomes Iatora. A black jaguar then comes in his direction, head lowered: "I entered it, the true me, I went as a jaguar," Iatora tells me (1993: tape 10). I ask whether it had been his double (*-a'owa*) that had entered the jaguar's skin. He repeats what he had already said: "the true me" (*ije-eté*). The transvestment is physical just as much as the actions of the "jaguarized" dreamer: As a jaguar, he hunts and eats, so much so that his teeth hurt in the morning. Those who transvest are dangerous, since they can act as the predator for real. One of the songs that I collected speaks of the ambivalence of the "jaguarized" dreamer:

Ije pota te we'yra	Shall I make my other-mother
Amoja'a he'ynia-rehe weha	Cry for her family?
Wepinimohoa-po	With my spotted skin
Wepinimohoa-po	With my spotted skin
He he	He he
He he	He he

The theme of convalescence and thinning, which appears in the narratives on jaguar metamorphosis, announces the main purpose of the allomorphy: to feed oneself by acquiring the feline's capacity to hunt.

Cosmological Axes

The foregoing analysis of dreams applies only in part to the eastern Parakanã. The relational structure is the same, the gifts are also songs and names, the interlocutors are also called *akwawa*, and they likewise considered that the transformation into jaguars occurs on the same level of reality as waking life.[25] An important difference exists, though. There is no figure of the dreamt human-enemies, whose primary function is to effect a material cure through suction. There is no need to reconcile the immateriality of dreams and the materialistic conception of the therapy, since they accept the extraction of *karowara* by kinpersons who momentarily place themselves in the role of shamans. Among the western Parakanã, by contrast, we can observe a radical eclipsing of the kin-shaman as shamanism became generalized. Such a development is akin to the sociopolitical process experienced by the group over the course of the twentieth century, particularly their centrifugal vertigo.

Yet however important the differences between western and eastern Parakanã conceptions of dreaming may be, the dominant axis of their cosmologies is horizontal. This dominance expresses a unity in the operations of shamanism and warfare: The Parakanã conflated the warrior and shaman functions. Whereas the Araweté killer establishes a special relationship with his victim, as does the shaman with the divinized spirits of the dead, the Parakanã warrior does not form any special relationship with *his* victim, but rather with the set of existing entities that can be generically denominated *akwawa*. Instead of being a way of appropriating the victim's spirit, killing opens the way for the familiarization of dreamt enemies.

The vertical sky-earth axis has a residual place here, although there are dreams of anthropomorphic astral bodies and natural phenomena: moon, sun, "solar wind" (*kwarywytoa*), and rain are all song givers. Most knowledge of the cosmos derives from these dream experiences, which are fragmentary and subject to individual variations. There is no overarching depiction of the cosmos as we often find among other Amazonian peoples. Dreams of cosmic figures are little elaborated: Whereas those of human-enemies or jaguars result in long narratives, the encounters with astral bodies and

25 The Asurini of the Tocantins express the difference between common dream experiences and the metamorphosis into a jaguar as different "divisions" within the dream: "To turn into a jaguar there is another division in the dream. The jaguar has its skin. Who knows, explains: he wears its clothing, consumes its food" (Andrade 1992:155).

natural phenomena are described in few words. Such dreams are similar to those of the majority of animals: rapid images followed by songs.

There is one exception to this rule: the rain, Amyna, also known as Topoa, who is an important pet in a dreamer's career. Here is one of his songs, heard by Ajowyhá:

Eawyripé ke enaro-narongoho eha	To your own house, go thunder-under
Enaro-narongoho eha	Go thunder-under
Enaro-narongoho eha	Go thunder-under
Paranomokoa eremono-monon-owé	The long river you made overflow-flow
Paranomokoa eremono-monon-owé	The long river you made overflow-flow

The song is a cosmographic sketch of rainfall. Whenever Topoa plays his great gourd the long celestial river shakes and the water spills over, running from the border of the sky to the earth. It rains. Lightning is produced by the blinking of his eyes or, in another version, by arrows hurled by him from the sky.[26] There is a myth recounting that Topoa lived on earth with his *awaeté* kin, who could not stand his passion for thundering. One day they told him to stop the noise, and he decided to leave. He asked the naked-tailed armadillo to shoot the moon and climbed the line of arrows, going to live in the sky. This inverts the classic Tupi theme of the abandonment of humans by the demiurge: Instead of the latter becoming irritated with the former and leaving, it is the humans who are vexed with the demiurge's din and send him away: "Go thunder-under to your own house!"

Topoa is the rain-thunder, like his predecessor, the sixteenth-century Tupã, who became God in the Jesuits' hands. He occupies a particular place in the Parakanã cosmos. He represents a trace position outlining the divinized celestial plane whose importance remains residual in the current cosmography. He is sometimes mentioned as the recipient of human souls that arrive in the sky, although the Parakanã are quite uncertain about any posthumous celestial destiny of the person. Topoa thus marks the place that would be occupied by a celestial entity were the vertical axis of the cosmology to be activated – which is not the case at present. It is a structural position, albeit of low contemporary productivity, expressed in various ideas relating to death and shamanism. One of the epithets given to great dreamers is *amynjarohoa*, "great master of rain." Having Topoa as a pet is an attribute of those who truly dream.

---

26 A modern version states that thunder is the sound of a giant pan similar to an oven used to toast flour and that lightning is produced by Topoa's immense camera flash. He is said to have been the "first to carry a photographic camera" (*morejakawa-rerekatar-ypya*).

The shamanic potency of individual dreamers is evaluated according to various criteria. Dreaming of Topoa is one of them, whereas another is dreaming of human-enemies or jaguars and interacting with them in their "true skin." These are unusual experiences for younger people, who typically only see *ma'ejiroa*, a category that includes artifacts, natural objects, and game; that is, entities that, though capable of communicating in dreams, lack pronounced subjective potency. The vast majority of songs come from this category and result from dream experiences composed of fragments of everyday events: During periods of abundant fish catches, dreams of fish are frequent; when honey is being gathered, the number of songs of bees multiples, and so on. Dreaming of human-enemies, the jaguar and Topoa, on the other hand, only occurs in special circumstances. These *akwawa* possess greater potency, consciousness, and autonomy, which are manifested in their predatory capacity. Inexperienced dreamers are unable to familiarize them. Only those with a surplus of agency, acquired through warfare and a rich dream life, can control pets of such power.[27]

There is one category of beings, however, who are entirely irreducible, even to great dreamers: the dead. In contrast to enemies, dead kin cannot be familiarized. The predominance of a horizontal axis in Parakanã cosmology is linked to an eschatology that does not postulate any immortal celestial soul appropriable by the living. The dead play no part in shamanism.

Soul Matters

I have been drawing attention to certain peculiarities of Parakanã shamanic and warfare conceptions – such as the absence of the classic theme of soul capture, the inexistence of a victim's spirit to be incorporated by the killer, the substitution of this relation for one with the dream *akwawa*, and, finally, the materialist interpretation of curing dreams. We can now examine how these elements are connected to the constitution of the person and its posthumous fate.

Coming-to-Be

In many Amerindian cosmologies, the corporal substrate is animated by immaterial principles that can be liberated under certain conditions (such as dreams, trances, morbid states) and, definitively, after death. The Parakanã use two terms to designate these immaterial components of the

---

27 The shamanic capacity of dreamers is not only indexed by the types of *akwawa* with which they interact, but also by the quality and quantity of songs that they offer to the collectivity. Quality here involves an evaluation of the beauty of the songs – whether they are "tasty" (*heekwen*) and "perfumed" (*-pi'e*) – and of their complexity, which may be indicated by the enunciation of the name of more than one animal or by an internal reference to therapeutic techniques.

person: The first is -'*onga*, the second -*a'owa*. In Tupi-Guarani languages, we often find cognates of these terms (whose protoforms are **anga* and **a'uva*) to refer to "the incorporeal aspect of animated beings or the representational mode of things" (Viveiros de Castro 1992a:208). The cognates of **anga* are more common, possessing the double meaning of vital principle and image, designating both the soul and the shadow projected by the body or the photographic image.[28]

Viveiros de Castro (1992a:209) distinguishes these two meanings in the Araweté concept of "soul" (*i*) and links them to eschatology: On one hand, we have an active component internal to the body, which animates it (a vital image); on the other, a passive aspect, external to the body, which accompanies it (a shadow image). In death, these aspects separate into two components with different destinations: a soul that becomes celestial and immortal, and a terrestrial specter that is doomed to fade. This spiritual duality is reencountered in modern Guarani cosmologies, in which the cognates of **a'uva* predominate, referring exclusively to the soul with a celestial destination, as opposed to the other soul, which is animal, telluric, and regressive.[29]

Whereas the Araweté postulate the existence of one soul with two posthumous destinies, the Guarani conceive the person to be divided from the outset into two principles with different origins and fates. For their part, the Parakanã refer to two incorporeal aspects of the person (-'*onga* and -*a'owa*) but only know of one posthumous destiny: the putrescence of the specter. The -'*onga* loses many of the features attributed to its congeners in other Tupi groups: It is impersonal, is not linked to consciousness, and does not have the attributes of a free soul. It lacks the activity that would characterize it as a vital image, as an autonomous cause, leaving it simply with the condition of a projected shadow. There are just two moments when the active attributes of the -'*onga* are highlighted: in conception and death.

In conception, the -'*onga* emerges as a virtuality of existence, an uncreated principle responsible for its own placement. The Parakanã theory holds that women become pregnant when an -'*onga* penetrates the vagina and settles (-*je'om*, "places itself") in the womb (or, in another version, penetrates the penis and, through the sexual act, the woman herself). It is not rare for someone to state that he "placed himself" inside his mother, as a man once told me while explaining why another man was his maternal

---

28 These include the Wayãpi *ã*, the Araweté *i*, the Asurini and Tapirapé -*unga*, the Asurini of the Xingu -*ynga*, the Kayabi -*ang*, and so on. Some of these peoples employ another term to refer to photos and anthropomorphic representations, such as the Wayãpi *ta'anga* and the Asurini of the Xingu *ta'yngava* (see Gallois 1988; Viveiros de Castro 1992a; Andrade 1992; Wagley 1977; Oakdale 1996; Müller 1990).

29 See, for example, the opposition between *ayvu(cué)* and *acyiguá* among the Apapocuva and the Ñandeva (Nimuendajú 1987:33–4; Schaden 1954:132).

uncle: *heninté-popé aje'om*, "I placed myself inside his true sister." There is, then, no generation, but a placement of a potential life, which occurs through the penetration of the -*'onga* into the female body.

In contrast to the shamans from other Tupi groups, who are capable of capturing souls to fertilize women, the Parakanã dreamers do not control the -*'onga*, nor do they interfere in female fertility.[30] All that is known about the -*'onga* is that they inhabit water courses and that they enter women when they bathe in rivers. The dreamers only interact with the fetus shortly before birth, in order to ease a delivery that is proving difficult. In dreams, they can speak to the baby and repeat their words during labor, telling the fetus that the mother is good and beautiful, that it should not be angry with her, and that it should come out slowly and smoothly.

Once the -*'onga* has placed itself in the uterus, the father is responsible for fabricating the baby through a continuous injection of semen (called *ta'yra*, "son"). This fabrication is divided into two moments: There is an initial act that makes the woman pregnant and a repeated process that makes her belly grow ("makes her swell up completely"). Like other Tupi-Guarani peoples, the Parakanã embrace a strictly agnatic theory of fetal fabrication: The mother is a "container" (-*yroa*) in which the child is formed by the semen of the father, whom it should resemble physically. The -*'onga* is not conceived as an entity inhabiting the body of the baby or as a soul separable from its physical substrate. After birth, it will be referred to merely as a shadow, which can be neither lost nor liberated during life. In accordance with this, all the precautions undertaken for the newborn focus on the body. Absent here are the common Amazonian themes of the precarious fixing of the soul in the baby and the danger derived from its volatility.

The strictest period of seclusion (-*jekoakom*, "seclude oneself") lasts roughly three months. During this interval, the mother and child are said to still smell of blood (-*pyji'o*) and therefore present a danger to the father. The wife should not cook for her husband, since the food contaminated by the smell-taste of blood would cause his spleen to swell, as occurs with the killer during seclusion. Most prohibitions, however, apply to both the father and the mother and look to preserve the health of the newborn child: Certain honeys cause fever in the child, certain meats make the spleen swell, others cause pains in the liver, and so on. There are two interdictions that apply exclusively to the father: He should not smoke, since the baby's belly would swell, nor can he kill jaguars, since this would make the child cry constantly. The most long-term prohibition is on sexual relations: Women

---

30 Except during the rhythm baton ritual (*waratoa*), also known as *moropyhykawa*, "catching people" (see Chapter 6).

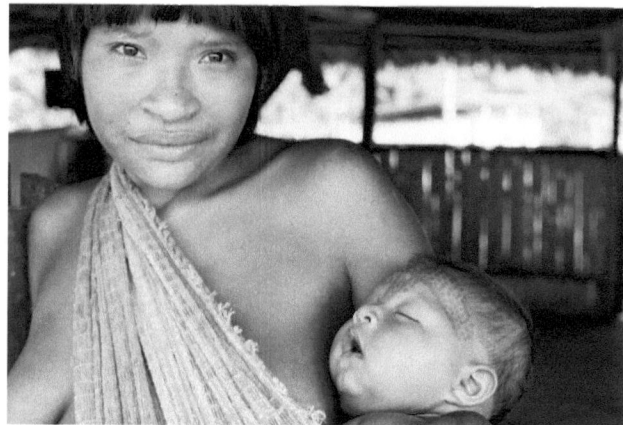

Photo 5. Orowojora and her daughter, the latter's forehead painted with the
jaguar's motif (western Parakanã, Apyterewa village, 1988).

say that this should last until the child starts to walk, whereas men affirm
that it is sufficient to wait until the infant starts to crawl.

The baby is a malleable being, which needs to be shaped (-*mongatyro*)
to acquire human characteristics and conform to Parakanã standards of
bodily perfection. The mother and close kin dedicate themselves to this
art: They squeeze the skull, stretch the ears and cheeks, pass their fingers
over the lips, massage the back, buttocks, calves, genitals, and feet. These
operations work to distinguish human bodies from animal bodies, which
are not shaped (except for those of pets). As well as moldable, the baby is
hot and needs to be bathed continually, especially its head. The infant is
also painted with genipap, which helps the process of maturation called
-*piteram*. The strictest period of reclusion ends when the child -*piterapam*;
that is, "-*piteram* completely," a state opposed to "immaturity" (-*akyn*), a
term that also applies to unripe fruits. The process of maturation is linked
to motor and sensory development and to the constitution of the flesh. The
newborn is said "to have no flesh" (*naha'ai*): This is formed by the mother's
breast milk, completing the process of fabrication begun with the male
injection of semen. "To have flesh completely" (-*a'amam*) is, however, a
moment prior to the finalization of the -*piteram* process.

During the period of seclusion, the dreamers do not interfere in the
production of the person: All the emphasis falls on the constitution of
the flesh. The prohibition on smoking indicates that the father must not
dream during this period. The dream experiences only surface again at the
moment of naming, which occurs when the child is between three and six
months old. No formal ceremony exists for imposing this name, which is

Photo 6. The boy Jorohewera ("Mouth-corpse") named after one of Koria's dream
enemies (western Parakanã, Apyterewa village, 1993).

termed *terypya* ("first name") or *tereté* ("true name") and corresponds to the
childhood name. This is strictly individual: No other living person may
have the same name.

Among the western Parakanã, most of the names come from outside –
they are *akwawa* names. Like songs, they are appropriated rather than
transmitted. The most common form of capture is through dreams, and
the most prolific dreams are those of human-enemies. Koria, for example,
named various children on the basis of his experience with the Karajá:
Jorohewera (his WSS), Piroroa (his BDS), Wiriri (another BDS), and so on.
Among the eastern Parakanã, some of the names are names from people
who died long ago (*imawe-rera-ren-kwera*, "ex-name of the remote past").
The names of the recently deceased cannot be recycled as this would harm
the child. Reusing a name requires a certain lapse of time in which it
remains as a memory, separating itself gradually from the singular existence it once represented.[31] This precaution has two outcomes: On one
hand, the person bearing the name does not know who its previous bearer
was, nor whether some kind of kinship tie connects them (in this sense,
we cannot really speak of inheriting or transmitting names). On the other
hand, young people are dependent on older people to name their children:
"Search for the future name of my child" (*emomyro jera'yra-renroma*), a young
man will ask an older relative.

---

31 For a long period of time the name will occur with the suffix *-away'yma* ("nonperson"), indicating
   that it is connected to a dead person. Only decades later, when the genealogical links have been for-
   gotten and its former bearers have become figures in ancient narratives, can the names be reused.

The capturing of names in dreams implies the same dependency on older people, since young people are less able to dream. A child often remains nameless for a long period. When someone who has yet to find a name is asked what his child is called, he will reply somewhat ashamed: "He/she hasn't got a name yet." Normally an older relative – a father, father-in-law, brother, or brother-in-law – ends up offering a name to the child's father. The offer follows a standard formula: The namer says to the father, "I heard his future name in a dream" (*aenom wekewyri henroma*). To which the father replies: "So name him" (*eipo rapo ke eenoi*).

These names heard in dreams are not necessarily from humans-enemies: They may be from any kind of dream *akwawa*. Ajowyhá, for instance, dreamed of a bat and subsequently named his grandson. The name given was not "bat," though, but the proper name of the dream interlocutor: Reroa, an individual name, not a species name. However, some names are identical to the designations for animals: Ararona (hyacinth macaw), Iwangyrá (silky anteater), Marakajá (ocelot), Jejoa (golden trahira), and so forth. These names do not form a separate class. If questioned, the Parakanã say that they are names and have nothing to do with species designations, though they recognize the homonymy. No connection is made between the named person and the animal's characteristics.

Names taken from real enemies are classified as *akwawa-renwera* ("ex-names of enemies"). There are two ways of acquiring them: through the conversation that may precede an armed conflict or through captive enemy women.[32] Such names are not usually given to a child, but supplement a childhood name, sometimes in association with warfare renown. Experienced killers can give a new name to a young killer, as Awanamia did when his son-in-law, still a youth, killed an Araweté man: "True killer. Receive an ex-name, my son-in-law. Look, you made a beautiful eagle feather." However, rather than the name of *his* particular victim, the young killer receives an old enemy's name, preserved in memory for many years.[33]

New names supplementing the childhood one are called *terakawa* or *tera-iroa* ("kind of name" or "equal-other name.") There is no fixed occasion for name changing, although there is a diffuse notion that new names are acquired around adolescence. These can come in the form of nicknames imposed by use or can be requested by the youth from a dreamer. Awanga,

---

32 However, only those who speak the same language as the Parakanã can function as namers. There are, for instance, no Araweté names among the western Parakanã.

33 Awanamia renamed his son-in-law in the 1970s as Awajowa, which was the name of the older brother of the eastern Parakanã headman Arakytá, about whom he had not heard since the 1950s. The namer himself possessed an ex-name from another Awanamia, killed during the fission of the Parakanã blocs.

for example, dreamed of jaguars and renamed his daughter. Learning about
this, some youngsters asked him to narrate the dream. They then claimed
names for themselves. Tatoa, a preadolescent, said to him: "Name me, so I
can throw away Tatoa." The Parakanã typically say that they have "thrown
away" a particular name; a person never pronounces his or her own name,
except when claiming to have discarded it. In most cases, though, names
accumulate: The closest kin will continue to use the childhood name, peers
use a nickname, and a more distant kindred will refer to the person by a
third name.

Naming does not mark any social distinction. All names have the same
value and are not organized in classes. Instead, they are the condition for
the person to exist in singular form. For this to occur, the Parakanã have to
rely on the *akwawa* since they espouse a radical exonymic system in which
the conservation and transmission of names is severely limited. Names are
continually appropriated through warfare and shamanism, and then transmitted just once, from the dreamer or warrior to a junior relative, without
establishing a juridical or ceremonial bond between namer and named.
Viveiros de Castro distinguishes such a "cannibal" naming system from a
"dialectical" one, mainly represented by Ge onomastics, in which names
circulate in an almost closed system and transmission replaces appropriation. Whereas in a cannibal system the value of names resides in their
origin and means of capturing, among the Ge their value derives from the
possibility of retransmission, since it is through it that ceremonial relations are established and the person acquires prestige (Ladeira 1982:43,
Lea 1992).

Parakanã naming and musical systems are part of the same sociocosmic
configuration, which takes to an extreme the need to capture wealth from
the outside. Parakanã songs are transmitted within the group just once –
from the dreamer to the singer, who executes them and cannot transmit
them further, since, once killed in the ritual, they lose their potency. This
is why the songs taught by captured foreign women cannot be incorporated into ceremonial life. This stands in contrast to what occurs among
the Kayapó, where songs, dances, adornments, and ritual routines are introduced from other indigenous groups (Verswijver 1992a:155). In the Kayapó
case, these appropriated wealth items acquire an additional value through
the ritual performance, and enter into a complex social network based on
intergenerational transmission and the concession of ceremonial prerogatives. Furthermore, ritual performances imply the establishment of a hierarchy, expressed in the opposition between "beautiful people" (*memex*) and
"common people" (*mekakrit*), the former being defined as those who received
"beautiful names" in a collective naming ceremony (Turner 1991).

The Kayapó rituals produce differences in ranking: Their inscription is
sociological and visible, whereas among the Parakanã it is ontological and

invisible. In the first case, a mark is imprinted as a distinctive emblem of the person; in the latter, a putative transformation occurs, which can only be confirmed by future acts. This is why *opetymo* is not a rite of passage, despite its association with male maturation. It is certainly central for acquiring the full productive capacity of an adult man, which means above all being a warrior-singer and a dreamer-giver of songs. Those who never danced in *opetymo* are said to be like children; they feel ashamed. Yet this shame does not disappear all at once: One needs to participate in the festival numerous times, which demands a continual supply of new songs given by the *akwawa*. In the past, the external mark of this gradual development of male agency was the placement of the lip-plug, which took place around the age of eight. However, oral and oneiric skills develop much later: in general, in the man's thirties. It is at this moment that the other incorporeal aspect of the person emerges: the *-a'owa*.

My Double and I

In the majority of Tupi-Guarani peoples, the same term is used to designate the "dream soul" and the "vital image" responsible for activity and consciousness. This term is usually a cognate of **anga*, except among the Parintintin, where it is called *ra'uv*. The Parakanã possess both forms, differentiating the aspect of the person that acts during dreams (*-a'owa*) and its existential principle (*-'onga*). This bifurcation is consistent with the eclipsing of the active characteristics of the latter, which are partially transferred to the former. The *-a'owa* possesses attributes of a "wandering self" (Basso 1987:88) – a free form of consciousness, which interacts actively in dreams with the *akwawa* in a communicative context.

Onga and *-a'owa* are not only aspects of the person. They also designate modes of representation: The first applies to two-dimensional images such as shadows and photos, which retain a visual correspondence with the entity represented; the second applies to three-dimensional substitutes that maintain a more complex correlation with it. The dramatization or personification of an other-self is a presentation of the *-a'owa* type. In the myth of the origin of fire, Máira pretends to be a rotting victim to trick the vultures into descending: He is *temiarema-ra'owa*, "representation of stinking-prey." Toys and miniatures are the same: A doll is *konomia-ra'owa*, "representation of a child"; a hunting hide constructed by boys for play is *tokaja-ra'owa*, "representation of a blind." The same applies to the few dream symbols that need to be interpreted. Dreaming of killing an animal indicates that a real enemy will be killed – the dream prey is a "representation of the enemy" (*akwawa-ra'owa*), or, more precisely, a "representation of the future enemy" (*akwawa-ra'owoma*). People also say that the song performed in *opetymo* is a "representation of the dreamt enemy" (*akwawa-ra'owa*).

What all these examples share is the idea that the relation between the representation and the thing represented is not based exclusively in iconic similarity. The correspondence is more complex and implies a relation of substitution. It is in this sense that we can translate the -a'owa as the person's "double" or "substitute": It is not a simple inert image (like the -'onga) but a principle endowed with activity. It is a free form of the self manifested in altered states of consciousness. The -a'owa possesses the qualities of the soul associated with activity and shamanism, which correspond to one of the aspects of *anga among other Tupi-Guarani peoples.

One could suggest that the Parakanã merely separate into two concepts characteristics that other peoples attribute to a single principle, whose dual character is only revealed after the person's death, when it divides into an immortal soul and a dwindling specter. This is not the case, though. There are three important differences: First, the -a'owa is an epiphenomenon of the capacity to dream, not a component dwelling in the body and liberated during dream activity. The fact that children, young people, and women do not dream (or dream little) cannot be translated into possessing or lacking -a'owa. Second, it is not a vital principle and hence does not occupy the functional place of *anga in relation to sicknesses caused by soul loss. It cannot be lost: What is lost is the capacity to dream, but this does not threaten the person's existence. Finally, -a'owa does not have a specific posthumous destiny.

The Enemy Dead

The person is the product of a vital image (-'onga) that penetrates the vagina and places itself in the uterus. Semen transforms this image into a being with a body (-eeté), and breast milk into a being with flesh (ha'a); a being that can present itself in two forms during life: as a skin-covered person (-piretê) accompanied by a passive shadow (-'onga) and as a dream double (-a'owa). Death produces the dissolution of the person into three components: the ex-body (teewera), whose destiny is to turn into bones (-kynga), ex-dreams (-poahipawera), and, finally, a new autonomous and dangerous image called -'owera, which I translate as specter. The term is composed of the nominal past tense suffix -wera and the radical -'ong, with elision of the velar nasal /ng/: 'owera would thus translate as ex-'onga.

Death is announced when people see themselves pursued by their own image, no longer a passive shadow but an active future specter. This haunting anticipates death. Someone who sees herself outside of herself will say to her kin, "I became a specter, I shall probably die" (je'owen, amano rapo pota). One can also say that she has seen her future-ex-'onga (-'owenroma) or, simply, her future -'onga (-'ongoma). These two expressions are equivalents and seem to express the idea that the -'onga only exists as an autonomous entity when the body ceases to exist, just as it existed independently before the body came to be. Its condition of existence is always past or future, as a corruption or generation of the living being. It only *is* at the fleeting moment in which it enters the womb or separates from the body. Yet it immediately transforms into something that already is not it: into a fetus or into a specter. The Parakanã do not espouse the idea that death results from the exiting of an animic principle from some region of the body. They say, instead, that the specter undresses (*-jyroekyi*) in the grave and departs: The bones remain in the earth, and the ex-image is freed into the world. The emphasis once again is the act of removing a skin, a piece of clothing.

Although the specter is a posthumous transformation of the *-'onga*, it is endowed with activity like the *-a'owa*. Following death, what were two separate aspects of person – activity and passivity – are united. The Parakanã postulate two incorporeal aspects of the living person, but only one posthumous destiny: the ineluctable putrescence of the specter, whose most common epithet is "large opossum" (*toymyohoa*). They also conceive of just one relationship between the living and the dead: predation. The *'owera* are the quintessence of the killer: For the western Parakanã, they shatter the skulls of their ex-kin with an enormous black club, as the late Arona did with one of his children:

I was extracting honey when the *'owera* of my father came to show himself to me. I didn't see him when the snake killed him, which is why he came to me [Arona died of a snake bite in the mid-1980s]. He removed my bow. I gave him my machete. He took two things: bow and machete. Then I fled from him as he sat eating the honey. But he came after me again when I was killing tortoises. I was killing tortoises when he came after me again:

– Why are you accompanying me? I asked.

The opossum is a dangerous thing, very dangerous. It had an enormous warclub. So I killed him while he ate, I killed his *'owera* truly. I returned home and recounted [what happened] to my maternal uncle:

– The opossum almost crushed my skull with his enormous warclub.

The specter's blow is expressed as fever, loss of consciousness, and death. Among the eastern Parakanã, we find, as well as the violent club blow, the crushing of the victim's bones by manual compression.[34] With their relish for land turtles and honey, the *'owera* are inveterate killers; head smashers and grillers of the living, they cease being kin to become enemies. The

---

34 It is told, for example, that the *'owera* of Takorahá appeared to his older brother, Mino'oa, while the latter was hunting tortoises. He approached from behind, calling him *-pajé* rather than brother. He smashed him completely. Mino'oa returned to the village and announced: "The enemy grilled me" (*jemoka'é ngyngé*). He rotted alive – his skin peeling off and teeth falling out.

homicidal compulsion is less a desire to reencounter the living than the posthumous expression of the ambivalence inherent to the warrior. It is the *kawahiwa* doctrine taken to an extreme, the final resolution of the fate that hovers over the killer: He is an enemy, his destiny is to become an adversary. All dead kin produce a specter. In the event previously described, for instance, Arona was accompanied by a boy who had died around the same time in an accident. But only the *'owera* of adult men possess autonomous activity and offer a real danger; in other words, only the warriors have a significant posthumous destiny.

There is just one way of dealing with specters – killing them again. This second death makes them transform definitively into an opossum or rat or simply disappear, never to return. Before being rekilled, the *'owera* may appear in the form of certain animals, such as the large blue morpho butterfly, the lesser anteater, and the nightjar. The prototypical animal form of the specter, however, is that of icterid birds generically called *japoa* (oropendola), the most specific association being with the *karara'oré* (the green oropendola).[35] It stays in the trees talking, and if someone is imprudent enough to reply to its call, it descends and "makes itself a person" (*-jemoawa*) in order to club to death the ex-relative. Hence, the specter is a bird that transforms itself into a person and, when killed again, turns irreversibly into an opossum.

If the specter relates to the warrior as a posthumous image of the person's predatory power, is there not a representation of the other cardinal capacity, namely, the ability to dream and familiarize enemies? This capacity is indeed present in two other eschatological notions: the idea that dreams possess a continuity after death and that graves offer danger to the living. The death of a dreamer, in particular those who were "great masters of the rain" (*amynjarohoa*), can cause torrential rainstorms, accompanied by lightning and gales, and can lead to flooding similar to that of mythic times. The rain results from both the past dream activity and its posthumous continuation, meaning it comprises a kind of persistence of the deceased's shamanic capacity. According to Iatora, there is a certain intentionality involved here: "When an *amynjarohoa* dies, he makes the rain return. In the house of sleep, he sees very well, so he makes the rain return on his ex-kin. Then, in his ex-place, he makes the earth soften until it bursts." The death of a great dreamer reenacts the myth of the primordial flood, when men

---

35 Most probably, *Psarocolius viridis*. This identification matches that obtained by Jansen (1988:38) among the Wayãpi, who denominate the species *P. viridis* as *karamaramoré* and *P. Decumanus* as *japu*. Both are gregarious birds whose nests, shaped like long bags and built in groups hanging from branches in the same tree, are reminiscent of a cluster of upside-down houses (Frisch 1981; Meyer de Schauensee & Phelps Jr. 1978). Another kind of *japu*, the yellow-rumped cacique (*Cacicus cela*), is usually noted for its capacity to imitate a wide variety of sounds.

punctured the earth via their dreams in retaliation for women's aggressive behavior toward them.

The other risk posed by the death of a dreamer is the sending of diseases against the living. This danger is linked to the grave and is manifested in two forms: One is passive and relates to the notion of mephitic emanations deriving from the burial place, which produce sicknesses known as *tywya-rahya* ("grave pains"). The other form is active and relates to the notion of ensorcelled objects: The deceased hurls *karowara* against the living through his ex-dreams.[36] Certain funerary practices aim to minimize these risks. The deceased must be buried facing the direction opposite to the village with a bowl covering his/her eyes, safeguarding the living against diseases and a cataclysm: "so he will have no shamanic power," "so he will have no pathogenic agents," or "so he will not puncture the earth." Before contact, whenever a dreamer died, the people would disperse, abandoning the village for a couple of months until the corpse "was completely mature-rotten" (*-kwepam*).

The risks diminish after the corpse's decomposition. The western warriors used to return to the location of attacks on enemy groups to check the number of dead. They did this only after these had *-kwepam*: "Then we weren't afraid of sicknesses," Iatora explained to me, "since only the skeleton remained." If the war victims had been buried, they were exhumed. All the attention was focused on the skull, which was removed from the grave and deposited on the ground, where it was said to hiss to its dreams and make it rain. Although it is impossible to know whether the enemies have a specter (and if they do, they would only appear to their own kin anyway), they undoubtedly possess dreams that extend beyond death.

There is a positive association between the *-a'owa*, its space-time (the dream), the skull, and consciousness. Its posthumous existence, however, is not as a personalized image like that of the *-'owera*, but as a representation of the dream activity itself. The *-a'owa* persists as a dream endowed with efficacy, linked to the grave and the skull. Its action is simultaneously wider and narrower: wider because it threatens the collectivity of the living with rainstorms and hurls sicknesses at anyone approaching the grave (whereas the specter only targets its nearest ex-kin); narrower because it acts at close range, given that it does not move about like the *'owera*. This is a curious inversion of the aspects of the person in life: The *-'onga*, a faceless image stuck to the body, becomes autonomous and personalized, whereas the *-a'owa*, a free representation of consciousness, becomes impersonal and associated with the corpse.

---

36 The deceased is said to obtain the *topiwara* in a dream while alive, but use them after death. These *topiwara* are called *-pao'ywa*, a term that seems to be composed of "hand" (*paa*) and "arrow" (*-o'ywa*).

The Parakanã represent an extreme case within the set of Tupi-Guarani cosmologies. Some of these postulate the splitting of the person into two aspects after death: on one hand, the terrestrial specter, a sign of the putrid fate of humans; on the other hand, the divinized immortal soul, a sign of the permanence of consciousness.[37] Parakanã eschatology swept away the celestial-perfumed-immortal plane entirely, reducing the fate of the person to a single outcome: an opossum-becoming. The eschatological machine is not veered toward immortality but toward a desire for persisting in the present. It does not aim at the definitive overcoming of the human condition, remaining content in claiming small temporary victories over the driving forces of life: pain, sickness, and rottenness. The only transcendence possible is not reserved for a vital principle destined to become an immortal soul but for the dream double. Yet this transcendence is the condition for immanence, for persisting in this life, in this world. Longevity is an attribute "of those who persist" (*iteka wa'é*), a condition sought and produced with each killing and each dream. It is by means of the *akwawa* that the eschatological machine is halted, albeit temporarily.

Parakanã eschatology put the whole emphasis on the -'*owera*'s regressive destiny and its homicidal compulsion, which blocks the appropriation of the dead for the production of social life. The end of life demands a radical separation: The dead cannot be mediators between humans and gods (as among the Araweté) or between humans and the jaguar (as among the Asurini of the Tocantins). They are irreducible. All entities can be familiarized, but the ex-kin must be nullified so as not to hinder the continuation of life.

In order to round off this exposition of Parakanã eschatology, I shall now systemize the comparison I have been developing with two other Tupi-Guarani peoples: the Asurini of the Tocantins and the Araweté.

The Eschatological Jaguar

The Asurini postulate a single incorporeal principle of the person during life, called *iunga*. This is the same word as the Parakanã's, but endowed with those characteristics that were in ellipsis among the latter: It is the vital image, which the divinity (Mahira) deposits in women, and also the dream soul. Its fate is correspondingly different. At death, it separates into a celestial aspect and a terrestrial one: The former joins Mahira in *Tupana*; the latter turns into a specter. The celestial part is denominated both *iunga* and '*owera*; the terrestrial part, both '*owera* and *asonga*. '*Owera*

---

37 This model occurs among the Araweté, the Guarani, and the Wayãpi. Among other peoples, an immortal destiny is a privilege of certain categories of persons, in general shamans or warriors, the remainder being doomed to wander the forest as specters (Viveiros de Castro 1992a:259–69).

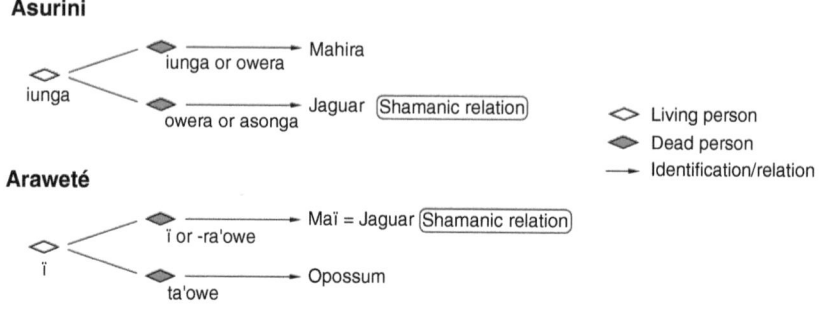

Figure 5.1. Asurini and Araweté theories of the soul.

designates, therefore, both aspects of the dead person (which is not surprising since they are equally ex-*'onga*, ex-vital image). The spectral form of the *'owera* is also called *asonga*, a cognate of the Tupinambá *anhanga*, a necrophagic spirit associated with the dead.[38] What is remarkable here is not the fact that the Asurini postulate a celestial destiny for the soul, but that they establish a shamanic relation with its spectral form. The *'owera* that goes to *Tupana* ceases to have any meaning for the living, whereas the rotten specter becomes an auxiliary of the shamans, mediating their relations with the jaguar, a central figure in shamanic apprenticeship (Andrade 1992:217–9).

The Araweté, by contrast, assert that it is the imperishable portion of the person that acts as an intermediary between the living and the gods (called Máï, another cognate of Maíra). They believe that at death the soul (*ï*) divides into two components: a posthumous projection of the shadow (the specter, *ta'o we*) and a spirit (also called *ï*), which journeys to the sky. There, it is eaten and immortalized by the gods, who are considered "eaters of the raw," that is, jaguars (Viveiros de Castro 1992a:90; 201–14) (see Figure 5.1).

Cannibal appropriation is associated with different values in each case. The Araweté equate the gods with the jaguar and celestial immortality with omophagy, founding shamanism on the relation with this plane. The Asurini, on the other hand, link the cannibal-function to the perishable

---

38 Métraux claims that the chroniclers incorrectly identified the *anhang* with the specter of the dead due to the similarity of this word to the term *anguera*, which means "ex-soul" (Métraux 1979:50). However, if we analyze the cognates of *anhang*, we can note that all of them contain the root for "vital image." Thus in Tupinambá, *ang* → *anhang*; in Araweté, *ï* → *äñï*; in Asurini of the Xingu, *ynga* → *anhynga*; in Asurini of the Tocantins, where the [ñ] changed to [s], *onga* → *asonga* (Viveiros de Castro 1992a; Müller 1990; Andrade 1992). Hence, the identification is not the result of any confusion: **anhang* is the impersonal and collective form of the specter of the dead.

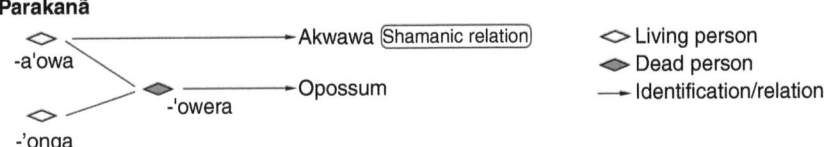

Figure 5.2. Parakanã theory of the soul.

portion of the person, and found shamanism on a relation with a jaguar distinct from the divinity, which is both an "eater of the raw" and an "eater of the rotten." Omophagy and necrophagy appear as equivalent alimentary forms. The Parakanã system is structured in yet another way, swapping around these same values (Figure 5.2).

The Parakanã postulate two incorporeal components to the person in life, which transform into a single specter linked to rottenness. The latter cannot be recuperated by the living through shamanism, which is shifted to the horizontal relation with enemies, conceived in similar fashion to the Asurini 'owera (that is, as eaters of the raw and the rotten): The Karajá are thus a synthesis of the jaguar and the vulture. The cannibal-function among the Parakanã and the Asurini turns on the same alimentary mode, but the terms are organized in a different way, perhaps because in one case warfare encompasses shamanism (Parakanã) and in the other shamanism encompasses warfare (Asurini).

The association of the jaguar-function with rottenness is also found among the contemporary Guarani (Viveiros de Castro 1992a:260), but with an entirely negative connotation. An absolute disjunction exists between cannibalism and shamanism, which is expressed in the opposition between the two animic principles constitutive of the living person: the "divine soul" and the "animal soul." I suggest that, among the Guarani, contact with mission-based Christianity and the experiences of colonialism led to a growing denial of cannibalism as a source of shamanic knowledge, whereas among the Parakanã (especially among the western bloc) their sociopolitical experience during the late nineteenth and early to mid-twentieth centuries led to exactly the opposite; that is, to a general "jaguarization" of the shamanic field.

A New Approach to Amazonian Shamanism

The master-pet relation in dreams points us to a relational schema recurrent in Amazonia and neighboring regions, which has still to receive due attention. I refer to the asymmetric relations of real or symbolic control conceptualized as a form of adoption; or, more precisely, the conversion of a predatory relation into another of control and protection, schematized as a transition from affinity to consanguinity. This schema has a considerable productivity in four domains of social life: hunting, shamanism, ritual, and warfare.

Historically, the peoples of the South American lowlands have never domesticated animals, but have always practiced the familiarization of the offspring of game animals.[39] The importance, diffusion, and symbolism of this type of adoption has been thematized by a few authors, in particular by Erikson (1987, 2000) and Descola (1986, 1994), but globally it has received little attention in Amazonian ethnology. This would not have been the case had we consistently connected it to another, more productive modality of familiarization, which occurs in shamanism and which defines the shaman's relation with his auxiliary spirits, frequently denominated "familiars" in the literature. Some examples will suffice to illustrate this point.

The Wayãpi refer to the shaman's auxiliaries as "pets" (-rima), of which there are two categories: The nearest (õpi-wan) are taken to be consubstantial with the shaman, as kinds of children, and they act as messengers in the contact with more distant pets, such as the masters of animals, who themselves are thought of as shamans. The Wayãpi shaman is a master of masters, controlling his auxiliaries by means of invisible threads, the tupãsã (Gallois 1996:46–7). Among the Tapirapé, some "demons of the forest" (anchunga) become pets of the shaman: "These less harmful anchunga, to a certain degree domesticated by the Tapirapé, come to live for spells during the year in the large central men's house." Dreaming, conceived to be an out-of-body experience of the soul, is the main way of contacting these spirits: "After a visit, in dreams, entire categories of demonic spirits may become the shamans' familiars, obeying their appeals for help" (Wagley 1976:241).

We find the same relation beyond the Tupi-Guarani family. Among the Jívaro-Achuar, the familiar spirits are the shaman's pet animals. These are organized in a hierarchy, at the top of which are the blue anaconda and the black jaguar, which confer maximum power to the shaman (Descola 1993:356–7). Likewise among the Arawak-speaking Mehinaku, the shamans' familiars are conceived as pets. Gregor writes:

Kupatekuma, like all traditional Mehinaku shamans, did not consciously choose to become a yetamá. His career began with an encounter with a spirit. In the course

---

39 Throughout the book I use the terms domestication and familiarization interchangeably. Here, though, I refer exclusively to the domestication of animals for the purposes of consumption or as a substitute for human labor.

of a dream the monkey demon (Pahikuma) came to him and said, "My grandson, I will stay with you; I will be your pet" (Gregor 1977:335).

This adoption, always ambivalent (since one never knows exactly who adopted whom, nor who controls whom), can also be schematized by the father-son relation, as revealed in the dream of a great Tapirapé shaman, Ikanancowi:

He wandered far, reaching the beaches of a great lake in the depths of the forest. He heard dogs barking and ran towards the place from which the noise was coming, encountering many forest spirits, called *munpí anká*. They were pulling a bat from a tree for food. They spoke to Ikanancowi, inviting him to go to their village.... The *anchunga* had various pots of *kauí* and invited Ikanancowi to drink with them. He refused because he perceived that the *kauí* was made from human blood. Ikanancowi saw a spirit drink the *kauí* and vomit blood immediately afterwards; he saw a second one drink from another pot and immediately evacuate blood. The *munpí anká* vomited their intestines and threw them on the ground, but Ikanancowi straight away realized that it was a trick: they were not going to die because they had more intestines. After this visit, the *munpí anká* called Ikanancowi father and he called them children; he often visited them in his dreams and always had a *munpí anká* alongside him.... Other shamans have had familiar spirits, but none had such dangerous ones as the *munpí anká*; the people were very afraid of Ikanancowi, because these *anchunga* are very dangerous (Wagley 1976:242).

In this narrative, we can recognize various themes present in the Parakanã dreams: the bestiality of the oneiric pets connoted by their hematophagy and by their scatological habits (vomiting, defecation); the capacity for organic renewal (the never-ending intestines); the danger posed to kin by the shaman's privileged relation with the spirits; and the consanguinization of the relationship. The shaman is a "father" to his pets (whereas among the Parakanã he is a "child," an inversion linked to the absence of powerful specialist-shamans).

This relationship of adoptive filiation can also be observed among the Yágua of Peru. Chaumeil narrates the vision of a shaman taken to an underground village by an anthropomorphic creature, who tells him: "Don't be scared, I am your son.... From now on you are my father.... I shall accompany you until your death." The Yágua shaman calls his auxiliaries "my people" (*anihamwo*), and the relation is "marked by the fidelity, obedience and assistance shown by the child to the father" (1983:120).

In some groups, the spirit's adoption by the shaman may be transformed into an effective relation of paternity. Thus, among a Ge people of southern Brazil, one of the ways in which mortals may establish permanent and friendly relations with the spirits is to adopt one of their children.... Sometimes men take the children of spirits and put them into their wives' wombs, from which they later emerge in the form of human children. Even if a spirit is adopted in its animal form ... it is loved like a pet. (Henry 1964:73)

In sum, all these culturally and linguistically distinct peoples conceive the acquisition of shamanic power as a process of familiarization of nonhuman entities frequently associated with predation and cannibalism. The most potent familiar spirits are predatory animals such as the jaguar and the anaconda, or bestial beings, eaters of raw flesh and blood. The "familiar" relation is modeled by two asymmetric relations involving control and protection: that between father and son, and that between owner and pet.

The relation of symbolic control schematized by familiarization also applies to ritual objects and body adornment. Among the Ikpeng, for instance, the same term (*egu*) is used to designate familiarized animals, captured children, war trophies, bamboo flutes, and the melodies played on them (Menget 1988:67). Similarly, the Tukano call body adornments and certain musical instruments, in ceremonial and shamanic contexts, "familiar animal" (Hugh-Jones 1996:141). These objects allow the presentation of alien subjectivities, placing them under the control of the ritual specialists.

Finally, the other context in which the schema of familiarization is pervasive is that of warfare. The fact that captives are frequently conceived as pets is well known. Viveiros de Castro (1992a) called attention to this association in Tupinambá ritual anthropophagy, whereas Menget (1988) and Journet (1995:200–205) indicated the same in relation to the capture of children among the Ikpeng and the Curripaco, respectively. The latter call the enemy children taken during a war expedition *hmairruwa*, a term that also designates the animal young captured during a hunting trip. More importantly, the schema of familiarization in warfare also defines the relation between the killer and the victim after the homicide. Among the Araweté, the killer captures the dead enemy's spirit and learns to control it over the course of seclusion. At first he is taken over by the spirit and loses control of himself, but ends up domesticating it and placing it in the service of the community, since it is through the enemy's spirit that new songs and names enter the Araweté world (Viveiros de Castro 1992a). The Wari' conceive the killing as a form of consubstantialization leading to adoptive filiation (Vilaça 1996:120–3). The victim's spirit-blood penetrates the killer's body, fattening him, a process compared to female gestation (Conklin 1989:239–41). At the end of seclusion, the enemy's blood, now transformed into semen, impregnates the killer's wife. The killing thus allows the constitution of a double relation of filiation: In addition to becoming a father to his victim, the killer fertilizes his own wife with the blood-made-semen of the enemy.

These examples reveal the meaning of the predatory act: It is not a simple negation of the other, but the appropriation of an other-agency, which fuses with that of the killer. This explains the recurrent identification between predator and prey, permeated by a dialectic of control in which the victim is not merely a passive pole, but a source of capacities that are simultaneously necessary and dangerous to social life. This bond of control established by the killer with his victim should be compared to the shaman's relation with his familiar spirits. Both connections are conceived as an adoption, as the transformation of a relation of predation into control and protection. An adoption, though, that is *necessarily* ambivalent, as are shamanism and the figure of the shaman: It is not known who adopted whom ("Don't be scared, I am your child," says the spirit) or who controls whom.[40] The same ambivalence is found in the relation between the killer and the victim's spirit, which needs to be tamed but cannot be entirely so (when this happens, it loses its genetic potency). The Parakanã *karahiwa* doctrine or the Araweté killer's other-becoming express the ambiguity of the operation of familiarization in warfare, marking the killer as a dangerous and necessary being, just like the shaman.

The overall thesis espoused by this work is that the operations of domestication in shamanism and in warfare are of the same nature, and that both are part of a generalized economy for producing persons. The main themes are ontological: the acquisition of new existents, naming, the development of agentive capacities, maturation, the control of sickness, immortality. There are differences in the way in which relations with the auxiliaries are constituted: In warfare, there is a continuity between predation and familiarization – a death is followed by seclusion during which the victim's capacities are appropriated. In shamanism, predation and familiarization are connected in a mediated and generalized form. Under the conditions of the current cosmos, the relation of cynegetic predation between humans and nonhumans is correlated with the adoptive relation between shamans and their auxiliaries, most of which are animal spirits. The dialectic of predation and familiarization is the possible, and always ambivalent, mode of being in *this* world.

In conclusion, although we can indeed speak of a symbolic economy of predation (Viveiros de Castro 1993), we also need to develop its complement, which is not a theory of balanced reciprocity, but rather of the

---

40 The shaman's initiation can itself be conceived as the result of a predatory act in which he occupies the position of prey. Among the Wari', for instance, the future shaman is devoured by the animal, becoming its consubstantial, which allows him to make use of the capacities of the devouring animal (Vilaça 1992:81).

asymmetric relations of the father/son or master/pet kind, constituted through homicide and the dream-trance. Predation is one moment in the process of producing persons of which familiarization is another. We cannot understand the meaning of Amerindian warfare through its reduction to the symmetric relations of exchange, but we may succeed through the construction of a *model of the asymmetric relations of control and protection.*

6

Death Producing Life

They tied the cord around my neck high up in a tree, and they lay around
me all night and mocked me calling: schre inbau ende [Chê reimbaba indé],
which in their language means: You are my bound animal [pet].

Hans Staden, True History (1557)

The journey that brings us now to the analysis of Parakanã rituals began
in Chapter 4 with the hypothesis that indigenous warfare is a form of consumption intended to appropriate the victim's capacities. I called this
mode of appropriation *familiarizing predation*, since the relation established
between killer and victim is conceived as a bond of control and protection, modeled on the relation between master and pet, itself conceived
as adoptive filiation. I suggested that the destruction of the enemy was a
fertile negation, insofar as warfare enabled a productive process at a wider
scale: production not of material goods, but of persons and capacities that,
although subjective, are simultaneously objective. The master-pet dialectic
is a version of the master-slave relation in societies in which the production
of immaterial and/or symbolic goods – virtualities of existence, names,
songs, ritual objects, emblems – encompasses the production of material
goods and utilities. This analysis would be incomplete without a description of Parakanã rituals, moments when this entire economy is manifested
in a public and collective form.

Warfare Rituals, Shamanic Rites

I use the term "festival" for activities differentiated from those of quotidian life as involving greater coordination of actions, requiring the
performance of predetermined functions and routines, mobilizing the
collectivity in a wider form, and associating music and dance in specific
ways. The Parakanã term closest to this definition is *morahaitawa*, a nominalization of the verb *-porahai*, "to dance." Music and dance are associated on innumerable occasions. Three of them, however, are distinguished
from the rest by their greater elaboration and duration. These are the

"clarinet festival" (*takwara-rero'awa*), the "tobacco festival" (*opetymo*), and the "rhythm baton festival" (*waratoa*).[1] Here we could also include the "beer festival" (*inata'ywawa*), although in this case music and dance appear to be less important. Besides these four rituals, there are a series of small festivals associated with the hunting of a particular animal or the collective gathering of wild honey. There are no agricultural ceremonies, and indeed swidden products are avoided in the preparation of ritual drinks: Beer is made from babassu coconut, and sweet porridge from the heart of the same palm. The only cultigen used in festivals is tobacco, placed inside the cigar made from the inner bark of the tauari tree.

Dancing with Animals

Dances with animals are not intended to interfere in the natural world or control the fertility of the game: they are neither propitiatory ceremonies, nor forms of compensation for predation. Instead, they aim to appropriate some feature of the animal as a way of producing transformations in human beings. The most important of these festivals is the "cayman race" (*jakaré-rerojonawa*) – a rarely performed ritual since it is considered extremely dangerous.[2] It involves bringing these animals to the village still alive, tied to a post, in order for men to dance with them while women sing. Pubescent girls and children must stay inside the houses, since the cayman songs are bearers of *karowara*. After being raced, the prey are killed and cooked by older women. Caymans can only be eaten if they are danced, though an exception is made for older people. The festival is performed to ensure a long life, "for us to remain, people say" (*tajenetekaoho oja*). Men dance with the giant land turtle for the same purpose, believing that the longevity of these animals will be transferred to humans. Both foods are prohibited to young people, but when eaten ritually they induce a long life rather than early aging.

Men also dance with armadillos to close the body and avoid being struck by enemy arrows. The species chosen are the long-nosed armadillo (*D. novemcinctus* or *kappleri*) and the giant armadillo (*Priodontes maximus*), also deemed edible for elders. Other danced animals include the electric eel, which enables the dancer to dream (the shock being propitiatory) and the jaguar, which enables him to metamorphose into the feline.

---

1 I took part in two *opetymo* (1988 and 1989) and two *takwara-rero'awa* (1988 and 1993), all among the western Parakanã. I never witnessed the *waratoa* ritual, and my account here is based on second-hand descriptions.

2 For a description of the ritual among the eastern Parakanã, see Magalhães (1995:250–5); among the Asurini, see Andrade (1992:114–16).

Together all these operations look to prolong life, either by avoiding violent death or by acquiring oneiric powers that allow access to the shamanic science of enemies.

The avoidance of cultigens and the absence of propitiatory ceremonies for horticulture become comprehensible in this context: The aim is to transfer wild, untamed, and entirely other capacities to people (especially males) in order to transform them ontologically. People also dance with animals making up part of the daily diet, but here no transformative power is involved. These festivals seek to produce an intersubjective space positively invested with the values of sharing and generosity, rather than transfer dangerous powers from outside to inside. Men dance because game was abundant and the hunt was a collective undertaking; people gather to redistribute the produce on the patio and celebrate because they "are happy" (-orym).

A distinction appears to exist, then, between quotidian and ritual foods: Whereas the former are already proper for consumption, the latter need to be danced before eaten. Dancing with these animals produces an ontological transformation centered on the idea that rituals can mature a person, thereby placing the inexorable movement toward death under human control. This image is vividly expressed in the killer's corruption-maturation (-kwepam) during seclusion. For this reason, older men – who are no longer "unripe" (-akyn) – can eat without harm those foods that need to be danced by younger men.

Drinking Beer

Beer festivals are infrequent among the Parakanã. Between the 1930s and 1980s, the western group held three or four, whereas the eastern group recall a few more. Just one has been held since official contact. The drink is prepared with babassu coconut, which accounts for its name: inata'y'a, "babassu coconut water." The coconuts were gathered in large quantities and their kernel left to ferment naturally. It was then crushed in a mortar and sieved. The fatty extract was cooked only by older women, otherwise the beer would not make the drinkers jump-fly (-wewe), which is the festival's explicit goal. After cooling, the drink was taken to the tekatawa, where a pole had been placed at a certain height, parallel to the ground, over which the drinkers would jump as they gulped down the beer.

For the Parakanã, beer induces lightness rather than drunkenness. Its ability to "make people jump-fly" (-mowewé) is essentially derived from its emetic effect: They say that vomiting expels that which makes people heavy or, according to the eastern Parakanã, the "stomach's inhabitants," notably the miniscule beetles associated with pathogenic agents.

The festival unfolded during the day, with the men drinking and jumping and the women singing. One of the songs went as follows:

Ere ewewe-wewe	Go fly-fly
Ere ewewe-wewe	Go fly-fly
Awewe	I'm flying
Awewe	I'm flying

There were also dramatic improvisations, such as shooting arrows at *akwa-wa-ra'owa* ("the enemy's double"). The primary function of the beer festival, however, was to produce hunters, not warriors. The morning after the festival, the drinkers left to hunt. Having become light, they easily caught the tapirs they pursued and brought the game back to the women as "payback for the beer" (*inata'y'a-repya*). The fermented drink – just like the action of transvesting into a jaguar – makes the hunter quicker than his prey.

Beer (*inata'y'a*) contrasts with sweet porridge (*kawonia*), made from babassu palm heart and honey. Porridge leaves people heavy, diminishing their capacity to hunt (enabled by fermented drink) and their ability to dream (stimulated by tobacco). The contrast opposes a food and an antifood, or indeed breastfeeding and anti-breastfeeding. The Parakanã say that only "those who have no milk" (*ikamy'ym wa'é*), referring here to postmenopausal women, can prepare beer. The lightness induced by vomiting is opposed to breastfeeding, which provides the nursing child with weight, flesh, and substance. The mother's milk would ruin the beer, just as drinking porridge after the beer festival ruins the drinker.

So when they stopped flying:

– Don't consume porridge, that which was mixed [with honey], he said, but to no avail.
– Let's go after Itakyhé to consume porridge, Arapá said.

That's what he said.

– I'm telling you the truth. Your powers may vanish (*-pajé'an*). You flew really well. Just eat what hasn't been mixed.[3]

But they ate the mixture and made themselves weak. This doesn't make us quick.

(Arakytá 1992: tape 17)

There are occasions, though, when the Parakanã want to avoid becoming light, preferring to look inward to themselves, and not to the animals hunted in the forest or familiarized in dreams.

---

3 Arakytá uses here the term *-pajé'an* ("to lose shamanic power"), which normally implies losing the capacity to dream.

The Clarinet Festival

Takwara-rero'awa, "fetching bamboo," is a nocturnal festival thematizing the relations between men and women. Its performance lasts just one night, but the preparations start fifteen days earlier, when the clarinets are made from a dark green bamboo called *jitywojinga*. This marks the start of a period of nightly rehearsals. The musicians are divided into three categories according to the type of clarinet played. The longest and deepest sounding – called *towohoa* ("big father") – is played by the main instrumentalist, who sets the theme and the tempo. He takes up position in the middle of the semicircle, flanked by two people who play smaller and higher pitched clarinets called *haty'a* ("his wives"). Spreading out to the right and left of the wife-clarinets are a varying number of "children" (*ta'yra*): small bamboo clarinets with even a higher pitch that accompany the *haty'a*. The structure is that of a prolific polygamous nuclear family – a father, two wives, and more than a dozen children – but also a viricentered one, since *ta'yra* means "a man's son."

Only a few people know how to play the father-clarinet, since the themes to almost eighty musical pieces as well as their order need to be memorized. Each of these has an owner (*-jara*), normally an animal, and the music is said to be "its song" (*ije'engara*).[4] In conjunction, these pieces are known as *takwara-je'engara* ("bamboo music") and, in contrast to the vocal songs, form a fixed repertoire. Though conceived as an ordered and closed set, variations occur from one performance to the next. Their origin lies deep in the past: People say they were appropriated from the Wyrapina, an enemy group attacked by their ancestors and today identified with the Asurini. Of the seventy-five pieces of music I registered, the owners include thirty-three birds, eighteen mammals, three reptiles, one amphibian, one insect, and a fish. These fifty-seven animals are joined by a heteroclitic set that includes the moon and the demiurge Maira, the cajá fruit and vine, ex-timbó-juice and fire, and so on. There are two elements that call attention in this list: the absence of two large classes of predators – the eagles and the jaguars (only the ocelot appears) – and the marked presence of one class of birds, the vultures (the final two musical pieces are owned by the king vulture and the yellow-headed vulture).

After some days of rehearsal, those who are set to dance in the festival (the *takwara-pyhykara*, "bamboo fetchers") begin to collect and store honey. On the eve of the ritual, they must abstain from sex or else risk vomiting the sweet porridge. In the morning, they leave in search of babassu palm

---

4 They may also sometimes be called *jawara* ("jaguar") and their performance said "to kill" (*-joka*), but only as an extension of the terminology of vocal music. Their structure is simple: The *towohoa* marks the entry of the other clarinets and sets the tempo; the smaller clarinets play an AABBCC sequence, where BB is the distinctive theme of the music and AA and CC are constant musical segments.

heart and deliver the ingredients to the women, who prepare the porridge. During the cooking, the *takwara-pyhykara* must stay away from the locale. In the early afternoon, the women paint the dancers with genipap, and before dusk the men head off to an area behind the houses. There they finish decorating each other, gluing white king vulture or harpy eagle feathers on their legs and tying rattles to their ankles. Thus adorned, they enter the patio where the women await them with pots of porridge. Advancing toward the women, playing the clarinets noisily, the dancers take over the patio and perform the first complete cycle of musical pieces. The execution is then interrupted for elder men to mix honey into the porridge.[5]

Honey and porridge are called the "pets" (*te'omawa*) of the *takwara-pyhykara* and of the clarinets themselves. To take part in the festival, everyone must have their own porridge, not to eat themselves, but to distribute. The ritual's main injunction is that the porridge owner cannot taste his own pet, since this would bring him bad luck. Hence, after mixing in the honey, each dancer must begin the arduous task of distributing the porridge – arduous because the women come forward with every variety of container, asking for a little of the porridge, while more audacious youngsters dip their spoons inside the pots. Suffocated by the flurry of hands, elbows, spoons, and banter, the dancer offers all his pet and has little time to try the food of his companions.[6] In structural terms, giver and taker form a brother-sister pairing, and the porridge distribution can be likened to men breastfeeding women. Iatora told me of a festival in which one woman said to the porridge owners: "I'm thirsty, brother, I want to be breastfed, give it to me now so I can be the first to feed."

Once the food is over, the festival starts up again, lasting until dawn with the nonstop repetition of various complete cycles of the musical pieces. During the night, some women from the audience are grabbed by the men, who force them to enter the dance circle. Some resist bravely but always eventually succumb. Each woman is put next to a dancer, who embraces her, the couple remaining that way until dawn. Structurally, the relation between those who embrace is that of lovers, conceived prototypically as a relation between the husband's brother and the brother's wife. Embracing another man's wife has a strong sexual connotation. This is the act that remains in people's minds, with some capable of remembering who embraced whom in festivals held decades earlier.

---

5 Among the western Parakanã, the festival can be performed from the female viewpoint, symmetrically reversing the sexual roles; all that this requires is a woman who knows how to play the father-clarinet (in Apyterewa village, in the 1990s, there were two). The eastern Parakanã do not admit this inversion.

6 The experience of distributing porridge compares to that of distributing presents, which I performed many times in the role of researcher-giver. The attitude of receivers is similar to – the comparison is Itaynia's, not mine – vultures swooping down on meat.

Embracing in the clarinet festival constitutes a man and a woman as lovers, whereas in the *opetymo* festival formal friendship is established between persons of the same sex. Both relations are called *-pajé* and imply a form of intimate predation: A man may refer to his girlfriend as "my food" (*jeremi'oa*) since he is "eating" (*-'o*) her; likewise, the killer, who conceives of his victim as a *-pajé*, also consumes the latter symbolically, although the verb to eat cannot be applied to the act of killing. The term common to killing and sex is "to pierce" (*-kotong*). Here we can recall that, among the western Parakanã, a wife – especially after having given her husband a child – is affectionately called "my related enemy" (*weakwawa'yn*). "Piercing" one's wife transforms her into "enemy-kin," whereas "piercing" the adversary transforms him into an "enemy-pet." Real children issue from the first relation, and virtual ones issue from the second through the appropriation of names and songs that propel the rituals.

The woman's familiarization through sex is expressed in the clarinet ritual, when the captured enemy women were introduced into the group. The first ritual held after the ending of the killers' seclusion was precisely *takwara-rero'awa*, which marked the public entry of the captured women into the field of kinship relations (since they drink the porridge of their "brothers" and embrace their husband's brother). In these festivals, another type of clarinet was used – one made from white bamboo (*takwajinga*) – since blowing the *jitywojinga* clarinet would provoke vultures to defecate on the dancers. As we have seen in Chapter 4, the ritual's goal was to make the enemy women "place their hearts inside the clarinet" to ensure they would stay among them for a long time.

Performance of the clarinet ritual for the captured women reveals its overall aim, which is the introduction of women into the dance circle in order for them to have a long life as sexual partners. This explains why most of the embraced women are pubescent girls. Nonetheless, everyone looks to take part in the rite's action in some form. When the first signs of dawn appear, mothers give their babies to the women in the circle for them to dance with their children. Again, the goal is for the infants to have a long life: "so they will remain, people say" (*taiteka oja*). Similarly, boys more than eight years old are encouraged to take part as instrumentalists: "so they will grow, people say" (*tojemotowi oja*). The ritual allows women and children access, albeit in a weakened form, to an ontological transformation intrinsic to the homicidal action of the warrior.

As morning looms, the tempo speeds up so that the final music coincides with the dawn. Playing the yellow-headed vulture song, which states *arahaté penohi*, "we're going away from you," the players leave by the way they came, heading toward the forest. There they play a noisy blast on the clarinets and hurl them into the forest. They cannot be blown again, as doing so would harm the musician's throat. Time to bathe and rest.

The Tobacco Festival

The clarinet festival is danced collectively at night, is associated with honey and the brother's breastfeeding of the sister, and involves the establishment of cross-sex -*pajé* relations and sexual predation. The *opetymo* festival inverts each of these terms: It involves vocal music and is danced individually, is predominantly diurnal and associated with tobacco, and involves sisters singing for their brothers, the establishment of same-sex -*pajé* relations, and warfare predation.

The performance of the tobacco festival lasts for three to four days and engages five to ten people dancing. The reasons for performing the ritual are varied: abundant game, the celebration of a warfare event, or the resolution of internal conflicts. The preparations begin fifteen days earlier, when an experienced man decides "to stand up" (-*po'om*). This man will be the owner of the festival, the first to dance and the one responsible for sponsoring the nocturnal rehearsals. Among the eastern Parakanã, these rehearsals are held in the *tekatawa*, out of earshot of the women who remain in the houses. The same appears to have once been the norm among the western Parakanã, but for some time now the preparations have taken place on the patio between the houses, within hearing range and sight of the women.

The first nocturnal meetings involve giving songs: The men sit in a circle, armed with bows and arrows or shotguns, the older men occupying the center. One of the latter begins to chant a song in a low, deep voice. He then announces which *akwawa* gave him the *jawara* in a dream and immediately resumes the song, which is repeated numerous times accompanied by the other men until it is finally memorized. This act is designated -*pyro jawara*, "to raise [nourish] the jaguar," in the same sense in which the husband "raises" (-*pyro*) his prepubescent wife by giving her game. In both cases, the nourishing precedes a future act of predation. Memorizing songs through repetition provides the model for all learning ("to memorize" is said -*jawapyhyng*, "to seize the jaguar").

Several songs can be given each night. Some of them will be repeated in later sessions, others will be lost. After two or three nights, the dance rehearsals begin. At this moment, the songs are offered to those individuals willing to participate in the ritual. The dreamer sings and then says: "Here is your jaguar, my nephew" (or friend, brother-in-law, etc.). The man receiving the song confirms his acceptance and refers to it from now on as "my jaguar" (*jejawara*), "my prey" (*jeremiara*), or "that which is mine" (*jeremireka*, a term also applied to a wife).[7] When standing up to dance in the

---

7 Or "deceased" (*away'yma*) and "bastard" (*awarawera*). A man once compared the latter insult to the Portuguese expression *filho da puta* (son of a bitch). The gloss is perfect since *awarawera* is used both in a purely negative form and in an ambiguously positive way ("Ah! That bastard never misses!"). The female form is *kojarawera*.

rehearsals, a man may say: "I'm going to kill the great bastard" (*ajokapota awarawerohoa*) or something similar. The audience remarks on the execution, encouraging him: "This is what a true killing is" (*eipo ijokatawaeté*), "the song is very tasteful" (*heekweneté jawara*), and so on. The musical pieces performed in the run-up to *opetymo* cannot be reused in the festival, since they have already been "killed." Some of them therefore need to be reserved for the ritual itself.

Giving a song implies its "enemization": It ceases to be the pet of the giver and becomes the prey of the receiver, who must finish it off through a public execution. This movement has a double meaning. First, the requirement to transmit the song arises from the fact that no dreamer can "kill" his own jaguar. The reason is identical to the one that makes it imperative to distribute porridge in the clarinet festival: Song and porridge are pets and cannot be eaten by their masters. Second, it manifests the recurring opposition between enmity, ferocity, and self-awareness on one hand, and familiarization, tameness, and alienation on the other. There is no reason to execute a captive that has relinquished its own perspective in favor of the captor's. The mode of cannibal appropriation supposes that the other possesses his/her own point of view, evinced by ferocious and independent behavior.

During the rehearsal period, the ritual's participants are gradually defined. These are called *opetymo wa'é* or *metymonara*. Ideally, the group is formed by pairs of "friends" as in warfare expeditions: The *-pajé* of the man who stood up first will be the second to dance. A third man will stand up, to be followed by his friend, and so on. As the ritual approaches, the nocturnal sessions become longer and the preparations intensify. Inner bark of the tauari tree is fetched to make the cigars, king vultures are killed to obtain their white plumes, and genipap is brought. On the morning of the festival, the ritual house is constructed, called *tokaja*, a term that, as we have seen, designated both the game screen used to ambush certain animals and the wooden cage in which certain kinds of pets are held. Among some Tupi-Guarani peoples, cognates of this term also designate small houses where shamans shut themselves away to attract their familiar spirits.

Mid-afternoon, the performers' sisters paint them with genipap, and at dusk the men are taken to the area behind the *tokaja*, facing the sunset. They remain outside on mats, separated from the inside by a rope (see Figure 6.1a). An older man enters the ritual house wearing leg and arm bands and ankle rattles, carrying the *arawy'a* headdress and a cigar.[8] He

---

8 *Arawy'a* probably translates as "blood-macaw," but the word also designates a fish, the red-bellied pike cichlid (*Crenicichla* sp.). The headdress rim is formed by a babassu strap to which eight red macaw fathers are attached. The tips of the longest are decorated with a flower made from the crest of the female bare-faced curassow. The ornamentation among the eastern Parakanã – from the body painting to the decorations – is more sophisticated, though the general pattern is the same (see Magalhães 1982; 1995).

Photo 7. Iatora dancing inside the ritual house (western Parakanã, Apyterewa village, 1989).

then begins to sing one-by-one the musical pieces set to be "killed" in the festival. This act is known as "cornering" (*imongetawa*), and the old singer is said to be the "cornerer" (*imongetara*). He introduces the songs and dancers inside the ritual house, his performance being not an execution but a conduction: "He corrals the jaguars, he doesn't finish them off," Koria explained to me. When the *imongetara* finishes singing, young people approach the performers, who continue standing behind the ritual house, and push them over, pulling them by the waist and pretending to bite them on the back and nape of the neck. Next they carry them inside the *tokaja*, where they are placed in hammocks. The festival opening is over.

Next morning before sunrise, the performers are decorated with white king vulture or harpy eagle feathers from the ankle to the waist. Donning leg and arm bands, rattles, and a headdress, the owner of the festival starts the execution. Each *metymonara* then dances in turns. They leave the *tokaja* by the front end, facing the sunrise, and enter it from the rear, facing the sunset (see Figure 6.1b).

The standard execution is as follows: Each *metymonara* chants one of his two songs in a very deep guttural voice and at a slow tempo. The women then sing in conjunction in a very high-pitched voice, at an accelerated tempo and more loudly than the dancer. Structurally, the relation between the female choir and the soloist is one of sister and brother: One of the defining activities of sisters is to sing to men during *opetymo*. In so doing, the women cover their head or mouth with a piece of fabric because, they say, "we feel ashamed." The standard dance step involves three small diagonal jumps forward with the feet together and knees

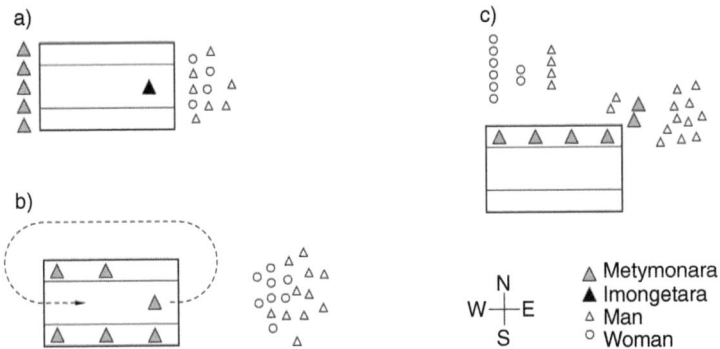

Figure 6.1. Choreographic formations.

slightly flexed, followed by three jumps along the opposite diagonal, and so on successively. There are variations of incidental importance here. What is worth emphasizing is that each dancer produces a dramatization of the *akwawa* he represents: Thus, for example, one of the musical pieces sung by Koria in 1989 was owned by the red-tailed catfish (*Phractocephalus hemioliopterus*). The spectators threw imaginary hooks that he swallowed, initiating a struggle between the fishermen and the fish: The former pulled in the line while the latter thrashed about; they pretended to strike the fish until finally it escaped triumphant and recommenced its dancing and singing. After ten or twenty minutes of nonstop dancing, the *metymonara* finishes his execution with the same short, high-pitched cries used to celebrate the killing of a game animal or a human victim, simultaneously slapping his thigh with the palm of his hand. The next participant immediately begins his performance.

This sequence takes the entire morning, with an interval at midday. The cycle is quickly restarted. Mid-afternoon, young men from the audience start to join in. They form a circle around the performer and stop him from leaving. Circling rapidly, they sing at a faster tempo and at high pitch. New dramatizations take place. In 1989, for example, Wara'yra executed a song called "Temonohoa" ("Great Liar"). While the young men danced around him, the spectators began to shout: "Talk to him." The youths stopped and forced the dancer to stand still. Then a dialogue began in which the performer-as-enemy became angry and spoke strongly while the youths tried to calm him by speaking softly. They soon discovered the reason for the enemy's anger: One of the youths had slept with Temonohoa's sister. As the dialogue progressed, the young lover spoke strongly to Temonohoa, threatening to take his sister away from him. He then pretended to leave with her and was pursued by the enemy.

Photo 8. Wara'yra, the Great Liar, circled by youths (western Parakanã, Apyterewa village, 1989).

Structurally, the relation between the youths and the dancer is one of a junior affine (*tekojara*) and a senior affine (*totyra*). As we saw in the analysis of dreams, the latter is strongly associated with the jaguar. Thus, here the enemy-performer is simultaneously the dream *akwawa*, the maternal uncle, and the cannibal father-in-law. This series of associations is inverted on the second day of the festival, when women are pulled from the audience to dance. The *metymonara* grabs one of them by the wrists, and together they perform a song face-to-face. Other women circle the couple. The relation between the performer and his partner is likewise a *totyra-tekojara* one, but now the maternal uncle assumes the position of a wife-taker in relation to the male audience (which refers to his dancing partner as a sister). In each of these ritual motifs, there are two pairs of cross-sex siblings. Together they comprise a symmetrical predatory exchange (see Figure 6.2 on the next page).

These motifs are repeated from dawn to dusk. At night, a new motif may take place. Inside the ritual house (*tokaja*), the *metymonara* begin to chant new songs. Next, two lines are formed, with the members standing face-to-face on the patio outside the ritual house: One is a line of women, turned to the east; the other of young men, turned to the west. Positioned behind the latter are two men in their early twenties who listen to the *metymonara*'s new songs and chant them in a loud voice (see Figure 6.1c). The young men then form a circle and revolve around different pairs of women successively – an adult woman and a girl – who dance and sing the *jawara* being given at that moment. The interval of time between giving the song and executing it is compressed. The ritual contact with the *akwawa* accelerates the dreaming machine. Each night more than ten songs are given, all

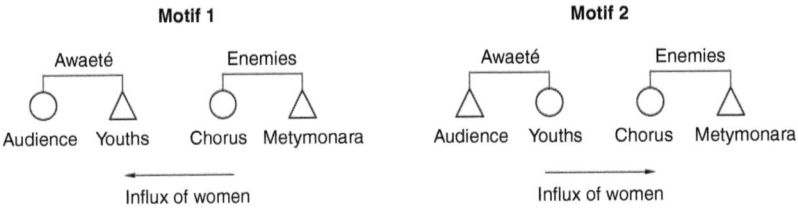

Figure 6.2. Diurnal ritual motifs.

of them immediately killed. The women take now the *akwawa*'s position, but their relation with the circle of men is the same as motif 2: The men are *totyra*, the women *tekojara*. The nocturnal phase therefore involves a gender inversion between the role of soloist and the chorus, as summarized in Table 6.1 on the next page.[9]

The festival continues with the repetition of these motifs for three or four nights, during which the *metymonara* sleep in the ritual house. When the final morning arrives, they dance for the last time and soon leave for the forest to fetch tortoises for their hungry wives.

The focal relation in *opetymo* is not those of ritual motifs 1, 2, or 3, but the relation between the performer and himself, or, more precisely, between the two aspects of his personage: He is at once executioner and victim, killer and prey. The song he chants is the "double" (-*a'owa*) of the dream enemy, and the vocal act is a homicide. The dramatization is equally an embodiment of the enemy, but the performance is the enemy's own execution. In the synthetic language of the ritual, the terms of the predatory relations merge: The pairs killer-victim and hunter-game are amalgamated in a single person, the *metymonara*, thus producing a complex ritual personage (Houseman and Severi 1998).

In the previous chapter, I referred to the Araweté as an example of familiarizing predation: The killer preys ontologically on the victim, who becomes his "auxiliary spirit," providing him with the ritual *pirahë* songs in dreams (Viveiros de Castro 1992a:238–48). The Parakanã construction differs through its greater elaboration, concatenating a higher number of intermediary operations: (a) Warfare predation does not establish a direct relation between the killer and the victim's spirit, but opens up the possibility of the former relating with enemies (*akwawa*) through dreaming;

9 As I stated previously, among the western Parakanã, women can perform the *opetymo*, reversing the gender polarities in all the ritual motifs. In 1996, I witnessed the female rehearsals for performance of the festival, which had not been held by women since 1977, when the Kayapó killed a number of elder women. The eastern Parakanã refuse this inversion, although there are older women who dream and offer songs for men to dance in the ritual.

Table 6.1. *Diurnal and Nocturnal Ritual Motifs*

	Soloist	Chorus
motif 2	men	women
(diurnal)	*akwawa*	*awaeté*
	totyra	*tekojara*
motif 3	women	men
(nocturnal)	*akwawa*	*awaeté*
	tekojara	*totyra*

(b) in dreams, enemies are familiarized and the songs received from them are conceived as the dreamer's pets; (c) these songs need to be reenemized so they can be ritually killed, which is achieved by giving them to a third person; (d) in *opetymo*, this person (embodying both the enemy-victim and the kinsperson-executioner) kills the song-jaguar. This gives us:

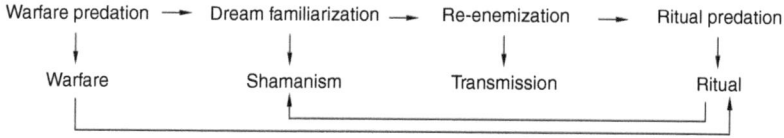

Figure 6.3. Model of familiarizing predation among the Parakanã.

The moment of transmission is crucial since it allows a short-circuit in the system: The predation in *opetymo* also enables the maturation that leads to the development of the person's capacity to dream (represented by the reverse arrow). At the same time, ritual predation is connected to warfare since it realizes the ontological predation eclipsed in the killer-victim relation (represented by the bottom arrow), just as the active "soul" is eclipsed in the theory of the person. The ritual, therefore, operates in two registers: bellic and shamanic.

Nature, Culture, Supernature

The word *opetymo* can be analyzed as "to eat tobacco" (*o-petym-'o*, 3p-tobacco-eat). The ingestion of tobacco smoke is a central element in the rite and is thought to induce dreaming. The dancers may even fall unconscious from tobacco intoxication, a state called -*pikajym*, which also designates the dreamer's state of altered consciousness in waking dreams. The cigar opposes the honey that sweetens the porridge in the clarinet festival. Whereas the honey leaves people heavy and sleepy, tobacco makes them light and prone to dreaming. Inhalation of the smoke is also opposed to the consumption

Table 6.2. *Parakanã Rituals (Shamanic Register)*

Fermented Drink (*inata'ywawa*)	Clarinet Festival (*takwara-rero'awa*)	Tobacco Festival (*opetymo*)
coconut	honey	inner bark of tauari + tobacco
alcoholic drink	sweet porridge	cigar
vomiting	breastfeeding	fainting
induces lightness (-*mowewe*)	induces fattening (-*mokam*)	induces dreaming (-*mopoahim*)

of the porridge itself, since tobacco neutralizes hunger and treats digestive disturbances caused by the excessive consumption of honey. To this opposition we can add another, between fermented drink and sweet porridge: The former is an antifood, an emetic that has to be cooked by "those who have no milk," whereas the latter food expresses the intimate relation between kin (making it comparable to breast milk). Finally, comparing fermented drink with tobacco, we find an opposition in their relation to vomiting: In the former case throwing up causes lightness, whereas in the latter case it prevents dreaming.[10]

In sum, sweet porridge is associated with sex and intimacy between men and women, whereas tobacco and fermented drink enable relations with alterity. The lightness produced by tobacco and beer have distinct characteristics, though: Tobacco induces a state of intoxication focused on relations with familiarized dream enemies, whereas beer produces a state of physical excitement focused on alimentary predation. This set of oppositions can be summarized within a triadic model in Table 6.2.

The shamanic function of *opetymo* is expressed by another term by which the ritual is also known: *pajé*, a word with a thousand meanings – the festival, the songs, the kin-friends (cross-cousins), the enemy-friends, the lovers, but also shamanic power. This designation reveals that the Parakanã *opetymo* is also a form of shamanic initiation. Among the Asurini of the Tocantins, indeed, *opetymo* is explicitly a shamanic apprenticeship ritual in which a well-established shaman administers *karowara*, the source of curative power, to initiates via the cigar. This transmission is strongly correlated with the capacity for predation. The cigar is prepared by the shaman, who inserts small animal teeth animated by his breath. One of the neophyte's possible reactions on inhaling the cigar is, instead of controlling its cannibal drive, to be dominated by it, running wildly and unconsciously

---

10 According to an Asurini shaman, someone is considered to have a shamanic vocation if his smoking during the ritual, instead of inducing the urge to vomit, causes him to fall unconscious under the sway of the *karowara* (Laraia 1986:251).

after raw meat. This is why menstruating women (who smell of blood) should avoid watching the ritual: to prevent the risk of being attacked by the apprentice shaman (Andrade 1992:128). As we have seen in Chapter 5, the Asurini shaman, who controls the *karowara* and dreams of the celestial jaguar, is an eater of raw and bloody meat. The Asurini *opetymo*, a ceremony for initiating new shamans, is hence a cannibal ritual.

In the Parakanã case, the link with warfare is immediate. In the past, *opetymo* was held at the start and end of the killers' seclusion. "I'll dance for you, my sister, and make the hair of my victim fall out" (*apetymo neopé, wetenyn, imongoita wetemiara'awera*), people said. Or: "so that I can become truly ferocious-effective for you, sister" (*tajerahyetene neopé wetenyn*).[11] The fusion between killer and victim in the ritual performance, as well as the idiom of homicide applied to the song, show that *opetymo* is a warfare rite, a renewed presentation of an original predation. It should be recalled that the other designation for the dream *akwawa*, apart from "pet," is precisely "magic-victim" (*temiahiwa*): In the ritual, the "double" (*a'owa*) of the quarry of warfare and hunting is preyed upon. In Table 6.3 on the next page, we reformulate Table 6.2 from the warfare perspective.

Both registers – bellic and shamanic – are expressed in *opetymo*, whose dominant idiom is warfare among the Parakanã and shamanism among the Asurini. The triadic structure of the Parakanã rituals can be related to the Tupi-Guarani model proposed by Viveiros de Castro (1992a:260), in which the values of death, life, and immortality correspond to the warrior, chief, and shaman functions, and more generally to the domains of nature, culture, and supernature. According to the author, this model does not describe any specific case, but comprises a deductive construction from which existing cosmologies can be described as permutations. Its closest example, though, is the contemporary Guarani cosmologies, where we find a clear disjunction between the first and third domains that usually overlap among other Tupi-Guarani peoples. As I argued elsewhere, in response to mission experience and Christian soteriology, the Guarani ended up opposing the two modes of surpassing the human condition: the "low" route, as a regression to nature (animality, cannibalism, warfare); and the "high" route, as a progression to supernature (ascetecism, divinization, shamanism) (see H. Clastres 1975:116–17; Viveiros de Castro 1992:305). This dichotomy is expressed in two Guarani ideal characters: the man who allows himself to be dominated by the animal soul and the desire to eat raw

11 *Tajerahyetene* means literally "so that I truly hurt." *Ahy* means "to hurt," but as an adverb means "effectively." A therapeutic song is only effective if it "hurts." Nimuendajú (1987:33–4) analyzes the Apapocúva term for the "human animal soul" (*acyiguá*) as a participle of *acy*, a cognate of -*ahy* with the same range of meanings. The capacities mobilized by the Parakanã are those that the Guarani seek to elide through asceticism.

Table 6.3. *Parakanã Rituals (Warfare Register)*

Fermented Drink (*inta'ywawa*)	Clarinet Festival (*takwara-rero'awa*)	Tobacco Festival (*opetymo*)
coconut	honey	inner bark of tauari + tobacco
alcoholic drink	sweet porridge	cigar
hunter-game	men-women	predator-prey
alimentary predation	sexual predation	warfare predation

meat, whose fate is to transform into a jaguar; and the ascetic who searches for maturation-perfection in life, whose fate is to become immortal. The dichotomy possesses an ethical and alimentary correlation: The former is the selfish hunter who eats the animals killed in the forest to avoid sharing them; the latter is the generous hunter who gives all the game to kin, since he abstains from meat.

Comparing the Guarani and Parakanã models, we can see that the supernature complex is absent from the latter, meaning that the shamanic ritual is immediately a warfare ritual, just as the familiar spirit is an enemy. Warfare and shamanism are part of the same operation, dominated, though, by the first term, since strictly speaking there are no shamans, only warriors among the Parakanã.

A Blend of Blood and Tobacco

What is the relation between the blood that contaminates the warrior and the tobacco swallowed by the shaman? In Chapter 4, I stated that the killer's dream potential is developed by killing and by the fact that he smells of blood. At the same time, we have seen that tobacco, the substance par excellence of shamanism, can be thought of as an antiblood. It belongs to the world of fragrant resins (*ihynga*) and sweet perfumed (*-pi'e*) things, and is opposed to both the fetid and rotten (*-nem*) and to the things that exude the bloody smell of the raw (*-pyji'o*). Among the Parakanã, tobacco is used to neutralize the odor-taste of blood that impregnates the killer's mouth. Among the Asurini, the shaman-to-be who ingested the jaguar's food cannot eat the following day, limiting himself to smoking, like the Parakanã killer in seclusion. Fragrant resins and tobacco are also used to calm the *karowara* of the initiate shaman who enters into a state of cannibal excitation during the ritual (Andrade 1992:135).

However, although tobacco indeed neutralizes the smell of blood, it also potentializes hematophagy. Among the Asurini, the *karowara* is transmitted by means of cigar smoke, which enables the dream interaction with the jaguar. Among the Parakanã, the tobacco festival is a predatory ritual in which the performers execute jaguar-songs. Intoxication from tobacco during the ritual causes the person to "die" (-*mano*) and "lose consciousness" (-*pikajym*). For the Parakanã, the typical dream of these "tobacco victims" (*petyma-remiara*) is that of "fetching peccaries" to be hunted by their kin. For the Asurini, the loss of consciousness during the ritual can provoke the neophyte to act as an eater of the raw. Here we have the two counterpoised ideal-types in Guarani thinking: the selfish man who transforms into a jaguar and the generous man who brings food for his kin (or the warrior and the shaman, the cannibal and the ascetic).

Among the Parakanã, tobacco is a kind of white and perfumed blood. So much so that when no tobacco was available to make the *opetymo* cigar (a common enough occurrence during their nomadic periods), they used the leaves from a vine called *ipowy'rona* ("like the blood vine"). This vine exudes a large quantity of white sap and is similar to another, called *ipowy'a* ("blood vine"), which possesses a sap with the same consistency but with an intense red color. The leaves of the latter cannot be used as a substitute for tobacco, but its sap is used to glue the charcoal staining on the inside of the pointed tip in the manufacture of arrows. The concave side of war arrows was completely blackened as the combination of the "blood vine" with charcoal was thought to provoke lethal bleeding.

The disjunction between warrior and shaman observable among the contemporary Guarani can also be observed among a non-Tupian people, the Bororo, in the form of a shamanic dualism. The Bororo used to have two types of shamans: the *bope* shaman, master of becoming, capable of transforming into a jaguar and hunting for himself; and the *aroe* shaman, master of pure forms, who has the power to lure herds of peccaries toward his kin (Crocker 1985). In contrast to the Guarani dichotomy, the Bororo antithetical principles are represented by two opposing but complementary shamans. It is this complementarity that we find among Amazonian Tupi-Guarani peoples, though not in dualist form, but in the necessary overlapping of warfare and shamanism, as a blend of blood and tobacco, predation and familiarization.

The Model of Familiarizing Predation

It is now possible to understand why beer festivals are seldom held among the Parakanã. *Opetymo* absorbed both the values of regression to "nature" and those of progression to "supernature," elucidating a basic equation of the Tupi structure: The jaguar is the divinity and vice-versa, since both are figures of wild exteriority, ferocious enemies that must be familiarized in order to transform them into a source of fertility. This equation is pervaded by a tension between the jaguar-function and the demiurge-function, a tension upon which most Tupi cosmologies thrive, and the Guarani strive to dissolve by means of a radical disjunction.[12] Such conflation of the first and third columns of the foregoing tables leads us, however, to a static dichotomy – between life and death, sex and homicide, inside and out-side – that needs to be overcome. We must explain how one passes from inducing death to producing life, from a cannibal symbolic to a symbolics of fertility.

Opetymo induces an ontological transformation. The ritual contact with the *akwawa* enabled by the vocal killing and the swallowing of cigar smoke precipitates a transformation that gradually allows the person access to exterior powers – powers that he or she will learn to control to achieve a long and productive life. Productive because it is this capacity to establish relationships with the *akwawa* that allows the performer to pass on names (that is, singularity) and songs (that is, victims) to children and grand-children. The ritual also promotes a maturation of the person in a broader sense: It develops his or her oral capacities through songs, enables dream-ing, makes young people lose their shame, and allows the children who accompany the dancers to grow. Although the ritual seeks to develop male capacities rather than female, these capacities are not exclusive to men, as shown in the performance of *opetymo* by women among the western group and women's giving of songs to men among the eastern group. Moreover, whereas one of the ritual's focal points is the relation with exterior powers (the *akwawa* embodied and executed by the dancer), the relation between brother and sister or between maternal uncle and niece is equally central to the ritual's realization. In a sense, *opetymo* is performed in order for men to be able to embody the *akwawa* for their sisters and for the latter to be able to pay them back by singing.

Ontological transformation is not the same, though, as a symbolics of fertility. In order for us to see more clearly how the model of warfare as *productive consumption* and the general schema of *familiarizing predation* apply to the analysis of the Parakanã data, we need a further element. To this end, I turn to another ritual, one that functions as a synthesis of the tobacco fes-tival and the clarinet festival. In contrast to these, which take place almost annually, the rhythm baton ritual is somewhat rare as it is considered very "costly."[13] Just six performances were held among the western Parakanã

---

12 As a norm, the two main Tupi-Guarani divinities are assigned differently to the homicidal and curative powers: When the emphasis falls on producing death, Tupã, dominates; when it falls on saving life and gaining immortality, Maíra dominates. This tension is also present in the Parakanã case, although the first pole dominates. In Chapter 7, we shall see how the whites came to occupy predominantly the Maíra's pole.

13 Among the western Parakanã, *opetymo* is usually held at the end of October/beginning of November, and is followed by *takwara-rero'awa*, celebrated about a month later. Among the eastern Parakanã, *opetymo* is held between the end of the rainy season and the onset of the dry season.

between the 1920s and 1980s, all of them in celebration of warfare feats (apart from one performed after contact "for the whites to watch").

The Baton's Children

The ritual is called *waratoa* or *moropyhykawa*. *Waratoa* is the name of the two-meter-long baton, made from the same light-colored bamboo (*takwajinga*) used to make arrow points and the clarinets for the ritual of initiating the female war captives. The upper end, called "mouth," is engraved with a design and covered with annatto (the opposite end, struck against the ground and called "anus," is left undecorated). The design is an example of the *imojywakawa* pattern, considered the most beautiful and sophisticated decorative motif.

In contrast to other patterns that reproduce the pelt or shell of certain animals (such as the jaguar, paca, young tapir, or tortoise), *imojywakawa* is not a figurative pattern but rather "pure design". It is applied to two surfaces, the human body and bamboo, and is associated with three specific contexts: warfare, the tobacco festival, and the rhythm baton festival. The best arrow tip for the warrior is held to be that made from *takwajinga*, with the inner part blackened and the outer part decorated with the *imojywakawa* motif. This is also the pattern most valued in the body painting used by the dancers in *opetymo*: The eastern Parakanã invariably apply the design at mouth height in a band running from ear to ear, which is the same painting applied to the killer during seclusion.[14] Finally, the same design is applied to the upper end of the *waratoa*, which is made from *takwajinga* like a war arrow but rounded with an inside like a mouth. In contrast to the killer's mouth, however, which is covered with black genipap, the fertilizing mouth of the *waratoa* is colored with red annatto. We can identify, then, an idiom associated with the *imojywakawa* design that connects the arrow that kills, the mouth that sings, and the baton that fertilizes. The first preys on beings in their "real skin" (*-pireté*), the second preys on the "doubles" (*ta'owa*) of dream enemies, and the third captures virtual existences. Hence the other name for the rhythm baton festival: *moropyhykawa*, "capturing people." *Waratoa* is a ritual for acquiring children-to-be.

Its structure is a synthesis of the tobacco and clarinet rituals. Divided into three parts, the first is an *opetymo* with shorter duration, concluding at the end of the afternoon of the first day. The second part then begins, inaugurated by the distribution of porridge prepared on the patio. The *opetymo* performers transform into porridge owners and distribute their pets

---

14 The western Parakanã paint just one black circle around the killer's mouth so that "the vulture does not defecate on him." During *opetymo*, the women paint the mouths of all men with a killer status.

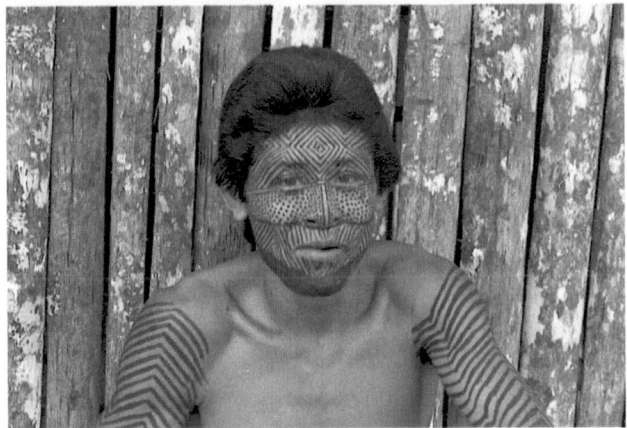

Photo 9. Apytera with the typical eastern Parakanã painted facial design
used during the *opetymo*. Forehead: land turtle motif; across the cheeks:
jaguar motif; across the mouth: *imojywakawa*; chin: black
(eastern Parakanã, Paranatinga village, 1992).

to their sisters. These men pass from the enemy-function to the brother-
function; from providers of vocal songs to providers of food. When the
porridge is finished, those with child-batons remain on the patio, while the
father-baton and wife-baton enter the ritual house.[15] The festival continues throughout the night, but its actual officiants do not take part, since
they also head off to sleep in the ritual house. Before doing so, they hand
over the *waratoa* to the other men, telling them: "Carry our great magic-
prey but don't yell in celebration," or in other words, don't kill our dream
prey.[16] The rhythm baton is the "magic-prey" (*temiahiwa*) of the executors and the relation between the baton and its carrier is analogous to the
relation between the singer and the "double" of the enemy in the tobacco
festival. The ritual action is also analogous to the execution of the song in
opetymo: The baton carrier is a killer. This is why only the true masters of
waratoa can shout as though celebrating a homicide. The nocturnal part
excludes predation: It is merely a simulacrum of the effective ritual action,
a *divertissement* involving men and women alike.

As dawn arrives, the third part of the festival begins. The *opetymo* performers once again assume command of the ritual. The one who began
opetymo the previous day takes the baton and starts to dance and sing. On

15 As in the case of the clarinets, there are three types of rhythm baton: *towohoa*, *haty'a* and *ta'yra*
("father," "his wife" and "children"), all made from *takwajinga*. Only the father is called *waratoa*.
16 I translate as "yell in celebration" the verb *-joropeteng* ("to strike vocally"), which designates the act
of emitting the short, high-pitched shouts that mark the end of an act of predation.

the patio, he clutches the *waratoa* under his armpit; a woman (generally, his wife) tries to pull out the instrument, which he carries tied to his neck by a red cord. Freeing himself from her, he resumes dancing, beating the bamboo on the ground. This routine is repeated several times until finally he heads off to his house. He enters. There he sings one last time and celebrates the homicide with a series of final cries. He is then said to have "truly killed" (*-jokaeté*) or "finished off" (*-apiji*). He sits down and his wife comes over to remove the white down from his legs. Meanwhile, the wife of the next performer fetches the baton and carries it back to the *tokaja*, where the sequence begins again. When the last dancer enters his house and sits down, the *waratoa* is taken to the ritual house and stored. The festival ends and the executors leave to hunt.

The songs chanted in the third part of the ritual, known as *waratoa-je'engara* ("rhythm baton songs"), differ thematically from those performed in the first. They speak of the children seized during the festival, who cry inside the *waratoa*. The following song refers to a child whose wrists are painted with the *imojywakawa* motif and shines like the golden parakeet:

Pepyhyngeme ke konomikatohoa	Don't seize the good child
Opaapyjywangoho-eroramo	Bringing him by his painted wrists
Opaapyhon-eroramo	Bringing him by his blackened wrists
He he he	He he he
ipapa'awa:	coda:
Konomi-tarawewajingohoa	Great golden-parakeet-child
Ojepotarimo jerehe	Could he be coming to me?

This other song refers explicitly to the child's crying inside the rhythm baton:

Aha pota rimo	Perhaps he will go
Pemana pota rimo	Perhaps you'll send him away
Oja'a-oho	He cries too much
Oja'a-oho	He cries too much

In striking the bamboo against the ground, the performer produces a variety of sounds. Some are associated with the howl of the howler monkey, others with the whistles of a marmoset. Still other sounds are taken to be the cry of the baton child. Various individuals are identified as having been brought by the *waratoa* during the ritual. They are called *oja'a-wa'e-kwera* ("the ex-criers") or, alternatively, *waratoa-memyra* ("baton children"). The bamboo – called "father" during the second part of the ritual – is also a "mother": The virtual existences contained inside the *waratoa* are its *memyra*, a term used by women for their children.

The dancer therefore carries a female-baton that, like a uterus, contains "children-to-be" (*konomiroma*).[17]

No precise theory exists to explain how the baton becomes "pregnant" or for the ontological status of the virtual existences contained inside it. Some people argue that these are the child's "vital principles" (*-'onga*), but older people merely say that they are "children-to-be," rejecting any classification of them according to one of the three presentation modes of living being: *-'onga*, *-a'owa*, or *-pireté*. When I asked Akaria about this, he simply said to me that "the child cries inside the baton, just like the child crying on the ground." The crying announces its exiting from inside the *waratoa* and entry into the womb of the "mother-to-be." The attempt by women to take the dancer's baton fertilizes them. For this reason, pubescent girls take no part in this action: "A child might enter inside me, they say." The precaution is useless, however, because as Akaria explained to me, "the child will cry inside the father-to-be and will enter her later."[18] That is, it will penetrate the mother-to-be during sex: Instead of introducing itself directly via the vagina, the vital principle enters first the man and is then deposited inside the woman.

The dancer fertilizes the women, and from this point of view the baton is also a "great father" (*towohoa*), or, more exactly, a penis. The child imprisoned in the *waratoa* is the carrier's "magic-prey" (*temiahiwa*), a prey that he transfers to the uterus of the women. Men state explicitly that "our [excl] magic-prey enter inside them." Simultaneously penis and womb, the baton expresses the procreative relationship between husband and wife. Whereas the tobacco and clarinet festivals emphasize the relations between cross-sex siblings and lovers respectively, the *waratoa* ritual highlights the dancer and his wife, who brings him the bamboo and, at the same time, tries to pull it from him.

The cycle of the three main Parakanã rituals expresses the male capacity for producing persons in a collective and public way. In the clarinet festival, the men appear as nursing mothers, breastfeeding the collectivity; in *opetymo*, as providers of immaterial values (songs and names); and in *waratoa*, as those responsible for female fertility. Through these rituals, the general conditions for producing persons appear as the outcome of the male activity of predation and familiarization in warfare

17 The "children-to-be" are also called *waratoa-popiara*, "the contents of the baton," in the same way that one says of someone that s/he is the son or daughter of a particular woman: X is the "ex-content" of Y (Y-*popiarera*).

18 Adolescent girls look to postpone their first pregnancy since, on one hand, they fear a difficult birth, and on the other, they have no desire to assume the responsibilities of maternity so soon. Hence as they approach puberty, their mothers give them remedies to delay their biological maturation. These remedies include the infusion of quinine (cinchona bark), which, as we have seen, is a neutralizer of blood.

Table 6.4. *Comparison between the Tobacco and Clarinet Rituals*

Opetymo	Takwara-rero'awa
diurnal	nocturnal
bamboo	honey
cigar	porridge
vocal music	instrumental music
mouth	clarinet
new songs	fixed repertoire
individual dance	collective dance
sisters sing to brothers	brothers feed sisters
ritual house	absence of ritual house
enemies "imprisoned" in the *tokaja*	kin dancing on the patio
homicide	sex between lovers

and shamanism.[19] In contrast to secret male initiations, however, the Parakanã rituals do not exclude women from their execution. Much the opposite, they are necessarily performed by men and women, strongly thematizing the cross-sex relations between brother and sister, husband and wife, and lovers. The point is that, through ritual, men present themselves publicly as capable of mediating the conditions required for the group's reproduction.

Cannibal Productions

We can now explain what the native theory leaves unsaid: how the baton captures people. How does it appropriate virtual existences and transmit them within the group? The answer is found in the synthesis of two apparently opposed rituals: *opetymo* and *takwara-rero'awa* (Table 6.4).

These rites, normally consecutive, are combined in the baton ritual, which possesses the following sequence (see Table 6.5): The first part is an *opetymo* properly speaking, whereas the second is already a transformation of the clarinet festival, since the wind instruments turn into the rhythm baton. However, the characteristics of the latter ritual are retained: It is nocturnal, collective, and held outside the *tokaja*. In the third part, the

---

19 The fact that these rituals are held by women among the western Parakanã, with a symmetrical inversion of roles, does not substantially alter this affirmation for two reasons: first, due to the low frequency with which they are performed; second, due to the fact that the change of sex does not affect the *gender* of the ritual. The lower asymmetry between men and women among the western group owes less to the valorization of traditionally female activities and more to women's involvement in male activities. The system as a whole was masculinized not by a greater control of men over women, but by the emphasis on male-gendered roles and activities.

Table 6.5. *Structure of the Rhythm Baton Ritual*

First Part		Second Part		Third Part
1st night	1st day	End of 1st day	2nd night	2nd day
entry into the *tokaja*	individual execution of the *opetymo* songs	distribution of the porridge	collective circulation of the baton on the patio	individual execution of the *waratoa* songs

baton substitutes for the cigar carried by the dancers in *opetymo*, and is trans-formed from an attractor of dream *akwawa* into an attractor of children.

The analogy between the two is expressed by the shared terminology: *temiahiwa*, "magic-prey," which applies to the dream enemy and the baton alike, to the song received by the dreamer and the child captured by the *waratoa*. From an enabler of shamanism, *opetymo* becomes, by means of its opposite (the clarinet festival), an enabler of female fertility. Thus although the outcomes of *opetymo* are indirect, *waratoa* directly transfers future per-sons to the collectivity.

The baton ritual expresses the equivalence of the relation between mas-ter-pet and father-son, manifesting the shift from warfare to shamanism or, generically, from predation to familiarization. The conversion of the killer-victim relation into a master-pet relation equals its conversion into a genitor-offspring relation. Thus:

killer-victim → master-pet : : killer-victim → father-son

We can rewrite the formula: The master-pet relation can be substituted by its products (songs and names) or, more generically, by the production of personal capacities. The relation of procreation can also be substituted by its product: concrete existences. Finally, the killer-victim relation can give way to the notion of consumption, in the sense of a destruction-appropriation of bodies and capacities. This gives:

consumption → production of capacities : : consumption → production of existences

Amalgamating the homologous terms, we arrive at a simplified formula of the cannibal mode of production:

consumption of persons → production of persons (existences and capacities)

This is the formula of *producing persons by means of destroying persons*. The Parakanã terminology clearly expresses this outcome: The word *temi-ahiwa* – applied to the dream *akwawa*, the song, the baton, and the child of the ritual – is analogous, but not identical, to that of pet or son. Why is it

not a perfect synonym if it points to the same referents? Because it retains
a trace of the movement of fabricating persons by means of their negation;
that is, the shift from death to life. *Temiahiwa* is the familiarized victim,
the magic-victim that converts itself into life. The relation between the
first moment (predation) and the second moment (familiarization) is one
of contradiction, such that the shift from the former to the latter implies,
simultaneously, negation and conservation of the negated moment; that is,
familiarization "affected" by predation. The arrow of the formula indicates
this negative movement realized through symbolic work, which gains
public and collective expression in rituals.

A New Approach to Amazonian Warfare Rituals

At the end of Chapter 4, I suggested that Amerindian warfare rituals are
the culmination of a logic of socializing the homicidal act that aims to multiply the productive effects of this predation. As an apex to bellic action,
they express, by means of a generative symbology, the movement spanning from the destruction to the production of persons. Over the course of
this chapter, I have sought to decompose the operations involved in this
movement and at the same time provide it with an empirical content. To
generalize the results obtained from my ethnography, I turn now to other
Amerindian warfare rituals.

The Tupinambá, who inhabited the Atlantic coast in the sixteenth century, became renowned for their anthropophagic ritual complex (Fernandes
1970, Métraux 1979, Fausto 1992). How does the movement that led
from Tupinambá warfare to the cannibal feast compare with that which
leads from Parakanã warfare to ritual predation in the *opetymo*? To answer
this question, we must return to Figure 6.3, and define more precisely
the operation denominated "reenemization" into three moments: First,
the *jawara-pyrotawa* ("nourishing the jaguars"), which involves giving and
memorizing the songs before the ritual; second, the specific moment of
reenemization, which involves the taking of the jaguar by the person who
will "kill" it in the festival; and finally, the moment of capture, *imongetawa*,
when the executors and their songs are imprisoned in the ritual house.
Distinguishing these three moments, we arrive at the following model:

Warfare predation ⟶ Dream familiarization ⟶ Nourishment ⟶ Re-enemization ⟶ Capture ⟶ Ritual predation

Figure 6.4. Extended model of familiarizing predation among the Parakanã.

The same schema applies to Tupinambá cannibalism if we substitute
dream familiarization by actual familiarization: The captive was adopted
by his future executioner's family, which fed and protected him (Métraux
1979:118). His condition was that of a taker of women in an uxorilocal

regime: a man controlled by his father-in-law and brothers-in-law, a situation compared to that of a pet (Viveiros de Castro 1992a:280). Hans Staden narrates that, on the return journey after his capture, a warrior told him precisely: *xe remimbaba in dé*, "you are my pet" (Staden [1557] 1974:84). Arriving at the village, the captive was introduced into his new family. He received a wife, was fed, and enjoyed a reasonable degree of freedom. His social condition only altered on the eve of execution, when he was converted into an enemy again (reenemized). They seized him, separated him from his "adoptive family," forcing him to assume once again the position of enemy: He was submitted to a pantomime of escape and capture, given hard fruits to throw at those who would eat him, and allowed him to insult them by saying that his kin would avenge his death. Finally, he was executed and devoured. We have thus the following sequence:

Warfare predation ⟶ Actual familiarization ⟶ Nourishment ⟶ Re-enemization ⟶ Capture ⟶ Ritual predation

Figure 6.5. Model of familiarizing predation among the Tupinambá.

This predation-familiarization-predation movement corresponds to the process of socializing and multiplying the effects of the homicide and is completed with its subproducts: new names and warfare renown. In fact, each ritual action (capture, reenemization, recapture, execution) allowed new names to be acquired. As far as we know, Tupinambá ritual anthropophagy did not possess a symbolics of fertility. Its effects were turned instead to the transformation and maturation of personal capacities, as occurs in the Parakanã *opetymo*. The very execution of captives' children born of women from the capturing group indicates that the main point was not to produce new existences, but to confer additional singularities to those already existing.

A clear generative symbology can be encountered in other warfare rituals such as the Munduruku head-hunting complex. The ritual cycle was composed of three parts. The first, called *inyenborotaptam* ("decorating the ears"), took place soon after the arrival of the war party and involved decorating the trophy with feather ear-plugs. In contrast to the depilation and shaving of the Tupinambá captive, which identified him with the captor group as a whole, the decoration of the Munduruku head introduced it into a particular segment of the society. Each killer adorned his trophy with feathers specifically attributed to his clan. In addition to introducing the head, the rite consecrated its owner as a *dajeboishi* ("white-lipped peccary mother") and marked the beginning of a long period of seclusion, which, if not completed, would cause the killer to lose his ability to provide game.

The second part of the ritual was held in the rainy season: *yashegon*, or "skinning the head," when it was cooked and its skin peeled away. Finally, the following winter the cycle was completed with the *taimetoröm* festival ("hanging the teeth"), in which the teeth extracted from the trophy were sewn onto a cotton belt. This third part was the most elaborate and allies from other villages were invited to eat the "hide of the game of the *dajeboishi*." The theme of reenemization and recapture was also enacted: Painted and tonsured young men ran to the forest to be captured by adults from the opposite moiety. After this enactment, there was a collective banquet, followed by singing in front of the men's house. The seclusion of the *dajeboishi* was then terminated (Murphy 1958:53–8).

The powers of the head and the killer were not limited to the fecundity of game. The trophies were also associated with the physical reproduction of the group itself and the renewal of warfare, since the tooth belt was supposed to increase the chances of the bearer killing new victim.[20] The ritual had two outcomes – new lives and new deaths – the latter inaugurating a new cycle. Menget's comparison (1996:134–5) between the killer's seclusion and the *couvade* is apposite, since acquiring the trophy evinced the male capacity to produce life through warfare.

We find the same genesic motif among the Jívaro of Peru and Ecuador. The *tsantsa* trophy ritual cycle comprised three parts. The initial festival occurred soon after the return of the expedition and was called *numpenk* ("his true blood"). In the festival, chicken blood was dribbled on the killers' thighs, while the women chanted songs thematizing this fictive menstruation (Taylor 1994:82). The ritual publicly inaugurated the killers' seclusion and introduced the head into the group, marking, by means of a "menarche," the beginning of the development of the head takers' reproductive capacities. The maturation process was concluded a year later during the third and final part of the ritual, called *amiamu* ("accomplishment").

Over the course of the cycle, the trophy was also transformed: First, the traces of its origin were erased so that it could embody a generic Jivaroan identity. All the orifices were sewn up and "it was [then] forced to learn its new social space: it was carried through the house by the cardinal points and made familiar, according to the formula employed in the songs, with its 'adoptive land'" (Descola 1993:305). In the rituals, the head occupied different positions as though assuming different roles in a sociological theater: enemy, giver of women, taker of women, the killer's lover, his wife's lover. The trophy condensed a series of positions and relations, which among the Parakanã are embodied by the dancer himself.

After being adopted and occupying different affinal positions during the ritual, the head was killed one more time, through an oral re-creation

---

20 In the nineteenth century, a Munduruku man gave Gonçalves de Tocantins two reasons for going to war: "I'm going because I need a woman to marry" and "I need a child for my wife." As Menget notes, this latter assertion not only refers to the children to be captured, but also to the head itself (1993:314–15).

of the attack in which the enemy had been decapitated (Taylor 1993:673). The theme of reenemization appears here in dislocated form. Before the final festival, domestic pigs were bred to be subsequently freed and recaptured during the ceremony. Pork meat was then served to the guests as the enemy's "substitute" (*imiak*) (Descola 1993:303). The process of familiarizing the head ended with their transformation into "children" of the killer's group, their final destiny being that of a fetus: "[M]ore than a literal child, we need to see this embryo as a concrete representation of the conditions of possibility of birth of a human being in general, or, if one prefers, a metonymy of all the children generated in the future by the group's women." (Taylor 1994:96). The process that had started with a male menarche was completed with the production of new lives in the bellies of women.

In the warfare rituals, the appropriation of alien agency, subjectivities, and/or capacities is enabled through the transformation of the killer-victim relation into a father-son or namer-named relation. Some rites contain both possibilities, but not all of them emphasize these possibilities in the same way. *Opetymo* is not as explicit as *waratoa* in terms of the capturing of children; Tupinambá anthropophagy does not revolve around the production of a new life, as occurs in the Jivaroan head-hunting ritual. Some systems directly associate the killer's genesic potency with digested enemy blood; others require the intervention of an additional substance, such as sweet porridge (the Parakanã case) or fermented drink.[21] Additionally, the movement that leads to warfare predation may or may not be conceived as a process of mastering the victim's spirit. As I showed in the Parakanã case, there is no need to postulate a "soul" of the enemy in order for the homicide to be conceived as a means of appropriating others' agency. This is merely the most explicit case.

Outside the Tropical Forest, in the Chaco region, the Nivakle established an explicit parallel between the transformation that occurred to the victim's spirit and those occurring to the trophy. The scalp and the killer were inaugurated in a festival, soon after the arrival of the war expedition. Women danced with the still-bloody trophy so that "a little of the victim's soul-spirit" passed on to them (Sterpin 1993:42). Only "bloodless" older women could take part in the dance, which allowed them to acquire "melodic fertility" (that is, new songs to initiate new scalps). The trophy's

---

21 The Arara, a Carib group of the middle Xingu, perform a ritual in which the enemy is represented by a post on which the skull of a war victim is placed. The post serves as a prop for the same operations described previously: It is beaten as an enemy and embraced as kin; it is an affine to men (its name means "wooden affine") and a lover to women (who rub their vulva on the post). At the high point of the festival, a pot of fermented drink is placed at its base for the women to drink. On downing it, they say: "I'm drinking a child … I'm drinking a newborn" (Teixeira-Pinto 1997:128).

genesic potency was expressed in the blood transferred to postmenopausal women as though it were a new menstruation. Afterward the scalp began to be prepared so as to remove all traces of blood, leaving it dry. During this period, the killer "had to remain alert to the arrival of the spirit, placate its homicidal intentions and master it" (Sterpin 1993:44). When the scalp had completely dried and the killer learned to master his victim's spirit through songs, a beer festival was held.

This ritual marked the promotion of the killer to the *caanvacle* ("war leader") status, the superlative father of the Nivacle communities, compared to the Fathers or Mothers of the Animals. According to Sterpin, the reciprocal term for *caanvacle* is *cataôclaj* ("follower," "disciple'), which breaks down into *ca-* (possessive marker) and *taôclaj* ("child"): "The *caanvacle* finds himself, vis-à-vis his own people, in a position analogous to the adult in relation to the child" (Sterpin 1993:42). Among the Nivacle, where chiefly status was based on warfare activity, familiarizing an enemy was equivalent to promoting the warrior to the condition of master-father of the community, controlling its reproduction just as the animal masters control the reproduction of their species.

This parallel between individual seclusion and the collective rite among the Nivakle can be generalized for all the rituals already analyzed. Such a parallel confers a public character to familiarizing predation, making it the general schema of producing persons and sociopolitical units in these societies. The trophies function as a support for the mediation between allies and for the separation between rivals, shaping nexuses of proximity and distance. Hence the multicommunity nature of warfare closure rituals, normally glossed as the "big festival." A maximum moment of reunion and the constitution of networks of amity and enmity that structured the total universe of social relations of a specific group. Ritual activities not only allowed homicidal acts to acquire a maximum productivity – socializing and multiplying them – but also turned them from a juxtaposed series of isolated acts into a generalized mode of social reproduction.

In the process spanning from the bloody scalp to the dry trophy, from the vengeful soul to the familiar spirit, there is a degradation of the enemy's creative potency, which is transferred to the killer and diffusely to the collectivity. This appropriation of the enemy's agency is commonly conveyed by two recurrent images: the digesting of the victim's blood and the controlling of his spirit. This process is invariably ambivalent, since one always runs the risk of being seized by the desire to eat raw meat or of ending up controlled by the enemy's spirit. The alteration of the killer (Viveiros de Castro 1992a), his identification with the other (Lévi-Strauss 1984:143), is a finely tuned exercise that demands appropriating an other subjectivity without oneself becoming entirely other.

7

Gods, Axes, and Jaguars

Tyger! Tyger! burning bright / In the forests of the night, / What immortal hand or eye / Dare frame thy fearful symmetry?

William Blake, *Songs of Experience* (1794)

In the last three chapters, I have analyzed the universe of external relations, which differ from relations between kin. Kinship is defined both by genealogical connections and appropriate behavior. Being kin means acting in accordance with an ideal of peaceful exchange and sharing, which in turn delineates an exclusive "we" (*ore*) from which predation is excluded. This ideally secure sphere of sociability is, however, an *ens incompletum*, incapable of reproducing itself in isolation. Every kin group sees itself surrounded by a world of others who are simultaneously the condition for and a threat to its perpetuation. Five centuries ago, a new figure irrupted into this universe, occupying more and more space thanks to their investment in the "sarcastic predominance of matter": the whites, called Toria by the Parakanã. This book closes by returning to the history of contact; a return under new conditions, for our concern now is to determine the place the whites came to occupy within the broader framework of the symbolic economy of alterity described in the preceding chapters.

The Origin of Pain and the Whites

The Parakanã inserted the whites into their mythology in many ways. Two narratives exist that deal exclusively with their origin, as well as brief inclusions in two stories with broader themes.[1] This proliferation is part of the effort to conceptualize not only the difference between Indians and

---

[1] I discussed these two inclusions in Chapter 2: the myth of the deluge (the whites are those who flew away with the house during the floods) and the mytheme of the bad choice (the ancestor of all Indians takes the darker-skinned woman as his wife, letting the lighter-skinned woman leave, who becomes the mother of the whites).

non-Indians but also the diversity of the latter. Each of these myths tells of different whites who took diverging paths and who sometimes behave in distinct ways. The narratives were already fully formed at the end of the nineteenth century since they are told by both Parakanã blocs. This seems to indicate that, despite their isolation during the period, the experience of contact had been intense in the past and that the mythology bore the scars of this history.

The Toria are classified in the encompassing category of *akwawa*, but with such unique features that I rarely heard the Parakanã refer to us by this term. Although the designation *akwawa* is omnipresent in the accounts of interactions with other indigenous groups, it is extremely rare in the narratives of encounters with nonindigenous people. How should we explain the salience of the Toria category?

In the myth "The taking away of the nephews," the origin of the whites is narrated as a horizontal spatial distancing, leading to an "ethnic" differentiation. The myth tells how an unmarried woman had sexual relations with animals, her pets brought in dreams. Her brothers, however, recurrently killed these animals to feed their families. To avenge herself, the woman decided to transform her own nephews into dream pets. She dreamt of them and the next day invited them to bathe in the river. The children dived into the water and emerged repeatedly to warm themselves by a fire. These bathing sessions were held over several days, each time farther away from the nephews' parents. One day, the mothers called for their sons to return. In vain. The men then left in pursuit of their sister but she escaped, departing forever with her nephews, who turned into whites. This distancing is conceived less as a sociological modality of producing enmity than as a transformation of bodies and capacities: The boys who bathe in the water and warm themselves by the fire gradually metamorphose until they turn completely other.[2] Not just any kind of other, though. Their special transformative capacities will be revealed in the future through the ability to produce industrial goods. The difference between the indigenous *akwawa* and the Toria resides in the proliferation of objects, indexing a specific form of agency.

If we compare the vocatives used in war narratives with those employed during interactions with whites before pacification, another difference becomes apparent. Indigenous enemies were addressed using affinal terms, such as *wepajé* ("my friend"), *wetairo'yn* ("my brother-in-law") and *miatyrange* (formal vocative for a maternal uncle/father-in-law). For whites, the Parakanã reserved the term *miangá*, a formal vocative for father or paternal uncle. The term already appears among the few indigenous words

---

2 This cold-hot river bathing sequence is reminiscent of other transformative baths in Amerindian mythology, which are commonly associated with immortality and skin-changing.

recorded by SPI employees from the 1930s onward.[3] Curiously, thus, the Parakanã addressed the whites in the same way as their enemies domesticated in dreams. Could this mean that they conceived the relations with whites according to the model of relations with dreamt enemies?

Of Twins and Opossums

To start answering this question, let us turn now to another myth, "The small opossum who killed his mother," which could also be called the "Origin of pain and the whites." This myth is a transformation of the classic saga of the twins, one in which the ancestor of the whites occupies the place of Maíra (the demiurge who represents the maximal shamanic potency in Tupi-Guarani mythology). The story goes as follows:

The Small Opossum who Killed his Mother
(The Origin of Pain and the Whites)

They were inside the house. There was a small opossum that nobody was able to kill. Its mother-to-be was sat near the doorway. The opossum ran out of the firewood and entered her vagina.[4]

– Hey, did the opossum enter my daughter's vagina?
– No, it ran past over there.
– Yes, it entered her, I saw him entering her.

Her belly grew that night. She was very young and her mother was worried about the birth.

– Go on, have sex with her. Penetrate her and make her soft so that her son can be born.
– Wait, it'll be born by itself, they replied.

The girl's mother insisted and they had sex with her. So her belly swelled up fully. They took her outside and waited for the pain.

– My child is hurting me, said the girl.

---

3 "As for the language that they speak, probably affiliated to the Tupi group, there are very few references to the subject. In old reports from the Tocantins Post, dated 1930, the only term we find recorded is 'miancá.' ... From the second phase of relations, commenced in 1953, we find mention of the expression 'karapia-miangá'" (Arnaud 1961:21). The latter expression means: "metal axe, my father."

4 This form of conception is not confined to mythic narratives. A child from the Apyterewa village, for example, is called "ex-paca." His mother had accompanied her husband on a hunting trip. They cornered a paca in its burrow, but the animal escaped, running between the woman's legs and disappearing. As she became pregnant soon after, it was concluded that the moment of conception had been the hunt with the paca performing the function of the preexisting vital principle (-'onga). This is a literal version of the transformation of the victim into a child, a topic discussed in earlier chapters.

At birth, the child tore the mother's vagina and she bled to death. They dug a grave, buried her and moved away. Time passed. One day, the grandfather left to go hunting with his other wife. The child stayed behind alone with his grandmother, swinging in the hammock. He looked at her and said:

- How did my mother die, grandma?
- The bullet ant killed your mother, grandson.
- Let the bullet ant hurt, grandma!

Soon after:

- How did my mother die, grandma?
- A snake killed your mother, grandson.
- Let the snake hurt, grandma!

Again he asked:

- How did my mother die, grandma?
- The tarantula killed your mother, grandson.
- The tarantula doesn't hurt, grandma. What killed my mother, grandma?

The child continues to ask the same question, and his grandmother lists many other dangerous species: snakes, pit viper, ants. The child makes these "hurt."[5] Finally, the grandfather's other wife returns and seeing them talk, asks:

- What did you tell our grandson?
- "A snake killed your mother," she told me – the boy replied.
- Hum. And you, what did you say, grandson?
- Let the snake hurt, grandma!

The woman admonished the boy's grandmother:

- Why are you telling our grandson nonsense? He'll make the forest dangerous for us.

She turned to the boy:

- You killed your mother, you wretch![6]
- Hum. Let the child hurt, grandma!

Then he began to cry, striking his temples.

- Did I kill my mother, grandma?
- Yes, you killed her.
- Where's her grave?
- Over there, look.

---

5 The Parakanã do not have a word for "poisonous." "To hurt" also means here "to be venomous" and "to have efficacy."
6 When a woman dies giving birth, people say that "the child killed her." This death is conceived to result from the child's anger at being made to abandon the womb.

— Let's go so I can dance over the grave and remove her from there, grandma.

— Okay.

Just before dawn.

— Give me your cigar, grandfather, so I can take out my mother from the grave for us.

His grandfather gave him the long cigar. He left with his grandmother:

— Look, there's where you killed your mother, grandson.

He began to dance.

— Stay away from me, grandma. Look from over there. Come when I call you.

He built a cabin from tucum palm leaves over the grave and went inside.

— What side did you place the head, he asked his grandmother.

— That side, my grandson.

— Okay then, I'll start here at the heart.

— Okay, his grandmother replied.

— Move away, grandma, he insisted.

The boy began to dance, stamping rhythmically and blowing out the cigar smoke. He removed the pot that covered his dead mother's face, lifted her up and holding onto her, they danced together. They span round and round everywhere. But then the grandmother interrupted them:

— You're going to break your mother, grandson.

— Hum. Wait, grandma, go away for now.

His mother let go of him and, turning into a paca, disappeared into the woods. The boy yelled at his grandmother:

— I told you to wait over there, grandma. Now my mother has been lost to me forever!

With that they headed back.

— What happened? asked the grandfather.

— My wretch of a grandmother made my mother leave for good, grandpa. She told me that I was going to break her. But I was going to make her stop and sit down. I was going to clean her face, blow on her, remove the secretion from her eyes and talk to her.

The grandfather spoke to his wife:

— I told you to stay away from him.

— Wait, we'll leave when dawn comes and leave him here.

— Okay, let him die lying down.

Before departing, the grandfather shot the boy with an arrow. At daybreak:

— Let's go, the grandfather said.

— Why are you all going to abandon me, grandfather? the boy asked.

– I'm going to leave you behind. Lie down and die.
– I shall not die, grandfather. I'll remain. Why are you all going to abandon me, grandfather?

Turning to the women, the grandfather said:

– Let's go, leave him to die here lying down.

The boy insisted:

– Let's stay together, grandma, come and lie next to me.

They departed. The boy was left alone, still speaking:

– Why are you abandoning me, grandma. Stay with me. In the future, we're going to make ourselves whites, he said in vain.

He turned completely white. The others had all gone away. Time passed and those that had left asked themselves:

– Do you think the small opossum has died by now?
– Go and see his skull.
– Let's go and see.
– Maybe he's still alive. Let's shoot him.

The grandfather and his brothers went to see what had happened. On the way they saw a felled tree:

– What?
– Hum, perhaps he cut it down with stone, brother.
– Do you think he became white?

They continued along a wide path. They found bananas growing and a house further on. He had dug his future kin from the earth and brought his mother in a dream, transforming her into a person once more.

– The wretch turned into a white?
– Let's go there and see. Let's join him.

As they approached the house – poo poo poo poo – they met a hail of bullets.

– He's become completely white.

The grandfather shouted in vain to his grandson:

– It's me, grandson.

But he shot in the direction of the voice. They decided to leave and went to meet the women:

– He's become completely white, he shot at us, they said.

(Iatora 1993: tape 20)

This version describes the origin of animal venom, the pain of childbirth and the emergence of non-Indians. In a sense, it is a myth on the origin of pain in general, and this is how some narrators interpret the myth, explaining there was no pain until the protagonist spoke strongly and effectively (which resulted from the grandmother's verbal incontinence). This is the myth's first major theme. The second is the failed resurrection of the mother, which prepares the way for the third: the transformation of the boy into a white. The figure linking these three themes is the small opossum, *angoja*, who becomes human and at the end of the myth turns into a Toria. The movement leading from opossum to whites is manifested by two other names for the myth: *Angoja-kwera* ("ex-opossum") and *tori-roma* ("white-to-be").

Here is a summary of the events:

1. Angoja enters the vagina of the future mother, a virgin, inside the house;
2. the mother dies during labour and is buried;
3. Angoja is raised by his grandmother and grows rapidly;
4. his grandfather goes hunting and the grandmother lies to him about the mother's death;
5. he "talks strongly," making life painful;
6. his grandfather's other wife returns and reprimands his grandmother for her verbal incontinence;
7. she tells the boy the truth. He makes childbirth painful thereafter;
8. Angoja tries to revive his mother but is disrupted by his grandmother;
9. the mother transforms into a paca and leaves;
10. the grandfather tries to kill Angoja, but he survives;
11. Angoja is abandoned and transforms into a white, extracting his kin from the earth and transforming his mother back into a person;
12. his former kin go to check whether he is dead and are met by a hail of bullets.

Revival (item 8) is a classic theme among the Tupi-Guarani and can be traced directly to the famous saga of the twins. In the following, I provide an outline of this saga for comparison with our reference myth:

1. The demiurge Maíra abandons his wife who is pregnant with twins (one of them his son, the other the son of Mucura, an opossum);
2. the woman leaves in his search but takes the wrong path (because Maíra's son, still in her womb, fails to tell her the correct way);
3. she arrives in the village of the jaguars who end up killing her;
4. the twins survive and are raised by the jaguar grandmother;
5. they grow quickly and one day, while hunting, a bird tells them how their mother died;
6. they decide to resuscitate their mother, but the younger brother approaches too soon and the mother decomposes;
7. they kill the jaguars and leave in search of their father.

Maíra's wife is a superlative mother who bears two children, the outcome of two different sexual relations. She carries a child of the demiurge and

Table 7.1. *Comparison of the Origin Myth of the Whites (Parakanã) and the Tupian Twin Saga*

Origin of the Whites	Twin Cycle
virgin mother made pregnant by a small opossum	mother pregnant by Maíra becomes pregnant by opossum too
dies during childbirth	death is a birth
child raised by grandmother	twins raised by false grandmother
grows rapidly	grow rapidly
grandfather leaves to hunt with other wife	twins leave to hunt
boy learns the truth	twins learn the truth
tries to resuscitate mother	try to resuscitate mother
grandmother disrupts the attempt	younger brother disrupts the attempt
grandfather tries to kill him	twins kill the jaguars
grandparents leave	twins leave
boy turns into a white man	twins encounter demiurge-father

another of opossum, and converses with the former while still in the womb, as though he is already outside. In contrast, Angoja's genetrix is a deficient mother: a virgin with a narrow vagina who dies during delivery. The theme of labor pains indicates that her condition is the inverse of a marsupial mother's, though she is actually the mother of an opossum.[7] However, the fates of Angoja's mother and the demiurge's mother are identical: The first dies in childbirth, whereas for the second her death is a birth. In a Wayãpi version, the jaguar-grandmother carefully removes the boys from their mother's belly before eating her (F. Grenand 1982:67). Angoja is raised by his real grandmother and knows nothing about the cause of his mother's death. The twins are raised by the false grandmother without knowing who killed their mother. In both cases, the infants grow rapidly.

In the Parakanã myth, the grandfather goes hunting with his second wife and the grandmother lies to the boy, who "speaks strongly," provoking the venom of some animals. Next the other wife returns and tells the truth to Angoja, who makes childbirth painful. In the Tupi twin cycle, the boys go hunting and a bird tells them how their mother died. In both narratives, learning the truth leads to an attempted revival. In the Parakanã version, the grandmother assumes the role of the opossum-twin who disturbs the

---

7 In the Apapocuva version of the twins myth, this theme appears in an inverted form: After realizing that he would be unable to resuscitate his mother, Maíra's son asks the opossum to breastfeed his younger brother. As a sign of his thanks, he grants the wet nurse "the faculty of giving birth to its offspring painlessly and carrying them around with her effortlessly in a natural pocket" (Nimuendaju 1987:58).

demiurge brother. The mother turns into a paca, a nocturnal, subterranean animal; that is, she "dies" again, as in most of the Tupi versions of the twins myth.[8] After this episode, the grandfather tries to kill Angoja and goes away, while the twins kill the jaguars and leave. Angoja transforms into a white man; the twins find their demiurgical father (see Table 7.1).

In sum, the Parakanã myth of the origin of pain and the whites is a transformation of the saga of the twins in which twinship disappears. Its trace is left behind though: The protagonist is both a marsupial *and* a shaman. The Parakanã possess two broad taxa for marsupials (and rats), according to size: *Toymya* are large; *angoja* are small. Our protagonist is thus a weaker version of the younger twin, Opossum's child. At the same time, he possesses capacities that also belong to the older twin, Maíra's child, in particular the science of resuscitating the dead. He thus combines aspects of both figures: He is a "small opossum" and a "small shaman." We should recall that the same ambivalence marks the protagonist of the maize origin myth, analyzed in Chapter 2: He is called Máira like the demiurge but behaves like an opossum.

In producing these oxymoronic figures, the Parakanã myths generate new meanings in which the twins' distinction functions as a background: In the origin of the maize, we have a mixture of two extreme potencies (Máira-Toymya); in the origin of the whites, we have a tiny opossum who becomes a diminished demiurge (Angoja-Toria). The Parakanã bifurcated the myth of the twins into two different stories, distributing their capacities differentially: The opossum-function predominates in the maize myth, whereas the Maíra-function prevails in the origin of the whites. But why is the latter also a myth about the origin of pain? If the protagonist is a dilute version of the Tupi twins, pain is likewise a dilute version of the origin of the short life, a basic motif in all versions of the twins saga.

Many of these myths begin with the demiurge's departure, which in some narratives accounts for the origin of death and agriculture. In fact, in most Tupi-Guarani cosmogonies, the human condition is inaugurated with the departure of the culture hero who, as Thevet wrote ([1575] 1953:39), had previously lived among humans "fort familierement." In some versions, the abandonment is prompted by the incredulity of humans who distrust Maíra's words, a theme that reappears in the Parakanã myth: The separation occurs because true humans (*awaeté*) disbelieve what the boy says: "I shalln't die," he says, "stay here because in the future we're going to make ourselves into whites." Indigenous peoples are left without industrial goods because they failed to listen-believe.

---

8 A Mbya version collected by Cadogan (1959:77–8) features the same ending as the Parakanã version: The shaman-son transforms the mother into a paca after the failed attempt to revive her.

At their close, both myths return to the theme of separation: The boy becomes white, the twins become gods. This is the final disjunction between Indians and non-Indians or between mortals and immortals. However, there is no simple homology between the two oppositions that would allow us to write [Indians : whites : : humans : gods]. The first opposition is a weak form of the second: Angoja is a dilute version of Opossum and the whites a dilute version of Maíra, just as the origin of pain is a weak version of the origin of the short life.

The Parakanã myth can also be read as ontogenetic metamorphosis: It starts out from an infrahuman condition (the small opossum), passes through the properly human, and veers toward a suprahuman potency. We can interpret this metamorphosis as a movement within the triadic model proposed by Viveiros de Castro (1992a:260) for the Tupi-Guarani:

opossum	→	Indian	→	white
infrahuman	→	human	→	suprahuman
death	→	life	→	immortality

This analysis evinces the identification in a weak register of the demiurge with the whites, indicating that the key to interpreting the story is the separation between humans and suprahumans. This outcome also surfaced as a lapse. When telling me another version of the same story, Pykawa made no reference to the hero's final transformation into a white man. So I asked him:

- Didn't he transform into a white man?
- Yes, he transformed into a white man, he turned himself into Máira. No! Into Tarewa, he replied.
- He transformed into a white man? I repeated.
- The small opossum turned into a white man. That's right, he became Tarewa. The true chief went up above, becoming Topoa. Máira went to the sky and turned into Topoa. He was afraid of arrows, that's why he entered the sky. (Pykawa 1995: tape 42)

Pykawa conflates the whites with Máira and then the latter with Topoa, referring to the episode when he left for the Sky. The conflation is suggestive since the first association generated the second; that is, the figure of the whites evoked Máira, who is the supreme shaman. At the same time, the separation between Indians and non-Indians evoked the humankind-demiurge disjunction, which in Parakanã mythology corresponds to the theme of Topoa's departure to the Sky. The initial mistake generated the entire short-circuit: The white man is Máira who is Tupã, identifications that the Parakanã would never consciously make. The slip also conjures up a fourth figure: Tarewa.

Mortal Immortals

Tarewa is the name of a white man who resuscitated people from bones. His story was told to the Parakanã by a woman captured from Moakara's group. This is how Akaria narrated it to me:

Tarewa and the Resuscitated People

Moakara was the first to talk to the whites. He was the first master of the whites. Our grandparents cleared swiddens with stone axes, Moakara used a real axe. He brought machetes, hammocks, tobacco, flour. Our grandmother Jororawa told us that. She was Moakara's daughter. He shouted at the whites and they gave him things. He returned and distributed them to his kin. One day, a severe fever killed two of his sons:

— Let's take them to the whites so they can resuscitate our children. They are the ones who make the axes.

They exhumed Moakara's sons and put the bones in a basket, carefully packing the teeth. They set off, slept, carried the basket, slept, carried the basket. They left our grandmothers behind:

— Stay here, we're going to take our children for the whites to resuscitate.

They took them and shouted to the whites.

— Are you there, my father (*miangá*)?

They had a canoe. The whites lived on the other side of the river. They had brought things. Moakara asked the white man:

— Are you the one who makes axes?
— That's me, we make axes.
— Okay then, in the same way resuscitate my child for me. I brought my child for you to revive, father.
— Where is he?
— Here, look.
— Pass him to me.

He took him:

— What was his skin like? he asked Moakara.
— Very white. Are you going to resuscitate him?
— I'm going to take him to a white man, to Tarewa so he can resuscitate him.

In the past Tarewa resuscitated people.

— Okay then, Moakara agreed.

He gave him the other child:

— What was his skin like? the white man asked.
— Brown.
— Tarewa will resuscitate your children.

They went away, heading back to meet our grandmothers:

- So what happened? Did you give the children to them?
- Yes, we did. "We're going to resuscitate them," he said to us. He told us to return in a short while and call for them.

They returned to the village. There they slept a few nights. When it was time, they set off again.

- Let's see if they've been resuscitated, Moakara said to his kin.

They went. They shouted to the whites:

- Are you there, my father?

He clambered into the canoe and crossed the river. Arriving, Moakara recognized his children:

- He resuscitated them, look, he's bringing them.

He arrived:

- Did you resuscitate my children for me?
- Tarewa resuscitated them, come here and look.

He looked at them. They were exactly as they had been. Except for their eyes, which were a little bloodshot.

- You really did resuscitate my children, father? Moakara asked him.
- We said we would resuscitate them.

Moakara was extremely happy with the children and said they were ready to leave:

- Take care of them, don't take them hunting, a tinamou could cause them to become lost from you for good, the white man warned him.

They left, taking the children to meet their mother. They found her:

- I've brought our children for you to see. The white man resuscitated them.
- Bring my children for me to see.

She recognized them. They talked:

- What happened to me, mother? one of them asked.
- A strong fever killed you, son, so the white man resuscitated you for me.

They departed, camping en route. Their parents went in front, making the tinamous fly off. One day the mother left to catch tortoises and one of the children wanted to go with her.

- Stay behind, the mother said to no avail.
- I'm going with you to catch tortoises.

They walked and walked until the tinamou caused him to become lost for good. The other went hunting with his father and also became lost forever.

(Akaria 1995: tape 9)

As we saw in Chapter 1, Moakara was an *awaeté* killed by the Parakanã at the end of the nineteenth century, in the Pucuruí River basin. He had been visiting the Toria for a long time, and instructed the Parakanã how to interact with them to obtain metal tools without bloodshed. This is why Moakara is considered the first "master of the whites" (Torijara). His interaction with them is reminiscent of the relation between a dreamer and a dream enemy, since predation is replaced by protection with the same inversion: The whites are controlled by Moakara (which is why they offer their objects) but are more powerful than him. Moreover, like the Karajá, the whites are thought capable of giving life to the dead.

Tarewa's story echoes the interpretation of the small opossum myth, where I suggested that the whites occupy diachronically the place reserved to Maíra's son synchronically. The salience of the Toria category derives, then, from a recurrent association between the whites and the great shamans capable of crossing the line between life and death. This association evokes a classic theme in the history of the conquest of the New World: the identification of the conquerors with gods. On the Brazilian coast, this assimilation first appears in the chronicles from the mid-sixteenth century and is consolidated in the later historiography. Interpreting the behavior of the Tupiniquim on the arrival of Pedro Álvares Cabral's expedition, Friar Vicente do Salvador wrote:

There the foresaid captain disembarked with his soldiers armed for battle, because he had first sent a boat with some men to survey the land, and they had given news of the many people they saw; but the arms were unnecessary, since by just seeing men dressed and shodden, white with beards (which none of them have) they took them for gods rather than men, and thus calling them caraíba, which means divine thing in their language, they arrived peacefully before ourselves. (Salvador [1627] 1982:56)

Coming from overseas in large ships, the Europeans would have been associated with more-than-human beings, masters of the secrets of immortality and abundance. They brought metal tools and firearms, and claimed to speak with an all-powerful God who had revived after death and who could multiply food (Abbeville [1612] 1975:88).[9] Already in the sixteenth century, Thevet ([1576] 1953) registered the conquerors' identification with the demiurge in a Tupinambá cosmogonic myth in which the whites appear as *les sucesseurs et vrays enfans* of the culture hero Maire-monan. The identification is consistent with the term by which the Europeans came to be known: Irrespective of nationality, they were called "caraíba," the Tupian

---

9 Ironically enough, whereas the Tupinambá sought the science of the long life from the whites, the latter supposed that the Indians lived for more than a 150 years!

designation for the great shamans who wandered from village to village, curing, prophesizing, and speaking of an edenic life.[10] This set of evidence gave rise to the classical interpretation repeated by various authors: The Portuguese expansion was seen on this side of the Atlantic as the arrival or return of gods, with the Europeans thus revered as such.

Gods and Conquerors

The conflation of European conquerors with native gods is a recurrent and controversial theme in anthropology, which I do not intend to review here.[11] I just wish to investigate, in the specific Parakanã case, if it merely reflects a European myth of themselves as gods-to-the-savages, or if it also corresponds to some long-held indigenous belief on the nature of whites. If the conquerors' identification with divinities is indeed a pervasive topos in colonial narratives, does it automatically imply its absence among the conquered peoples?

In relation to the Tupinambá, Viveiros de Castro (1992b) has consistently argued that the European interpretation partially coincided with the native view: They agreed in terms of the identification (whites equal demiurges) but not in terms of the relationship between humans and divinities. The humankind-gods separation among the Tupi was not a question of being but one of state: "[O]ne can be a man and yet become a god, mortal and yet immortal" (H. Clastres 1975:110). This ontology allowed certain individuals (not necessarily a single one, a Messiah) to be circumstantially identified with the demiurges. The equation should be read in both directions since it not only tells us about shamans, but it also tells us something crucial about the divine: The demiurges were above all great shamans of the past. Moreover, the Tupinambá did not have faith in their shamans in the same sense that the missionaries believed in God or in the scriptures. The missionaries' topos of the "inconstancy of the savage soul" as an impediment to evangelization corresponded to a style of indigenous religiosity adverse to any orthodoxy: They could believe in everything simultaneously and thus never believe in one thing only (Viveiros de Castro 1992b:36–7).[12]

---

10 In the sixteenth-century chronicles, the term is translated as "prophet" or "sanctity." The Tupinambá differentiated the French, called *Mair*, like the demiurge himself, from the Portuguese, known as *Peró*.

11 See the debate between Obeyesekere (1992) and Sahlins (1995), which was followed by a number of articles taking sides.

12 Disbelief lies at the origin of the human condition. In mythology, the inauguration of mortality and work is caused by an act of incredulity: Humans question the capacities of the demiurge (Thevet [1575] 1953:39; Évreux [1612] 1985:205; Abbeville, [1612] 1975:60–1). The predicament for every Caraíba – demiurge, shaman, or European – was the impossibility of monopolizing belief.

The problem of belief raises another question. Let us accept that Tupinambá ontology enabled them to believe Europeans possessed extraordinary capacities (like demiurges and great shamans), but that their style of religiosity did not lead them to revere the conquerors. Now how do we explain their recurrent belief in whites' shamanic capacities without implying that they were trapped in an illusion immune to experience? Did they not evaluate "the implications of a problem in terms of a practical criteria" (Obeyesekere 1992:19)? The cosmographer of the king of France, André Thevet, thought so: "[W]hen the scoundrels saw that the Christians sickened, died and were subject to the same passions, they began to disdain and mistreat them systematically" (Thevet [1575] 1978:100).

The chronicler interprets the hostile attitudes of the Amerindians to be the result of an awakening to the reality of human mortality. They went from blind belief to total disbelief. Seventy years after Thevet's voyage, however, the Capuchin priests in Maranhão were still describing the same voracious Tupi desire to become Christians, welcoming the priests and asking to be baptized. Still more curious, the Tupinambá from that region had possibly arrived from the Brazilian northeast, having fled from there due to the epidemics and violence of the Portuguese. They not only knew that the Christians died, but they had already been killed by them.

Almost five centuries later, the Parakanã were surely well aware of this fact. So how do we make then sense of this strange continuity without attributing it to a conceptual framework impermeable to history and the materiality of lived experience? Why was the assumption that "the whites are capable of resuscitating people" so pregnant and salient? To answer these questions, I now turn from myth to actual events that occurred during the eastern Parakanã contact process.

The Bones Affair

The year was 1970. The Transamazonian highway had cut through the eastern Parakanã territory. The Indians were ransacking the construction camps. In response, the military government sent Funai to place them under state administration. The agents penetrated deep into Parakanã land, discovering numerous campsites and swiddens. The head of the team was the *sertanista* João Carvalho, who had some grasp of Parakanã since he spoke a related Tupi-Guarani language. They also had indigenous interpreters, including an Asurini man who spoke a dialect of Parakanã.

On November 30, they made the first contact. Three weeks later, the Parakanã started visiting the Funai camp. They received gifts and reciprocated with tortoises. During the first months of 1971, the interaction between the Indians and the agents intensified, and a degree of mutual trust was established. Men, women, and children visited the camp, where

Photo 10. João Carvalho (painted with genipap) shows a Parakanã man how to use a shotgun (eastern Parakanã, Contact process, 1971 – Photo Yves Billon).

they obtained axes, knives, glass beads, dogs, and food. The agents worked for the Parakanã, hunting for them with guns, cooking for them in aluminum pots, and sharpening their metal tools. In all these encounters, the natives asked the agents to sing and dance but refused to allow them to visit their village. In April, they finally took them there.

After this visit, the contact process advanced at a steady pace. On May 6, the Parakanã once more came to the Funai camp.

I saw a woman carrying our bottle of *Específico Pessoa* [a regional phytotherapeutic agent used against snake venom]. I said it would be no use to her, since it was a medicine against bushmaster snakes. Then Picaua asked me to treat his wounded foot. I cut the skin with a razor blade and pressed cotton wool soaked with *Específico* against the wound. When I finished, Jauarauaquaí said: "let's raise the buried one." At first I didn't understand. Then the captain [the headman] invited me to go.... When we arrived at the grave, he ordered Gerson [another Funai agent] to remove the stuff covering it and dig.... When they uncovered the kneecaps ... Gerson placed these bones and then grabbed the shins, I asked what they were going to do. The captain said it was for me to *murrem*, which means to take out. I was to make the body rise up. I understood the goal: I was to revive the dead. (Carvalho 1971: May 6)

Did the Parakanã actually believe the whites could resuscitate the dead? If not, why exhume the bones? Had Carvalho misunderstood their intentions? To obtain a better grasp of the situation, let's return to some of the events prior to May 6, when the bones affair first surfaced.

April 17 would mark the first visit of Funai agents to the village. Early on that same day the Indians came to the Funai camp, where they received bunches of banana and machetes. Carvalho offered them a quarter of a paca. They were puzzled by the smallness of the hole made by the bullet in the animal's flesh and asked how he had killed it. For the first time Carvalho showed his rifle and how it worked. The Parakanã invited the whites to dance. The women cut the agents' hair in the native style and painted them. As they were about to leave, Carvalho asked if he could go with them:

They asked me, "what for?" I said that I wanted to stay with them. But before they allowed me, they asked if I smoke tauary [the Parakanã cigar], if I sing and dance. I said yes, so they decided to take me with them. Nelson, Josias and Piauí were forced to go, while the others were pushed back and told to stay. (Carvalho 1971: April 17)

The agents arrived at the village and started to dance and sing. The Parakanã then asked Carvalho to sharpen their axe blades. The women brought food. At dusk, the men came over to him with a meter-long cigar, and the dancing recommenced. Eventually they went to sleep, but before dawn he was summoned again: "Before rising, I spoke and found my voice was hoarse. The same happened to the Indians, so I stretched the throat of eight of them, rubbing my hands and then blowing away the disease" (Carvalho 1971: April 17).

After this fake shamanic performance, Carvalho and Nelson started to sing again, the former chanting songs of the Urubu-Ka'apor people (among whom he had worked for many years) and the latter singing those of the Tembé. Since both are Tupi-Guarani peoples, the Parakanã were probably able to grasp some of the words. The headman Arakytá became Carvalho's ritual friend, his *pajé*. Over the ensuing months, Arakytá would insistently ask Carvalho to sing: "[B]efore dawn," the Funai agent writes, "the captain always comes to my hammock and asks me to sing." As we have seen, songs are the sensory evidence of a special relationship between a person and the *akwawa*. Songs can only be obtained through interaction with these alien persons in dreams and hence are a sign of shamanic power. Names are obtained in the same way, and young parents ask dreamers to name their child, just as Arakytá's son would ask Carvalho later on:

Piriaré ... arrived with his wife and newborn son. I asked him what the child's name was. He told me to give the name. I thought and gave the name of an Urubu-Ka'apor warrior: Tameré. They found it so beautiful that they asked me to name a girl of the same age. (Carvalho 1971: July 13)

One week after the visit, the Parakanã took them back to the village, but then something new happened:

Around 9pm, we were dancing and suddenly Miarin [another Funai agent] fell down.... This was like a bath of cold water. Every young Indian got a machete and asked if he had *caruara* (if he was a shaman). We said, "no." ... They ordered everyone to go to sleep and they kept their machetes under their hammocks. (Carvalho 1971: April 25)

Miarin's faintness could be interpreted in two ways: He may have been attacked by pathogenic agents (*karowara*) or he may have been dreaming as a result of the dancing and tobacco intoxication. Both interpretations converged on the same conclusion: For better or worse, powerful shamanism (and witchcraft) was involved. So they stopped for a while, only to start again before daybreak:

By dawn, almost every single Indian was singing and dancing. They performed the song of the howler monkey, the rail, the tayra, the anteater, the peccary and others, and finally the white man song. They asked me to sing the last one with them until I had learnt it. (Carvalho 1971: April 25)

Carvalho had to learn a song given by a white man in a dream: He was representing the dream enemy in his "real skin" (*ipireté*). This conflation between dreaming experience and wakeful interaction was fueled by the positive responses of Carvalho and his team. Finally, on May 6, the Parakanã asked Carvalho to *murrem* the dead; that is, to *mo-hem*, "to make [someone or something] leave." His reply – which I omitted from the first quotation – was as follows:

[T]he captain said it was for me to *murrem*, which means to take out. I was to make the body rise up. I understood the goal. I was to revive the dead. I informed them that I was not a shaman. They told us to leave the grave as it had been before, and ordered Gerson to wash his hands. (Carvalho 1971: May 6)

Were the Parakanã convinced by Carvalho's answer? Apparently yes, since they told him to close the grave. Yet what if he was only unwilling to display his powers? Perhaps it was just too early to ask him to perform this feat. In any case, Carvalho knew that a great shaman could resurrect the dead, otherwise he would not have denied being a shaman.

One Who Dies Never Lives Again

May 1971 was a sad month. The epidemic that would kill 30 percent of the eastern Parakanã population began to take hold. Within a couple of weeks, at least 9 people had died from a total population of about 140. The Parakanã stopped visiting the whites. By the end of the month, the agents had decided to track them. They found graves and one corpse covered with no more than a cloth. In the first days of June, the Parakanã reappeared at the Funai camp, and Carvalho wrote in his diary that "the captain said something about taking the bones out. I had no real idea what he meant." The remark had been prompted by the difficulty in dealing with so many deaths over so short a time. The contact process continued. The agents started to visit the village again. Whenever they passed near a grave, the Parakanã ordered Carvalho to sing, "probably so I would not ask questions," he writes.

On June 18, a new gadget was introduced to the Parakanã: a radio connecting the camp to the Funai administration. Carvalho made the Parakanã listen to it and later talk.

[T]hey were happy, everyone wanted to listen to it, even the children. Every man spoke his name to hear the radio reply. Whenever a word imitating their names came out, it was sheer happiness. I turned on the radio at 8:10am, and at 11:30 the captain [Arakytá] told the women to leave. As soon as they left, he invited me to remove some bones from a grave. When we arrived there, he asked me to dig and the other Indians encircled the grave. The captain started to blow smoke from his cigar.... I asked him why he wanted the bones. He told me he was going to take them and brought a basket to put the bones inside, all the while blowing smoke. When I had already laid the arm and leg bones inside, I noticed that they were still clammy.... I told the captain it was not a good idea to take them out yet, since they stank. He said to put the bones back in the grave and asked me to come back later, remove the bones and bring them to him. I think they are going to perform a symbolic burial in one of those large pots I've seen in the village. (Carvalho 1971: June 21)

They were not, however. The Parakanã do not practice secondary burial. Carvalho based this interpretation of events on what he knew about other Amerindian peoples. As for the Parakanã, the deaths and the radio had stirred their assumptions about white people's powers once more. This time, though, Carvalho made no attempt to deny he was a shaman. He was unsure about Arakytá's purpose and said it was not yet the right time (thus implying that there would be a right time). If we assume that it is possible to cross the Great Divide between us (the living) and them (the dead), the crucial question is: Who can do this and when?

From July to August, influenza struck. This time the Parakanã came to the Funai camp immediately to ask for medicines. It was the high season of antiflu, anticatarrh, and antibiotics injections. They eagerly took medicines, particularly penicillin injections whose rapid effect had a considerable impact on them. Finally, on October 2 the Parakanã abandoned their village to live with the whites. During the trip, the bones affair came to the fore for the final time:

When we passed by the grave of an old shaman, which has a beautiful shelter over it, we sat down to rest and talk. I asked the captain who was there. He said it was my grandfather and asked if I was going to take him out. I said it wasn't the right time yet, since he would still be stinking. He agreed, but asked me to give the body an injection. I said it was impossible to inject into the bones and that, besides, one who dies never lives again, and the medicines can only cure while there is still life. They agreed, but even so wanted me to take the bones out. I asked them why they wanted the bones, but failed to obtain a satisfactory answer, and I still have no real idea. (Carvalho 1971: October 2)

Arakytá asked Carvalho to open the grave and inject medicines into the bones. They were both uncertain. Carvalho questioned his initial assumption that he was supposed to *murrem* the dead. Arakytá wanted to know if the injections were the whites' well-guarded secret of immortality. This time Carvalho was clear: Death is irreversible. "One who dies never lives again." However, when he left the region five days later, he was still in doubt: Why did they want the bones?

Crossing the Great Divide

Among the Tupi-Guarani speaking peoples, the assumption that some individuals, especially great shamans, can come back to life has been well documented since the sixteenth century, already in a context of widespread cultural transformations. In some cases, special funerary practices were employed to facilitate the resurrection. In the seventeenth century, the Jesuit priest Ruiz de Montoya found a house where the Guarani of Paraguay preserved the bones of powerful shamans, who were believed capable of coming back to life, "recovering their former flesh, now beautified by juvenile freshness" (Montoya [1639] 1985:108). In the same period, the Tobajara, a Tupi-Guarani people of northeastern Brazil, conserved the bones of the Jesuit Francisco Pinto, whom they considered to be a "master of the rain" (see Carneiro da Cunha 1996, Castelnau-L'Estoile 2000).

In the nineteenth and twentieth centuries, there are reports of double funerals among Tupian peoples, including the Juruna (Lima 1995:209–15) and the Cocama (Métraux 1928:274). Among the Mbyá-Guarani, this practice was associated with revivification. Cadogan writes that the corpse had to be buried in a basket until the flesh had putrefied completely, when the body was then exhumed. The bones were washed and placed in a cedar container, which was stored in the ritual house (Cadogan 1959:51–2). It was believed that through songs and incantations, the bones could receive the soul of the deceased once more, returning the person to life.

The closest example to the Parakanã are the Asurini do Tocantins, where double funerals were reserved for great shamans. Dead shamans were ideally not buried but put into a basket. After the flesh had putrefied, the bones were collected and preserved. The women would then make sweet porridge for the soul, night after night, until the soul became accustomed to the living again and came back to life (Andrade 1992:220–2). Despite their cultural proximity to the Asurini, I have never heard the Parakanã refer to this kind of funerary practice. They say instead that a great dreamer can resurrect a person by dancing on his or her grave and intoning revivifying songs known as *ywy-je'engara* ("songs of the Earth"). While dreaming, he learns from an enemy how to "make [the dead] leave" (*-mohem*, precisely the term that Carvalho transcribes in his diary as *murrem*). He then repeats the act when awake, singing the songs he received from the dreamt enemy. All great dreamers can become a *moromohemara*, "one who makes people leave," an ability that is not exclusively attributed to the whites, since all powerful *akwawa* are capable of performing the feat.

What was then the status of the proposition "The Whites can revive the dead" for the eastern Parakanã during the contact process? This proposition was based on deep-rooted ontological assumptions and on historical and dream experiences, crystallized in narratives, and represented in rituals. Many other propositions were implicated in this one, such as "One who dies can live again"; "Some shamans can resurrect the dead"; "Shamans interact with powerful enemies"; "the Whites are powerful enemies"; "the Whites may be powerful shamans"; "Carvalho may be a shaman"; and finally "Carvalho may know how to resurrect the dead." As we move from the general to the specific, the truth value of these propositions becomes increasingly conditional, setting in motion an inferential process based on empirical evidence.

From an epistemological standpoint, therefore, the eastern Parakanã's "belief" in the whites' capacity to revive the dead was an empirical proposition, based on the perceived nexuses between cosmology and concrete historical experiences. Such nexuses did not imply the deductive application of general principles contained in the former to explain particular events occurring in the latter. The assimilation of white people with demiurges was not made deductively but abductively, as Boyer (1994:142–8) suggests for all magical-religious explanations. Abductive inferences are triggered by the need to explain new data, leading to the formulation of a proposition, which, if confirmed empirically, accounts for the observable data. Hence it is necessarily tested in context.

We can derive a further consequence from this idea that premises such as "the whites are demiurges" are based on abduction. If they are not divorced from experience, then their truth-value is conditional. Abductive explanations are conjectural, inasmuch as the process of making inferences is triggered by the explanatory needs of particular situations (Boyer 1994:217–18). Conditionality implies flexibility but also resilience. If a conditional truth-value accounts for both behavioral flexibility and practical engagement, it also accounts for the stability of magico-religious assumptions, since no single piece of evidence is ever enough. No particular situation can disprove a general assumption.

During the first months of contact, the veracity of the network of propositions supporting the idea that whites can revive de dead was boosted by a number of facts. Carvalho was able to master songs and names as only dreamers could. The question then became: Just how powerful is he? If he cures with injections, controls the flow of goods, operates the radio, and is the head of the whites, he may be very powerful indeed. So why not convert this possibility into action in a moment of hope and distress? Many years later, I asked the headman Arakytá if they had really imagined the possibility of Carvalho resurrecting the dead. He replied: *Oporowa'a pa rimo Toria, oroja rakokwehe*, which can be translated as "Can the whites really resurrect people? This we asked ourselves at the time." This conditional reasoning was grounded in a series of assumptions about the nature of whites and enemies in general, which were combined together within a shamanic ontology. The final test was to ask Carvalho to resurrect the dead. Unfortunately, he failed three times.

What did this failure mean for the eastern Parakanã? They concluded that either Carvalho himself or the whites in general were unversed in the shamanic art of resurrection. Yet they remained impressed by white people's power to cure, and even more so by their power to cause diseases. For many years, the eastern Parakanã suffered from acute epidemics and many of them died. They never asked the whites to resurrect their kin again. In 1998, however, the death of a teenager provoked a tremendous commotion among them. They buried him and built a shack over the grave. For many days his father and other elders danced on the grave, smoking their long cigars and singing the Songs of the Earth. The whites remained at the Post, keeping a respectful distance. The elders danced again and again. In vain.

What about the western Parakanã? Did they too draw on these same premises about the whites to make sense of the initial moments of contact? As I discuss later, as early as the 1930s they had equated the agents of the SPI with dream enemies too, just as years earlier they had associated Tarewa with the revival of the dead. Such an association was also present in dreams. The old man Pi'awa once narrated me one of his oneiric experiences, in which he went to see his father's brother's grave and met a white man, who showed him how to resurrect the dead. By dancing and singing, Pi'awa made his father's brother rise out of the earth: "Very well, I made a human leave [the grave]." When Pi'awa eventually finished telling me his dream, he fixed his eyes on me and asked: "How do *you* make the dead leave (-*mohem*)?" I had no answer and remained in silence.

Soon after definitive contact in the 1980s, the western Parakanã start to "deshamanize" the Funai staff and other whites with whom they lived on a day-to-day basis. They no longer referred to them as *miangá*, having replaced this vocative with the one used for traditional enemies: *wepajé*, "my friend." However, dream familiarization continued to serve as a way to capture the secret powers of the whites. One day my friend Karája became sick. In the dream, he brought a white man who placed him on a table and, instead of sucking out the pathogenic agents, gave him serum and injections, singing the following song:

Kaohoa mohangohoa	Here is the great medicine
Imotororo orerehe herota	Which he brought and dripped in us
Ka nemorokytykawa-homohoa.	Here is the long string of your people-polisher.[13]

Later, Karája sung this *karahiwa* for his cross-cousin who had been bitten by a snake. The presence of the remedy and its owner in the dream suggests how concrete figures (such as the Funai nurse) can be dislocated to the word of dreams, simultaneously enabling the persistence of general ontological premises and pragmatic action in the daily interaction with state agents. After all, so long as there are dreams, there is hope. Poenakatu, an Asurini Indian, once explained to an anthropologist why his father, who was a great shaman, did not return to life: "Our father always told us not to bury him, but to make a basket and leave him in there until all the flesh was gone.... That is why our mother did not want to have him buried. He was going to live again for us." The whites, however, urged them to bury him, and Poenakatu laments, "The whites, they didn't know that he dreamt" (Andrade 1992:220).

The Enchantment of Technology

The identification of the whites with shamanism was restaged many times during the process of conquest, associating either with curing or with the lethal epidemics. In the Tupinambá case, the identification with the Caraíba was based on a convergence of actions, dispositions, and signs, but also on the Europeans' perceived technological superiority. The impact of material goods, though, went beyond their immediate use value. Here we can recall the observation of the Norman captain Paulmier de Gonneville on how he persuaded the Carijó chief Arosca, in the distant year of 1504, to allow one of the latter's children to accompany him on his return trip to France:

[T]hey convinced him that they would teach artillery techniques to those from this side [of the ocean]; this is something they desire intensely as a means of dominating their enemies, as well as learning to make mirrors, knives, axes and everything that they see and admire of the Christians; which was just like promising a Christian gold, silver and precious stones, or instructing them in the ways of the philosopher's stone. (Paulmier de Gonneville [1505] 1992:24)

---

13 "String of the people-polisher" is a metaphor referring to the plastic tubing of the intravenous drip. The Parakanã consider the treatment with serum to be more "reviving" than injections. "People-polisher" (*morokytykawa*) is also the word for soap.

The captain attributes a practical interest in possessing these objects and, at the same time, compares knowing how to make them with knowledge of the philosopher's stone (one of the foundations of the alchemic project, along with – suggestively – the elixir of long life). Ontological inferences are not an impediment to evaluating the practical implications of artifacts. Knowing a technique implies more than knowing how to use a tool; it implies knowing who produced it, how, and why. Objects can function as the grounds for abductive inferences concerning the nature of their producers, indexes that enable the abduction of a nonordinary agency (Gell 1998).

Akaria's narrative about Tarewa is wonderfully explicit on this point: "Let's take them to the white man so he can resuscitate our children. They are the ones who make the axes."[14] The passage from axes to resurrection implies an abductive inference: The observable capacity to produce the tool confirms the identification of white people with the great shamans who are capable of crossing the frontiers between life and death. "Are you the one who makes axes?" Moakara asks Mojiajiga, the artifact-giver. When the latter replies yes, he gives him the bones of his sons and demands: "In the same way, resuscitate my child for me" (*einon jera'yra ewa'a jeopé*).

Like People You See in a Dream

The story of Tarewa is connected to a historical event described in Chapter 1: the killing of Moakara, the man who supposedly taught the Parakanã how to obtain metal tools peacefully. After the construction of the Tocantins Pacification Post in 1928, the western Parakanã had numerous opportunities to play out Moakara's lesson. In the 1929 report, the head of the Post seems still ambivalent in describing their behavior. Although he claims that they are "happy," their attitude does not strike him as being "as peaceful as we had expected, given the information at my disposal, since they made a large racket, as well as clutching their bows and many arrows in their hands" (SPI 1929). In later reports, though, he invariably describes the camaraderie shown to the Post's workers. This trust seems to have been gradually shared by the Indians who, during this first period of contact, visited the locale with greater frequency, accompanied by women and children. In 1930, for example:

14 The Parakanã do not have a notion of invention like our own: Explaining to them that objects such as airplanes, antibiotics, or radios had been "recently" invented demanded an effort in cultural translation. I used to resort to an asociological explanation of invention as an *ex nihilo* creation by a talented individual. The Parakanã transformed such explanation into an externalist theory of dreams as an effective interaction with enemies possessing valuable knowledge. Instead of the creative insight of the individual genius, they postulated an enemy capable of teaching a new technique to a great dreamer.

[T]hey once again visited this Post, when we distributed everything that we had for them: machetes, axes, knives, hammocks, clothing, flour, bananas, maize and various other objects, all of it in large quantities. But as there were many of them (I would calculate one hundred), including a lot of women and children, not everyone received gifts. (SPI 1930a)

On February 5, 1931, they returned in even bigger numbers, totaling one hundred and fifteen, "composed of sixty men, thirty women, fifteen nursing infants carried in slings and ten boys between ten and fifteen years old." Alípio Ituassu, the head of the Post, states that they stayed for four hours at the Post, "always with great displays of contentment, singing, dancing, jumping and running festively" (SPI 1930). On November 21, 1931, they appeared again, but only twelve men went to fetch the gifts while the bulk of the group – also formed by women and children – stayed waiting about a kilometer away. A year later, they appeared twice: First about forty people arrived, mostly men and a few boys. Two days later another eighty came, comprising men, women, and children, the latter including nursing infants (SPI 1932).

The fact they took women and small children indicates that they discarded the possibility of both physical and shamanic aggression from the whites. The association between diseases and the Toria only slowly took hold during the course of the twentieth century, becoming consolidated after the post-pacification depopulation. The reports describe a feeling opposite to fear – joy: "On the 31st of July, we were ... visited by the Indians who usually emerge at this Post.... After a short stay, they departed with the same display of joy as when they arrived: singing, dancing and talking wildly" (SPI 1933). These joyous outbursts became hallmarks of the western Parakanã's visits to the Pacification Post, along with their voracity for industrial goods. The gifts offered were not few in number, and they acquired an exceptional dimension given that the Parakanã had until then scant access to merchandise. The visits were great festivals of goods that needed to be celebrated in indigenous fashion: with song, dancing, and words.

This experience cemented a particular view of the Toria, which would come to mark interethnic contact. The whites, "masters of objects" (*ma'ejiroajara*), emerged as generous providers who could not be killed without the risk of losing access to their goods. Historically, the western Parakanã avoided killing non-Indians whenever they could, considering them to be *ma'e ijokapyrahe*, "that which you don't kill." This avoidance had three motives: First, rather than being strengthened, a white person's killer became exhausted, sometimes even dying of weakness (a fact indicating that nonindigenous victims ill-suited the goals of Parakanã warfare). Second, it struck the Parakanã as irrational to kill the providers of goods (at least before discovering how numerous the whites were). Finally, the manner thought to be the most suited to obtaining the tools was to leave some retribution for the goods obtained (as Moakara had taught them). This does not mean that they did not circumstantially kill whites, only that they tried to avoid doing so, desiring to establish peaceful relations instead. They used the SPI Post just as the owner of a pet bird uses its feather: They plucked the objects and returned after six months or a year when the stock of goods had been reconstituted.[15]

In the indigenous narratives on the visits to the Pacification Post, the most prominent image is that of a festive occasion involving an abundant and voluntary distribution of presents. Iatora was still a boy when he visited the Post in the 1930s:[16]

I was Japia's age [about twelve years old]. I said to my grandfather for us to go to see Toria. I asked him:

– What are the Toria like?
– Just like us, you'll see, he replied.

Mojiajinga's house was as a high as the tree tops. We spotted it:

– Let's go there and ask him for goods.

So the late Tapi'awa shouted to them:

– Are you there? Can I visit your house, *miangá*?

I went on as far as the train tracks and shouted:

– I'm arriving, father (*wetom*).

A Toria came out of the house carrying machetes. We approached and took the goods. The machete had a red handle. We took axes too. The Toria told us to enter and take hammocks. We entered the Post. We found red hammocks:

– Give me that hammock, father, I've been sleeping on the ground, I said to the Toria.

The Toria told me to stay there first, so I stayed in his house, but afterwards he suggested:

– Take it to your kin, let's pacify them first and then we can live together.

He put the hammock inside a bag and offered me some tobacco:

– Do you smoke this? he asked me.
– I came to your house because I was after this, father.

---

15 It was not all camaraderie, though. The Parakanã did not limit themselves to taking the offered goods; they also plundered everything they could: "[A]s always, they came peacefully, displaying pure camaraderie. Though this didn't stop them from looting. They took all the hammocks which had been set aside for them, a large quantity of machetes, axes and knives; flour, bananas, plus most of the different objects belonging to our staff for their own use." (SPI 1932).

16 As was his custom, Iatora places phrases in the mouths of his interlocutors and creates an image of free-flowing communication, like in a dream, to the extent that one child asks him: "Grandfather, did you use to know how to speak their language?"

Then I said to Tapi'awa:

     – Let's take the hammocks, let's get tobacco so we can perform *opetymo*.

We danced a little:

     – That's how we dance in *opetymo*, father.

So the Toria asked us if we would return. We said yes.

     – Bring me tortoises so we can give you tobacco, so we can retribute you with hammocks, rice and coffee.

...

Our fathers remained on the other shore of the river and the Toria threw tobacco over the river to them. The older people were afraid. Then my maternal uncle told me to bring him some things. I took a hammock, an axe, tobacco. Arona moved a bit closer and the Toria grabbed him by the wrist:

     – Why are you afraid of us? he asked him. Come and take these things. Look at the children, they're not scared of us.

So Arona said to me:

     – Let's go, nephew, so I can take some things too.

I went ahead and we entered. We picked up a lot of things and went away. The Toria accompanied us as far as the railroad and told us to bring tortoises so we could swap them for hammocks.

     – Bring them soon, he told us.

So, I, Tapi'awa, my late -*'ai'wera*, my late -*taja*, my late -*pajé* Awokoa, the late Jakaré and my late father-in-law Arona soon returned with the tortoises. My father-in-law Inajokyga and Arakoria were the expedition leaders. We caught many tortoises and caica parrot fledglings. We returned and shouted to them:

     – We brought you tortoises, father.

We took the tortoises and they were pleased, giving us tobacco in exchange. They gave me a mosquito net when I told them that they swarmed all over me. We stayed there with the Toria, eating tortoise liver with manioc flour.... They told us to stay with them so we could take knives, axes, hammocks, mosquito nets, sandals, and so on. We danced with them. The song was *Jirawohoa* from my late -*ai'wera* Ata'a.

     – This is what you told me, father, Ata'a said to them.

     – This is what we told you. It was I who told you, son, one of them replied.

So *Toria* gave me a hat as protection from the sun. Then he brought me a machete, telling me to use it for weeding. We ceased dancing and ate more tortoise and flour. When we were leaving, we told them we would return. They told us to bring more tortoises. As we went, they asked us to sing for them.

(Iatora 1993: tapes 36–8)

The trip to the Pacification Post is described as a visit to Mojiajinga's house, a character from Moakara's story. Although the Parakanã knew the workers at the Post were not Mojiajinga, they behaved like the latter in that they were distributing gifts. The visitors, for their part, acted out what Moakara had taught them – not only behaving peacefully, but also offering something in exchange for the gifts: tortoises and the offspring of wild animals. Fifty years after the attack on Moakara, they were still reproducing the same relational mode toward the whites. These increased the goodwill that Alípio Ituassu held for the Indians: "[W]here there had been an object they had taken, they left a tortoise in substitution, or an agouti, or some small birds perhaps. In other words, they didn't so much take as exchange." (SPI 1930a).

Actually, the Parakanã did not believe they were "exchanging" (-*ponekwam*) but "paying" (*wepy*) to keep the necessarily asymmetric flow of goods going. Rather than being a matter between brothers-in-law or even generic affines, it was a relation between familiarized enemies. This was an unequal redistributive relationship in which the whites figured as providers. If visits confirmed the asymmetry existing between whites and Indians, they allowed a glimpse of its reversal: The whites' control over goods was overdetermined by the Parakanã's capacity to control the whites' will. The latter extracted from the former a voluntary action, making them behave as dream *akwawa*: givers, not of songs and names, but of material goods. For sure, they were non-kin, but for this reason they could also be father-providers, *miangá*. This latter premise needed to be reasserted in each concrete situation to prevent the underlying alterity – hostile by default – from surfacing. When people made statements such as "we don't kill Toria because they provide us with artifacts," I would recall for them the occasions when they had actually killed a white person. My interlocutors would then retort that, in these cases, the Toria had been miserly, refusing to give them any of their things. In other words, by failing to behave as providers, they acted as enemies.

The Pacification Post constituted a unique setting: an open space surrounded by dense forest, bordered by a rail track whose terminal points remained invisible, where a profuse number of objects were freely distributed, replaced, and distributed again. This interactional context reinforced powerful assumptions concerning the whites, making them similar to dream enemies, providers of immaterial goods, and masters of the shamanic science. The experiences at the Post were like those found in the second part of dreams, the waking dream. In his narrative, Iatora renders this association explicit. Ata'á, after dancing and singing, turns to one of the employees and exclaims: "This is what *you* told me, father," a formula similar to the one used by dreamers when they transmit their songs in the *tekatawa* (for instance, "this is what the Karája told me, my nephew").

Now awake, Ata'á encounters the enemy that he had seen (and heard) when dreaming, something that was not only plausible, but a relatively common experience for great dreamers. The SPI workers were in all likelihood "like people you see in a dream" (Schieffelin & Crittenden 1991).

Forget about Violence

Throughout this chapter, I showed that the equivalence between whites and demiurges in the myth of the small opossum is part of a more general identification of the former with shamanic capacities. This equation was not only mythical but full of practical consequences, motivating collective action and informing interethnic strategies. They did not only see whites as potentially great shamans, but acted according to this premise and tested it in many practical situations. Eventually, the whites came to occupy the place of the great enemy shamans in the Parakanã world, echoing what happened five centuries earlier with the Tupinambá, who associated them with their indigenous Caraíba. The resilience of this idea is surprising given the violence of the historical process of conquest. Why is this so? Why is violence not a predominant feature of Parakanã perceptions of whites?

This question invokes two lines of reasoning, one historical, the other relating to comparative ethnology. The first concerns the actual experience of the Parakanã in relation to colonial and, later, national society. As we have seen in Chapter 1, the peoples living in the Pacajá-Tocantins interfluvial region were plunged into relative isolation from at least the beginning of the nineteenth century, a situation that would only change with the surge in Brazil-nut extraction and the construction of the Tocantins Railroad in the 1920s. The Parakanã narratives contain no evidence of attacks perpetrated by slave hunters or large-scale conflicts with the regional population. In the twentieth century, the Parakanã suffered just four losses in interethnic conflicts, and these were from the 1960s onward. It is not surprising, therefore, that violence is not a dominant theme in their representations of whites.

The second line of reasoning, however, cannot be dismissed so easily. In Chapter 5, I focused on the close intertwining of shamanism and warfare to show that – aside from the contemporary Guarani – Tupi peoples combine these two modes of surpassing the human condition. The prototypical figure of regression to nature, the jaguar, is always associated with the condition of shamans and divinities. Should we not expect predation to figure prominently in the identification of whites with shamanism? In fact, among the Parakanã there is a vague assumption that the Toria eat people. They are sometimes said to slice open the thorax of their victims to remove the heart and eat it. People claim, for example, that one of the employees at the

Pucuruí Post in the 1960s was a cannibal and say that they saw human meat hanging in a storage shed. In oral tradition, however, what predominates is the figure of a shamanism disconnected from the principle of cannibal appropriation. This point is of special interest for comparative ethnology, since some Amerindian peoples did associate the whites with cannibalism while simultaneously expressing moral disapproval of their behavior.

Whites as Jaguars

This is particularly the case of the mythologies of the Upper Xingu and Upper Negro River. In the former, the identification of whites with jaguars appears at the end of the cosmogonic cycle, which differentiates the peoples according to their technology and moral disposition. The narrative is structured around the famous motif of the bad choice (Lévi-Strauss 1964): The Sun asks the ancestor of the Xinguanos to choose between the bow, the warclub, and the shotgun. The Xinguano prefers the bow, the "wild Indian" picks the warclub, and the white picks the shotgun. Next follows a new choice: The Sun passes around a gourd and asks each man to drink. The Xinguano notices that the gourd is full of blood and refuses to drink, but both the "wild Indian" and the white drank it down (Ireland 1988:166). Hematophagy is linked here to predatory dispositions: After drinking blood, whites and wild Indians (the Ge-speaking people) became warlike and prone to violence. In a Kamayurá version of the same myth, the demiurge Mavutsinin expels the white man from the Upper Xingu for having chosen the rifle (Agostinho 1974:180–1).

The same theme appears in the final sequence of the Tukanoan-speaking Barasana creation myth, in which the indigenous ancestor proceeds to make a series of bad choices: He refuses to bathe in the ever-rejuvenating water, chooses the bow instead of the revolver, and does not eat what is offered by the demiurge. These episodes explain why the whites are more numerous, longer-living, healthy, and technologically adept than the Tukano, but also why they are more violent: Equipped with firearms, the ancestor of the whites became a threat to Indians, and the culture hero sends him far away (Hugh-Jones 1988).

It is not by chance that we find this association between jaguars and whites among those societies that became structured into pacific, multilocal, pluriethnic, and multilinguistic complexes.[17] Both in the Upper Xingu and the Upper Rio Negro, indigenous peoples constructed wider and more durable systems of integration than the unstable networks found in other

---

17 For the historical transformations of Upper Rio Negro system and the balance between violence and peace, see Wright (1990), Hugh-Jones (1994), and Hill (1996). For the Upper Xingu, see especially Gregor (1990), Heckenberger (1996), and Franchetto and Heckenberger (2001).

parts of Amazonia. These complexes tended to develop a clearly defined ethics and aesthetics that characterize the proper human life in contrast to outsiders. In contrast to those groups that located the source of power and vitality in the familiarizing predation of others, in these societies a centripetal cosmology prevailed over the cannibal dynamic, meaning that their reproduction did not depend on the *violent* appropriation of external subjectivities. The amplification of the space of safe sociability beyond the local group, the expansion of the sphere of exchange, and the constitution of an internally differentiated social system served to dynamize social life. It is in these contexts that whites came to be defined via predatory characteristics and explicitly associated with the jaguar.

We arrive here at a curious general result: "Pacific" systems, with their centripetal cosmologies and centrifugal sociologies, identify the whites with jaguars and, secondarily, with other elements of shamanism. "Warrior" systems, on the other hand, with their centrifugal cosmologies and centripetal sociologies, identify the whites with great shamans and, residually, with cannibalism, as if regarding them not with censure but desire. By defining themselves as jaguars, the Parakanã projected onto whites the shadow of the demiurge.[18] If this is the answer to the question concerning the non-identification of whites with jaguars in Parakanã mythology, we are still faced with a problem: Where does the jaguar stand?

Losing the Jaguar

I now turn to a myth in which a man undergoes a literal process of jaguarization. This jaguar-becoming story is a variant of the bird-nester motif analyzed by Lévi-Strauss (1964). Among the Parakanã, the narrative is known as "The Macaw Nester" (*Araramokajinara*) or "The one who was taken by the Jaguar" (*Jawararemirakwera*), depending on whether the beginning or end of the myth is emphasized. Below I provide a summary of the initial and final events of this long narrative.

The Macaw Nester who Turned into a Jaguar

Two men go to capture macaw nestlings. One of them climbs a Brazil-nut tree. He reaches the nest and removes a small bird. Its feathers have only just started to develop. The man below asks about the small birds. The one above replies:

18 As much as these identifications and values are part of a long and enduring tradition, they are not fixed and isolated from the historical processes in which they developed. Just remember my description of how the eastern and western Parakanã diverged in terms of war practices, a divergence that primarily stemmed from ethical-political choices. The role of social reform among indigenous peoples of the Americas is a topic deserving closer investigation.

"The feathers have started to emerge." The one below repeats the question, to which the other replies again. This continues numerous times until the nester becomes irritated and says: "The macaw feathers are growing now, just like your wife's pubic hair." The man below knocks over the scaffold, leaving his companion trapped in the Brazil-nut tree, and goes away.

The man spends days in the tree until eventually the red squirrel finds him: "Come here and I'll help you get down," the squirrel says to the nester. "No, you'll make me fall," he replies fearfully. Finally, after displaying his proficiency in scaling trees, the squirrel convinces the man and brings him down to the ground. The nester asks about his kin, but the squirrel did not see them leave. He departs in search of them.

The story goes on to recount the protagonist's adventures while searching for his kin: how he learns to weave baskets, how he crosses a river on the back of a cayman who wants to eat him, how he lives in the village of the tapirs, and how the armadillos finally spot the locale to which his kin have moved.

He finally encounters his sisters. The men have gone hunting. He recounts his story. The women tell him to wait inside the house. When the hunters arrive they tell them: "Our brother returned, the one we left behind." The next morning, his brothers-in-law leave to hunt while the nester remains in the village making his bow. The brothers-in-law return empty-handed. The next day, they set off again. The nester stays behind making his arrows. The sisters leave to fetch babassu coconuts. On the path, they notice that the inajá palm fruit is falling and the agoutis are eating them. They tell their brother, who replies, "Hey! I'm going to kill the agoutis to make a chisel [with their teeth]."

He builds a hunt screen and lies in wait. No agoutis appear. He returns to the village at dusk. The next morning, he returns to the hide. Nothing. Then the *korowiré* bird sings. A jaguar approaches. When he is about to take aim, the animal stands up and transforms into a woman. She says that she came to fetch him so that he could become her husband. He replies that he has just returned to his sisters. "Let's go first, we can return later for you to see your sisters," the jaguar suggests. He drops his bow and departs with her.

They reach the village of the jaguars. She presents her new husband to her mother, who tells her daughter to hide him in a hammock suspended high up in the house so the father cannot see him. The male jaguars arrive the next day bringing smoked tapir. They smell the man. The daughter says to her father: "I told you that I would bring the unloved-one [rejected by his kin] to be my spouse." He asks the daughter to bring his son-in-law to him. He approves her choice and decides to take him to the village plaza in order to transform him into a jaguar. The jaguar father-in-law says to the man: "Come here so I can dress you, son-in-law." He transforms him first into an ocelot, then into a cougar, then into a spotted jaguar, and finally into a black jaguar. The daughter approves: "This one turned out great, father. You can stop."

Some time later, the jaguar-wife has a son by the nester. When the child is already crawling, the father decides to visit his sisters with his new family. In the village, he reencounters his brothers-in-law and sisters. The next day, he leaves to hunt and bring deer back for their kin. The following day, the brothers-in-law want to join him to hunt tapir and peccary, but the jaguar-wife warns them not to shoot him when he turns into a jaguar. However, while he is chasing a tapir, the brothers-in-law end up shooting him. He stands up, pulls out the arrows, and undresses. He reprimands the brothers-in-law: "I told you to wait for me to catch the tapir." "We thought you were another jaguar, that's why we shot you," the brothers-in-law reply.

The nester warns them: "Wait for her [the jaguar-wife] to come here because she'll smell my blood." The wife hands the son to the sister-in-law, advising her not to wake him up as he bites too much. She leaves to meet up with her husband. The jaguar-wife admonishes the men: "I told you not to shoot him, I said to wait for him to catch the tapir for you." She then announces that she will never bring him back again. They return to the village. The child had awoken and bitten the aunt. The jaguar also advises her sisters-in-law that they will never return. And thus they went away forever.

(Summary of Akaria 1995: tapes 3–4)

I have omitted the middle section of the myth not only for reasons of space. By passing directly from the first section to the last, we end up with a narrative very similar to other Tupi-Guarani myths using the bird-nester motif as a framework. The most famous of these is a Parintintin legend collected by Nunes Pereira (1967:582–5) and analyzed by Lévi-Strauss in *The Raw and the Cooked* (1964:319–22). The myth, which explains the origin of bird colors, enables Lévi-Strauss to draw a comparison between the Bororo reference myth (which relates to the establishment of a meteorological order), the Ge myths on the origin of cooking fire (which relate to the cultural order), and the myths that explain bird coloring (which relate to the zoological order).

These Ge and Parintintin myths can be compared in another correlated way. They establish (dis)continuities between the human and animal conditions, conceived in distinct ways in Ge and Tupi cosmologies. In both cases, the narratives begin with the hero leaving his human social condition and passing through a long period of isolation, leading to a peaceful interaction with predatory animals (jaguars in the Ge case, eagles in the Parintintin case). After this point, the myths take opposite directions. In the Kayapó version, the bird-nester is adopted by the jaguar, who feeds him cooked meat. He also receives a bow and arrow to protect himself from the jaguar-wife. One day, though, he ends up killing his adoptive father's

Table 7.2. *Comparison of the Ge and Parintintin Bird-Nester Myths*

Ge	Parintintin
brothers-in-law go to capture macaw nestlings	friends go to capture eagle nestlings
insult	insult
young brother-in-law trapped in tree	man trapped in tree
jaguar adopts the young man	eagle "adopts" the man
jaguar gives the man a bow and arrows to protect himself from the jaguar-wife	eagle transforms the man into an eagle for him to take revenge on his companion
young man kills the jaguar's wife	bird-nester kills his human companion
returns to human social life	returns to social life with the birds
they organize an expedition to steal the jaguar's fire	birds are tattooed with blood from the human victim
men eat cooked meat	birds eat a raw human

wife and flees in fright, though not before grabbing the bow he had been given and a piece of roasted meat. He returns to live with the humans. An expedition is then organized to steal the cooking fire, an act that inaugurates the separation between humans and jaguars according to their predatory and dietary modes: Thereafter, the former will hunt with bows and arrows and will eat cooked meat, while the latter will use their claws to kill and will become eaters of raw food.

The Parintintin bird-nester, by contrast, abandons his human condition by assuming the form and habits of falconiform birds. Adopting the hero, the eagle transforms him into a bird of prey so he can take revenge on the man who had left him trapped in the tree. Instead of returning to live with his kin, bringing a "cultural" element that inaugurates the human condition, the bird-nester kills his companion and takes him to the birds for them to feast on his flesh, with the condition that they agree to be tattooed (inaugurating a zoological order: the colors marking the discontinuity of birds). The human diet is defined here only in negative. What is positively asserted is a nonhuman alimentary mode: omophagy (and cannibalism). In Table 7.2, I summarize these two narratives.

The systematic oppositions reveal that the myths diverge as they unfold. In the Ge case, eating raw food is defined as a lack, whereas in the Tupi case it is positively affirmed as a way of exacting revenge. In the latter myth, the perspective accompanies the metamorphosis: The viewpoint is that of the protagonist who becomes an eagle, not that of those who remain human. The killer possesses the point of view, not his victim.

The Parakanã myth of the bird-nester seems to oscillate between the Ge and the Tupi-Guarani mythic series: the former thematizing the acquisition

Table 7.3. *Comparison of the Ge, Parintintin, and Parakanã Myths*

Ge	Parakanã	Parintintin
brothers-in-law	indeterminate	friends
macaw	macaw	eagle
jaguar father	jaguar father-in-law	eagle father
adoptive father gives "cultural instruments"	father-in-law gives "natural instruments"	father-in-law gives "natural instruments"
to protect him	to feed the daughter	to be able to exact revenge
man preys on jaguars	jaguar-man hunts for humans	eagle-man preys on humans
horizontal separation	horizontal separation	vertical separation
jaguars – humans	jaguars – humans	eagle – humans
human alimentation	(human alimentation)$^{-1}$	cannibalism

of cooking fire as a positing of the human condition against which the dietary mode of the jaguar is defined; the latter exploring the theme of cannibal cooking not as a "natural" form of alimentation, but as a culinary expression of the asymmetric predator-prey relationship. As in the Ge myth, the Parakanã bird-nester goes to capture macaws rather than eagles, has privileged relations with the jaguar, and does not try to take revenge on his kin (on the contrary, he returns to visit them peacefully). Like his Tupi congeners, however, he is metamorphosed, receives "natural tools," returns only provisionally to human social life, and remains definitively animal. Furthermore, inversely to the Ge hero who receives the jaguar's bow, the Parakanã hero abandons his bow in the hide before leaving with his future jaguar-wife, since he will learn how to hunt with the jaguar's "natural" instruments. Table 7.3 presents a summary of these myths.

If the Parakanã story employs elements from the two mythic series – the Ge and the Tupi-Guarani – what is its message after all? Rather than describing the acquisition of a human alimentary mode, the narrative explains humanity's loss of the jaguar's predatory capacities. In contrast to the Ge versions, it is not a civilizing myth: It does not describe the acquisition of an art that makes possible society and culture.[19] On the contrary, it accounts for the loss of a nonhuman capacity, which could be employed as a means of obtaining food for humans. Instead of describing the danger of a regression to animality, the myth emphasizes what humanity loses by

19 In neither case, however, are we dealing with a generic disjunction between nature and culture, but rather the difference between the *human and jaguar predatory codes*. The Parakanã hero's journey is interspersed with other possibilities for becoming animal: In the villages of the tapirs and the armadillos he also receives a wife but avoids eating with them. This earlier trajectory marks the specificity of the jaguar metamorphosis.

being abandoned by the jaguar brother-in-law – a loss that, today, can only be individually restored by the capacity of the great dreamers to transform into felines or collectively restored through rituals.

Closing the Circle

If the Parakanã bird-nester myth describes the loss of a "natural" predatory capacity and the disjunction between humans and jaguars, what is the relation between this myth and the cosmogonic ones describing the separation of humans and gods? Is there a homology between the former and the latter loss? Both the Parakanã jaguar myth and the Tupi twins myth turn on the surpassing of the ordinary human condition: the immanent mode of the cannibal-jaguar and the transcendent mode of the immortal-shaman. As we have seen, the small opossum myth, which describes the origin of the whites, absorbed the latter theme, whereas the bird-nester myth elaborates the former. They take opposite but intersecting paths. Our problem, therefore, is how to close the circuit, connecting the stories of the jaguar and the small opossum.

Let's then consider yet another version of the bird-nester story, one collected by Wagley & Galvão (1961:151–2) among the Tupi-speaking Tenetehara. The hero is abandoned on a tree by his brother. Adopted by an eagle, he marries the latter's daughter, and exacts revenge by taking his own brother to be eaten by his eagle-affines. After the revenge, he notices that his ex-kin are sad. He then returns to the village and takes on a human form. He invites everyone to sing, but only his parents accompany him. At sunset, the dance house rises into the air, and they are taken to the celestial village of the eagles. Those who refused to sing are transformed into small birds to be hunted by the birds of prey, and a flood covers the former *maloca*. The opposition between humans and animals gives way entirely to the asymmetric relation between predator and prey. As in the Parintintin version, the point of view follows the predator.

The Tenetehara finale is *sui generis*: It echoes the Tupi-Guarani myths of the flood, in which the first inhabitants sing and dance to make the house to rise into the air above the water. Those left on the ground die, with the exception of two men who climb a palm tree: These will become the ancestors of the Indians. In some versions, those who leave with the house reach a promised land in the sky or in some other region on the earth (Nimuendajú 1987:156; Cadogan 1959:57). In the Parakanã version, as we have seen in Chapter 2, they are unable to enter the sky and set down in a distant land from where they later return as whites. The comparison of the Tenetehara myth with other Tupi-Guarani myths suggests that the bird-eagle relation is homologous to the human-demiurge relation and the Indian-white relation, as shown in Table 7.4.

Table 7.4. *Comparison of Tupi Myths: Gods, Whites, and Predators*

Tenetehara	Guarani	Parakanã
small birds : eagle	humans : gods	indians : whites
↓	↓	↓
predation	Mortality	interethnic contact
(bird-nester)	(universal flood)	(universal flood)

In order to finally close our demonstration, we need now to present another myth that narrates the origin of the whites using the framework of the bird-nester myth. This is exactly what the Wayãpi saga of Ulukauli does: It begins with the episode of the bird-nester and ends with the origin of the whites. The story starts with Ulukauli going to fetch eagle nestlings with his brothers-in-law. He offends them by comparing the little birds' feathers to their sister's juvenile pubic hair. The brothers-in-law break the scaffold and leave him stranded in the tree. When the harpy eagle comes back, the nestlings tells her that Ulukauli is their guardian. So instead of eating the hero, the harpy eagle gives him food. After a few mishaps, he manages to descend the tree by holding onto the mucus dribbling from the oropendola. This bird provides him with a magical tool to exact revenge on his brothers-in-law. Ulukauli returns then to the village and invites his affines to go hunting. He places the oropendola's magical tool in a hole, as if it were an armadillo. The brothers-in-law try to tug it out, but the magical armadillo drags them underground. Next Ulukauli kills his wife, cuts her into pieces, and grills her. He places the meat in a basket and returns home, only to recuperate his children. He then builds a new village and raises birds with the remains of his dead wife. Her surviving kinfolks go in pursuit of Ulukauli numerous times. Each time, he relocates his village farther away until, one day, they can no longer track him. The myth then comes to an end with this elegant conclusion: "Ulukauli and his family ... were in their canoes in the sea. He is the one ... who the whites later called Christopher Columbus" (F. Grenand 1982:252).

Myth and Antimyth

I began this chapter with the Parakanã myth of the small opossum, which narrates the origin of the whites. I showed that the narrative is a transformation of the twins cycle, in which an equivalence between whites and the demiurges is established. Throughout the chapter, I described the enactment of this identification in eastern and western Parakanã history, particularly as it was played out during specific moments of their contact processes. I then returned to mythical realities and analyzed the story of the "Bird-Nester who Turned into a Jaguar," whose framework is the same as the Ge myths on the origin of cooking fire, but whose message is inverted: Whereas the latter deal with the acquisition of a human mode of predation and alimentation, the Parakanã narrative describes the loss of an extrahuman mode for obtaining food. I finally compared the Parakanã jaguar myth with their myth on the origin of whites, since both deal with a disjunction that negatively defines the indigenous social condition. Now what kind of myths are these in which proper human social life is seen as the result of loss, in which the point of view always remains outside human society?

Contrasting the Ge myths on the origin of cooking fire with those on the origin of whites, DaMatta coined the concept of antimyth. According to him, a myth establishes a relation of complementary opposition between nature and culture, in which a natural element is appropriated to found the social order, whereas an antimyth describes a contradiction born from within society itself, but which cannot be absorbed by its structures and must therefore be expelled. The dichotomy in the antimyth is not reciprocal and complementary, like the opposition between nature and culture; rather, it is hierarchical and contradictory, like the contrast between Indians and whites (DaMatta 1970:100–5). Myth describes how an extrahuman power is obtained in order to found social life once and for all; antimyth, by contrast, deals with the birth of powers within society that cannot be absorbed and that it will ultimately lose. Such loss is precisely the final message of the Parakanã myths analyzed in this chapter. So let me conclude by comparing the Ge and Parakanã stories on the origin of the whites.

Becoming White

This comparison takes us to some Ge narratives that became widely known by the Timbira name of their protagonist, Auke. I start by providing a summary of this story, basing it on a Canela version collected by Nimuendajú (1946:245–6):

1. A "public girl" hears the cry of a mouse while bathing in the river;[20]
2. once home, she realizes she is pregnant, when the mouse-child talks to her from the womb, announcing the moment of its birth;
3. the mother utters the fateful sentence: "If you're a boy, I'll kill you, but if you're a girl, I'll raise you";
4. a boy, Auke, is born and the mother buries him;

---

20 As in the Parakanã case, the animal in question may be a mouse or a small opossum. "Public girl" refers here to those Ge women who must remain unmarried and at the disposal of members of a specific male ritual society.

5. the grandmother scolds the mother, digs up the grandchild, and breastfeeds him;

6. Auke grows rapidly, he has the gift of transforming himself into various animals;

7. for this reason, his maternal uncle kills and buries him, but he returns and asks the grandmother why they want to kill him;

8. finally, after a number of attempts, the maternal uncle strikes Auke and burns him;

9. everyone then leaves;

10. after a while, the mother asks them to bring her son's ashes;

11. two messengers go back and discover that Auke has turned into a white, creating black people, horses, and cattle from wood;

12. he welcomes them warmly and invites his mother to live with him.

Both the Canela and Parakanã myths on the origin of the whites start out from an initial transformation (animal into child) and terminate with a second transformation (Indian into white). The plot line is the same, but various elements appear in inverted form: Angoja's mother is a virgin, whereas Auke's mother is a sexually promiscuous woman. Angoja enters via the vagina but cannot leave except by tearing it at birth, whereas Auke speaks with his mother from inside her. In the Parakanã myth, the son kills his mother at birth (and the grandmother buries her), whereas in the Canela myth, the mother kills her son (and the grandmother unearths him).

Both narratives call attention to the boys' exceptional powers: They grow rapidly, and whereas Auke transforms himself into animals, Angoja makes some of them venomous. Two events confirm their shamanic capacities: The maternal uncle kills Auke and buries him, but he resuscitates; Angoja exhumes his mother and brings her back to life (but the grandmother disrupts him). The maternal uncle tries to kill Auke again and burns him; Angoja's grandfather shoots him with arrows. Finally, a separation occurs: Their kinfolk abandon them and go away. The endings, however, are again inverted: Auke recognizes his kin and welcomes them, showing them his farm. Angoja, by contrast, does not recognize his kin; his grandfather shouts his name, but he shoots back in return. There are no gifts: Thereafter, industrial goods will belong to whites rather than Indians. I summarize this point in Table 7.5 on next page.

The narratives oppose each other at the outset only to converge on the same final outcome: the whites. At the end, the initial difference internal to each myth is converted into a maximal difference that implies a hierarchical inversion: The son of the "public girl" with an inferior status transforms into an outsider with superior power, just as occurs with Angoja, who, orphaned and abandoned by his grandparents, becomes the owner of industrial goods. Both myths thus describe a loss for indigenous societies, and both are opposed to the Ge founding myth of cooking fire.

Table 7.5. *Comparison of Ge and Parakanã Myths on the Origin of Whites*

Angoja myth	Auke myth
mother without sex life	mother with intense sex life
made pregnant inside house by an opossum (or mouse)	made pregnant outside house by a mouse (or opossum)
son kills mother during birth	mother kills son after birth
grandmother raises the boy	grandmother unearths the boy and breastfeeds him
boy grows rapidly	boy grows rapidly
transforms animals into dangerous beings	Transforms into animals
tries to resuscitate mother	is killed and resuscitates
grandfather shoots him but he does not die	maternal uncle burns him but he does not die
kin go away	kin go away
the boy transforms into a white man	the boy transforms into a white man
kin return but are not recognized	kin return and are recognized
greeted with gunshots	greeted with presents

In the Tupi-Guarani case, however, the notion that the indigenous social condition is founded on a loss is not exclusive to the myth on the origin of whites. This even applies to narratives on the origin of cooking fire. Take the eastern Parakanã myth presented in Chapter 2: After the flood, their ancestor finds himself alone. He lacks fire but does not eat raw meat; he grills the fish under the sun. The demiurge Máira pretends to be dead so the ancestor can steal fire from the vultures, but warns him to take the fire from the king vulture. The man errs and takes the fire from the yellow-headed vulture instead. Although the myth fails to specify the consequence of this bad choice, it seems to imply that the flame of the latter is inferior to that of the chief of the vultures.

This Parakanã myth describes thus an imperfect acquisition. Rather than founding a definitive form of human cooking, this ambivalent act gives rise to an equally ambivalent form of cooking. By contrast, the Ge fire myth is a foundational act: It implies that ever since its acquisition, society, as Turner says, can "reproduce itself as a reflexively self-generating cultural pattern" (1988:256). This is certainly not the message of the Parakanã narratives analyzed in this book. Rather, they mark the constant need for interaction with the exterior of society in order for it to be reproduced. There is no foundational act: All beginnings imply a lack against which social life has to be continuously produced. In this sense, then, what comprises an anti-myth for the Ge is precisely what myth is for the Tupi-Guarani.

Conclusion

There is the sarcastic predominance of matter With its immense silence suf-
focating the spirits of the air...

We must contemplate it, and patience, Little brother, will allow us to
glimpse the clearest visions.

Mário de Andrade, Rito do Irmão Pequeno (1931)

We are finally in a position to complete our journey by reassessing some of
the problems raised over the book's course. Not resolving them, for sure, but
generalizing them provisionally for more elaboration in the future. First,
I provide a synthetic formulation of the contrast between the two types of
sociocosmic regimes that I have been developing at various points of the
book. I then return to the concept of familiarizing predation, highlighting at a more abstract level its value in terms of understanding indigenous
South American sociocosmic configurations and, at a more concrete level,
its place in the theoretical discussion with which I wish to engage. Finally,
I return to the Parakanã and ask about the transformations now taking
place and what the future may hold.

Sociocosmic Regimes

As a heuristic device, I propose distinguishing between two sociocosmic
regimes: one centrifugal, the other centripetal. In the former, familiarizing
predation predominates, and social reproduction depends on the external
appropriation of agentive capacities; in the latter, the focus falls on the
internal accumulation and transmission of agentive capacities and wealth.
Both aim at the production of persons as a generalized mechanism for
reproducing social life, but in diverse manners: In the first mode, the ideal
person is constituted by the acquisition of potency outside society, whose
transmission is limited and constitutes ontological rather than sociological
differences; in the second, the ideal person is constituted through the ritual transmission and confirmation of distinctive social attributes that confirm sociological differences. Whereas centrifugal systems depend on the

continual replacement of new elements acquired from the exterior, centripetal systems emphasize a founding event in which the conditions of reproduction are given once and for all.

No indigenous social formation is entirely one or the other – not only
on the pragmatic plane, but also on the conceptual plane. There are innumerable gradations between the poles. The evidence for this continuum
is given in the ethnographic material itself: We find predominantly centrifugal peoples, such as the Araweté, with a stock of names that is continuously put back into circulation, and centripetal peoples, such as the
Xinguanos, with traditional mechanisms for introducing new names into
the system. The fundamental distinction is that in a centripetal system, the
sphere of circulation occupies the place reserved in a centrifugal system for
productive consumption: The horizontal and vertical circulation of symbolic wealth replaces its appropriation from the outside. Transmission and
exchange become more important than predation.[1]

This expansion of the sphere of circulation can take place in various
forms. A more detailed analysis of the correlation between modes of social
organization and cosmological systems would show a range of formations
more complex than the simple opposition between centripetal and centrifugal. In the Tukanoan case, for example, the expansion in the sphere
of circulation is historically linked to the formation of a pacific multi-
lingual system connecting localized patrilineal exogamic units. In the
Ge-Bororo case, social segmentation is internal to the village, structuring
a network for transmitting and perpetuating symbolic attributes between
units, which enable the group's self-renewal. At the same time, as the
Munduruku example shows, internal differentiation does not necessarily
imply the absence of a strong centrifugal mechanism for appropriating
principles of subjectification through warfare.

Globally, warfare tends to occupy a minor space in centripetal systems,
which depend less on cannibal appropriation to reproduce themselves:
Exchange and mechanisms of intergenerational transmission between
clans, houses, ceremonial groups, and villages ensure the internal dynamic
of the system. Here I am not suggesting a correlation between the *frequency*
of warfare and a mode of social reproduction. On one hand, there are centrifugal societies that, for specific historical reasons, adopt a more timid
approach to warfare, looking for other forms – in general, associated with

---

1   If I were to compare comparisons, I would say that this contrast between two modalities of social
    reproduction in Amazonia bears a striking parallel with the contrast between the Western and Eastern
    Highlands in Papua New Guinea proposed by Godelier (1982) and further developed by Lemmonier
    (1990). One could also observe that the Southern Fringe Highlands and the pretwentieth-century
    South Coast (Knauft 1993) would compare well with the predatory modality of social reproduction
    described in this book.

shamanism – for ensuring social reproduction. On the other hand, there are predominantly centripetal systems that practice systematic offensive warfare, the best known example being the Kayapó.

Among this people, warfare is a mechanism for increasing the stock of wealth, which serves as ceremonial insignias and enable the acquisition of status. The value of such wealth does depend on their foreign origin, but they must be transmitted and ritually confirmed to become socially productive (Turner 1993:62). Moreover, the Kayapó centrifugal drive is limited to this area of the prestige system, excluding nomination that is predominantly centripetal. Although all names can be considered to have an external origin, the system distinguishes those that have been in circulation since time immemorial from those that were more recently acquired.[2] It is the vertical transmission and ceremonial confirmation that adds value to names, a process similar to the flow of kula shells, whose value depends on their beauty and size, but also their antiquity. This inverts the rule of the renown and prestige of the Tupinambá killer, which involved accumulating new enemy names rather than receiving them from an ascendant kinsperson and transmitting them to a descendant.

Centripetal systems are characterized by the greater transmissibility of wealth items and attributes, as well as the greater productivity of the "substitution principle" (Lemonnier 1990). The latter, though, has a lower yield among the Ge (characterized by a local integration in which each village is ideally an autonomous microcosm divided by multiple internal differences) when compared to the Upper Xingu and the Upper Rio Negro (characterized by a regional integration that forms open and potentially unbounded systems). In the Upper Xingu, for example, certain luxury artisanal objects function as a means of payment for services performed by shamans and ritual specialists, to compensate for perceived injuries and even as a form of bridewealth to be paid by the young man when the girl marries after emerging from puberty reclusion during an intertribal ritual.

The existence of objects with a transcontextual value has been described historically for other parts of Amazonia. The most well-known example is the Montaña Central in Peru, organized around the mines of the Cerro de la Sal, the center of a vast trade system controlled by the pre-Andean Arawak and connected to the Pano peoples of the Ucayali (Varese 2002, Santos-Granero 1992). This is probably where the substitution principle reached its maximal point in Amazonia, since the salt cakes produced in fixed sizes apparently functioned as a general exchangeable equivalent for any other object (Renard-Casevitz 1993:34). The similarities between this

2 According to Lea (1986:105), recently acquired names are considered "inauthentically beautiful" because of their origin in dreaming, in contrast to names obtained in mythical times from nonhuman entities.

system, known historically, and the Upper Xingu system, known ethnographically, are noteworthy. Of particular interest is the dynamic of the exchanges, which generates a dense social network founded on the transaction of luxury items and artisanal specialties, on marriage alliances, and on mutual participation in rituals, defining a zone of peace where internecine warfare is prohibited. This complex reappears in other areas, such as the Upper Rio Negro, suggesting that its existence is associated with the presence of Arawak peoples.

Were these systems of regional integration – based on the widespread circulation of goods and persons – hegemonic in the precolonial past? Were centrifugal formations with their cannibal symbolic a marginal phenomenon that only became visible under the colonial gaze and after the destructuring of native social systems? Answering the first question with any certainty is impossible, but the response to the second is clearly negative. Here we simply need to recall the existence of the Tupinambá, one of the examples I used to construct my model of familiarizing predation. With an estimated population of more than a million, they dominated the entire Brazilian coast at the moment of Conquest.

It would be interesting to try to understand what happened in those regions where different social formations bordered each other. Here we can identify a distinction between the centripetal quality of the Ge systems and those of the Xinguano type: Whereas the latter are constituted by the capacity to attract, incorporate, and acculturate enemy peoples as groups (explaining their multilinguistic and pluriethnic nature), the former tend to capture and incorporate isolated members of foreign peoples, dissolving their identities in preexisting internal differences. It remains to investigate, therefore, how these mechanisms for absorbing persons and symbols are distinguished from the movement of familiarizing predation, and what place the latter occupies in the reproduction of centripetal systems. These are questions that I leave for a future work.

Predation and Perspective

Whether internal or external, difference is the motor of life, since without the benefit of alterity "there can be no fertility and no productive capacity" (Overing Kaplan 1996:54). There are different others, though. Human and nonhuman beings are scaled according to their degree of activity or subjectivity, being distinguished in terms of their creative potency, positively associated with ideas such as "autonomy," "ferocity," and "self-awareness" and negatively with "domesticity," "tameness," and "alienation." These oppositions surfaced earlier in this book in Sterpin's analysis of the Nivacle concept of *nitôiya*, where she opposes the captive "unconscious" animal to the "correct" animal, "which 'has consciousness' of what it is" and is therefore both ferocious and wild (Sterpin 1993:59–60). Allow me to rephrase this idea using a less idealist terminology by resorting to the notion of perspective as elaborated by Viveiros de Castro (1998).[3]

In Amazonia, predation is the main mode of determining the point of view in any relation between entities possessing agency and intention, resolving which of the subjects is capable of imposing its own perspective on the other. Vilaça highlights this point in analyzing two categories central to the Wari' people: "[W]ari' is the *subject* position, schematized as the position of a *devourer*; *karawa* is the *object* position, archetypically the position of prey, the *devoured*" (Vilaça 1992:51). Instead of positing a subject-object distinction, though, I would rather say that predation determines an asymmetric relation between two beings that both possess subjectivity. This is why killing game is not enough to reduce it to the condition of food: Additional treatment is needed to desubjectify and turn it into an inert object. Only then can it serve to produce individual bodies and the body of kin. Inversely, in warfare, the victim's subjective condition must be affirmed in order to be appropriated all the more effectively. Warfare and hunting are distinct forms of consumption: The first aims at acquiring principles of subjectification for the production of active persons; the second implies the prior extraction of these same principles to ensure the physical growth of the individual.

The development of the person's reproductive capacities depends on the appropriation of a surplus of agency, which exists in dissimilar degrees in the human and nonhuman world. Generally, this surplus is linked to the predator position and to an alimentary mode: hemato-omophagy. Eating raw bloody meat is the equivalent, in substantialist language, of ontological predation. It involves consuming the activity of the subject not neutralized by fire, in contrast to everyday eating in which all residues of blood need to be extinguished by cooking. This is why cannibalism is defined as omophagy, despite the fact human flesh is always consumed cooked. The same applies to divine cannibalism, such as the Araweté celestial devouring in which the gods are defined as "eaters of raw meat" although they always devour the dead cooked (Viveiros de Castro 1992a:211).

Predation is a subjugating act that determines who possesses the point of view in a relationship. The predator's greater subjective potency allows it to impose its perspective and thereby control the other. Predation establishes a power asymmetry, which is positional and can therefore be reversed, though this possibility of reversion does not imply equivalence and symmetry between the terms of the copula. The asymmetric content of the predatory relationship should not be obscured by the idea that perspectives can be interchanged since they possess the same ontological status. Predation is

3 See also Arhem (1993, 1996), Carneiro da Cunha (1998), and Lima (1999),

a moment in a productive process that aims at mastering other-persons in order to produce new persons at home. The prototypical relation of control in Amerindian societies is not that of master and slave, but that of master and pet, exercised practically in the familiarization of animals and the capture of enemy children. These, however, are no more than particular cases of a much wider relational structure that involves the familiarization of the victim in warfare and animals in shamanism (Fausto 1999).

As Descola (1994) pointed out, there is a close correlation between treatment of the human and nonhuman other, a correlation that he expresses in the form of a structural homology:

> affine : consanguine : : enemy : captive child : : prey : pet

This formula can be generalized as the conversion of predation into familiarization for producing new persons. Substituting the two points of the structural formula with arrows to represent the passing movement between the terms, we have:

affine → consanguine : : enemy → victim's spirit : : prey → familiar spirit
     v   v   v
   kinship   warfare   shamanism

By comparing warfare with shamanism, I am not suggesting that specific prey animals become the shamans' familiar spirits, but that the counterpart of cinegetic predation between humans and nonhumans is the relation of familiarization between shamans and animal spirits. The same applies to warfare: As we have seen, the Parakanã conceive themselves to be establishing a generic relationship with their victims rather than familiarizing specific individual souls.

The movement of familiarizing predation is not a mere identification with the other or simply its negation. The predator negates its prey at the same time as it affirms it, since the predator emerges from the relation as a new person *affected* by the victim's agentive capacities. Several authors have called attention to this transitional period in which the killer turns into the victim. Viveiros de Castro (1992a) explores the idea via the Deleuzian notion of becoming, whereas Taylor employs a more Hegelian language, speaking of the "temporary alienation of Self, its transmutation into the Other in order for it to become fully Self" (1985:160). This "transitory alienation" or "alteration" does not translate as empathy or as an abstract opening to alterity, but rather as a movement of appropriating alien principles of subjectivization. It involves mobilizing the other's perspective as a means of reproducing one's own group, an act that involves a dialectic of control in which the predator risks becoming definitively other.

The risk of alienation that leads to seeing adversaries as friends and kin as enemies is a recurrent theme in indigenous warfare. This clash over perspective is also endemic to shamanism. As we saw, one of the dangers faced by the Parakanã dreamer in his interaction with the *akwawa* is, precisely, to become a "nonperson" (*-awa'y'ym*) by assuming the enemy's point of view. Likewise, the Wari' shaman may become confused in his capacity to interchange points of view, momentarily seeing kin as though they were prey (Vilaça 1992:92–3). Predation does not imply, therefore, a simple negation of the other's perspective and the imposition of one's own. Hence the ambiguity of the shaman and the warrior: At the same time as they control other-persons, they are affected by them. The relation is always ambivalent since the alterity of the other can never be entirely neutralized. Its difference has to be maintained as a condition for a creative action to be extracted from it. Such ambiguity projects the specter of predation onto the inside: The fully controlled, completely alienated, and domesticated other has no use. To remain powerful, shamans and warriors can never entirely control their pets: Rather, they must ensure their subjective condition and run the risk of losing their own.

The Sarcastic Predominance of Matter

The continuance of cannibal systems in the absence of warfare is not difficult to imagine. All such systems possess a degree of flexibility, allowing them to be reproduced in the absence of human victims. Their reproduction does not mean they remain self-identical, but rather that any transformation takes place within a certain limit – a limit that, if surpassed, results in the death of the formation and the emergence of a new one. The problem of exceeding this limit comes to the fore when indigenous societies are definitively inserted in a system whose ontology, structure, and mode of operation are radically different to their own. This is what the Parakanã and other Amerindian people face today, obliging us to pose new questions. The issue is not how mythic thought becomes inserted into history. Historical experience always invaded the context of myth and, at the same time, myth was always sufficiently flexible to absorb new historical facts and act on history. What interests us is the global meaning of the potential transformation of a particular symbolic economy.

The new situation of interethnic contact affects the whole Parakanã perceptive universe, beginning with scale. Until pacification they conceived us to be relatively limited in number and diversity. When I began my research in 1988, four years after permanent contact, the western Parakanã had begun to apprehend this new dimension. When they told me about their encounters with isolated members of the regional nonindigenous population, stretching back two, three, or four decades, they would frequently end by asking me: "Has he died?" or "Didn't he tell you?" or "Was he your kin?" When another white person arrived in the village, they would ask me what our relationship was. And I would reply "I don't know, I've never seen him/her before." Undoubtedly, my reply failed to match the local conception of a relationship. What I presumed to be neutral, the Parakanã presumed to be necessarily qualifiable: Someone is either a kin or an *akwawa*. Yet my reply was also unsatisfactory because the scale of our society was incomprehensible to them: Until their first visits to the city of Altamira, they had never seen more than a dozen non-Indians at any one time. Although there had been frequent contacts, they were unable to apprehend our real number: We were scattered in all directions – and so we must have been numerous – but in concrete interactions we were always in the minority.

Hence the first real shift in scale came with trips to the city of Altamira. This was when they began to realize that we all lived in a different world to the one they had imagined. People were surprised by the amplitude of this "clearing" in the forest and by the number of people living there. My *pajé* Japokatoa, then a restless young man, told me that on seeing so many people in the city he immediately calmed down: "My anger went away," he told me. The closed world of the forest and the village, opened up only through dreams and warfare, was plunged into a universe of unknown limits, entirely peopled by the Toria, who proved to be increasingly diverse: Loggers and anthropologists, Funai workers and river-dwellers, priests and prospectors. The world of gestural interaction gradually gave way to verbal communication: from vision to speech and, very slowly, to writing.

Traditionally, the native system functioned as an *ens incompletum*, unable to ensure its own reproduction without interaction with the outside. However, the new contact situation did not allow a simple permutation of the figures of alterity, a mere adaptation of the cosmology to new figures. In effect, the Parakanã now appear as a part-society (Redfield 1960) within an encompassing national society. Learning about the "great tradition" has become an imperative for political survival and for redefining the hierarchical relations between Indians and whites. Obtaining industrial goods requires more than just "strong talk" or having access to a generous white person: It requires understanding the meaning of money, government, trade, logging, and the politics of identity. It demands knowing their constitutional rights and how to fight for them. They need to memorize the price of a cubic meter of mahogany or a gram of gold and learn about the harm caused by mercury. And there is no turning back, since in a very concrete sense the reproduction of the group depends today on the outside in the form of medicines for flu, pneumonia, hepatitis, and malaria.

A world in which relations were seldom mediated by objects has become definitively immersed in a system of objects whose mechanism lies beyond their control. Until pacification, this system was represented in a limited way by axes, machetes, and some small items acquired sporadically. Now they find themselves faced with an endless variety of tools, motors, pens, watches, T-shirts, torches, cars ... a profusion of objects at once frightening and dazzling, which confirms the power of the whites at the same time as it makes the asymmetry less bearable. Money, whose existence was once unimaginable, emerged as a universal mediator. The Parakanã quickly realized that the philosopher's stone was not the capacity to produce objects, but the capacity to obtain them through an equivalent. The question then became how to acquire money, since everything circulates around it. Comprehending and dominating money became essential to participating in a world of objects. Numerous times in the *tekatawa* or in the classroom, in private or public conversations, I was asked to explain something that even for ourselves always remains somewhat mysterious. It was simpler to teach the value of each note, yet in the early 1990s, the nominal value of the Brazilian currency was voraciously devoured by inflation, and the notes regularly changed their look and name. What object was this that allowed all other objects to be obtained, but which was never in a fixed relation with a determined quantity or quality of objects?

My aim in this work has not been to determine how the Parakanã system is transforming and where it is heading. Perhaps it is too early to reach any conclusion, although it is undoubtedly a good moment to begin looking at it more closely. Yet what about the model I have proposed here? How will a mode for producing persons based on familiarizing predation change? Will it shift to functioning entirely on the plane of dreams and rituals? How does a system centered on the appropriation of alien creative agency become part of a world of objectified objects?

These are questions to which I have no sure answers. Presuming that these processes will involve a simple adaptation of traditional cosmology to new objects and facts would be to foreclose the analytic possibilities from the outset. The transformations of indigenous systems also respond to the structure of the historical process in which they are immersed. And this structure is part of a wider dynamic in which, to quote Marx,

nature becomes purely an object for humankind, purely a matter of utility.... In accord with this tendency, capital drives beyond national barriers and prejudices as much as beyond nature worship, as well as all traditional, confined, complacent, encrusted satisfactions of present needs, and reproductions of old ways of life. It is destructive towards all of this, and constantly revolutionizes it, tearing down all the barriers which hem in the development of the forces of production, the expansion of needs, the all-sided development of production, and the exploitation and exchange of natural and mental forces ([1857] 1973:409–10).

At last the sarcastic predominance of matter. Can it be digested? We must contemplate it, and patience, my friend, will allow us to glimpse the clearest visions.

References

Abbeville, Claude d' 1975 [1614]. *História da Missão dos Padres Capuchinhos na Ilha do Maranhão e Terras Circunvizinhas*. São Paulo: Itatiaia/Edusp.

Agostinho, Pedro 1974. *Kwaríp: Mito e Ritual no Alto Xingu*. São Paulo: epu/Edusp.

Albert, Bruce 1985. Temps du Sang, Temps des Cendres: Représentation de la Maladie, Système Rituel et Espace Politique chez les Yanomami du Sud-Est (Amazonie Brésilienne). Thèse de Doctorat. Paris: Université de Paris-X (Nanterre).

Almeida, Mauro W. B. de 1988. "Dilemas da Razão Prática: Simbolismo, Tecnologia e Ecologia na Floresta Amazônica". *Anuário Antropológico*, 86:213–26.

Anchieta, José de [1554–1594] 1988. *Cartas: Informações, Fragmentos Históricos e Sermões (1554–1594)*. Belo Horizonte: Itatiaia/Edusp.

Andrade, Lucia M. M. de 1992. O Corpo e os Cosmos: Relações de Gênero e o Sobrenatural entre os Asurini do Tocantins. Dissertação de Mestrado. São Paulo: Universidade de São Paulo.

Araújo, Pe. Antonio [1623] 1937. "Informação da Entrada que se pode fazer da Vila de São Paulo ao Grande Pará (...) dada por Pero Domingues, um dos trinta portugueses que da dita vila foram descobrir no ano de 1613 (...)." In: S. Leite, *Páginas de História do Brasil*. São Paulo: Cia. Ed Nacional.

Arhem, Kaj 1993. "Ecosofia Makuna." In: F. Correa (org.), *La Selva Humanizada: Ecología Alternativa en el Trópico Húmedo Colombiano*. Bogotá: Instituto Colombiano de Antropología / Fondo FEN Colombia / Fondo Editorial CEREC. pp. 109–126.

———. 1996. "The Cosmic Food Web: Human-Nature Relatedness in the Northwest Amazon." In: P. Descola and G. Pálsson (orgs.), *Nature and Society. Anthropological Perspectives*. Londres: Routledge. pp. 185–204.

Arnaud, Expedito 1961. "Breve Informação sobre os Índios Asurini e Parakanan, Rio Tocantins, Pará". *Boletim do Museu Paraense Emílio Goeldi* (Antropologia), n.s. 11.

———. 1967. "Grupos Tupi do Tocantins". *Atas do Simpósio sobre a Biota Amazônica* (Antropologia). Vol. 2. pp. 57–68.

Arvelo-Jiménez, Nelly and Biord, Horacio 1994. "The Impact of Conquest on Contemporary Indigenous Peoples of the Guiana Shield: The System of Orinoco Regional Interdependence." In: Anna Roosevelt (ed.), *Amazonian Indians: From Prehistory to the Present*. Tucson, AZ: The University of Arizona Press. pp. 55–78.

Aspelin, Paul 1975. External Articulation and Domestic Production: The Artifact Trade of the Mamaide of Northwestern Mato Grosso, Brazil. Latin American Studies Program Dissertation Series, n° 58. Ithaca, NY: Cornell University.

Ayres, Carneiro, J. R. [1849] 1910. "Intinerário da Viagem da Expedição Exploradora e Colonizadora ao Tocantins em 1849." *Annaes da Bibliotheca e Archivo Publico do Pará*. Vol. VII.

Baena, Monteiro, A.L. 1848. "Respostas dadas ao Exmo. Presidente da Província do Pará sobre a Comunicação Mercantil entre a Dita Província e a de Goyaz." *Revista do Instituto Histórico e Geográphico Brasileiro*, 10: 80–107.

[1829] 1969.*Compêndio das Eras da Província do Pará*. Belém: Universidade Federal do Pará.

Bailey, Robert et al. 1989. "Hunting and Gathering in Tropical Rain Forest: Is It Possible?" *American Anthropologist*, 91:59–82.

Bailey, Robert and Headland, Thomas 1991. "Have Hunter-Gatherers Ever Lived in Tropical Rain Forest Independently of Agriculture?" *Human Ecology*, 19(2):115–286.

Baldus, Herbert 1970. *Os Tapirapé: Tribo Tupi no Brasil Central*. São Paulo: Companhia Editora Nacional.

Balée, William 1984a. The Persistence of Ka'apor Culture. PhD Thesis. New York: Columbia University.

1984b. "The Ecology of Ancient Tupi Warfare." In: R. B. Ferguson (ed.), *Warfare, Culture and Environment*. New York: Academic Press. pp. 241–65.

1985. "Ka'apor Ritual Hunting." *Human Ecology*, 13(4):485–510.

1989. "The Culture of Amazonian Forests". *Advances in Economic Botany*, 7:1–21.

1992. "People of the Fallow: A Historical Ecology of Foraging in Lowland South America." In: K. H. Redford and C. Padoch (eds.), *Conservation of Neotropical Forests: Building on Traditional Resource Use*. New York: Columbia University Press. pp. 35–57.

1994. *Footprints of the Forest: Ka'apor Ethnobotany*. New York: Columbia University Press.

1995. "Historical Ecology of Amazonia." In: L. Sponsel (ed.), *Indigenous Peoples and the Future of Amazonia: An Ecological Anthropology of an Endangered World*. Tucson: University of Arizona Press. pp. 97–110.

Balée, William and Gély, Anne 1989. "Managed Forest Succession in Amazonia: The Ka'apor Case". *Advances in Economic Botany*, 7:129–58.

Balée, William and Moore, Denny 1991. "Similarity and Variation in Plant Names in Five Tupi-Guarani Languages (Eastern Amazonia)". *Bulletin of the Florida Museum of Natural History Biological Sciences*, 35(4):209–62.

Barnard, Alan and Good, Anthony 1984. *Research Practices in the Study of Kinship*. London: Academic Press.

Barth, Fredrik 1987. *Cosmologies in the Making: A Generative Approach to Cultural Variation in Inner New Guinea*. Cambridge: Cambridge University Press.

Basso, Ellen 1988. *The Kalapalo Indians of Central Brazil*. Prospect Heights, IL: Waveland Press.

1987. "The Implication of a Progressive Theory of Dreaming." In: B. Tedlock (ed.), *Dreaming: Anthropological and Psychological Interpretations*. Cambridge: Cambridge University Press. pp. 86–104.

1995. *The Last Cannibals: A South American Oral History*. Austin: University of Texas Press.

Bateson, Gregory 1972. *Steps to an Ecology of Mind: Collected Essays in Anthropology, Psychiatry, Evolution, and Epistemology*. Ballantine Books.

Beckerman, Stephen J. 1987. "Swidden in Amazonia and the Amazon River." In: B. L. Turner II and S. B. Brush (ed.), *Comparative Farming Systems*. New York: The Guilford Press. pp. 55–96.

1980. "Fishing and Hunting by the Bari of Colombia." In: R. Hames (ed.), *Working Papers of South American Indians*, vol. 2. Bennington, Vermont: Bennington College. pp. 67–111.

1994. "Hunting and Fishing in Amazonia: Hold the Answers, What are the Questions?" In: A. Roosevelt (ed.), *Amazonians Indians from Prehistory to the Present*. Tucson: The University of Arizona Press. pp. 177–200.

Bergman, R. W. 1980. *Amazon Economics: The Simplicity of Shipibo Indian Wealth.* Dellplain Latin American Studies 6. Syracuse, NY: Syracuse University Department of Geography.

Berlin, Brent and Berlin, Ann 1980. "Adaptation and Ethnozoological Classification: Theoretical Implications of Animal Resources and Diet of the Aguaruna and Huambisa." In: R. Hames and W. Vickers (eds.), *Adaptative Responses of Native Amazonians.* New York: Academic Press. pp. 301–25.

Berredo, Bernardo Pereira de [1718] 1849. *Annaes Históricos do Estado do Maranhão, em que se dá Noticia de seu Descobrimento, e Tudo o Mais que Nelle tem Succedido desde o Anno em que Foy Descuberto até o de 1718.* 2ª Edição. Maranhão: Typographia Maranhense.

Betendorf, João Filippe [1698] 1910. *Chronica da Missão dos Padres da Companhia de Jesus no Estado do Maranhão.* Rio de Janeiro.

Betts, La Vera 1981. *Dicionário Parintintín–Português / Português–Parintintín.* Brasília: Summer Institute of Linguistics.

Boomert, A. 1987. "Gifts of the Amazon: 'Green Stones' Pendants and Beads as Items of Ceremonial Exchange in Amazonia and the Caribbean." *Antropologica,* 67:33–55.

Boster, James S. 1986. "Exchange of Varieties and Information between Aguaruna Manioc Cultivators." *American Anthropologist,* 88(2):428–35.

Boudin, Max 1966. *Dicionário de Tupi Moderno (Dialeto Tembé-Ténêtéhara do Alto do Rio Gurupi).* São Paulo: Faculdade de Filosofia, Ciências e Letras de Presidente Prudente.

Bourdieu, Pierre 1972. "Esquisse d'une Théorie de la Pratique." In: P. Bourdieu, *Esquisse d'une Théorie de la Pratique (précédé de trois études d'ethnologie kabyle).* Genève: Librairie Droz. pp. 154–267.

1980. *Le Sens Pratique. Le Sens Commun.* Paris: Minuit.

Boyer, Pascal 1994. *The Naturalness of Religious Ideas.* Berkeley: University of California Press.

Buscaglioni, Luigi 1901. *Una Escursione Botanica nell'Amazzonia.* Roma. Societá Geográfica Italiana.

Butt-Colson, Audrey 1973. "Inter-tribal Trade in the Guiana Highlands." *Antropologica,* 34:5–69.

Cadogan, Leon 1959. *Ayvu Rapyta: Textos Míticos de los Mbyá-Guarani del Guaira.* Faculdade de Filosofia, Letras e Ciências Humanas da Universidade de São Paulo, Boletim 227, Antropologia 5. São Paulo: Universidade de São Paulo.

1965. "En Torno al Bai-ete-ri-va Guayakí y el Concepto Guaraní de Nombre". *Suplemento Antropológico de la Revista del Ateneo Paraguayo,* 1:3–13.

1966. "Animal and Plant Cults in Guarani Lore". *Revista de Antropologia,* 14:105–24.

1968. "Chonó Kybwyrá: Aves y Almas en la Mitología Guaraní". *Revista de Antropologia,* 15–16: 133–147.

Carneiro, Robert 1973. "Slash-and-Burn Cultivation among the Kuikuru Indians and its Implications for Cultural Development in the Amazon Basin." In: D. Gross (ed.), *Peoples and Cultures of Native South America.* Garden City, NY: Doubleday. pp. 98–123.

1979. "Factors Favoring the Development of Political Leadership in Amazonia". *El Dorado,* 4:86–94.

1994. "Kuikuru." In: Johannes Wilbert (ed.), *Encyclopedia of World Cultures.* Vol. VII. Boston, Ms: G.K. Hall and Co. pp. 206–209.

1995. "The History of Ecological Interpretations of Amazonia: Does Rooosevelt have it Right?" In: L. Sponsel (ed.), *Indigenous Peoples and the Future of Amazonia: An Ecological Anthropology of an Endangered World.* Tucson: University of Arizona Press. pp. 45–70.

Carneiro da Cunha, M. Manuela 1978. *Os Mortos e os Outros: Uma Análise do Sistema Funerário e da Noção de Pessoa entre os Indios Krahó.* São Paulo: Hucitec.

1996. "Da Guerra das Relíquias ao Quinto Império: Importação e Exportação da História no Brasil". *Novos Estudos do CEBRAP*, 44:73–87.

1998. "Pontos de Vista sobre a Floresta Amazônica: Xamanismo e Tradução". *Mana: Estudos de Antropologia Social*, 4(1):7–22.

Eduardo Viveiros de Castro 1985. "Vingança e Temporalidade: os Tupinambás". *Journal de la Société des Américanistes*, LXXI:191–217.

Chagnon, Napoleon 1968. "Yanomamö Social Organization and Warfare." In: M. Fried, M. Harris, and R. Murphy (eds.), *War: the Anthropology of Armed Conflict and Aggression*. New York: Doubleday. pp. 109–159.

1973. "The Culture-Ecology of Shifting (Pioneering) Cultivation among the Yanomamö Indians." In: D. Gross (ed.), *Peoples and Cultures of Native South America*. Graden City, NY: Doubleday. pp. 126–42.

1992. *Yanomamö*. New York: Harcourt Brace College Publishers (4th Edition).

Chaumeil, Jean-Pierre 1983. *Voir, Savoir, Pouvoir: Le Chamanisme chez les Yagua du Nord-Est Péruvien*. Paris: École des Hautes Etudes en Sciences Sociales.

1985. "L'Échange d'Énergie: Guerre, Identité et Reproduction Sociale chez les Yagua de l'Amazonie Péruvienne". *Journal de la Société des Américanistes*, LXXI:143–57.

Clastres, Hélène 1975. *La Terre Sans Mal: Le Prophétisme Tupi-Guarani*. Paris: Seuil.

1985. "Introduction." In: Évreux, Yves d' [1613] 1985. *Voyage au Nord du Brésil: Fait en 1613 et 1614*. Paris: Payot. pp. 9–21.

Clastres, Pierre 1972. *Chronique des Indiens Guayaki*. Paris: Plon.

1978. *A Sociedade contra o Estado*. Rio de Janeiro: Francisco Alves.

1982. *Arqueologia da Violência: Ensaios de Antropologia Política*. São Paulo: Brasiliense.

Clendinnen, Inga 1991. *Aztecs: An Interpretation*. Cambridge: Cambridge University Press.

Collier, Jane F. and Michelle Z. Rosaldo 1981. "Politics and Gender in Simple Societies." In: S. Ortner and H. Whitehead (eds.), *Sexual Meanings*. Cambridge: Cambridge University Press. pp. 275–329.

Collier, Jane and Yanagisako, Sylvia 1987. "Toward a Unified Analysis of Kinship and Gender." In: J. Collier and S. Yanagisako (eds.), *Kinship and Gender: Essays Toward a Unified Analysis*. Stanford: Stanford University Press. pp. 14–50.

Combés, Isabelle 1992. *La Tragédie Cannibale chez les Anciens Tupi-Guarani*. Paris: Presses Universitaires de France.

Conklin, Beth 1989. Images of Health, Illness and Death among the Wari' (Pakaas-Novos) of Rondonia, Brazil. PhD Dissertation. San Francisco, CA: University of California.

Coudreau, Henri 1897. *Voyage au Tocantins-Araguaya*. Paris: A. Lahure.

Crocker, Jon Christopher 1985. *Vital Soul: Bororo Cosmology, Natural Symbolism, and Shamanism*. Tucson: University of Arizona Press.

Dal Poz, João 1991. *No País dos Cinta Larga: uma Etnografia do Ritual*. Dissertação de Mestrado. São Paulo: Universidade de São Paulo.

DaMatta, Roberto 1970. "Mito e Antimito entre os Timbira". In: Lévi-Strauss et al. *Mito e Linguagem Social. Ensaios de Antropologia Estrutural*. Rio de Janeiro: Tempo Brasileiro. pp. 77–106.

1976a. *Um Mundo Dividido: A Estrutura Social dos Apinayé*. Petrópolis: Vozes.

1976b. "Uma Reconsideração da Morfologia Social Apinayé". In: E. Schaden (ed.), *Leituras de Etnologia Brasileira*. São Paulo: Cia. Editora Nacional. pp.149–63.

Daniel, João [1776] 1976. *Tesouro Descoberto no Rio Amazonas* (2 vols). Rio de Janeiro: Biblioteca Nacional.

Davis, Shelton 1978. *Vítimas do Milagre: O Desenvolvimento e os Índios do Brasil*. Rio de Janeiro: Zahar Editores.

Descola, Philippe 1986. *La Nature Domestique: Symbolisme et Praxis dans L'Écologie des Achuar*. Paris: Maison des Sciences de L'Homme.

1992. "Societies of Nature and the Nature of Society." In: A. Kuper (org.), *Conceptualizing Society.* Londres: Routledge. pp. 107–26.

1993. *Les Lances du Crépuscule: Relation Jivaros.* Haute Amazonie. Paris: Plon.

1994. "Pourquoi les Indiens d'Amazonie n'ont-ils pas Domestiqué le Pécari? Généalogie des Objets et Anthropologie de l'Objectivation." In: B. Latour and P. Lemonnier (eds.), *De la Préhistoire aux Missiles Balistiques: L'Intelligence Sociale des Techniques.* Paris: La Découverte. pp. 329–44.

1996. "Constructing Natures: Symbolic Ecology and Social Practice." In: P. Descola and G. Pálsson (eds.), *Nature and Society. Anthropological Perspectives.* Londres: Routledge. pp. 82–102.

Dreyfus, Simone 1993. "Os Empreendimentos Coloniais e os Espaços Políticos Indígenas no Interior da Guiana Ocidental (entre o Orenoco e o Corentino) de 1613 a 1796." In: E. Viveiros de Castro and M. Carneiro da Cunha (orgs.), *Amazônia: Etnologia e História Indígena.* São Paulo: NHII-USP / Fapesp. pp. 19–42.

Dumont, Louis 1983. "Stocktaking 1981: Affinity as a Value." In: *Affinity as a Value: Marriage Alliance in South India, with Comparative Essays in Australia.* Chicago: The University of Chicago Press. pp. 145–214.

Eisenberg, John F. 1989. *Mammals of the Neotropics. The Northern Neotropics.* Vol 1. Chicago: The University of Chicago Press.

Emídio-Silva, Claudio 1998. A Caça de Subsistência Praticada pelos Índios Parakanã (Sudeste do Pará): Características e Sustentabilidade. Dissertação de Mestrado. Belém: Universidade Federal do Pará.

Emmons, Louise 1990. *Neotropical Rainforest Mammals.* Chicago: The University of Chicago Press.

Erikson, Philippe 1987. "De l'Apprivoisement à l'Approvisionnement: Chasse, Alliance et Familiarisation en Amazonie Amérindienne". *Techniques et Cultures,* 9:105–40.

1986. "Alterité, Tatouage et Anthropophagie chez les Pano: la Belliqueuse Quête de Soi". *Journal de la Société des Américanistes,* LXII:185–210.

1996. *La Griffes des Aïeux: Marquage du Corps et Démarquages Ethniques chez les Matis d'Amazonie.* Paris: Peeters.

Évreux, Yves d' [1613] 1985. *Voyage au Nord du Brésil: fait en 1613 et 1614.* Paris: Payot.

Fausto, Carlos 1991. Os Parakanã: Casamento Avuncular e Dravidianato na Amazônia. Dissertação de Mestrado. Rio de Janeiro: PPGAS/Museu Nacional/UFRJ.

1992. "Fragmentos de História e Cultura Tupinambá: Da Etnologia como Instrumento Crítico de Conhecimento Etnohistórico." In: M.Carneiro da Cunha (ed.), *História dos Índios no Brasil.* São Paulo: Fapesp/Companhia das Letras/SMC. pp. 381–96.

1995. "De Primos e Sobrinhas: Terminologia e Aliança entre os Parakanã (Tupi) do Pará". In: E. B. Viveiros de Castro (ed.), *Estruturas Sociais Ameríndias: Os Sistemas de Parentesco.* Rio de Janeiro: Editora da UFRJ. pp. 61–119.

1996. História, Subsistência, Contato e Expoliação dos Parakanã da T.I. Apyterewa. Relatório do Grupo Técnico para Estudos Complementares sobre a T.I. Apyterewa. Rio de Janeiro: Funai.

1997. A Dialética da Predação e da Familiarização entre os Parakanã da Amazônia Oriental: Por uma Teoria da Guerra Ameríndia. Tese de Doutorado. Rio de Janeiro: PPGAS, Museu Nacional, UFRJ.

1999a. "Cinco Séculos de Carne de Vaca: Antropofagia Literal e Antropofagia Literária". *Nuevo Texto Crítico,* 23/24:73–80.

1999. "Of Enemies and Pets: Warfare and Shamanism in Amazonia", *American Ethnologist,* 26(4):933–56.

2001. *Inimigos Fiéis : História, Guerra e Xamanismo na Amazônia.* São Paulo, SP, Brasil: Edusp.

2002a. "Faire le Mythe: Histoire, Récit et Transformation en Amazonie". *Journal de la Société des Américanistes*, 88:69–90.

2002b. "The Bones Affair: Knowledge Practices in Contact Situations Seen from an Amazonian Case". *Journal of the Royal Anthropological Institute*, 8(4):669–90.

2004. "A Blend of Blood and Tobacco: Shamans and Jaguars among the Parakanã of Eastern Amazonia." In: N. Whitehead and R. Wright (eds.), *In Darkness and Secrecy: The Anthropology of Assault Sorcery and Witchcraft in Amazonia*. Chapell Hill, NC: Duke University Press. pp. 157–78.

2007a. "Feasting on People: Cannibalism and Commensality in Amazonia". *Current Anthropology* 48(4):497–530.

2007b. "If God Were a Jaguar: Cannibalism and Christianity among the Guarani (XVI-XX Centuries)." In: C. Fausto and M. J. Heckenberger, *Time and Memory in Indigenous Amazonia: Anthropological Perspectives*. Gainsville, FL: University Presses of Florida. pp. 74–105.

2008. "Donos Demais: Maestria e Propriedade na Amazônia". *Mana: Estudos de Antropologia Social*, 14(2):280–324.

2011a. "Le Masque de l'Animiste: Chimères et Poupées Russes en Amérique Indigène". *Gradhiva*, 13:49–67.

2011b. "Mil años de Transformación: La Cultura de la Tradición entre los Kuikuro del Alto Xingú". In: Jean-Pierre Chaumeil y Oscar Espinosa. *Por donde hay soplo*. Lima, Peru: IFEA-PUCP.

In press. "The Friend, the Enemy and the Anthropologist: Hostility and Hospitality among the Parakanã (Amazonia, Brazil)". *Journal of the Royal Anthropological Institute*.

Fausto, Carlos and Michael J. Heckenberger 2007. "Introduction: Indigenous History and the History of the 'Indians'." In: C. Fausto and M. J. Heckenberger, *Time and Memory in Indigenous Amazonia: Anthropological Perspectives*. Gainsville, FL: University Press of Florida. pp. 1–46.

Bruna Franchetto et Tommaso Montagnani 2011. "Art Verbal et Musique chez les Kuikuro du Haut Xingu (Brésil)". *L'Homme*, 197:41–69.

et Isabel Penoni. In press. "La Représentation de l'Humain en Amazonie : Les Effigies Rituelles chez les Kuikuro du Haut Xingu". In: Carlo Severi et Carlo Fausto, *L'Image Rituelle: Agentivité et Mémoire*. Cahiers d'Anthropologie Sociale. Paris, France.

Fausto, Ruy 1987. *Marx: Lógica e Política*. tomo 2. São Paulo: Brasiliense.

Ferguson, R. Brian 1989. "Game Wars? Ecology and Conflict in Amazonia". *Journal of Anthropological Research*, 45(2):179–206.

1990. "Blood of the Leviathan: Western Contact and Amazonian Warfare". *American Ethnologist*, 17:237–57.

1995. *Yanomami Warfare: A Political History*. Santa Fé: School of American Research Press.

Ferguson, Brian R. and Neil L. Whitehead 1992. *War in the Tribal Zone: Expanding States and Indigenous Warfare*. Santa Fé, New Mexico: School of American Research Press.

Fernandes, Florestan 1963. *A Organização Social dos Tupinambás*. São Paulo: difel.

1970. *A Função Social da Guerra na Sociedade Tupinambá*. São Paulo: Pioneira/Edusp.

Fisher, William 1991. Dualism and its Discontents: Social Process and Village Fissioning among the Xicrin-Kaiapo of Central Brazil. PhD Thesis. Ithaca, NY: Cornell University.

Fortes, Meyer 1978. "An Antropologist's Apprenticeship." *Annual Review of Anthropology*, 7:1–30.

Franchetto, Bruna and Michael J. Heckenberger. 2001. *Os Povos do Alto Xingu: História e Cultura*. Rio de Janeiro: Ed. UFRJ.

Frisch, J. Dalgas 1981. *Aves Brasileiras*. Vol. 1. São Paulo: Dalgas-Ecoltec.

Funai. 1971a. Relatório Anual das Atividades da Base de Pucuruí de 14/09/70 a 17/01/71. Cel. Clodomiro Bloise, Delegado Especial da Base de Pucuruí. São Paulo: Instituto Socioambiental.

1971b. Relatório das Atividades da Base de Pucuruí de 17/01/71 a 20/03/71. Cel. Clodomiro Bloise, Delegado Especial da Base de Pucuruí. São Paulo: Instituto Socioambiental.

1971c. Relatório do Primeiro Contato e Pernoite na Aldeia dos Parakanãs em 30/03/71. Cel. Clodomiro Bloise, Delegado Especial da Base de Pucuruí. São Paulo: Instituto Socioambiental.

1971d. Relatório da Concretização da Pacificação dos Índios Parakanã (julho de 1971). Cel. Clodomiro Bloise, Delegado Especial da Base de Pucuruí. Brasília: Funai – Setor de Documentação.

1971e. Cópia do Relatório do Sertanista João Evangelista Carvalho sobre as atividades e a situação dos Índios Parakanan e da Frente Especial de Penetração. 20/11/70 a 21/02/71. São Paulo: Instituto Socioambiental.

1971f. Cópia Fiel do Diário Pertencente ao Sertanista João Evangelista de Carvalho da Frente de Penetração nº 1, Índios Parakanã. 27/05/71 a 30/06/71. São Paulo: Instituto Socioambiental.

1971g. Cópia Fiel do Diário Pertencente ao Sertanista João Evangelista de Carvalho da Frente de Penetração nº 1, Índios Parakanã. 01/07/71 a 07/10/71. São Paulo: Instituto Socioambiental.

1971h. Relatório de Lauro Menescal de Souza, Atendente da Base Pucuruí, sobre Saída de Parakanãs na Vila de Repartimento (09/09/71). Brasília: Funai – Setor de Documentação.

1971i. Relatório quanto a Ocorrências com os Índios Parakanan. (24/10/71). Cel. Clodomiro Bloise, Delegado Especial da Base de Pucuruí. Brasília: Funai – Setor de Documentação.

1978. Relatório da Frente de Atração Parakanã Ipixuna. João Evangelista Carvalho, 21/03/78. Brasília: Funai – Setor de Documentação.

1982. Relatório de Viagem de Reconhecimento ao Grupo Indígena Arredio que Atacou a Fazenda Castanhal no Igarapé São José, rio Xingu. Fiorello Parise. São Paulo: Instituto Socioambiental.

1983a. Relatório de Atividade da Frente de Atração Parakanã, dezembro de 1982 a março de 1983. Fiorello Parise. São Paulo: Instituto Socioambiental.

1983b. Expedição Parakanã. Sydney Possuelo, 13/09/83. Brasília: Funai – Setor de Documentação.

1984. Relatório de Atividades da Equipe Volante de Saúde (EVS). Dr. Roberto Madeiro. Belém: Funai – 4ª SUER.

1988. Relatório Conclusivo sobre a Retirada de Madeira nas Áreas Indígenas Apyterewa, Araweté do Igarapé Ipixuna e na Área Pretendida Denominada Xingu/Bacajá, 19/11/1988. Antonio Pereira Neto, titular da ADR Altamira. Altamira: Funai.

1995. Relatório sobre a Invasão da AI Apyterewa, 05/01/95. Walter Coutinho. Brasília: Funai.

e CEDI. 1993. Avaliação de Danos Causados pela Exploração Madeireira nas Áreas Indígenas Araweté/Igarapé Ipixuna, Apyterewa e Trincheira Bacajá (Pará). São Paulo: Instituto Socioambiental.

Gallois, Dominique T. 1988. O Movimento na Cosmologia Waiãpi: Criação, Expansão e Transformação do Mundo. Tese de Doutorado. São Paulo: Universidade de São Paulo.

1996. "Xamanismo Waiãpi: Nos Caminhos Invisíveis, a Relação I-Paie." In: J. Langdon, Xamanismo no Brasil: Nova Perspectivas. Florianópolis: UFSC. pp 39–74.

Gandavo, Pero de Magalhães [1576] 1980. *Tratado da Terra do Brasil/História da Província de Santa Cruz*, Belo Horizonte: Itatiaia/Edusp.

Gell, Alfred 1998. *Art and Agency: An Anthropological Theory*. Oxford: Clarendon Press.

Gellner, Ernest 1988. *Plough, Sword and Book: The Structure of Human History*. Chicago: The University of Chicago Press.

Godelier, Maurice 1982. *La Prodution des Grands Hommes*. Paris: Fayard.

Gonçalves, Marco Antonio 1993. *O Significado do Nome: Cosmologia e Nominação entre os Pirahã*. Rio de Janeiro: Sette Letras.

Good, Kenneth 1995a. "The Yanomami Keep on Trekking." *Natural History*, 4:57–65.

1995b. "Yanomami of Venezuela: Foragers or Farmers — Which Came First?" In: L. E. Sponsel (ed.), *Indigenous Peoples and the Future of Amazonia: An Ecological Anthropology of an Endangered World*. Tucson: University of Arizona Press. pp. 113–120.

Gow, Peter 1989. "The Perverse Child: Desire in a Native Amazonian Subsistence Economy." *Man*, 24(4):567–82.

1991. *Of Mixed Blood: Kinship and History in Peruvian Amazonia*. Oxford: Clarendon Press.

Graham, Laura R. 1993. "A Public Sphere in Amazonia? The Depersonalized Collaborative Construction of Discourse in Xavante." *American Ethnologist*, 20(4):717–41.

1995. *Performing Dreams: Discourses of Immortality among the Xavante of Central Brazil*. Austin: University of Texas.

Gregor, Thomas 1977. *Mehinaku: The Drama of Daily Life in a Brazilian Indian Village*. Chicago: The University of Chicago Press.

1990. "Uneasy Peace: Intertribal Relations in Brazil's Upper Xingu." In: J. Haas (ed.), *The Anthropology of War*. Cambridge: Cambridge University Press. pp. 105–124.

Gregory, Chris 1982. *Gifts and Commodities*. London: Academic Press.

Grenand, Françoise 1982. *Et l'Homme Devint Jaguar*. Paris: L'Harmattan.

1989. *Dictionnaire Wayãpi-Français*. Paris: Peeters/SELAF.

Grenand, Pierre 1980. *Introduction à L'Étude de L'Univers Wayãpi: Ethno-écologie des Indiens du Haut-Oyapock (Guyane Française)*. Paris: SELAF/CNRS.

1982. *Ainsi Parlaient nos Ancêtres: Essai D'Etnohistoire Wayãpi*. Paris: ORSTOM.

Gross, Daniel 1975. "Protein Capture and Cultural Development in the Amazon Basin." *American Anthropologist*, 77(3):526–49.

Grünberg, Georg 1970. "Beiträge zur Ethnographie der Kayabizentralbrasiliens". *Archiv fur Volkerkunde*, 24. Viena.

Hallpike, C. R. 1973. "Functionalist Interpretations of Primitive Warfare." *Man*, 8(3):451–70.

Hames, Raymond 1983. "The Settlement Pattern of a Yanomamo Population Bloc: a Behavioral Ecological Interpretation." In: R. Hames and W. Vickers (eds.), *Adaptative Responses of Native Amazonians*. New York: Academic Press. pp. 393–427.

Harrison, Simon 1993. *The Mask of War: Violence, Ritual and the Self in Melanesia*. Manchester: Manchester University Press.

Hawkes, Kristen ; Hill, Kim and O'Connel, James 1982. "Why Hunters Gather: Optimal Foraging and the Aché of Eastern Paraguay". *American Ethnologist*, 9(2):379–98.

Headland, Thomas 1987. "The Wild Yam Question: How Well Could Independent Hunter-Gatherers Live in a Tropical Rain Forest Ecosystem?. *Human Ecology*, 15:463–91.

Heckenberger, Michael J. 1996. War and Peace in the Shadow of Empire: Sociopolitical Change in the Upper Xingu of Southeastern Amazonia, A.D. 1250–2000. PhD Thesis. University of Pittsburgh.

1998. "Manioc Agriculture and Sedentism in Amazonia: The Upper Xingu Example", *Antiquity*, 72(277):633–48.

Petersen, James B. and Neves, Eduardo G. 1999. "Village Size and Permanence in Amazonia: Two Archeological Examples from Brazil", *Latin American Antiquity*, 10(4): 353–76.

Heider, Karl 1991. *Grand Valley Dani: Peaceful Warriors*. Fort Worth: Holt, Rinehart and Winston.

Hemming, John 1987a. *Red Gold: The Conquest of the Brazilian Indians, 1500–1760*. Cambridge: Harvard University Press.

1987b. *Amazon Frontier: The Defeat of the Brazilian Indians*. London: MacMillan.

Henry, Jules 1964 [1941]. *Jungle People: A Kaingang Tribe of the Highlands of Brazil*. New York: Vintage Book. [2nd edition].

Hill, Jonathan D. 1996. "Ethnogenesis in the Northwest Amazon: An Emerging Regional Picture." In J. D. Hill (ed.), *History, Power, and Identity: Ethnogenesis in the Americas, 1492–1992*. Iowa City: University of Iowa Press. pp. 142–60.

Hill, Kim and Hawkes, Kristen 1983. "Neotropical Hunting among the Ache of Eastern Paraguay." In: R. Hames and W. Vickers, *Adaptative Responses of Native Amazonians*. New York: Academic Press. pp. 113–35.

Holmberg, Allan 1969. *Nomads of the Long Bow: the Siriono of Eastern Bolivia*. Garden City, NY: Natural History Press.

Houseman, Michael and Carlo Severi 1998. *Naven, or the Other Self, A Relational Approach to Ritual Action*. Leiden: J.Brill.

Hugh-Jones, Stephen 1988. "The Gun and the Bow: Myths of White Men and Indians". *L'Homme* 106–107, XXVIII(1–3):138–55.

1994. "Shamans, prophets, priests and pastors." In: C. Humphrey and N. Thomas (eds.), *Shamanism, History, and the State*. Ann Arbor: University of Michigan Press.

1996. "Bonnes Raisons ou Mauvaise Conscience? De l'Ambivalence de Certains Amazoniens envers la Consommation de Viande". *Terrains*, 26:123–48.

Humphrey, Caroline and Hugh-Jones, Stephen (eds.) 1992. *Barter, Exchange and Value: An Anthropological Approach*. Cambridge: Cambridge University Press.

Inspetoria Federal de Estradas 1937. Carta do Inspetor da Estrada de Ferro de Bragança, Virgínio Santa Rosa, ao Inspector Regional do Serviço de Proteção aos Índios. Belém.

Ireland, Emilienne 1988. "Cerebral Savage: the Whiteman as Symbol of Cleverness and Savagery in Waurá Myth" In: J. D. Hill (ed.), *Rethinking History and Myth: Indigenous South American Perspectives on the Past*. Chicago: University of Illinois Press. pp. 157–173.

Jensen, Allen Arthur 1988. *Sistemas Indígenas de Classificação de Aves: Aspectos Comparativos, Ecológicos e Evolutivos*. Coleção Eduardo Galvão. Belém: Museu Paraense Emílio Goeldi.

Johnson, Allen 1983. "Machiguenga Gardens." In: R. Hames and W. Vickers (eds.), *Adaptative Responses of Native Amazonians*. New York: Academic Press. pp. 29–63.

Journet, Nicolas 1995. *La Paix des Jardins: Structures Sociales des Indiens Curripaco du Haut Rio Negro (Colombie)*. Paris: Institut d'Ethnologie, Musée de L'Homme.

Kelly, Raymond 1993. *Constructing Inequality: The Fabrication of a Hierarchy of Virtue among the Etoro*. Ann Arbor: University of Michigan Press.

Kent, Susan 1989 . "Cross-cultural Perceptions of Farmers as Hunters and the Value of Meat." In: S. Kent (ed.), *Farmers and Hunters: The Implications of Sedentism*. Cambridge: Cambridge University Press.

Knauft, Bruce 1990. "Melanesian Warfare: a Theoretical History." *Oceania*, 60(4): 250–311.

1993. *South Coast New Guinea Cultures*. Cambridge: Cambrige University Press.

Koch, Klaus-Friedrich 1974. *War and Peace in Jalemo: The Management of Conflitct in Highland New Guinea*. Cambridge, MA: Harvard University Press.

Kracke, Waud 1978. *Force and Persuasion: Leadership in an Amazonian Society.* Chicago: Chicago University Press.

1984. "Kagwahiv Moieties: Form without Function?" In: K. Kensinger (ed.), *Marriage Practices in Lowland South America.* Urbana: University of Illinois Press. pp. 99–124.

1987. "Myths in Dreams, Thoughts in Images: An Amazonian Contribution to the Psychoanalytic of Primary Process." In: B. Tedlock (ed.), *Dreaming: Anthropological and Psychological Interpretations.* Cambridge: Cambridge University Press. pp. 31–54.

1990. "El Sueño como Vehículo del Poder Shamánico: Interpretaciones Culturales y Significados Personales de los Sueños entre los Parintintin." In: M. Perrin (ed.), *Antropologia y Experiencias del Sueño.* Quito: ABYA-YALA/MLAL. pp. 145–58.

La Condamine, Charles-Marie de [1745] 1992. *Viagem pelo Amazonas 1735–1745.* Rio de Janeiro: Nova Fronteira/Edusp.

Ladeira, Maria Elisa 1982. A Troca de Nomes e a Troca de Cônjuges: uma Contribuição ao Estudo do Parentesco Timbira. Dissertação de Mestrado. Universidade de São Paulo.

Lakoff, George 1987. *Women, Fire, and Dangerous Things: What Categories Reveal about the Mind.* Chicago: The University of Chicago Press.

Langness, L. L. 1972. "Political Organization." In: Peter Sack (ed.), *Encyclopaedia of Papua New Guinea.* Melbourne: Melbourne University Pess. pp. 922–35.

Laraia, Roque de Barros 1986. *Tupi: Índios do Brasil Atual.* São Paulo: FFLCH-USP.

Laraia, Roque de B. and DaMatta, Roberto 1967. *Índios e Castanheiros: A Empresa Extrativa e os Índios no Médio Tocantins.* São Paulo: Difel.

Lathrap, Donald 1968. "The 'Hunting' Economies of the Tropical Forest Zone of the South America: an Attempt at Historical Perspective." In: B. Lee and I. DeVore, *Man the Hunter.* Chicago: Aldine. pp. 23–9.

1970. *The Upper Amazon.* New York: Praeger.

1973. "The Antiquity and Importance of Long-Distance Trade Relationships in the Moist Tropics of Pre-Columbian South America". *World Archaeology*, 5:170–86.

Layton, Robert, Foley, Robert and Williams, Elizabeth 1991. "The Transition Between Hunting and Gathering and the Specialized Husbandry of Resources: A Socio-Ecological Approach." *Current Anthropology* 32(3):255–63.

Lea, Vanessa 1986. Nomes e Nekrets Kayapó: uma Concepção de Riqueza. Tese de Doutorado. Rio de Janeiro: PPGAS/Museu Nacional/UFRJ.

1992. "Mebengokre (Kayapó) Onomastics: A Facet of Houses as Total Social Facts in Central Brazil". *Man*, 27:129–53.

Lefort, Claude 1983. *A Invenção Democrática: Os Limites da Dominação Totalitária.* São Paulo: Brasiliense.

1987. "L'Oeuvre de Clastres." In: M. Abensour (ed.), *L'Ésprit des Lois Sauvages: Pierre Clastres ou une Nouvelle Anthropologie Politique.* Paris: Seuil. pp. 183–209.

Leite, Serafim 1943. *História da Companhia de Jesus.* Vol.III. Rio de Janeiro: Imprensa Nacional.

Lemmonier, Pierre 1990. *Guerre et Festins: Paix, Échanges et Compétition dans les Highlands de Nouvelle-Guinée.* Paris: Maison des Sciences de L'Homme.

Léry, Jean de [1578] 1980. *Viagem à Terra do Brasil.* Belo Horizonte: Itatiaia/Edusp.

Lévi-Strauss, Claude [1942] 1976. "Guerra e Comércio entre os Índios da América do Sul." In: E. Schaden (ed.), *Leituras de Etnologia Brasileira.* São Paulo: Companhia Editora Nacional. pp. 325–39.

1948a. "The Tupi-Cawahíb." In: J. Steward (ed.), *Handbook of South American Indians.* Vol. 3. Washington: Smithsonian Institution/Bureau of American Ethnology, Bulletin 143. pp. 299–305.

1948b. "Tribes of the Right Bank of the Guaporé River." In: J. Steward (ed.), *Handbook of South American Indians*. Vol. 3. Washington: Smithsonian Institution/Bureau of American Ethnology, Bulletin 143. pp. 371–80.

1955. *Tristes Tropiques*. Paris: Plon.

[1958]1974. "La Notion d'Archaïsme en Ethnologie." In: *Anthropologie structurale*. Paris: Plon. [2éme édition].

1960. "Introduction à l'Œuvre de Marcel Mauss." In: M. Maus, *Sociologie et Anthropologie*. Paris: PUF. pp. IX–LII.

1964. *Mythologiques I: Le Cru et le Cuit*. Paris: Plon.

1984. "Cannibalisme et Travestissement Rituel (année 1974–1975)." In: *Paroles Donnés*. Paris: Plon. pp. 141–50.

1991. *Histoire de Lynx*. Paris: Plon.

Lima, Tânia Stolze 1995. A Parte do Cauim. Etnografia Juruna. Tese de Doutorado. Rio de Janeiro: PPGAS/Museu Nacional/UFRJ.

1999. The Two and its Many. Reflections on Perspectivism in a Tupi Cosmology. *Ethnos* 64(1):107–31.

Lizot, Jacques 1989. "A Propos de la Guerre. Une réponse à N.A.Chagnon". *Journal de la Société des Américanistes*, LXXV:91–113.

1996. "Sang et Statut des Homicides Chez les Yanomami Centraux (Venezuela)". *Systèmes de Pensée en Afrique Noire*, 14:105–126.

Lorenzi, Harri 1992. *Árvores Brasileiras: Manual de Identificação e Cultivo de Plantas Arbóreas Nativas do Brasil*. Nova Odessa, SP: Ed. Plantarum.

Magalhães, Antonio Carlos 1982. Os Parakanã: Quando o Rumo da Estrada e o Curso das Águas Perpassaram a Vida de um Povo. Tese de Mestrado. Universidade de São Paulo.

1985. "Os Parakanã". *Povos Indígenas no Brasil*. Vol. 8: Sudeste do Pará (Tocantins). São Paulo: CEDI.

1991. "As Nações Indígenas e os Projetos Econômicos de Estado: a Política de Ocupação do Espaço na Amazônia." In: J. Hebette (ed.), *O Cerco está se Fechando: O Impacto do Grande Capital na Amazônia*. Petrópolis, RJ: Vozes.

1994. Os Parakanã: Espaços de Socialização e suas Articulações Simbólicas. Tese de Doutorado. São Paulo: Universidade de São Paulo.

Malinowski, Bronislaw 1941. "An Anthropological Analysis of War." *American Journal of Sociology*, 46:521–50.

Martin, M. Kay 1969. "South American Foragers: a Case Study in Cultural Devolution." *American Anthropologist*, 71:243–60.

Marx, Karl [1857] 1973. *Grundrisse (Introduction to the Critique of Political Economy)*. London: Penguin.

[1859] 1974. *Contribuição à Crítica da Economia Política*. (Coleção Os Pensadores). São Paulo: Abril. pp. 107–263.

Mauss, Marcel 1960. "Essai sur le Don. Forme et Raison de L'Échange dans les Sociétés Archaïques." In: *Sociologie et Anthropologie*. Paris: PUF.

Maybury-Lewis, David 1984. *A Sociedade Xavante*. Rio de Janeiro: Francisco Alves.

McCallum, Cecilia 2001. *Gender and Sociality in Amazonia: How Real People are Made*. Oxford: Berg.

Mead, Margareth 1940. "Warfare is only an Invention, not a Biological Necessity." *Asia*, 40:402–5.

Meggers, Betty J. 1954. "Environmental Limitation on the Development of Culture." *American Anthropologist*, 56:801–24.

Meggit, Mervyn 1977. *Blood is Their Argument: Warfare among the Mae Enga Tribesmen of the New Guinea Highlands*. California: Mayfield Publishing Company.

Mendonça Rodrigues, Patrícia de 1993. O Povo do Meio: Tempo, Cosmo e Gênero entre os Javaé da Ilha do Bananal. Dissertação de Mestrado. Brasília: Universidade Federal de Brasília.

Menget, Patrick 1985. "Jalons pour une Étude Comparative (Dossier: 'Guerre, Societé et Vision du Monde dans les Basses Terres de l'Amérique du Sud')". *Journal de la Société des Américanistes*, LXXI:131–41.

　　　1988. "Note sur l'Adoption chez les Txicão du Brésil Central". *Anthropologie et Sociétés*, 12(2):63–72.

　　　1993. "Notas sobre as Cabeças Mundurucu." In: E. B. Viveiros de Castro and M. M. Carneiro da Cunha, *Amazônia: Etnologia e História Indígena*. São Paulo: NHII-USP/Fapesp. pp. 311–22.

　　　1996. "De l'Usage des Trophées en Amérique du Sud: Esquisse d'une Comparaison entre les Pratiques Nivacle (Paraguay) et Mundurucu (Brésil)". *Systàmes de Pensée en Afrique Noire*, 14:127–43.

Métraux, Alfred 1927. *Migrations Historiques des Tupi-Guarani*. Paris: Société des Américanistes de Paris.

　　　1928. *La Civilization Matérielle des Tribus Tupi-Guarani*. Paris: Paul Geuthner.

　　　1979. *A Religião dos Tupinambás e suas Relações com as Demais Tribos Tupi-Guarani*. São Paulo: Nacional/Edusp.

Meyer de Schauensee, Rodolphe and Phelps Jr., William H. 1978. *A Guide to the Birds of Venezuela*. Princeton, NJ: Princeton University Press.

Milton, Katharine 1991. "Comparative Aspects of Diet in Amazonian Forest-Dwellers". *Philosophical Transactions of the Royal Society of London*, B, 334:253–63.

Mindlin, Betty 1985. *Nós Paiter: os Suruí de Rondônia*. Petrópolis, RJ: Vozes.

Monteiro, Jácome [1610] 1949. "Relação da Província do Brasil, 1610." In: Serafim Leite, *História da Companhia de Jesus*, vol.VIII (apêndice). Rio de Janeiro: Imprensa Nacional.

Monteiro, John Manuel 1992. "Escravidão Indígena e Povoamento: São Paulo e Maranhão no Século XVII." In: J. Dias, *Brasil nas Vésperas do Mundo Moderno*. Lisboa: Comissão dos Descobrimentos Portugueses.

　　　1994. *Negros da Terra: Índios e Bandeirantes nas Origens de São Paulo*. São Paulo: Companhia das Letras.

Montoya, Pe. A. Ruiz de [1639] 1985. *Conquista Espiritual Feita Pelos Religiosos da Companhia de Jesus nas Províncias do Paraguai, Paraná, Uruguai e Tape*. Porto Alegre: Martins.

　　　1876. *Vocabulário y Tesoro de la Lengua Guarani, ò mas bien Tupi*. Viena/Paris: Faesy y Frick/Maisonneuve y Cia.

Moreira Neto, Carlos de Araújo 1988. *Índios da Amazônia, de Maioria a Minoria (1750–1850)*. Petrópolis: Editora Vozes.

Moura, Ignacio B. 1910. *De Belém a São João do Araguaya: Valle do Rio Tocantins*. Rio/Paris: H. Garnier.

Müller, Regina 1990. *Os Asuriní do Xingu: História e Arte*. Campinas, SP: Editora da Unicamp.

Murphy, Robert 1958. *Mundurucu Religion*. Berkeley: University of California Press.

　　　[1960]. 1978 *Headhunter's Heritage*. Berkeley: University of California Press. [2nd edition].

Navarro, Aspicuelta et al. [1550–1568] 1988. *Cartas Avulsas (1550–1568)*. Belo Horizonte: Itatiaia/Edusp.

Nicholson, Velda 1978. *Aspectos da Língua Asurini*. Brasília: Summer Institute of Linguistics.

Nimuendaju, Curt U. 1946. *The Eastern Timbira*. Berkeley: University of California Press.

　　　1948a. "Little-Known Tribes of the Lower Tocantins River Region." In J. Steward (ed.), *Handbook of South American Indians*. Vol. 3. Washington: Smithsonian Institution/Bureau of American Ethnology. pp. 203–08.

1948b. "The Maué and Arapium." In J. Steward (ed.), *Handbook of South American Indians*. Vol. 3. Washington: Smithsonian Institution/Bureau of American Ethnology. pp. 245–54.

1956. "Os Apinajé". *Boletim do Museu Paraense Emilio Goeldi*. Tomo XII.

1987. *As Lendas da Criação e Destruição do Mundo como Fundamentos da Religião dos Apapocúva-Guarani*. São Paulo: Hucitec.

Oakland, Suzanne 1996. The Power of Experience: Agency and Identity in Kayabi Healing and Political Process in the Xingu Indigenous Park. PhD Dissertation. Chicago: University of Chicago.

Obeyesekere, Gananath 1992. *The Apotheosis of Captain Cook: European Mythmaking in the Pacific*. Princeton: Princeton University Press.

Ortner, Sherry 1984. "Theory in Anthropology since the Sixties." *Comparative Studies in Society and History*, 26(1):126–66.

Otterbein, Keith F. 1973. "The Anthropology of War." In: J. Honigmann (ed.), *Handbook of Social and Cultural Anthropology*. Chicago: Rand McNally College Publishing. pp. 923–57.

Overing Kaplan, Joanna 1981. "Review Article: Amazonian Anthropology." *Journal of Latin American Studies*, 13(1):151–64.

Overing, Joanna 1989a. "Styles of Manhood: An Amazonian Contrast in Tranquility and Violence." In: S. Howell and R. Willis (eds.), *Societies at Peace: Anthropological Perspectives*. London: Routledge. pp. 79–99.

1989b. "The Æsthetics of Production: The Sense of Community among the Cubeo and Piaroa", *Dialectical Anthropology*, 14:159–75.

1992. "Wandering in the Market and the Forest: An Amazonian Theory of Production and Exchange." In: R. Dilley (ed.), *Contesting Markets*. Edinburgh: University of Edinburgh Press. pp. 180–200.

1993a. "Death and the Loss of Civilized Predation among the Piaroa of the Orinoco Basin". *L'Homme* 126–128, XXXIII(2–4):191–211.

1993b. "The Anarchy and Collectivism of the 'Primitive Other': Marx and Sahlins in the Amazon. In: C. Hann (ed.), *Socialism: Ideals, Ideologies, and Local Practice*. London: Routledge. pp. 43–58.

1996. "Who is the Mightiest of Them All? Jaguar and Conquistador in Piaroa Images of Alterity and Identity." In: J. Arnold (ed.), *Monsters, Tricksters and Sacred Cows*. University Press of Virginia. pp. 50–79.

Paternostro, J. 1945. *Viagem ao Tocantins*. São Paulo: Cia Editora Nacional.

Paulmier de Gonneville, Binot [1505] 1992. "Relação da Viagem do Capitão de Gonneville às Novas terras das Índias." In: L. Perrone-Moisés, *Vinte Luas: Viagem de Paulmier de Gonneville ao Brasil: 1503–1505*. São Paulo: Companhia das Letras. pp. 15–29.

Peggion, Edmundo Antonio 1996. Forma e Função: uma Etnografia do Sistema de Parentesco Tenharim (Kagwahiv, AM). Dissertação de Mestrado. Campinas: Universidade Estadual de Campinas.

Pereira, Nunes 1967. *Moronguetá, um Decameron Iindígena*. vol. II. Rio de Janeiro: Civilização Brasileira.

Perrin, Michel 1992. *Les Praticiens du Rêve: Un Exemple de Chamanisme*. Paris: PUF.

Philipson, Jürn Jacob 1946. "Nota sobre a Interpretação Sociológica de alguns Designativos de Parentesco do Tupi-Guarani". *Boletim da Faculdade de Filosofia Ciências e Letras*. (série Etnografia e Língua Tupi-Guarani) vol. LVI 9:1–31.

Porro, Antonio 1996. "O Antigo Comércio Indígena." In: *Os Povos das Águas: Ensaios de Etno-História Amazônica*. Petrópolis, RJ: Vozes. pp. 125–41.

Price-Williams, Douglass and Degarrod, Lydia N. 1990. "El Contexto y Uso de los Sueños en Ciertas Sociedades Amerindias." In: M. Perrin (ed.), *Antropologia y Experiencias del Sueño*. Quito: ABYA-YALA/MLAL. pp. 277–99.

Redfield, Robert 1960. *The Little Community and Peasant Society and Culture*. Chicago: The University of Chicago Press.

Renard-Casevitz , France-Marie 1993. "Guerriers du Sel, Sauniers de la Paix". *L'Homme*, XXXIII(2–4):25–44.

Ribeiro, Berta G. 1979. *Diário do Xingu*. Rio de Janeiro: Paz e Terra.

Rival, Laura 1998. "Domestication as a Historical and Symbolic Process: Wild Gardens and Cultivated Forests in the Ecuadorian Amazon." In: W. Balée (ed.), *Advances in Historical Ecology*. New York: Columbia University Press.

Rivière, Peter 1969. *Marriage among the Trio: A Principle of Social Organisation*. Oxford: Clarendon Press.

  1984. *Individual and Society in Guiana: A Comparative Study of Amerindian Social Organization*. Cambridge: Cambridge University Press.

Roosevelt, Anna 1980. *Parmana: Pre-historic Maize and Manioc Subsistence along the Amazon and the Orinoco*. New York: Academic Press.

  1987. "Chiefdoms in the Amazon and Orinoco." In: R. Drennan and C. Uribe, *Chiefdoms in the Americas*. Lanham, Md: University Press of America. pp. 153–85.

  1993. "The Rise and Fall of the Amazon Chiefdoms". *L'Homme* 126–128, xxxiii (2–4):255–83.

Rosaldo, Michelle 1974. "Woman, Culture, and Society: A Theoretical Overview." In: M. Rosaldo and L. Lamphere (eds.), *Woman, Culture and Society*. Stanford: Stanford University Press. pp. 17–42.

Rosaldo, Renato 1980. *Ilongot Headhunting: 1883–1974. A Study in Society and History*. Stanford: Stanford University Press.

Ross, Eric 1978. "Food Taboos, Diet, and Hunting Strategies: the Adaptation to Animals in Amazon Cultural Ecology." *Current Anthropology*, 19:1–36.

Rousseau, Jean-Jacques [1755]1989. *Discurso sobre a Origem e os Fundamentos da Desigualdade entre os Homens*. São Paulo: Ática/Editora da UnB.

Sahlins, Marshall 1972. *Stone Age Economics*. New York: Aldine de Gruyter.

  1981. *Historical Metaphors and Mythical Realities: Strucuture in the Early History of the Sandwich Islands Kingdom*. ASAO Special Publications. Ann Arbor: The University of Michigan Press.

  1995. *How "Natives" Think: About Captain Cook, for Example*. Chicago: The University of Chicago Press.

Salvador, Vicente do [1627] 1982. *História do Brasil 1500–1627*. Belo Horizonte: Itatiaia/Edusp.

Santos-Granero, Fernando 1986. "Power, Ideology and the Ritual of Production in Lowland South America." *Man*, 21(4):657–79.

  1992. *Etnohistoria de la Alta Amazonia: siglo XV-XVIII*. Quito, Ecuador: Ediciones ABYA-YALA.

  1993. "From Prisoner of the Group to Darling of the Gods: An Approach to the Issue of Power in Lowland South America". *L'Homme* 126–128, xxxiii(2–4):213–30.

Schaden, Egon 1954. *Aspectos Fundamentais da Cultura Guaraní*. FFCL. Boletim 188, Antropologia 4. São Paulo: Universidade de São Paulo.

Schieffelin, Edward and Crittenden, Robert 1991. *Like People You See in a Dream. First Contact in Six Papuan Societies*. Stanford: Stanford University Press.

Seeger, Anthony 1980. "Corporação e Corporalidade: Ideologia de Concepção e Descendência." In: *Os Índios e Nós*. Rio de Janeiro: Campus. pp. 127–32.

  1981. *Nature and Society in Central Brazil: the Suyá Indians of Mato Grosso*. Cambridge, MA: Harvard University Press.

Seeger, Anthony DaMatta, Roberto and Viveiros de Castro, Eduardo B. 1979. "A Construção da Pessoa nas Sociedades Indígenas Brasileiras". *Boletim do Museu Nacional*, 32:2–19.

Soares, Manoel C. ; Menezes, R. Camurça de ; Martins, Sandro J. ; and Bensabath, Gilberta 1994. "Epidemiologia dos Vírus das Hepatites B, C e D na Tribo Indígena Parakanã, Amazonia Oriental Brasileira". *Boletín de la Oficina Sanitária Panamericana*, 117(2):124–35.

Soares de Sousa, Gabriel [1587] 1987. *Tratado Descritivo do Brasil em 1587*. São Paulo: Cia. Editora Nacional.

Souto Maior, J. [1656] 1916. "Diário da Jornada que fiz ao Pacajá no ano de 1656." *Revista do Instituto Histórico e Geographico do Brasil*, 77(2):157–79.

SPI (Serviço de Proteção ao Índio) 1929. Relatório do Posto de Pacificação José Bezerra. Alípio Ituassu, encarregado. Tucuruí. Rio de Janeiro: microfilmes do Museu do Índio.

1930a. Relatório do Posto de Pacificação do Tocantins. Alípio Ituassu, encarregado. Tucuruí. Rio de Janeiro: microfilmes do Museu do Índio.

1930b. Inquérito administrativo da Inspetoria do Pará e Maranhão sobre massacre sofrido por índios bravios na zona do Tocantins, entre 30 de junho e 1 de julho de 1930. Belém. Rio de Janeiro: microfilmes do Museu do Índio.

1931. Relatório do Posto de Pacificação do Tocantins. Alípio Ituassu, encarregado. Tucuruí. Rio de Janeiro: microfilmes do Museu do Índio.

1932. Relatório do Posto de Pacificação do Tocantins. Alípio Ituassu, encarregado. Tucuruí. Rio de Janeiro: microfilmes do Museu do Índio.

1933. Relatório do Posto de Pacificação do Tocantins. Alípio Ituassu, encarregado. Tucuruí. Rio de Janeiro: microfilmes do Museu do Índio.

1938. Telegrama de 18/01/38 do General Rondon ao Major Filadelpho Cunha, Inspetor Regional do Pará. Rio de Janeiro: microfilmes do Museu do Índio.

1939. Situação dos Postos Indígenas no Pará. Relatório do Major Filadelpho Cunha, Inspetor Regional do Pará). Rio de Janeiro: microfilmes do Museu do Índio.

1944a. Telegrama de 4/08/44 do encarregado do PIA Pucuruí à Agríndios, Belém. Rio de Janeiro: microfilmes do Museu do Índio.

1944b. Telegrama do encarregado do Posto de Pacificação do Tocantins à Agríndios, Belém. Rio de Janeiro: microfilmes do Museu do Índio.

1945. Telegrama do encarregado do Posto de Pacificação do Tocantins à Agríndios, Belém. Rio de Janeiro: microfilmes do Museu do Índio.

1953a. Relatório de T. Martins Fontes, Chefe da IR-2, à Diretoria do SPI (25/08/1953). Rio de Janeiro: microfilmes do Museu do Índio.

1953b. Telegrama de 04/1953 do encarregado do PIA Pucuruí a Agríndios, Belém. Rio de Janeiro: microfilmes do Museu do Índio.

1962. Telegrama do Encarregado do PIA Pucuruí de 23/11/1962. Documentos dos Postos Indígenas. Belém: Funai.

Staden, Hans [1557] 1974. *Duas Viagens ao Brasil*. Belo Horizonte: Itatiaia.

Stearman, Allyn M. 1989. *Yuqui: Forest Nomads in a Changing World*. San Francisco: Holt, Rinehart and Winston.

Sterpin, Adriana 1993. "La Chasse aux Scalps chez les Nivacle du Gran Chaco". *Journal de La Société des Américanistes*, LXXIX:33–66.

Stradelli, Ermano 1929. *Vocabulário da Língua Geral Portuguez–Nheêngatú / Nheêngatú–Portuguez*. Rio de Janeiro: Livraria J. Leite.

Strathern, Marilyn 1988. *The Gender of the Gift: Problems with Women and Problemas with Society in Melanesia*. Berkeley: University of California Press.

Taylor, Anne-Christine 1985. "L'Art de la Réduction. La Guerre et les Mécanismes de la Différenciation Tribal dans la Culture Jivaro". *Journal de la Societé des Américanistes*, LXXI:159–173.

1993. "Remembering to Forget: Identity, Mourning and Memory Among the Jivaro". *Man*, 28(4):653–78.

1994. "Les Bons Ennemis et les Mauvais Parents: Le Traitement Symbolique de L'Alliance dans les Rituels de Chasse aux Têtes des Jivaros de l'Equateur." In E. Copet and F. Héritier-Augé (eds.). *Les Complexités de L'Alliance, IV (Économie, Politique et Fondements Symboliques de L'Alliance)*. Paris: Archives Contemporaines. pp. 73–105.

Teixeira-Pinto, Márnio 1997. *Ieipari : Sacrifício e Vida Social entre os Índios Arara (Caribe)*. São Paulo: Editora Hucitec/Anpocs/Editora UFPR.

Thevet, Fr. André [1575] 1953. "La Cosmographie Universelle." In: S. Lusagnet (ed.), *Le Brésil et les Brésiliens: les Français en Amérique Pendant la Deuxième Moitié du XVIe Siécle.* Paris: PUF.

[1576] 1978. *As Singularidades da França Antártica*. Belo Horizonte: Itatiaia/Edusp.

Thomas, Nicholas 1991. *Entangled Objects: Exchange, Material Culture, and Colonialism in the Pacific*. Cambridge, MA: Harvard University Press.

Toral, André Amaral de 1985. "Os Índios Negros ou os Carijó de Goiás: a História dos Avá-Canoeiro". *Revista de Antropologia*, 27–28:287–325.

1992. Cosmologia e Sociedade Karajá. Dissertação de Mestrado. Rio de Janeiro: PPGAS/Museu Nacional/UFRJ.

Townsley, Graham 1987. "The Outside Overwhelms: Yaminahua Dual Organization and its Decline." In: H. O. Skar and F. Salomon (eds.), *Natives and Neighbours: Anhropological Essays*. Ethnographic Museum (Etnografiska Studier 38). pp. 355–76.

Turner, Terence 1984. "Dual Opposition, Hierarchy, and Value: Moiety Structure and Symbolic Polarity in Central Brazil and Elsewhere." In: J. C. Galey (ed.), *Différences, Valeurs, Hiérarchie: Textes Offerts à Louis Dumont*. Paris: École des Hautes Études en Sciences Sociales. pp. 333–70.

1988. "Commentary: Ethno-Ethnohistory: Myth and History in Native South American Representations of Contact." In: J. Hill (ed.) *Rethinking History and Myth: Indigenous South American Perspectives on the Past*. Urbana: University of Illinois Press. pp. 235–81.

1991. The Mebengokre Kayapo: History, Social Consciousness and Social Change. From Autonomous Communities to Inter-Ethnic System. Ms. inédito.

1993. "Da Cosmologia à História: Resistência, Adaptação e Consciência Social entre os Kayapó. In: E. B. Viveiros de Castro and M. M. Carneiro da Cunha (eds.), *Amazônia: Etnologia e História Indígena*. São Paulo: NHII-USP/Fapesp. pp. 43–66.

Varese, Stefano 2002. *Salt of the Mountain : Campa Asháninka History and Resistance in the Peruvian Jungle*. Norman: University of Oklahoma Press.

Varnhagen, Francisco Adolfo de 1959. *História Geral do Brasil antes de sua Separação e Independência de Portugal*. Tomo III. São Paulo: Melhoramentos.

Velho, Otávio G. 1981. *Frentes de Expansão e Estrutura Agrária*. Rio de Janeiro: Zahar Editores.

Vernant, Jean-Pierre 1985. "Introduction." In. J-P. Vernant (ed.), *Problèmes de la Guerre en Grèce Ancienne*. Paris: École des Hautes Études en Sciences Sociales. pp. 9–30.

Verswijver, Gustaaf 1992a. *The Club-Fighters of the Amazon. Warfare among the Kayapo Indians of Central Brazil*. Werken Uitgegen Door de Faculteit van de Letteren en Wijsbegeerte Rijksuniversiteit te Gent 179e Aflevering. Gent: Rijksuniversiteit te Gent.

1992b. "Toi et Toi seul Pourra Porter ma Parure." In: *Kaiapó-Amazonie: Plumes et Peintures Corporelles*. Tevuren: Musée Royal de L'Afrique Centrale. pp. 65–87.

Vidal, Lux 1977. *Morte e Vida de uma Sociedade Indígena Brasileira*. São Paulo: Hucitec/Edusp.

Vieira, Antonio [1654] 1943. "Carta ao Pe. Francisco Gonçalves, Provincial do Brasil." In: *S. Leite, História da Companhia de Jesus*. Vol. 3. Rio de Janeiro: Imprensa Nacional. pp. 316–37.

Vieira Filho, João Paulo Botelho 1983. Principais Diretrizes de Saúde para os Índios Xikrin, Parakanã do P.I. Marudjewara, Parakanã do P.I. Paranatinga, Suruí do P.I. Sororó e Gavião do P.I. Mãe Maria.

Vilaça, Aparecida 1992. *Comendo como Gente: Formas do Canibalismo Wari'*. Rio de Janeiro: Editora da UFRJ.

1996. Quem Somos Nós: Questões da Alteridade no Encontro dos Wari' com os Brancos. Tese de Doutorado. Rio de Janeiro: PPGAS/Museu Nacional/UFRJ.

Villa Real, Tomaz de Souza [1793] 1848. "Viagem pelos Rios Tocantins, Araguaya e Vermelho". *Revista do Instituto Histórico*, 4. Rio de Janeiro.

Viveiros de Castro, Eduardo 1986. *Araweté. Os Deuses Canibais*. Rio de Janeiro: Jorge Zahar/Anpocs.

1992a. *From the Enemy's Point of View: Humanity and Divinity in an Amazonian Society*. Chicago: Chicago University Press.

1992b. "O Mármore e a Murta: Sobre a Inconstância da Alma Selvagem". *Revista de Antropologia*, 35:21–74.

1993. "Alguns Aspectos da Afinidade no Dravidianato Amazônico." In: E. Viveiros de Castro and M. Carneiro da Cunha (orgs.), *Amazônia: Etnologia e História Indígena*. São Paulo: NHII-Usp/Fapesp. pp. 150–210.

1998. "Cosmological Deixis and Amerindian Perspectivism". *Journal of the Royal Anthropological Institute*, 4(3):469–88.

Wagley, Charles 1976. "Xamanismo Tapirapé". In: E. Schaden (ed.), *Leituras de Etnologia Brasileira*. São Paulo: Companhia Editora Nacional. pp. 236–67.

1977. *Welcome of Tears: The Tapirapé Indians of Central Brazil*. Prospect Heights, IL: Waveland Press.

Wagley, Charles and Galvão, Eduardo 1961. *Os Índios Tenetehara: Uma Cultura em Transição*. Serviço de Documentação do Ministério da Educação e Cultura.

Werner, Dennis W. 1983 "Why do the Mekranoti Trek?" In: R. B. Hames and W. T.Vickers (eds.), *Adaptive Responses of Native Amazonians*. New York: Academic Press. pp. 225–38.

Whitehead, Neil Lancelot 1984. "Carib Cannibalism: The Historical Evidence". *Journal de la Société des Américanistes*, 70:69–87.

1988. *Lords of the Tiger Spirit: A History of the Caribs in Colonial Venezuela and Guyana, 1498–1820*. Dordrecht, Holland ; Providence, U.S.A.: Foris Publications.

1990. "The Snake Warriors – Sons of the Tiger's Teeth: A Descriptive Analysis of Carib Warfare ca. 1500–1820." In: Haas, Jonathan. *The Anthropology of War*. Cambridge: Cambridge University Press. pp. 146–70.

1993. "Historical Discontinuity and Ethnic Transformation in Native Amazonia and Guyana, 1500–1900". *L'Homme*, 28:289–309.

Wright, Robin 1990. "Guerra e alianças nas histórias dos Baniwa do Alto Rio Negro", *Ciências Sociais Hoje*. São Paulo: Anpocs. pp. 217–36.

Annex

Table A.1. *Warfare Events*

Western Parakanã (1895–1983)

	Parakanã designation	Our Designation	Time	River	Setting
1	Makakawa	Asurini	1895–00	Pucuruí	Village
2	Makakawa	Asurini	1895–00	Pucuruí	Forest camp
3	Makakawa	Asurini	1895–00		Village
4	Amowaja	Eastern Parakanã	1910–15	Upper Bacuri	Swidden and forest
5	Akwa'awohoa	{no information}	1910–15	Pacajá headwaters	Village
6	Temeikwary'yma	{same language}	1915–20		Village
7	Makakawa	Asurini	1920	Pacajá headwaters	Forest camp
8	Yrywyjara	Araweté (?)	1920–25	West of Pacajá river	Village and forest
9	Jojywapokytaho wa'é	{no information}	1925–30	{no information}	Forest camp
10	Amowaja	Eastern Parakanã	1925–30	Upper Pucuruí	Village
11	Amowaja	Eastern Parakanã	1925–30	Upper Andorinha	Village
12	Ywywa	Xikrin of the Cateté	1930–35	Western Parakanã territory	Forest camp
13	Ywywa	Xikrin of the Cateté	1930–35	Western Parakanã territory	Village
14	Amowaja	Eastern Parakanã	1935–40	Upper Bacuri	Village
15	Amowaja	Eastern Parakanã	1935–40	Upper Bacuri	Village
16	Amowaja	Eastern Parakanã	1935–40	Upper Bacuri	Village
17	Makakawa	Asurini	1940–45	Pacajá headwaters	Forest camp
18	Makakawa	Asurini	1940–45	Pacajá headwaters	Village
19	Amowaja	Eastern Parakanã	1945–50	Upper Lontra	Village
20	Amowaja	Eastern Parakanã	1945–50	Upper Da Direita	Forest camp
21	Amowaja	Eastern Parakanã	1950–53	Upper Bacuri	Forest
22	Makakawa	Asurini	1950–53	Low Pucuruí	Forest camp

(continued)

329

Table A.1. (*continued*)

	Parakanã designation	Our Designation	Time	River	Setting
23	Amowaja	Eastern Parakanã	1953–55	Da Direita	Forest
24	Akwa'awa	{no information}	1969	{no information}	Forest camp
25	Akwa'awa	{no information}	1969	{no information}	Forest
26	Ywywa	Xikrin of the Bacajá	1970	Bacajá headwaters	Forest camp
27	Yrywyjara	Araweté	1974–76	Bom Jardim	Forest camp
28	Yrywyjara	Araweté	1974–76	Bom Jardim/Ipixuna	Village
29	Yrywyjara	Araweté	1974–76	Bom Jardim/Ipixuna	Village
30	Ywywa	Xikrin of the Bacajá	1977	Bacajá headwaters	Forest camp
31	Akwamojepé (Kynyjoa)	Eastern Parakanã	1977–78	Bacajá headwaters	Forest
32	Yrywyjara	Araweté	1983	Ipixuna	Funai Post
33	Yrywyjara	Araweté	1983	Ipixuna	Funai Post

Eastern Parakanã (1895–1971)

	Parakanã designation	Our Designation	Time	River	Setting
1	Jawarapy'a (2 people)	{same language}	1895–00	Middle Bacuri	Eastern territory
2	Tekope'oa	Western Parakanã	1910–15	Upper Bacuri	Eastern territory
3	Jimokwera (1 person)	mesma lingual	1920–25	Branch of Lontra	Eastern territory
4	Ngyngé	Western Parakanã	1925–30	Upper Pucuruí	Eastern territory
5	Ngyngé	Western Parakanã	1925–30	Andorinha	Eastern territory
6	Ngyngé	Western Parakanã	1935–40	Upper Bacuri	Eastern territory
7	Ngyngé	Western Parakanã	1935–40	Upper Bacuri	Eastern territory
8	Ngyngé	Western Parakanã	1935–40	Upper Bacuri	Eastern territory
9	Kagia (1 person)	{same language}	1940–45	Branch of Lontra	Eastern territory
10	Ngyngé	Western Parakanã	1945–50	Upper Lontra	Eastern territory
11	Ngyngé	Western Parakanã	1945–50	Upper Da Direita	Eastern territory
12	Iawohoiwa'é 1	Ge Indians	1950–60	Da Direita	Eastern territory
13	Iawohoiwa'é 2	Ge Indians	1950–60	Da Direita	Eastern territory
14	Ngyngé	Western Parakanã	1950–55	Upper Bacuri	Eastern territory
15	Ngyngé	Western Parakanã	1950–55	Upper Da Direita	Eastern territory

Table A.2. *Eastern Parakanã Villages (c. 1925–1995)*

	Village	Decade	Location	Observation
1	Jytyngopawa	1920	Upper Bacuri	{no information}
2	Akwawaja	1920	Upper Bacuri	Enemies suspected
3	Rokotawa	1920	Upper Andorinha	{no information}
4	Many'ywa-rakapa	1920	Middle Andorinha	Western group attack
5	Kakotawa	1930	Upper Bacuri	{no information}
6	Tawymyna	1930	Upper Bacuri	Western group visits
7	Tawya	1930	Upper Bacuri	Western group attack
8	[no name]	1930	Branch of Lontra	No swiddens
9	Kwajigitawa	1940	Lower Pucuruí Affluent	{no information}
10	Ypywawa	1940	Lower Pucuruí Affluent	Enemies suspected
11	Angapytawera	1940	Lower Pucuruí Affluent	Burnt down
12	Jero'a'enawa	1940	Lower Pucuruí Affluent	Death of children
13	Jamonynga	1940	Middle Lontra	{no information}
14	Ijemamawera	1940	Upper Lontra	Western group attack
15	Kojypy'a	1940	Upper Da Direita	{no information}
16	Ywytotawa	1940	Upper Da Direita	Western group attack
17	Toritawa	1950	Upper Bacuri	Re-occupation
18	Apinerenawa	1950	Upper Da Direita	Iawoho-wa'é swidden
19	Toriaremipojyka	1950	Middle Da Direita	Presence of whites
20	Piriji'oa	1950	Upper Da Direita	Western group attack
21	Kynyjoa-atawera	1950	Upper Da Direita	Internal conflict
22	Kopewe'e	1960	Upper Da Direita	{no information}
23	Rokotawa	1960	Upper Andorinha	Re-occupation
24	Orotawa	1960	Upper Andorinha	Presence of whites
25	Jawajia	1960	Upper Paranatinga	Presence of whites
26	Orowopetawa	1960	Upper Murici	{no information}
27	Tajahokokwera	1960	Upper Andorinha	Contact
28	Jepo'aranga	1970	Upper Lontra	Contact (no swiddens)
29	Piraka'anga	1970	Middle Lontra	Postcontact
30	Agy'oa	1970	Lower Lontra	Postcontact
31	[no information]	1980	Lower Andorinha	Postcontact
32	Paranajinga	1980	Lower Paranatinga	Postcontact
33	Paranowa'ona	1990	Upper Pucuruí	Division of village
34	Ita'yngo'a	1990	Middle Bacuri	Division of village

Table A.3. *Varieties of Species Cultivated as Food*

Eastern Parakanã

Generic Name	Parakanã	English
manioc	*Many'yweté*	true manioc
(*manyanga*)	*Ajoroa*	parrot
	Many'ywarakapá	manioc-root-?
	Many'ypironga	red manioc
	Joropironga	red mouth
	Manyokyra	green manioc (unripe)
	Hawiohowa'é	hairy-thing
sweet manioc	*Kanawapepironga*	?-flat-red
maize	*Awajieté*	true maize
(*awajia*)	*Awajipironga*	red maize
	Awajijinga	white maize
bean	*Komana*	broad bean
(*komana*)		
yam	*Karapá*	yam-?
(*kará*)	*Kara'ia*	small yam
	Karajákwera	ex-yam
	Karapiona or *Tepojikará*	black yam or faeces yam
	Karapetoa	collective flat yam
	Karapewa	flat yam
	Ikoijyngohowa'é	white crumbly thing
sweet potato	*Jytyngeté*	true potato
(*jytynga*)	*Erepia* or *Jytypironga*	?or red potato
	Jytyngapypema	potato-short-inside?
banana	*Jata'ia*	small banana
(*jata*)	*Jatapepokoa*	long flat banana
	Akawaijata	?-banana

Western Parakanã		
Generic Name	Parakanã	English
manioc	*Warejinga* or *Manyangeté*	?-white or true manioc
(*manyanga*)	*Ajoroa*	parrot
	Many'ywarakapá	root-manioc
sweet manioc	*Kanawapepironga*	?-red-flat
	Manyangatoa	manioc-collective
maize	*Awajieté*	true maize
(*awajia*)	*Awajipytonga*	red maize
bean	*Komana*	broad bean
(*komana*)		
yam	*Karapá*	yam
(*kará*)	*Kara'ia*	small yam
	Karajákwera	ex-yam
	Karapytonga	red yam
sweet potato	*Jytyngeté*	true potato
(*jytynga*)	*Jytypepirera*	potato-flat-ex-skin
	Jytypytonga	red potato
	Jytyjinga	white potato
banana	*Jata'ia*	small banana
(*jata*)	*Jatapewa*	flat banana

Tabel A.4. *Animal Species Consumed by the Parakanã (Excluding Fishes)*

	Parakanã	W. Parakanã edibility	E. Parakanã edibility	Postcontact diet
I. MAMMALS				
Perissodactyla				
Tapir	*Tapi'ira*	Yes	Yes	No change
(*Tapirus terrestres*)				
Artiodactyla				
White-lipped peccary	*Tajahoa*	Yes	Yes	No change
(*Tayassu peccari*)				
Collared peccary	*Jiwa'á*	Yes	Yes	No change
(*Tayassu tajacu*)				
Red brocket deer	*Mijara*	No with exceptions	No with exceptions	Yes
(*Mazama americana*)				
Grey brocket deer	*Maroje*	No	No	Yes
(*Mazama gouazobira*)				
Rodentia				
Paca	*Karowara*	Yes	Yes	More frequent
(*Agouti paca*)				
Brazilian agouti	*Akojia*	Yes	Yes	More frequent
(*Dasyprocta leporina*)				
Primates				
Howler	*Akykya*	No with exceptions	Yes with restrictions	No change
(*Alouatta*)				
Edentata				
Great long-nosed armadillo	*Tatoeté*	Yes	Yes	More frequent
(*Dasypus kappleri*)				
Southern naked-tailed armadillo	*Tatoraroa*	Yes with restrictions	Yes with restrictions	More frequent
(*Cabassous unicintus*)				
Nine-banded armadillo	*Tatorarojinga*	no data	Yes	No change
(*D. novemcinctus*)				
Seven-banded armadillo	*Tatoria*	No	No	Yes
(*D. septemcinctus*)				
Giant armadillo	*Tatokoapé*	Yes with restrictions	Yes with restrictions	No change
(*Priodontes maximus*)				
II. REPTILES				
Chelonia				
Red-footed tortoise	*Jaojieté*	Yes	Yes	No change
(*Geochelone carbonaria*)				
Brazilian giant tortoise	*Jaojikwajinga*	Yes	Yes	No change
(*Geochelone denticulata*)				

(*continued*)

Tabel A.4. (*continued*)

	Parakanã	W. Parakanã edibility	E. Parakanã edibility	Postcontact diet
Crocodilia				
Cuvier's Dwarf Caiman (*Paleosuchus palpebrosus*)	*Jakare'ona*	Yes with restrictions	Yes	No change
Spectacled caiman (*Caiman crocodilus*)	*Jakarejinnga*	Yes with restrictions	Yes with restrictions	No change
III. BIRDS				
Galliformes				
Curassow (*Crax spp.*)	*Mytoa*	Yes	Yes	More frequent
Guan (*Penelope spp.*)	*Jakoa*	Yes	Yes	More frequent

Index

For EU product safety concerns, contact us at Calle de José Abascal, 56–1°, 28003 Madrid, Spain or eugpsr@cambridge.org.

www.ingramcontent.com/pod-product-compliance
Ingram Content Group UK Ltd.
Pitfield, Milton Keynes, MK11 3LW, UK
UKHW040618240426
470322UK00010B/198

* 9 7 8 1 1 0 7 4 4 9 4 2 8 *